THE PURSUIT OF HAPPINESS IN TIMES OF WAR

THE PURSUIT OF HAPPINESS IN TIMES OF WAR

CARL M. CANNON

ROWMAN & LITTLEFIELD PUBLISHERS, INC.
Lanham • Boulder • New York • Toronto • Oxford

ROWMAN & LITTLEFIELD PUBLISHERS, INC.

Published in the United States of America
by Rowman & Littlefield Publishers, Inc.
A wholly owned subsidiary of The Rowman & Littlefield Publishing Group, Inc.
4501 Forbes Boulevard, Suite 200, Lanham, MD 20706
www.rowmanlittlefield.com

P.O. Box 317, Oxford OX2 9RU, UK

Distributed by NATIONAL BOOK NETWORK

British Library Cataloguing in Publication Information Available

Library of Congress Cataloging-in-Publication Data

Cannon, Carl M.
The pursuit of happiness in times of war / Carl M. Cannon.
p. cm. — (American political challenges)
Includes index.
ISBN 0-7425-2591-0 (cloth : alk. paper)
1. United States—Politics and government. 2. United States—Politics and
government—Philosophy. 3. United States—History, Military. 4. Iraq War,
2003. 5. National characteristics, American. 6. Civil rights—United States—
History. I. Title. II. Series
E183.C25 2004
973.931—dc22   2003015547

Printed in the United States of America

♾ ™ The paper used in this publication meets the minimum requirements of
American National Standard for Information Sciences—Permanence of Paper for
Printed Library Materials, ANSI/NISO Z39.48-1992.

This book is dedicated to the memories of
Michael Kelly, a journalist and friend;
and to a gallant young man from Massachusetts,
First Lt. Brian M. McPhillips, USMC.

Contents

Preface

For a Washington correspondent with initiative and imagination, covering the White House can be the best beat in town. Every national budget or policy decision must pass through the place, foreign policy is made there, and for the past two decades—coinciding with my time as a Washington reporter—the Oval Office has emerged as the communications center of the world. It was only natural that on September 11, 2001, and in the days that followed, foreign reporters based in Washington would look to the White House for the official reaction to the attacks against the United States. But twenty years earlier, during Ronald Reagan's first months in office, the same thing happened when Pope John Paul II was wounded in St. Peter's Square. That day, the city's foreign correspondents gathered in the White House briefing room, where bulletins were duly issued by the press office—so much so that many of the stories on the assassination attempt published in European capitals carried Washington datelines.

I have been assigned to the White House beat full-time since 1993, and was pressed into occasional spot duty there for the ten preceding years as well. Some of the longtime regulars on the beat, especially the broadcast reporters closeted in tiny West Wing booths near the James Brady Briefing Room, have been known to get cabin fever in that building. But I have been fortunate enough to work for bureau chiefs and editors receptive to my expansive views of a White House reporter's range. I have tracked wolves in Yellowstone, interviewed labor union activists trying to organize in the *maquiladoras* along the Mexican border, talked to the "hard men" of the Irish Republican Army about why they were finally taking steps to trade their Armalite rifles for ballot boxes in Belfast—and wrote those stories as part of my job as a White

House correspondent. The logic was simple: these events flowed out of specific decisions made by American presidents.

Having said that, I admit that there is something unnatural about covering a person—the President of the United States—with whom you speak only a few times a year, and then only in public. For that reason I jumped at the chance to write an article that would, with a little luck, entail talking privately with a sitting president—and communicating with most of the living former presidents as well. It came about when editors at *Forbes* magazine called me one day in the spring of 2001 to propose an interesting, if quirky, freelance assignment. Those editors, Patrick Dillon, Carol Pogash and Rodes Fishburne III, wanted me to convince President George W. Bush and the living ex-presidents to write essays on what the concept of *the pursuit of happiness* means to them. In lieu of that, I was to interview them on the same subject. The results were to appear, along with the words of wisdom of other prominent Americans, in a special end-of-the-year issue *Forbes* called "The Big Issue." It was an enticing prospect. In my time as a reporter, I had heard Gerald R. Ford, Jimmy Carter, Ronald Reagan, Bill Clinton and both Bushes employ the phrase "pursuit of happiness" in perhaps a hundred speeches. But until the *Forbes* editors asked me to get in touch with these men and solicit their views on what the concept actually means to them I had never given much thought to what Thomas Jefferson expected Americans to *do* with the Declaration's most soaring expression—or even what presidents had in mind when they repeated it.

Ultimately, I would communicate with all the living ex-presidents with the exception of Ronald Reagan, who was incapacitated in California with Alzheimer's disease. The project, which lasted over the summer of 2001 and into the autumn, was a welcome intellectual diversion from the daily grist of the White House beat; at least that was true until September 11. Then, suddenly, the question of how and whether Americans could pursue their hearts' desires somehow seemed to be at the crux of everything. It turns out that presidents knew this, and always had.

"The American people need to go about their lives," President Bush told his countrymen at a White House ceremony a month after the attacks. "Our government will fight terrorism across the seas, and we'll fight it here at home. And the American people need to fight terrorism as well by going to work, going to ballgames, getting on airplanes, singing with joy and strength. . . . They will not take this country down!"

Prior to the attacks, I had persuaded Bush's father (the elder Bush's staff refers to him as "Forty-One" as a way of distinguishing him from his son, who is the forty-third president) to cooperate with our project. The former president agreed to write something himself, and to e-mail it to me, which he did on Thursday, August 9, 2001. His essay was a poignant missive in which he described the journey of his own life as one of striving for success and happiness—a happiness he had, late in life, actually found.

"Dear Carl," the elder Bush began. "You ask about Pursuit of Happiness at a good time in my life. I have pursued life itself over many years now and with varying degrees of happiness. But now, at seventy-seven I find that I am perfectly content to let history be the judge of those things I got right and of my mistakes in life as well." Citing his pride in his children and grandchildren and, most of all, the love of his wife ("Our happiness together is . . . strong, unbendable and rock solid"), Forty-One went on to say that his quest was at a successful conclusion. "I have found happiness," he wrote. "I no longer pursue it, for it is mine."

"In competitive business I was very happy—though restless and somewhat driven," Bush added. "In politics I had victories and defeats but for the most part I was happy. In big government jobs here and abroad I was fortunate to get to live my life's creed which says public service is a noble calling."

Despite this intensely personal rumination, Bush revealed a keen awareness that the concept of pursuing happiness has a broader, civic application as well; that although happiness may be an individual experience, the social contract that allows us to pursue this goal is part of all Americans' heritage. Almost as if the right to pursue happiness is, in a sense, an obligation as well as an opportunity. Delia M. Rios, the only daily newspaper correspondent in Washington who covers American history as a primary beat, explained it to me this way: "This guarantee is, literally, in our founding documents. It's on our birth certificate." Vice President Hubert H. Humphrey often said virtually the same thing. So did Martin Luther King Jr.

Forty-One made the same point in an addendum to his first communication with me. It came about this way: After the nation was attacked—with his son as commander-in-chief—I worried that the first President Bush might find it jarring to read an essay he had penned prior to September 11, but which was being published *after* the world had changed so much. So I asked Bush's chief of staff, Jean Becker, if the former president wanted to revise what he'd written. She thought he might. But after thinking about it awhile, Bush decided, defiantly, not to do so. He sent another e-mail, dated Thursday, October 18. Here is the former president's note, which he asked me to simply add to the words he'd written on August 9:

> POSTSCRIPT: I wrote this "pursuit of happiness" essay before the tragic events of September 11th. When . . . asked [if] I wanted to revise it to reflect my post–September 11th thoughts, my first thought was that I probably should. But as I reread this, I realized that the "pursuit of happiness" is truly one of our inalienable rights as Americans. It's just as important now, as it was when I wrote this, that all of us participate in and celebrate one of our most treasured freedoms. It's just one of many reasons why I am so proud to be an American.

The elder Bush's response, in turn, made *me* proud to be an American, and whetted my appetite for further exploration of the meaning of Jefferson's evocative phrase. Where did he get it? What did he mean by it? How do we use it today, in a time of great wealth, but also a time of war and of great peril for ordinary American citizens? It was at this very time—after the war on terrorism had begun, but before the onset of the second war against Iraq in March of 2003—that Professor Larry J. Sabato, director of the Center for Politics at the University of Virginia, called and asked me if I wanted to write a book for a collection he was editing, a series called "American Political Challenges." The challenges faced by the American nation in these times are manifest, the connection to the university founded by Jefferson seemed a good omen, and so I accepted Larry's offer. The respected publishing house of Rowman & Littlefield, in turn, enthusiastically accepted my book proposal. In the process of writing it, which occurred as the war in Iraq was unfolding, I learned a great deal about my own birthright. This book also allowed me to pursue my own happiness, even in times of war, and my hope is that it will enlighten my fellow Americans a bit as well.

1

American Pie

In the first days after the September 11, 2001, attacks on the World Trade Center and the Pentagon, attacks that claimed more lives than were lost at Pearl Harbor, President George W. Bush told Americans that it was important for them—that it was, in fact, patriotic of them—to resume the rhythms of their daily lives. Once, Bush urged his fellow citizens to drive to Disney World.[1] On three occasions, the President encouraged Americans, specifically, to go see a baseball game.

This was very much in Bush's character. Baseball, not politics, was his first love; and managing a major league baseball franchise, not serving as governor of Texas, was his first significant foray into civic life. But the President's ministrations conformed to the kind of advice being offered by other public officials and national leaders. National Football League teams sat idle for one game, and then resumed their season with a patriotic fervor.[2] NFL commissioner Paul Tagliabue called the White House to make sure he understood the administration's wishes. He did, indeed, and the commissioner then publicly invoked the name and the example of Franklin D. Roosevelt, who had personally interceded to keep major league baseball operational during World War II. "At a certain point, playing our games will contribute to the healing process," Tagliabue said. "Our players recognize that."

So did the nation's tens of millions of sports fans, who set aside their safety concerns and packed college and professional football stadiums in the aftermath of the attacks. "You have to have a life," explained Atlanta Falcons' fan Ginny Wehunt, who had the Falcons' black team logo painted on one side of her face with a red, white and blue "USA" on the other. "You can't just stay home and live in fear." Surveying a jammed stadium at one game, longtime announcer and television per-

1

sonality John Madden said, "I've never been more proud to be an American. I've never been more proud of our people."

David Letterman returned to the air on September 17 after a six-night hiatus to assure his colleagues that it was all right for them to cry. ("You're a professional, but Christ, you're a human being too," Letterman told CBS anchorman Dan Rather, who had fought back his own tears while quoting "America the Beautiful," on-air, the day of the attacks: "thine alabaster cities gleam, undimmed by human tears.") More importantly, Letterman was there to show that it was all right to laugh. He made a joke at the expense of guest Regis Philbin, but only a small one, as Regis' son was in the Pentagon when it was attacked. Regis, in turn, proffered a gentle gag about the ability of his former partner, tough-cookie Kathie Lee Gifford, to straighten out Afghanistan all by herself. Letterman's most memorable remarks came when he praised New York Mayor Rudolph W. Giuliani for his courage.

Giuliani was generally considered the single most inspiring of the nation's elected officials, and he was also the one who made the most direct connection between Americans' continuing pursuit of happiness as a practical and effective way of asserting their freedom. Partly, this was because Giuliani was fighting for the very economic survival of his city. But the events surrounding September 11 also revealed that the famously belligerent mayor had a heroic streak as well as a keen appreciation for the many facets of patriotism. What history will record is that he found time in between officiating at hundreds of funerals to repeatedly urge New Yorkers and non–New Yorkers alike to keep coming to wounded Manhattan—and to go shopping or attend the theater.

"Go ahead and go about the everyday activities," Giuliani said. "If you go to a park and play with your children, do that. If you like to go out and spend money, I would encourage that. It's always a good thing." The mayor also emceed a series of light-hearted television advertisements featuring cameos by famous New Yorkers such as Robert De Niro and Billy Crystal. In one sense, the nation's top elected officials were responding on a pragmatic level. During World War II, Roosevelt had asked Americans to make material sacrifices—in everything from giving up silk stockings to rationing gasoline—for the war effort. At the same time FDR believed that an awakening U.S. economy, based on agriculture and manufacturing, would support the two-front military campaign while simultaneously leading America out of the Great Depression.

By contrast, George W. Bush and Rudy Giuliani held office in a post–Information Age America, in which a service economy that was the pride of the world had been shown to have a vulnerable underbelly: It could be crippled by business executives too fearful to get on airplanes and too worried about the future to make capital investments; or by consumers in no mood to travel, go on vacation or dine out. But if the ostensible purpose of the New York advertising campaign was to lure customers to the city and to other U.S. tourist destinations, those commercials also served a larger and more fundamental purpose. They were subtle but powerful reminders of the uniquely American notion that anybody can pursue any dream and that this knowledge is not a luxury, but a necessity. The ads conveyed the unspoken message that this ethic is the very source of American strength. To their artistic credit, the ad copywriters and the stars who produced them used a light touch, but their meaning was unmistakable and it was profound. In one of the skits, Barbara Walters is depicted auditioning, none too expertly, for a part in a Broadway show. In another, former Yankee great Yogi Berra conducts the New York Philharmonic Orchestra. The most humorous of the ads showed a portly Henry Kissinger running the bases at Yankee Stadium—in a business suit—and then sliding head first into home plate, *à la* glamorous Yankee shortstop Derek Jeter.

Kissinger then arises, dusts himself off and, German accent and all, indulges in some good-natured woofing.

"Derek Who?" asks the former Secretary of State with a sly smile.

Certainly, the hate-filled extremists who declared war on the United States, could hardly fathom such a response to the horror of September 11, 2001. In Manhattan—or in Las Vegas, for that matter—a call on the citizenry to go shopping or attend a musical strikes a free people as a logical, if vaguely unsatisfying, way of demonstrating resolve. To an embittered holy warrior in the caves of Afghanistan or in the shadows of fringe mosques in neighborhoods from Karachi to Hamburg, such a response is further evidence of the decadence and vulnerability of a people characterized by frivolousness, materialism, and a national absorption with having a good time. Sleiman Abou-Gheith, an al-Qaeda spokesman who appeared on Osama bin Laden's infamous October 9, 2001, videotape, gave voice to this alternate point of view: "There are thousands of our young people," he said simply, "who look forward to death like the Americans look forward to living." In late September, as the World Trade Center still smoldered, a thirty-five-year-old Afghan holy warrior named Maulana Inyadullah expressed that same sentiment in an interview with British journalist David Blair. "The Americans love Pepsi-Cola," he said from his stronghold in Peshawar, Pakistan. "But we love death."

Such statements, with their implication that blind zealotry gives Muslim terrorists a tactical advantage in their global war, were designed to be chilling. And they were. But America's sworn enemies were misreading both Americans' historical resolve and the true significance of American materialism. They weren't the first to make this mistake. Famed World War II correspondent John Hersey, who covered the war in the Pacific for *Life* magazine, once asked a group of U.S. Marines during a lull in a battle for control of Guadalcanal what motivated them while they were fighting. After a long silence, one of the Marines muttered, "Jesus, what I'd give for a piece of blueberry pie."

For a second, Hersey thought the Marine was changing the subject—or making fun of him. Until a second Marine, said quietly, "Personally I prefer mince." A third whispered, "Make mine apple with a few raisins in it and lots of cinnamon: you know, Southern style." In a book he wrote later, *Into the Valley: Marines at Guadalcanal*, Hersey filled in the scene:

> Fighting for pie. Of course that is not exactly what they meant. Here, in a place where they had lived for several weeks mostly on captured Japanese rice, then finally had gone on to such delicacies as canned corned beef and Navy beans, where they were usually hungry and never given a treat—here pie was their symbol of home.
>
> In other places there are other symbols. For some men, in places where there is plenty of good food but no liquor, it is a good bottle of scotch whiskey. In other places, where there's drink but no dames, they say they'd give their left arm for a blonde. For certain men, books are the thing; for others, music; for others, movies. But for all of them, these things are just badges of home. When they say they are fighting for these things, they mean that they are fighting for home—"to get the goddam thing over and get home."
>
> Perhaps this sounds selfish. It certainly sounds less dynamic than the Axis slogans. But home seems to most Marines a pretty good thing to be fighting for. Home is where the good things are—the generosity, the good pay, the comforts, the democracy, the pie.

Examining the same sentiment almost six decades later, financial writer and political commentator Robert J. Samuelson noted that Hersey understood American pie "as a metaphor not only for home comforts, but also for the assumed opportunities of a free society." Writing in the context of September 11, Samuelson added, "What Americans extol are not the abstractions of liberty and democracy but the personal blessings they bring."

In other words, *the pursuit of happiness* is not a celebration of materialism. It is, instead, the best working definition of freedom that has ever been devised. First Lady Laura Bush, in a November 8, 2001, speech at the National Press Club, said as much in a pointed rebuttal to the terrorists and their seventh century worldview.

"That's one of the major differences between our country and the people we fight against," Mrs. Bush said. "We believe every person matters; that every individual is valuable and has a right to life and liberty and the pursuit of happiness."

That this happiness depends on a willingness to wage war—and war is never a happy occurrence—is one of life's paradoxes. But, for Americans in the aftermath of September 11, it also became a truism. At a September 23, 2001, vigil at Yankee Stadium U.S. Navy Admiral Robert Natter, commander of the Atlantic fleet, promised a victory "Against a terrorist enemy, to whom we say: You picked the wrong city, and you picked the wrong country."

Yes, Admiral Natter is a warrior, but a seventy-three-year-old African-American poet renowned for her gentle ways said much the same thing: "I can see in the acorn the oak tree," proclaimed Maya Angelou, who had seen the smoke billowing out of the World Trade Center from her New York apartment. "I see the growth, the rebuilding, the restoring. I see that is the American psyche. There is so much we can draw understanding from. One of the lessons is the development of courage. Because without courage, you can't practice any of the other virtues consistently."

Thus did a diverse cross-section of Americans spanning several generations and the entire political spectrum give rebuttal to the terrorists' assumptions about the United States. The sentiments of a vast majority of Americans connected directly to the Declaration of Independence that Thomas Jefferson drafted in late June and early July of 1776, and which was signed by fifty-six patriots, most of them a month later, on August 2.

"All Americans can draw a straight line from the free lives we lead today to that one moment, when the world changed forever," President

Bush said in Ripley, West Virginia, on July 4, 2002—the first Independence Day after September 11. "From that day in 1776, freedom has had a home, and freedom has had a defender."

In such moments, American political and cultural leaders were giving expression to an idea that most Americans understand instinctively: namely, that chasing dreams, pursuing happiness, and even achieving material success, are not embarrassing by-products of American freedom; they are the *essence* of American freedom. The fierce Afghan holy warrior who invoked Pepsi-Cola so disdainfully also predicted—inaccurately—that the vast technology and firepower superiority of the coming American troops would prove no more decisive in his country than it had for the Russians who had marched into Afghanistan in 1979—and marched out, in defeat, ten years later. The Russians had technology and planes and tanks, too, he said, and the Russian soldiers were tough and they were fearless. But in the end, it availed them nothing, because "they had no purpose in life." Americans would be even easier to defeat than the Russians, he envisioned, because "the Americans lead lavish lives."

Lavish is a relative term, of course, and it would not normally be applied inside the United States to the predominately working-class young men and women who serve in combat positions in the all-volunteer U.S. military. But the more salient point is that the desire to share in the rich material gifts of American society is not the same thing as lacking a purpose. Nor has the desire for a materially successful life ever been an argument in American history for succumbing to tyranny; rather, it has been an argument for resisting it. In a series of letters written in the 1760s and 1770s, George Washington railed against the oppressive effects of the Stamp Act, the Townshend Acts and other measures imposed on the colonists by the British crown. His objections, originally, were that they constituted financial hardship on the New World planters. But grievances about economic freedom gave way, seamlessly, to arguments in favor of a more general freedom. On April 5, 1769, Washington wrote to fellow Virginian George Mason:

"At a time when our lordly Masters in Great Britain will be satisfied with nothing less than the deprivation of American freedom, it seems highly necessary that something shou'd be done to avert the stroke and maintain the liberty which we have derived from our Ancestors; but the manner of doing it to answer the purpose effectually is the point in question."[3]

George Washington, rarely, if ever, himself employed Jefferson's exact phrase *pursuit of happiness* in his writings, but by 1786, Washington was known to casually link American happiness to American prosperity. "I shall always be happy to give and receive communications on improvements in farming, and the various branches of agriculture," Washington wrote. "This is in my opinion, an object of infinite importance to the country; I consider it to be the proper source of American wealth and happiness."[4]

To this day, there are critics of American life who cannot reconcile Americans' love of materialism with their love of freedom. One impulse seems to them to be base, the other noble. How can a moral person serve both masters? And isn't the first of these concepts, the right to materialism, clearly subordinate in importance to freedom? These are not new questions. In 1774, Alexander Hamilton characterized the actual hardships of the Townshend Act as trivial in comparison with the passions provoked by taxation without representation. Writing in *A Full Vindication of the Measures of the Congress*, Hamilton posited: "How ridiculous, then, is it to affirm that we are quarreling for the trifling sum of three pence a pound on tea, when it is evidently the principle against which we contend."

But 170 years before the bombing of the World Trade Center, a Frenchman came to this country and concluded that American materialism and idealism are bolts of the same cloth. After observing the United States for nine months, less time than many of the September 11 suicide bombers from the deadly al-Qaeda cells spent here, Alexis de Tocqueville had the answer. When he left America, he not only understood the fundamental nature of what was then still thought of as the American "experiment," but he believed he had also unraveled the great riddle inside Jefferson's phrase. Ultimately, the French visitor reasoned, the high concepts of life and liberty are not actually at odds with the hedonistic-sounding "pursuit of happiness." Instead, those concepts strengthen and complement each other—Tocqueville actually suggests that one is hardly possible without the other. In a section in *Democracy in America* titled "How the Taste for Material Enjoyments Among Americans is United with Love of Freedom and Care for Public Affairs," Tocqueville wrote:

> An American occupies himself with his private interests as if he were alone in the world, and a moment later, he gives himself over to the public as if he had forgotten them. He sometimes appears animated

by the most selfish cupidity and sometimes by the most lively patriotism. The human heart cannot be divided in this manner. The inhabitants of the United States alternately display so strong and so similar a passion for their own welfare and for their freedom that it may be supposed that these passions are united and mingled in some part of their character. And indeed, Americans believe their freedom to be the best instrument and surest safeguard of their welfare; they are attached to the one by the other.

This passage is found in volume two, part two, chapter fourteen of Tocqueville's work. The first American writer to rediscover this passage in the wake of September 11 was Adam Gopnik. His piece appeared in the October 15, 2001, issue of *The New Yorker*. "In the end, Tocqueville had confidence in Americans' ability to defend their democracy, because he saw that they had something near at hand to love," Gopnik wrote. "He saw that the pursuit of happiness is still our most radical idea. The perpetual need to apologize for the 'material enjoyments' of the United States, or of the past decade, he would have recognized as a very American performance, but he would not have thought it much to the point. Instead of seeing America as a place that would be tempted by pleasure and need to be redeemed for it, he saw that the love of the good things of life was what gave Americans' love of liberty an object."

In the aftermath of the September 11 attacks, the president of the United States, four of the living ex-presidents and almost all of the nation's political and cultural leaders—whether they were liberal movie actors or conservative Republican politicians—understood this truth intuitively. George W. Bush took his own advice about seeing a baseball game, making a celebrated appearance at Yankee Stadium during the 2001 World Series. Among other Americans who heeded the call to take in a major league game were former President Jimmy Carter (Atlanta Braves), former President George Bush (Houston Astros), and former President Bill Clinton (New York Yankees). These men had previously pulled together in the wake of the new war, assembling, along with their wives, for a service at National Cathedral on the Friday after the attacks. Sitting in the pews with their wives, the former presidents presented a united front to the nation and to the world, a simple gesture that somehow conveyed a sense not only of America's unity at that moment, but of its power. Bush also invited Al Gore and his wife Tipper to attend, and they did so. The former presidents spoke to each other, quietly, before Bush's speech. When it was over, the former President Bush reached forward and silently squeezed his son's hand. For his part, George W. Bush seemed to have his father—and his father's World War II generation—in mind during his address.

"In every generation, the world has produced enemies of human freedom," Bush said. "They have attacked America because we are freedom's home and defender. And the commitment of our fathers is now the calling of our time."

During the year that followed, Bush returned again and again to this theme. He had come to office with a reputation for mangling the English language, a domestic agenda largely limited to cutting taxes and improving education and virtually no foreign policy agenda at all. Yet he found his voice as a wartime president, soaring to a 70 percent job approval rating, and staying there for a year—this is Eisenhower territory—even as his aides acknowledged publicly and privately that his popularity would inevitably decline. His approval rating did indeed decline prior to the war with Iraq, but the fall was not precipitous and did not occur until after the momentous 2002 congressional elections in which Bush led his party to unlikely midterm successes. But while certainly benefiting politically from the high poll numbers, Bush wasn't in much of a position to savor them. He knew his newfound stature came from the war against Islamic extremism. And he expressed concern that the attention of the media, the political community and even everyday Americans would move on to other issues. But as commander in chief, Bush realized he did not have such a luxury—and he said as much. In an October 2001 interview with editors from Asian media outlets Bush said bluntly that although others would tire of the war on terrorism he would not. And Bush rarely made an appearance in public without discussing the war. On June 18, 2002, for example, Bush was scheduled by his White House handlers to speak at a boilerplate made-for-television event touting his commitment to increasing the percentage of homeowners in the United States. The concept of owning a home brought forth his inner Jefferson, however, and the president riffed easily from this subject to the war to the pursuit of happiness.

> Let me first talk about how to make sure America is secure from a group of killers, people who hate—you know what they hate? They hate the idea that somebody can go buy a home. They hate freedom. That's what they hate. They hate the fact that we worship freely.

They don't like the thought of Christian, Jew and Muslim living side by side in peace. They don't like that at all. And—and therefore, they—since they resent our freedoms, they feel like they should take out their resentment by destroying innocent lives in this country, we'll do everything we can possibly do to protect America. . . . But the best way to secure the homeland is to hunt 'em down one by one—and I mean, hunt them down one by one and bring 'em to justice, which is precisely what America will do.

I want to thank the choir for coming, the youngsters for being here. I just want you to know that when we talk about war, we're really talking about peace. . . . We're going to be steadfast toward a vision that rejects terror and killing and honors peace and hope. I also want the young to know that this country—we don't conquer people; we liberate people, because we hold true to our values of life and liberty and the pursuit of happiness.

This language foreshadowed war with Iraq—as well as Bush's rationale for it—but few people outside the White House seemed to notice at the time. The nation's attention, understandably, was still on 9/11, and on the resurgent patriotism engendered by the attacks. And invariably, that patriotism harked back to the Declaration.

On July 4, 2001, the Advertising Council of America produced a series of public service announcements reminding the citizenry just what that means. The Ad Council is a private, nonprofit organization that, literally, pioneered the use of PSA during World War II. (Its first such ad memorialized the phrase, "Loose Lips Sink Ships.") Sixty years later, the Ad Council had another important message to convey. It produced a host of full-page newspaper ads that featured an American flag above a headline "READ THIS AD." Then, below that, in smaller type, it added: "Or, don't. An exercise in freedom." The text of the ad then commemorated Independence Day by reminding Americans that the "smaller liberties" of everyday life are no less important or worthy of celebration than the big ones. In words Tocqueville would have understood—as would the pantheon of American presidents—the Ad Council pitch continued: "Your right to backyard barbeques, sleeping in on Sundays and listening to any darned music you please can be just as fulfilling as your right to vote for the president. Maybe even more so because you can enjoy these freedoms personally and often. So take a moment to celebrate all the little liberties you enjoy in America."

John Hersey's Marines fighting in the jungles of the South Pacific islands couldn't have said it any better. One wonders what the reaction would have been from the holy warriors who were by then on the run from U.S. troops in the mountains of Pakistan and Afghanistan. Or, better yet, what those who sneered dismissively at American prosperity in general, and at Pepsi-Cola in particular, would have thought of Pepsi's recent ad campaign featuring the handsome countenance of a major-league baseball player named Ichiro Suzuki. Six decades after the Japanese invaded Pearl Harbor, Ichiro—he's so good he only uses one name—constituted a peaceful, one-man invasion of what we now incongruously call the American Homelands. In 2001, Ichiro left his native Japan and his professional baseball team in Osaka to join the Seattle Mariners. He was the first Japanese position player—that is, a player who isn't a pitcher—to make this jump.[5] In an era of hype, Ichiro is a quiet man, who will only occasionally let loose with a Zen-inspired bromide. In an era of sluggers, he is a singles hitter with a throwback theory of batting ("Hit 'em where they ain't!"), and an aggressive, old-school approach to fielding that hasn't been seen regularly in the majors since the days of Roberto Clemente and Willie Mays. In his first year as a pilgrim to the promised land of U.S. baseball, Ichiro led the American League in hitting, winning the rookie-of-the-year and Most Valuable Player awards. In the process, he became the most popular baseball player on two continents—eclipsing even the great Derek Jeter (not to mention Henry Kissinger). More important, Ichiro became a symbol of freedom and of the unlimited possibilities that freedom implies.

The ad featuring his handsome face doesn't say, "Drink Pepsi." It says, "Change the World."

2

A Felicitous Choice of Words

The famous phrase on happiness comes at the end of an equally famous sentence, possibly the most inspirational in the American language: *We hold these Truths to be self-evident, that all Men are created equal, that they are endowed by their Creator with certain unalienable Rights, that among these are Life, Liberty and the Pursuit of Happiness.*

That was the wording approved by a committee of five renowned patriots in Philadelphia in the summer of 1776 and ratified by the fifty-six signers of the Declaration of Independence. It comes in the second paragraph of the Declaration's preamble, the only section of that document with which most citizens of the United States are familiar today. That was not the case at the time it was drafted. In 1776, the preamble was considered the warm-up to the Declaration's main course, which was the forceful recitation of the colonists' grievances against Great Britain. It was in the building of this case that the phrase "United States of America" first appeared in history.

But the main theme of the document was not unity; it was justice. The Framers were making the argument—and openly appealing to the court of world opinion (especially France) for acknowledgement of the validity of that argument—that the purpose of their revolution was not to seize power from a duly recognized sovereign government. Rather, it was to reclaim political powers that the colonists possessed as their birthright. They already held these basic rights, they had said many times before, as "free" Englishmen. But that summer, with a worldwide audience in mind, they were broadening their claim. They did so by invoking the "natural rights" of all men—not just those who were English-born—and applying them to politics, an idea championed by a Dutch humanist Hugo Grotius and subsequently popularized by John Locke some eighty years before the American Revolution. In other words, it was not they, the Founders claimed, but the government in England that was guilty of usurpations. The Declaration uses that very word. Thus the preamble, only 340 words long, ends this way: "The History of the present King of Great Britain is a History of repeated Injuries and Usurpations, all having in direct Object the Establishment of an absolute Tyranny over these States. To prove this, let Facts be submitted to a candid World."

The main body of the Declaration then goes on at some length, nearly one thousand more words, listing the supposed grievances against the Crown, and ending with the well-known vow of solidarity in support of their work—and for each other. "And for the support of this Declaration, with a firm Reliance on the Protection of divine Providence," it reads, "we mutually pledge to each other our Lives, our Fortunes and our sacred Honor."

The plural pronouns at the end of the Declaration are worth noting. In the Revolutionary period, this document was never considered the work of one man. The popular perception has changed over time. It changed, in fact, while some of the signers still lived. The upshot is that for the better part of two centuries, authorship of that great sentence, indeed, of the entire Declaration of Independence, has been almost universally attributed to Thomas Jefferson. In modern America, schoolteachers, journalists, marble monuments, U.S. presidents and even historians, generally refer to the language of the Declaration—without qualification—as Jefferson's words.

Understandably, credit of authorship was an issue of contention with some of Jefferson's contemporaries, who viewed him more as a peer than a demigod. Jefferson's own friend and fellow Virginian Richard Henry Lee once remarked bluntly that the Declaration had been "copied" from John Locke's treatise on government.[1] And while he lived—and he and Jefferson died the same day—John Adams periodically took issue with the notion that the succinct eloquence of the Declaration of Independence was purely Jefferson's. "There is," Adams wrote much later to a friend, "not an idea in it but what had been hackneyed in Congress for two years before."

To be sure, provincial chauvinism played a role here, as it does today. Adams was a Massachusetts man. So was Timothy Pickering, the fellow patriot to whom Adams sent that acerbic letter. The rivalry between Massachusetts and Virginia was based on regional pride and partisan competition (Massachusetts was Federalist territory. Jefferson and his Virginians were Republican-Democrats) and, of course, the cosmic issue of slavery. Moreover, the complicated dynamics between Jefferson and Adams were invariably personal, even as their relationship traveled an arc from bitter adversaries (Jefferson unseated Adams in the nasty presidential race of 1800) to a friendship so deep and lasting that volumes of their letters to each other are still being released and sold in bookstores. Adams is supposed to have said on his deathbed, "Jefferson survives!" Whether that account is literally true or not one thing is certain: the rivalry survives.[2] To this day, a lively contingent of historians and political scientists from New England insist that Adams has been given short shrift in history while Jefferson of Virginia has been the beneficiary of what amounts to a free ride.

In truth, Jefferson has always had his challengers and would-be debunkers. But it is also true that at the turn of the current century, the influence of the Adams camp finally reached critical mass. In November of 2002, Congress unanimously approved the building of a monument in Washington honoring John and Abigail Adams. President Bush signed it on December 2. In the past five years three respected scholars, all of them from Massachusetts, have written critically acclaimed, well-researched and widely read works of history that serve to elevate Adams' role—and the role of other Founders—while diminishing Jefferson's. (The three are *Founding Brothers* by Mount Holyoke College professor Joseph J. Ellis; *John Adams*, by Pulitzer Prize–winning biographer David McCullough, who lives in West Tisbury, Mass.; and *American Scripture: Making the Declaration of Independence*, by Massachusetts Institute of Technology historian Pauline Maier.) Nevertheless, the "Charlottesville Mafia," as the keepers of the Jefferson flame were once called, have little to complain about. Even if Jefferson-mania were to end tomorrow—and it won't—their man has enjoyed one of the great public relations runs in history: 225 years of predominately positive press.

For our purposes, however, as seekers of happiness—or rather, as seekers of the intellectual origins of the notion that governments are instituted among men and women for the express purpose of guaranteeing us the right to pursue happiness—the relevant point is this: If we want to know what the author of the phrase had in mind when he wrote *Life, Liberty and the Pursuit of Happiness*, we will want to start by knowing who the author really was. Were the words original with Jefferson, or did he have help? It would also help to know in what context this language appeared, that is, what people understood it to mean at the time it was written. During our exploration, I will attempt to step gingerly. The rivalry between the partisans of Adams and Jefferson—or those of George Mason or Benjamin Franklin, for that matter—is not our fight. For one thing, it is a false choice, brilliance not being a zero-sum game. For another, what's actually in dispute in the drafting of the Declaration doesn't amount to so much if one looks at it with benefit of two centuries' perspective. Was Jefferson a sublime writer, much better than Adams? We know that he was because their respective prose lives on, because all of their contemporaries thought so and because Adams himself admits it. And he did so neither indirectly nor casually: Adams made this assertion in his own autobiography and in the very context of discussing authorship of the Declaration.

At the same time, do we know that Jefferson had lots of assistance in framing the ideas, and even precise phrasing, of the Declaration? Yes, because we can see these phrases and concepts in writings by other authors that predate Jefferson. We also know it because Jefferson freely concedes the point—and, like Adams, does so in the context of the discussion of authorship of the Declaration.

"Band of brothers" is one of the phrases Jefferson used when he looked back on his work with his fellow patriots, most especially with Adams. It is the inspiration for Joseph Ellis' memorable title, but even that evocative phrase is not original to Jefferson. The first "band of brothers" followed Henry V to war; the words are Shakespeare's. And in *Founding Brothers* Ellis brings us another ensemble cast of worthies, focusing in particular on seven men (Washington, Jefferson, Adams, Franklin, James Madison, Alexander Hamilton, Aaron Burr) and a woman, Adams' wife Abigail. In a question and answer session at the time of the publication of his book, Ellis was asked whom among them he considered "the most revolutionary." His inarguable answer: "They were *all* revolutionaries."

"They were trying to do something that had never been done before in modern history, and they were bold enough to take on the dominant military and economic power in the world, Great Britain, fully realizing that if they lost the contest they would all have been tried and hanged as traitors," Ellis continued. "Washington was probably the most indispensable character in the group. Without him, the effort would have most likely failed. Jefferson's legacy is most lustrous, because of those magic words he wrote in the Declaration of Independence. Franklin was, in my judgment, the wisest. Hamilton was the most brilliant, the one who would have scored the highest on the SATs. Madison was the sharpest political thinker, though I think Adams ranks right up there with him. In fact, Adams is probably the most underappreciated of them all and the Founder whose letters most fully reveal the hopes and fears and ambitions they all shared. But selecting one Founder over another misses the main point, which is that they succeeded because they were a collective."

In another interview, this one in October of 2000 with the *Boston Globe*, Ellis made a similar point about Adams while alluding obliquely to Pauline Maier's celebrated designation of Jefferson as being the most overrated of Americans. "I'm not sure Jefferson is the most overrated figure in American history," Ellis said. "But I am of the opinion that John Adams is the most underappreciated great man in American history."

For his part, McCullough has related how he started out to write a book about Jefferson and Adams, but decided that Adams was the "more compelling" character. But it's a bit more complicated than that. A presidential biographer whose training is in classic literature, not history, McCullough is a throwback: a storyteller who tends to fall in love with his subjects while researching their lives. In this way, the author of *Truman* and *John Adams* resembles the famed Dumas Malone, whose six-part biography of Jefferson was the accepted standard for two generations. But McCullough finds he cannot completely fall for Jefferson—because he's already in love with John and Abigail Adams.

"I set out to write a dual biography of Adams and Jefferson," McCullough told an engrossed audience at the Southern Vermont Art Center in July of 2001. "I quickly realized Adams was the one I wanted to focus on. In every respect he was a more fully developed, three-dimensional, warm-blooded, and compelling character than Jefferson. . . . Adams was the only Founding Father not to ever own slaves. He's good company, too. He was honest and everybody knew it. Adams is very much like a character in a Dickens novel. He is vivid, irritable, vain, stubborn to an extreme, brave, warmhearted, outspoken, humorous, affectionate and quite lovable. And so much of what he wrote dealt with the ideas and ideals that are the basis for our whole way of life, of our society as Americans. What more could a historian ask for?"

By way of rebuttal, Princeton historian Sean Wilentz suggested that there is much a scholar could find lacking in Adams as a hero, including a war record and a basic understanding of how the American Revolution changed the national character of the new nation by undermining the class system. Then there is Adams' central role in the enactment of the notorious Alien and Sedition Act. Wilentz also notes—and he is hardly alone—that in finding in the prickly Adams a high lovability quotient, McCullough is in a distinct minority. But McCullough's slave-owning line, tucked in the Vermont speech so casually, comes up repeatedly in interviews—and in his book itself. McCullough's stumbling block about Jefferson, it seems clear, was slavery. It's a good stumbling block to have.

Yet even these determined New England–based historians do not really contest Jefferson's claim to immortality. Remember Ellis' own description of Jefferson's contribution? *Those magic words he wrote in the Declaration of Independence.* And McCullough, in a post–September 11 appearance at Monticello, made tender remarks about Jefferson on the occasion of the dedication of a new Jefferson Library.

"In so lovely a setting as this, in such good company, in springtime, in Virginia, it would be easy to forget that we are at war—and that the merciless cause of the foe is enforced ignorance," McCullough said in his famously mellifluous voice.[3] The date of this speech was April 13, 2002—Jefferson's 259th birthday. "The ideals of Thomas Jefferson could not be more timely and to the point," McCullough continued. "Opening this magnificent new library in his name we again unfurl the banners of liberal education, the banners of the open mind, the pursuit of truth, freedom of religion, the free and open exchange of ideas and love of learning that were the very spirit of the 'good society' so eloquently and forever set forth by the lanky, bookish fellow from up the hill . . ."

Maier is no match for Ellis or McCullough as a public figure. Her books neither sell as well nor generate as much controversy. But she's probably a more formidable adversary—and Jefferson lovers know it. One even accused her in writing of "humbuggery," a rebuke so out-of-date that it must have caused a few chuckles in Maier's Boston social circles.[4] To be sure, Maier's book, the most definitive work on the writing of the Declaration in seventy-five years, constitutes a direct challenge to Jefferson's legacy. The reason is that she painstakingly documents the contributions made by other colonists in the preparation of the great document.

"I disagree with the notion that the Declaration of Independence is simply a reflection of the mind of Thomas Jefferson," Maier explains memorably in her text. "It was not an expression of his private convictions. It was an expression of the American mind."[5] Jefferson made that very point himself—as Maier points out, the phrase about the American mind is his—but the groundbreaking research in *American Scripture* is Maier's unearthing of some ninety documents in which states, counties, towns and militias crafted Declarations of their own before July 4, 1776. Ultimately, the historic record she constructs leads to an unmistakable conclusion: Whatever Jefferson's talents, the Declaration of Independence itself is indistinguishable from the political movement that made it possible—and that this is true both in its verbiage and its content. "That story is not of a solo performance or even, to extend the metaphor, a performance of chamber music with a handful of players," she writes. "What I had in mind was more the Boston Symphony Orchestra or, better yet, the Mormon Tabernacle Choir, a production with a cast of hundreds . . ."

Conceding all that, we must continue our quest. If Jefferson had help in the Declaration, if he had help even with the phrase *Life, Liberty and the Pursuit of Happiness,* then our questions only multiply. To the query, "What did Jefferson mean by the right to pursue happiness?" are now added the following questions: Who were his collaborators? Who, in turn, influenced *them*? And what exactly did they think a happy life entailed?

*   *   *

The lead players in this big cast convened in Philadelphia in the spring of 1776 for the Continental Congress. Jefferson himself arrived there on May 14. As summer enveloped the city, the tall, red-haired and somewhat diffident Virginian, then only thirty-three years old, was selected, along with four others, to draft the document declaring the colonists' intention, along with their reasons for doing so, to break away from England. The other four were Adams, Franklin, Roger Sherman of Connecticut and Robert R. Livingston of New York.

Jefferson, lodging alone, rented the middle floor of a newly built three-story brick house at the corner of 7th and Market streets owned by a man named Jacob Graff.[6] Although he possessed thousands of books, many of them on the philosophy of government and the rights of man, Jefferson brought none of them with him to Philadelphia at the time when, one might argue, he needed their vast stores of knowledge the most.[7] A bystander who happened up the stairs into Jefferson's quarters might have found that the only tangible clue of Jefferson's intentions to write something momentous was a small desk not much larger than today's laptop computers. It was on this desk that the young inventor, planter and intellectual from Virginia did his writing. The desk, which Jefferson designed himself and called his "writing box," measures 9¾ by 14⅜ inches, and is only 3¼ inches deep. There's a folding board, lined with green baize, attached to the top, which allows the writing surface to expand to 19¾ inches. A drawer in one end of the desk has space for paper, pens and a glass inkwell. Made of sturdy mahogany by a Philadelphia cabinet-maker, the writing box lives on. (For those who like to see the artifacts of history with their own eyes, it is on display at the Smithsonian Institution's presidency exhibit at the National Museum of American History.) With what must have been deliberate understatement, Jefferson described the desk this way: "It claims no merit of particular beauty. It is plain, neat, convenient, and, taking no more room on the writing table than a moderate quarto volume, it yet displays itself sufficiently for any writing." Yet Jefferson kept it for fifty years, evidently believing it might be a valued relic someday.[8]

But why was Jefferson chosen to labor away at this desk anyway? The most logical person to draft the document would appear to have been Richard Henry Lee of Virginia. Then forty-three years old, Lee was ten years senior to Jefferson and was the man in the Virginia delegation with the most established credentials as a patriot. In 1765, Lee's response to the hated Stamp Act was to round up his brothers—and four brothers of George Washington—and head to Leedstown, Va., in Westmoreland County on the Rappahannock River. The crowd, which grew in size to some 115 men, confronted a stamp collector, eliciting a promise that he would stop collecting taxes. Lee's band drew up the *Westmoreland Resolves*, which not only announced it would not pay the tax, but vowed to wreak "danger and disgrace" on anyone who did.

It was one of the first organized acts of sedition against the Crown—and it allied Virginia with Massachusetts as a hotbed of rebellion. Richard Henry Lee, born in Virginia but educated in England, was a planter, a lawyer and a gifted orator who mesmerized his audiences not only with his forceful and radical views, but by his lyrical voice and habit of waving his hand in the air as he spoke, a hand that was invariably covered in black silk to hide the scars of a hunting accident. Lee attended the First Continental Congress in Philadelphia in September of 1774, where he became allied with John Adams' cousin Samuel Adams.[9]

At the meeting of the Second Continental Congress the following year, Lee sat on the committee that made George Washington commander of the Continental Army, and in May of 1776, he was named to a three-man committee to draft a preface for a resolution on self-government. (The other two were John Adams and a South Carolinian, Edward Rutledge, who by the end of the year would be serving as a captain in the Charleston Battalion of Artillery.) And it was Richard Henry Lee who, on June 7, 1776, was given the honor of introducing to the Second Continental Congress the resolution that officially announced revolution to the world:

> Resolved: that these united Colonies are, and of right ought to be, free and independent States, that they are absolved from all allegiance to the British crown, and that all political connection between them and the State of Great Britain is, and ought to be, totally dissolved.

But Congress recognized that there needed to be a formal Declaration of Independence, and the task of drafting it was not given to Lee, nor to Adams. The former had returned to Williamsburg, either because his wife was ill or because independence was a foregone conclusion and he wanted to participate in the formation of Virginia's government. In *Jefferson the Virginian*, Dumas Malone weighs in on this question: "There is more reason to suppose that Jefferson envied Lee this opportunity than that Lee envied Jefferson," Malone wrote. "To both of them the proceedings in Williamsburg seemed more vital at the moment than the drafting of a document in Philadelphia. This particular document they undoubtedly regarded as important, but nobody then knew it would turn out to be immortal. It might not have been if Lee had drawn it."

Perhaps this claim is true, but it strikes me as overstatement. Jefferson was too astute a politician, not to mention a dedicated futurist, not to appreciate the historic significance of what was happening in Philadelphia, where *all* the colonies were represented. And as far as what Richard Henry Lee would have produced in the way of prose, suffice to say that we'll never know. Unless his reputation as an orator was overblown, why wouldn't he, too, have risen to the momentous historic occasion? In any event, Adams, along with Franklin, was given the job of being one of the advisers to the project. The writing assignment fell to

Jefferson, who, when paired by Congress on another writing project with the eloquent but more moderate Philadelphia lawyer John Dickinson the year before, had already exhibited the traits that would characterize his work on the Declaration: namely, a hardened attitude toward Great Britain, a talent for evocative prose and a prickliness about having that prose edited by anyone—even the highly respected Dickinson, or the brilliant Ben Franklin.

Many years after the fact Adams wrote down his recollections as to why Jefferson had been chosen. In his autobiography, published in 1805, Adams said that the committee of five appointed Jefferson to draw up the document "and clothe them in a proper dress." Adams said that he met privately with Jefferson, who in turn offered the older man the honor of being the author of record. In Adams' telling, he declined, citing several reasons: That Jefferson was a Virginian; that he was more popular with the Congress, meaning the draft would be subject to less scrutiny if Jefferson wrote it; and, finally, that "I had a great opinion of the elegance of his pen and none at all of my own."

Seventeen years later, it was the gist of this account that Adams was repeating in a letter to Timothy Pickering, a Harvard man who had been a local Whig politician in Salem and who had earned a reputation before the Revolutionary War as a pro-Independence pamphleteer. After joining the Revolution, Pickering served as Quartermaster General and later as Secretary of State under George Washington. Later, Adams dismissed Pickering from his own cabinet—the two Yankees were too irascible to work together harmoniously—but Pickering was a dedicated Federalist who spent the rest of his career opposing Jefferson-style Republicanism. In any event, Adams fleshed out his account of the drafting of the Declaration.

"You inquire why so young a man as Mr. Jefferson was placed at the head of the committee for preparing a Declaration of Independence?" Adams wrote Pickering on August 6, 1822. "I answer: It was . . . to place Virginia at the head of everything."

But that was not all, Adams said. "Mr. Richard Henry Lee might be gone to Virginia, to his sick family, for aught I know, but that was not the reason of Mr. Jefferson's appointment."

Adams continued:

There were three committees appointed at the same time, one for the Declaration of Independence, another for preparing articles of confederation, and another for preparing a treaty to be proposed to

France. Mr. Lee was chosen for the Committee of Confederation, and it was not thought convenient that the same person should be upon both. Mr. Jefferson came into Congress in June 1775, and brought with him a reputation for literature, science, and a happy talent of composition. Writings of his were handed about, remarkable for the peculiar felicity of expression. Though a silent member in Congress, he was so prompt, frank, explicit, and decisive upon committees and in conversation—not even Samuel Adams was more so—that he soon seized upon my heart; and upon this occasion I gave him my vote, and did all in my power to procure the votes of others. I think he had one more vote than any other, and that placed him at the head of the committee. I had the next highest number, and that placed me the second. The committee met, discussed the subject, and then appointed Mr. Jefferson and me to make the draft, I suppose because we were the two first on the list.

In Adams' telling, then, Jefferson and he were almost co-equals in the project—at least until they engaged in a kind of Alphonse and Gaston routine to see who would actually do the writing. The way Adams describes it to Pickering, their dialogue, in a "subcommittee" that apparently consisted only of the two of them, went like this:

Jefferson proposed to me to make the draft. I said, "I will not."
    "You should do it."
    "Oh! No."
    "Why will you not? You ought to do it."
    "I will not."
    "Why?"
    "Reasons enough."
    "What can be your reasons?"
    "Reason first, you are a Virginian, and a Virginian ought to appear at the head of this business. Reason second, I am obnoxious, suspected, and unpopular. You are very much otherwise. Reason third, you can write ten times better than I can."
    "Well," said Jefferson, "if you are decided, I will do as well as I can."
    "Very well. When you have drawn it up, we will have a meeting."
    A meeting we accordingly had, and conned the paper over. I was delighted with its high tone and the flights of oratory with which it abounded, especially that concerning Negro slavery, which,

though I knew his Southern brethren would never suffer to pass in Congress, I certainly never would oppose.

But after explaining to Pickering how he modestly stepped aside, Adams all but retracts the compliment about the "felicity" of Jefferson's prose, adding in the letter to his friend:

> As you justly observe, there is not an idea in it but what had been hackneyed in Congress for two years before. The substance of it is contained in the Declaration of Rights and the Violations of those Rights in the Journals of Congress, in 1774. Indeed, the essence of it is contained in a pamphlet, voted and printed by the town of Boston before the first Congress met, composed by James Otis, as I suppose, in one of his lucid intervals, and pruned and polished by Samuel Adams.[10]

Jefferson got wind of this letter because Pickering used it as the basis of a Fourth of July speech in Salem in 1823. The speech had generated some press coverage, which was brought to Jefferson's attention, especially the uncharitable characterization about its unoriginality. Now there were *two* grumpy old men: Jefferson, naturally, had a different recollection than did his old rival and collaborator, and he took pains to respond. In a letter to Madison, almost certainly written with one eye on history, Jefferson wrote his rebuttal:

> You have doubtless seen Timothy Pickering's Fourth of July observations on the Declaration of Independence. If his principles and prejudices, personal and political, gave us no reason to doubt whether he had truly quoted the information he alleges to have received from Mr. Adams, I should then say, that in some of the particulars, Mr. Adams' memory has led him into unquestionable error. At the age of eighty-eight, and forty-seven years after the transactions of Independence, this is not wonderful. Nor should I, at the age of eighty, on the small advantage of that difference only, venture to oppose my memory to his, were it not supported by written notes, taken by myself at the moment and on the spot. He says, "the committee of five, to wit, Dr. Franklin, Sherman, Livingston, and ourselves, met, discussed the subject, and then appointed him and myself to make the draught; that we, as a sub-committee, met, and after the urgencies of each on the other, I consented to undertake the task; that the draught being made, we, the subcommittee, met, and

conned the paper over, and he does not remember that he made or suggested a single alteration." Now these details are quite incorrect. The committee of five met; no such thing as a sub-committee was proposed, but they unanimously pressed on myself alone to undertake the draught. I consented; I drew it; but before I reported it to the committee, I communicated it *separately* to Dr. Franklin and Mr. Adams, requesting their corrections, because they were the two members of whose judgments and amendments I wished most to have the benefit, before presenting it to the committee; and you have seen the original paper now in my hands, with the corrections of Dr. Franklin and Mr. Adams interlined in their own handwritings. Their alterations were two or three only, and merely verbal. I then wrote a fair copy, reported it to the committee, and from them, unaltered, to Congress.

Pauline Maier has pointed out that Jefferson's recollection wasn't entirely accurate either. Also, Adams' reference to earlier documents that call for independence is a fair point. On October 14, 1774, the First Continental Congress issued a manifesto in support of the Boston Tea Party that invokes the rights to "life, liberty and property," and claims these rights are derived from "the immutable laws of nature." On the other hand, in fairness to Jefferson, in 1774 the colonists were invoking those rights as free Englishmen, and they cited "the principles of the English constitution" to back them up.[11] As for James Otis' 1765 manifesto, it's a stretch to suggest Jefferson was plagiarizing from that document—something he said he never saw—or even that he was directly influenced by it. True, Otis asserts that the colonists "are entitled to all the inherent rights and privileges" of native-born Englishmen and rails against taxation without representation, but the contrast in tone and substance with Jefferson's call to revolution in 1776—or even Jefferson's own earlier writings in "reminder" to the king in 1774—is quite stark. Otis doesn't call King George a "tyrant," he calls him "liege."[12] But if Jefferson, in his letter to Madison, objects to Adams' tone while attempting to correct Adams on many of the details, the Sage of Monticello doesn't really contest Adams' larger point: that the galvanizing ideas in the Declaration of Independence's preamble—and much of its language—had appeared many times before in many places. Moreover, Jefferson doesn't dispute that these words reflected the will, not only of the Second Continental Congress, but of the colonists themselves, and of many Englishmen as well. Some of them, like John Locke, were long dead. Others, such as Thomas Paine, were just off the boat.[13]

"But it was not the object of the Declaration to produce anything new," Daniel Webster protested in his conciliatory August 2, 1826, eulogy of Adams and Jefferson. "It was not to invent reasons for independence, but to state those which governed the Congress." While he lived, Jefferson made the same basic point, even while reacting defensively to some of the specifics of Adams' accusations. In his letter to Madison, he added:

> Pickering's observations, and Mr. Adams' in addition, 'that it contained no new ideas, that it is a commonplace compilation, its sentiments hackneyed in Congress for two years before, and its essence contained in Otis' pamphlet,' may all be true. Of that I am not to be the judge. Richard Henry Lee charged it as copied from Locke's treatise on government. Otis' pamphlet I never saw, and whether I had gathered my ideas from reading or reflection I do not know. I know only that I turned to neither book nor pamphlet while writing it. I did not consider it as any part of my charge to invent new ideas altogether, and to offer no sentiment which had ever been expressed before.

Two years later, Jefferson amplified on the larger point in a letter to Henry Lee Jr., the son of Henry "Light Horse Harry" Lee:

> When forced, therefore, to resort to arms for redress, an appeal to the tribunal of the world was deemed proper for our justification. This was the object of the Declaration of Independence. Not to find out new principles, or new arguments, never before thought of, not merely to say things which had never been said before; but to place before mankind the common sense of the subject, in terms so plain and firm as to command their assent, and to justify ourselves in the independent stand we are compelled to take. Neither aiming at originality of principle or sentiment, nor yet copied from any particular and previous writing, it was intended to be an expression of the American mind, and to give to that expression the proper tone and spirit called for by the occasion. All its authority rests then on the harmonizing sentiments of the day, whether expressed in conversation, in letters, printed essays, or in the elementary books of public right, as Aristotle, Cicero, Locke, Sidney, &c . . .

Sidney, a name barely recognizable to American audiences today, was Algernon Sidney, a British revolutionary and contemporary of Locke.[14] Sidney was beheaded on orders of the Crown in 1683 on trumped-up charges of conspiring to assassinate King Charles II, but his real crime—and the primary evidence against him—was his writing in support of liberty. In *Discourses Concerning Government,* Sidney wrote: "God leaves to Man the choice of Forms in Government; and those who constitute one Form, may abrogate it. The general revolt of a Nation cannot be called a Rebellion. . . . Laws and constitutions ought to be weighed . . . to constitute that which is most conducing to the establishment of justice and liberty." Sidney seems to have had few illusions that such a radical vision would ultimately only be instituted by force of arms. While at the University of Copenhagen, circa 1659, he wrote in the visitor's book

> *Manus haec inimica tyrannis*
> *Einse petit placidam cum liberate quietem.*
> (This hand, enemy to tyrants,
> By the sword seeks peace, but only peace under liberty.)

This slogan was printed beneath the frontispiece of early editions of *Discourses.* The second line was adopted as the official motto of Adams' beloved Commonwealth of Massachusetts, which retains that motto today. The *Discourses* were read by Jefferson and Adams, apparently more than once, and discussed by them in letters as late as 1823. Thus, even while defending his own reputation, Jefferson was freely reaffirming a reliance on those who came before him.

This is as it should be, notes Carl L. Becker, author of *The Declaration of Independence: A Study in the History of Political Ideas.* Becker's 1922 classic set the standard on scholarship of the Declaration—at least until Pauline Maier came along. "The primary purpose of the Declaration was not to declare independence, but to proclaim to the world the reasons for declaring independence," Becker states. "It was intended as a formal justification for an act already accomplished."

Becker goes on to dismiss the complaints of Adams and his loyalists about Jefferson's authorship not so much for being untrue, but as being beside the point. "The strength of the Declaration was precisely that it said what everyone was thinking," Becker wrote. "Nothing could have been more futile than an attempt to justify a revolution on principles which no one had ever heard of before."

It also should be acknowledged that the "principles" of revolution had been animate for a hundred generations before Jefferson & Co. arrived on the scene. A timeline tracing the origins of the American Revolution would take a diligent investigator intent on properly apportioning credit on an intellectual journey through Voltaire's France and the England of Locke and Hobbes and Milton. The road would travel through Scotland at the time of David Hume and to Holland in the early 1600s where Grotius was applying natural law to international affairs. It would include at least one visit to Italy, maybe more, and conversations—three hundred years apart—with Cardinal Bellarmine and Thomas Aquinas. It would entail many trips to ancient Greece as well, although some of the imagery invoked by the American Founders in Philadelphia is even older than that, having been committed to paper by the prophets and scribes who assembled the texts of the Old Testament.

John F. Kennedy, speaking in Philadelphia's Independence Hall on July 4, 1962, put it this way: "The theory of independence is as old as man himself, and it was not invented in this hall. But it was in this hall that the theory became a practice; that the word went out to all, in Thomas Jefferson's phrase, that 'the God who gave us life, gave us liberty at the same time.'"

We live today in an age where inclusiveness is considered a virtue, sometimes to the detriment of common sense. But in this matter of apportioning credit to the intellectual architects of the American Revolution, JFK had the right instincts. It is almost always a mistake to dismiss credible claims of assistance in the freedom business. Carl Becker, attempting to minimize the contributions from France, once asserted that there is little evidence that either Jefferson or Adams—or any of the Framers—"read many French books." But the implications of this claim are dubious, for the Framers could scarcely have been unaware of Rousseau's transformational 125-page treatise *The Social Contract*, unveiled in Amsterdam in 1762, or its electrifying opening line: *L'homme est ne libre, et partout il est dans les fers*" (Man is born free, and he is everywhere in chains.). This is an audacious opening salvo, all right, one that foreshadows not only the first sentence of the Declaration, but the closing lines of Friedrich Engel and Karl Marx's *Communist Manifesto* as well.[15] Another Frenchman, Denis Diderot, formulated the underpinnings of Jeffersonian's Deism. Educated by the Jesuits, Diderot was the chief editor of *L'Encyclopédie*, a seventeen-volume literary jewel of the Enlightenment that challenged the primacy of the Catholic Church over all aspects of French life.

"The good of the people must be the great purpose of government," reads one passage of *L'Encyclopédie.* "By the laws of nature and of reason, the governors are invested with power to that end. And the greatest good of the people is liberty. It is to the state what health is to the individual."

Voltaire, who poked fun of the monarchy in his plays and lived to tell about it, was a collaborator on *L'Encyclopédie*, and contributor to that work. So was philosopher Guillaume Thomas Francois Raynal, a priest who surprised even himself by surviving the French Revolution, which he had denounced for its excesses. Raynal died of natural causes in 1796, having lived long enough to see freedom take root on two continents. In the final volume of their epic history of western civilization, Will and Ariel Durant state flatly that Washington, Franklin and Jefferson and the other American patriots "were sons of the French Enlightenment."

Perhaps. But let us not go too far the other way and denigrate the English. It was while he was in England during one of his banishments that Voltaire was first exposed to the still-burning embers of Locke. Some of Voltaire's earliest purely political manuscripts, in fact, were written in the English language, including the 1727 *Essay Upon the Civil Wars in France.* In his *Histoire de Charles XII*, Voltaire disputes the notion that divine intervention guides kings—or is determinate in secular human affairs. His *Philosophical Letters*, published in 1734, contrasts the English system of government to that of France. Chagrined French authorities noticed that England comes off better in this comparison, and Voltaire found it necessary to flee Paris yet again. In 1748, another Frenchman, Baron de Montesquieu, published a book titled the *Spirit of Laws* extolling the English concept of the separation of powers, a doctrine that dates to 1215 and the signing of the Magna Carta at Runnymede.[16]

Ultimately the end of an inquiry into the origins of freedom depends mostly on how far back one wants to look. John Locke risked his life by saying, while postulating the existence of natural laws of men, that sensation was the only true means of knowledge. Two thousand years earlier, the Greek philosopher Protagoras made the same claim. "Man is the measure of all things—of those that are, that they are, and those that are not, that they are not," he said. Protagoras was not afraid to take his point to its logical conclusion, which was to question faith in the gods themselves. "With regard to the gods I know not whether they exist or not, or what they are like," Protagoras said at the end of a treatise he wrote—and then read—to a gathering of prominent Athenian intellectuals. "Many things prevent our knowing: the subject is obscure, and brief is the span of our mortal life."[17]

"To the historical eye, a whole world begins to tremble when Protagoras announces this simple principle of humanism and relativity," observed Will Durant. "All established truths and sacred principles crack; individualism has found a voice and a philosophy, and the supernatural bases of social order threaten to melt away."

It was not a straight line from the Greeks to the framers of the Declaration of Independence, of course. Nor does the fact that freedom has many intellectual fathers mean that all of the assertions about who influenced Thomas Jefferson are accurate, or even truthful. In 1819, Whigs in the state of North Carolina published a reconstruction of something called the "Mecklenburg Resolves," supposedly produced by militiamen in that county on May 20, 1775, and containing four verbatim quotations from Jefferson's Declaration. Adams, who should have known better, immediately seized on this clearly fraudulent claim, expressing shock, shock that Jefferson had plagiarized an earlier document. It was, of course, the other way around, but the controversy didn't finally die out in North Carolina until a last-ditch attempt in 1905 to establish the authenticity of the Mecklenburg Resolves proved instead that it was a hoax. It turns out that the North Carolinians who championed the Mecklenburg ruse were intellectual grifters who originally embraced the ruse specifically to sully Jefferson's reputation. Their aim was to promote Southern nationalism instead of American unity, a tainted cause if ever there was one. Long after the Civil War, the Mecklenburg myth lived on, at least in North Carolina, apparently owing to a less odious, but still petty, purpose: claiming authorship of snippets of Jefferson's prose became a source of misguided regional pride.

No sooner was the spurious Mecklenburg claim at long last laid to rest than another controversy presented itself concerning the origins of Jefferson's inspiration. This one was more worthy. In 1917, Gaillard Hunt, chief of the Manuscripts Division of the Library of Congress, published an article in *Catholic Historical Review* postulating that Jefferson, James Madison and George Mason drew from the writings of a sixteenth-century Italian priest, Robert Bellarmine. A classic Renaissance man, Bellarmine was the most influential theologian of the Catholic "counter-reformation," which he led with his four-volume work known as "the

Controversies." (Its full title, in Latin, was *Disputationes de Contro-versiis Christianae Fidei Adversus Hujus Temporis Haereticos*, which translates as "Disputations about the Controversies of the Christian Faith Against the Heretics of this Time.) Bellarmine was commissioned by Pope Clement VIII to write the catechisms of Catholicism, documents that constituted the Vatican's official rebuttal to Martin Luther, who had developed the catechism style to spread the Protestant faith. Bellarmine was made a Cardinal in 1598, a rare honor for a Jesuit, and later an archbishop. In 1605, when Paul V became pope, he brought Bellarmine back to Rome and installed him as head of the vast Vatican Library, one of the great repositories of learning in the world at that time.

In 1609, King James I of England published the rationale for—dare we say?—a self-serving little theory known as the "divine rights of kings." The notion had been bandied around Europe for three centuries or more, but as the continent's monarchies squared off against each other along lines demarcated by religion, the doctrine took on a new urgency. "The state of monarchy is the supremest thing upon earth; for kings are not only God's lieutenants upon earth, and sit upon God's throne, but even by God himself are called gods." So wrote James I. He added: "Kings are justly called gods, for that they exercise a manner or resemblance of divine power upon earth: for if you will consider the at-tributes to God, you shall see how they agree in the person of a king."

In Rome, the brilliant Bellarmine took aim. He wrote two pam-phlets, the first of which made fun of the poor quality of the king's Latin. In the second, *De Potestate Summi Pontifics in Rebus Temporalibus*, the priest attacked the arguments of James I frontally. But undermining the theological justification for kings is a slope that gets slippery pretty fast for any kind of authoritarian. Thus, even though Bellarmine (citing Plato) expressed fears that pure democracy would lead to anarchy, the Cardinal also penned several lines that sound as though they belonged in Philadelphia in 1776 instead of Rome in the late 1500s.

"For legitimate reasons people can change the government to an aristocracy or a democracy or vice versa," Bellarmine wrote in chapter six of *De Laicis*. "The people never transfers its power to a king so com-pletely but that it reserves to itself the right of receiving back this power."

To some, this might sound eerily like: "Whenever any form of gov-ernment becomes destructive of these ends, it is the right of the people to alter or abolish it, and to institute a new government. . . ."

It certainly did to Gaillard Hunt, a historian and a Catholic convert. Hunt also noted that Bellarmine provided a foretaste of the Declaration's claim that "governments are instituted among men, deriving their just powers from the consent of the governed." The Cardinal's version: "It depends upon the consent of the multitude to constitute over itself a king, consul, or other magistrate. This power is, indeed, from God, but vested in a particular ruler by the counsel and election of men."

Hunt then asked, somewhat playfully, "Did the Americans realize that they were staking their lives, their fortunes and their sacred honor in support of a theory of government which had come down to them . . . from a Catholic priest?"

This seems like mild fare today, but Hunt's article and his droll question set in motion a bitter academic exchange that sounds to modern ears more sectarian than scholastic in nature. Catholic educators chortled that their church was actually the seed of democracy; Protestant eminences, such as David S. Schaff, a professor at Union Theological Seminary in New York, scoffed at the "Bellarmine-Jefferson legend," and ended up attacking not only Hunt, but Bellarmine as well. The Protestant scholars' insisted indignantly that no work of Bellarmine ever appeared in Jefferson's library and that, in any event, Jefferson's grasp of Latin was not sufficient for him to have tackled Bellarmine, whose prose is pretty thick going. Ah, replied Catholic scholars, but there *was* a volume of Bellarmine at Princeton's library when James Madison was in attendance at that university. And so it went, back and forth.

A more dispassionate view (my own) is that Jefferson almost certainly knew of Bellarmine's writings. For starters, as Hunt pointed out, the library at Monticello did contain a copy of *Patriarcha: The Natural Power of Kings*, which Jefferson almost certainly read. This book, written by Robert Filmer, was an apologia of the divine right of kings and was published in 1680 upon the reinstitution of the Stuart monarchy.[18] *Patriarcha* quotes Bellarmine extensively, if only to rebut the good Cardinal, and does so prominently and in the table of contents, no less. It was Filmer's work, in part, that John Locke was responding to in his *Second Treatise*, the one that produced the memorable lines about life, liberty and property. And why exactly Jefferson changed the Lockean language to read "life, liberty and the pursuit of happiness"—here we are getting back to our original purpose—has been the subject of conjecture for more than two centuries.

Born in 1632 and educated at Christ Church, Oxford, Locke was a protégé of the liberal Lord Ashley (Anthony Ashley Cooper) who today is known in history as the Earl of Shaftesbury. Locke was trained as a physician, but his true interest was philosophy. In the *Second Treatise*, which was written earlier but published in 1690, Locke wrote that men unite in a society "for the mutual preservation of their lives, liberties, and estates, which I call by the general name 'property.'" Locke added: "Every man has a property in his own person. This nobody has any right to but himself. The labor of his body, and the work of his hands, we may say, are properly his."

Modern conservatives in the United States, concerned about what they see as an undemocratic erosion of property rights in twentieth- and twenty-first-century America, sometimes cite these words as a way of attempting to claim Locke as one of their own. They do the same with Jefferson, and with James Madison, who wrote about the concept of property after the Revolution: "In its larger and juster meaning it embraces every thing to which a man may attach a value and have a right; and *which leaves to everyone one else the like advantage.*"[19]

"In the former sense, a man's land, or merchandize, or money is called his property," Madison added. "In the latter sense, a man has a property in his opinions and the free communication of them. He has a property of peculiar value in his religious opinions, and in the profession and practice dictated by them. He has a property very dear to him in the safety and liberty of his person. . . . In a word, as a man is said to have a right to his property, he may be equally said to have a property in his rights." What is so striking about this passage is the expansiveness of Madison's understanding of "property." For him, clearly, the concept is wrapped up in intellectual freedom, a concept that in his time would have included freedom of religion.

There are strong hints that this was also true of Locke. In the waning days of the English Civil War, a group of brave idealists surfaced who came to be known as the Levellers. This name was given to them—accounts differ on whether it was Cromwell or Charles I—presumably because they wanted to level the estates of the rich. That wasn't in their platform, exactly, but the reforms they pushed were radical and they were democratic. The Levellers called for abolition of the monarchy and the House of Lords, suffrage for most Englishmen, direct elections of representatives to the House of Commons, an end to the class system, separation of church and state and an understanding that no one is above the law. For their troubles, Leveller leaders such as John Lilburne were tortured, flogged or imprisoned in the London Tower. But even if they are scarcely remembered in England today, and mostly unheard of in the United States, their ideas did not die with them. Among their members were some of Cromwell's former soldiers, men who grew weary of the sectarian violence that wracked England depending on the king's religion. The English Civil War pitted Parliament against the monarchy. But religious strife complicated and exacerbated the struggle. In 1648 while Cromwell was ruthlessly putting down a Catholic rebellion in Ireland, Charles Stuart made common cause with the Scots. As a result, Presbyterians were expelled from Parliament and, after Cromwell defeated the invading Scots at Preston Pride's Purge, Charles was tried and executed.

In such an environment, religious toleration was both the Levellers' most necessary and most radical creed. The best writer among them, John Overton, took direct aim not only at the harmful effects of government-mandated business monopolies, but also at the monopoly of the Church of England. In an essay called *An Arrow Against All Tyrants*, Overton equated the right to own property with liberty. "To every individual in nature is given an individual property in nature, not to be invaded or usurped by any," he wrote. "No man has power over my rights and liberties, and I over no man's."

Lilburne had invoked the precedent of Runnymede to give his movement legitimacy, but Overton's formulation sounds more like natural law than anything in the Magna Carta. William Walwyn, another Leveller theorist, called directly for religious freedom, predicting that tolerance would eventually produce more peace. The Levellers' emphasis on private property rights was a response to the frustrations of an emerging but stifled generation of middle-class merchants. But it also appears to have been tailored to fit into an intellectual framework designed to protect freedom of religion—and thus end religious-inspired violence: If an Englishman's home is his castle, and he practices his religion in the privacy of his home, then civic strife over religion would be kept to a minimum. This is the implication of Overton—that property rights relate directly to freedom of religion—and it is in this context that Locke was writing.

By the eve of the American Revolution, free thinkers in London took pride in knowing that one reason the colonists were so restive is that they had once been British themselves. Edmund Burke, speaking on March 22, 1775, put it this way. "This fierce spirit of liberty is stronger in the English colonies probably than in any other people of the earth; and this from a great variety of powerful causes; which, to understand the true temper of their minds, and the direction which this spirit takes, it will not be amiss to lay open somewhat more largely. First, the people of the colonies are descendants of Englishmen."

There is a paradox implicit in Burke's observation: Americans knew they didn't want to be oppressed by Parliament—or by King George III—precisely *because* their political sensibilities were English in origin. But if this sounds like a perverse boast, similar sentiments were uttered in America, too, by patriots as different in their outlooks as James Otis and George Washington. Less ironic, perhaps, is the contribution to the spirit of rebellion that came from Scotland, a land that still exhibits ambivalence about being part of Great Britain all these years later. In 1978, award-winning historian and best-selling author Garry Wills challenged the prevailing view that the Founders' primary philosophical underpinnings were Lockean in origin. In *Inventing America*, Wills examined the actual books that Jefferson read as a young man and discovered something fascinating: there were far fewer English writers and far more Scottish writers than had been previously supposed. This is a significant distinction for those interested in political theory because in the Scottish Enlightenment "moral sense" is the distinguishing human characteristic. It also is a more communal, and less individualistic, tradition. Wills, a gifted writer of prose in his own right, also pays close attention to the exact phrasings of Jefferson. He finds in the Declaration borrowings from the Scottish Enlightenment, including "all men are created equal," and "in-alienable rights." In so doing, he asserts that Jefferson—and his countrymen—had Scottish philosophers Francis Hutcheson and Thomas Reid to thank as much as they did Locke and Hobbes.

In the end, the point is that there was a wealth of freedom-loving philosophers on the European continent for the drafters of the Declaration to draw on. "Where Jefferson got his ideas, is hardly so much a question," Becker notes, "as where he could have got away from them."

In *American Scripture,* Maier picks up where Becker leaves off. She cites not only the contributions of philosophers such as Locke, but of Jefferson's contemporaries on this side of the ocean, including Lee, Paine, George Mason, both Adamses (Samuel and John), Josiah Bartlett, Elbridge Gerry and William Henry Drayton, the chief justice of South Carolina.[20] Once again, the point is that this was not strictly a Revolution led from on high by great men, but one that simultaneously worked its way up from the grassroots. It had to be so if the scattered colonists were to rouse themselves to defeat in battle the disciplined regulars of the British Crown. The townsmen of Massachusetts' villages such as Topfield and Malden and local officials in places such as Anne Arundel and Frederick County in Maryland beat the Continental Congress to the punch in calling for independence from England. Some of these connections are more immediate to Jefferson than others; the influence of George Mason appears to be the most direct.

Jefferson might not have brought any of the volumes in his vaunted library to Philadelphia, but he certainly had access to the Virginia Declaration of Rights, which Mason, with help from Madison—and Jefferson—had cobbled together weeks before in Williamsburg. Jefferson almost certainly had many of the most salient phrases of this document committed to memory. He may have had the Virginia document itself in his saddlebags. Even if he didn't, it was reprinted in Philadelphia's newspapers as he was writing.[21] The Virginia Declaration of Rights opens this way:

> That all men are by nature equally free and independent, and have certain inherent rights, of which, when they enter into a state of society, they cannot, by any compact, deprive or divest their posterity; namely, the enjoyment of life and liberty, with the means of acquiring and possessing property, and pursuing and obtaining happiness and safety.

Article II in this document continues in a vein that will sound familiar as well:

> That all power is vested in, and consequently derived from, the people; that magistrates are their trustees and servants, and at all times amenable to them.

And Article III goes on to say:

> That government is, or ought to be, instituted for the common benefit, protection, and security of the people, nation or community; of all the various modes and forms of government that is best, which is capable of producing the greatest degree of happiness and safety and is most effectually secured against the danger of maladministration; and that, whenever any government shall be found inadequate

or contrary to these purposes, a majority of the community hath an indubitable, unalienable, and indefeasible right to reform, alter or abolish it, in such manner as shall be judged most conducive to the public weal.

And Article VII posits:

That all power of suspending laws, or the execution of laws, by any authority without consent of the representatives of the people is injurious to their rights and ought not to be exercised.

This is the language, cumbersome to be sure, that Jefferson condensed into a more powerful and literary passage that begins, "When in the course of human events . . ." In this case, as Maier observed, less was definitely more. But was Jefferson merely rewriting Mason, editing the older man's words, as it were? Well, not exactly.

In 1766, while in England serving as a kind of unofficial ambassador to England, Benjamin Franklin had made a distinction between "internal" and "external" taxes while testifying before Parliament. His testimony helped convince Parliament to repeal the hated Stamp Act, but it did nothing to quell the growing appetite in the colonies for liberation. Writing in the *Pennsylvania Chronicle* under the nom de plume "Letters from a Farmer in Pennsylvania," John Dickinson had written that Franklin's dichotomy was the wrong way to look at the issue. To Dickinson, the crucial distinction was between taxes levied for regulation and those enacted for revenue. In other words, between taxes that simply helped facilitate the free flow of commerce and those designed to retain the Americans in a colonial, and thus subservient, state. Interestingly, the Dickinson letters were so thoughtful and provocative, they were initially believed by some to have been written by Franklin, as a way of showing the evolution of his own thinking. But Franklin himself was unsure of their authorship, even after he arranged for them to be reprinted in London. The Dickinson letters were written to justify opposition to the Townshend acts. But they got Franklin to thinking, and eventually he concluded that he and Dickinson—thoughtful moderates both—had been parsing this matter too closely, that there was no truly tenable intellectual middle ground. In March 1768, Franklin wrote:

The more I have thought and read on the subject, the more I find myself confirmed in my opinion that no middle doctrine can be well maintained, I mean not clearly with intelligible arguments. Something might be made of either of the extremes; that Parliament has a power to make *all laws* for us, or that it has a power to make *no laws* for us.

To his son William, Franklin confided: "I think the arguments for the latter more numerous and weighty than those for the former." By 1770, Franklin publicly asserted that it was clear that only the king had any basis in English constitutional law for governing the colonies; that it was self-evident that Parliament had "usurped" its rightful authority. In *Considerations on the Nature and Extent of the Legislative Authority of the British Parliament*, the Scottish-born James Wilson, a law partner of Dickinson's, followed Franklin's logic and answered his question in a 1774 essay:

All men are, by nature, equal and free: no one has a right to any authority over another without his consent: all lawful government is founded on the consent of those who are subject to it: such consent was given with a view to ensure and to increase the happiness of the governed, above what they could enjoy in an independent and unconnected state of nature. The consequence is, that the happiness of the society is the first law of every government.[22]

Here, in the prose of an Americanized Scot, was not just a tidy summation of Locke's natural law, but a fusing argument that applied those laws to the colonists' longing for independence. Moreover, it's all here, not just the argument that governments' authority is derived from the governed, but that "happiness" is its primary rationale for existence. In Article I of Virginia's Declaration of Rights, Mason also used the word "happiness," and the word "pursuing" as well. A year earlier, Jefferson had prepared what he characterized as "instruction" to the delegates appointed to the first Continental Congress as to what they should "remind" the king. Later printed as an essay, *A Summary View of the Rights of British America*, Jefferson also speaks of happiness in the context of political freedom—in July 1774. It was from this writing of Jefferson's that John Kennedy was quoting:

. . . our ancestors, before their emigration to America, were the free inhabitants of the British dominions in Europe, and possessed a right which nature has given to all men, of departing from the country in which chance, not choice, has placed them, of going in quest of new habitations, and of there establishing new societies, under such laws and regulations as to them shall seem most likely to promote public happiness. . . . That these are our grievances which we have thus laid before his majesty, with that freedom of language and sentiment which becomes a free people claiming their rights, as derived from the laws of nature, and not as the gift of their chief magistrate: Let those flatter who fear; it is not an American art. To give praise which is not due might be well from the venal, but would ill beseem those who are asserting the rights of human nature. They know, and will therefore say, that kings are the servants, not the proprietors of the people. . . . The God who gave us life gave us liberty at the same time . . .

So we can see that happiness in the context of making good government didn't arrive like a thunderbolt out of the Philadelphia summer, striking Jefferson in the noggin as he labored over his "writing box" in Jacob Graff's house. It came, instead, as beams of light from all over the colonies, from across the oceans and the centuries. Certainly, the notion that a government exists to guarantee a right to seek "happiness" is widely seen all over the world as being quintessentially American. And it is. The French, even though the Marquis de Lafayette (with Jefferson's help) participated in the drafting of their Declaration, didn't include happiness as a goal.[23] And yet, it's a concept and a desire that the Founders themselves considered universally human—and timeless. There is an Old Testament passage that was widely quoted in Revolutionary times, and still is today, especially in times of war, when it becomes a call for peace. It's from Micah, chapter four, verse three:

And He shall judge among many people,
and rebuke strong nations afar off;
and they shall beat their swords into plowshares,
and their spears into pruning hooks:
nation shall not lift up a sword against nation,
neither shall they learn war any more.

But there is more to this passage, and the part that follows was often cited, Framer-to-Framer, as an idealized description of what peace, independence and happiness would entail for them personally:

> *But they shall sit every man*
> *under his vine and under his fig tree;*
> *and none shall make them afraid*

This verse was a familiar reference in colonial America; it resonated particularly among the Virginia planters. On February 1, 1784,
after General Washington retired to Mount Vernon, for, as he mistak-
enly believed, the rest of his life, he wrote a poignant letter to Lafayette,
who had been like a son to him: "At length my Dear Marquis I am become a private citizen on the banks of the Potomac, and under the
shadow of my own Vine and my own Fig-tree, free from the bustle of a
camp and the busy scenes of public life . . ."

After leaving the presidency and returning to his beloved home for
a final time, Washington employed the same biblical imagery in a May
15, 1797, letter to Oliver Walcott Jr., directly equating it to his personal
happiness. He spoke of his farm not unlike the Marines on Guadalcanal
spoke of pie. Washington used the biblical language of the fig tree and
the vine no fewer than eleven times in the years 1796 and 1797.

We know that Jefferson also had a glorious Virginia home, more
stunning even than Mount Vernon, and that he loved it there. We know,
too, that Jefferson's phrase, the pursuit of happiness, encompasses so
much more than a happy farmer sitting under his tree. Historians who
have deconstructed the myth of Jefferson as a solitary genius have generally been more interested in where the *ideas* of the Declaration came
from, and less so with the rationale for his precise *words*. Pauline Maier
is an exception: she seems equally interested in both. And she is as charitable about Jefferson's writing about liberty as she is uncompromising
about his borrowing of its concepts.

"In the 18th century," she writes, "educated people regarded with
disdain the striving for novelty. Achievement lay instead in the creative
adaptation of pre-existing models to different circumstances, and the
highest praise of all went to imitations whose excellence exceeded that
of the examples that inspired them. Young men were taught to copy and
often to memorize compelling passages from their readings for future
use since you could never tell when, say, a citation from Cicero might
come in handy." And Thomas Jefferson, as Dumas Malone noted, had
"a rare gift for adaptation."

But even that is not enough of a defense of Jefferson. The power of the Declaration of Independence came from two sources. The first were its ideas, which as Adams, Jefferson and everyone else agree came from many great minds, spanning the centuries. The second was its language. When I was in college, my German language professor had a poster on his wall. It looked something like this:

When Cicero spoke, the people said, "How well he spoke."
WHEN DEMOSTHENES SPOKE, THE PEOPLE SAID, "LET US MARCH!"

Jefferson's challenge as a writer was to hit both these notes. On the one hand, history was watching, the French were waiting, the most brilliant men in the western world were judging the Americans by the power of their argument. On the other hand, General Washington and his troops were already on the march. These Continental Soldiers were not scholars of Greek and Latin. They were men who understood the language of Thomas Paine much better than John Locke—and they were in the field facing a better-equipped and highly feared army.

That was the challenge Jefferson faced in his rooms in Philadelphia. And he faced it alone, for that is the essential nature of the task. "Writing is a solitary occupation," said Jessamyn West, the Indiana-born and California-raised writer. "Family, friends, and society are the natural enemies of the writer." Jefferson himself might have included editors in that category, specifically South Carolina delegates, New England radicals and even a certain fatherly former newspaper editor from Pennsylvania. But such sentiments are common to gifted writers, even those without the responsibility of fomenting Revolution, for they know what non-writers do not: it is hard work. "Writing is easy," observed Gene Fowler, a biographer, novelist and screenwriter. "All you do is stare at a blank sheet of paper until drops of blood form on your forehead."

Other authors, without having Jefferson in mind, have paid homage to another truth: there aren't that many original ideas, even for original writers. "What moves men of genius, or rather what inspires their work, is not new ideas," said Eugene Delacroix, "but their obsession with the idea that what has already been said is still not enough." W. H. Auden put it this way: "Some writers confuse authenticity, which they ought always to aim at, with originality, which they should never bother about."

Perhaps that's the way we ought to think of Jefferson's 1776 rephrasing of John Locke and George Mason and James Wilson—and even the Thomas Jefferson of 1774. The prose in the preamble was authentic; it derived its power both from the force of the ideas and the vitality of the language. And the most resonant phrase of all was "Life, Liberty and the Pursuit of Happiness." Some scholars have wondered if Jefferson wasn't being deliberately vague with the third item on this list in order to avoid a semantic trap he had set for himself: How can something (property), which can be sold, lost or even renounced be described as an "unalienable" right? Jefferson was a stylist who prided himself on his phrasemaking, and might simply have solved this conundrum by substituting for the word property a more flowery—and elusive—concept. Maier implies as much: "In this case," she says, "Jefferson perhaps sacrificed clarity of meaning for grace of language."

She may be right, but my own view is that Jefferson's purposes in his word choices were more profound. Certainly that was their effect. A later generation would take heart in Jefferson's wording, noting that at the time black people were, legally, property, and that *pursuit of happiness* was, however inadvertently, a subversive word substitution that removed even by implication any tacit approval of the notion that the institution of slavery is compatible with a revolution based on a desire for liberty.

It was forward looking, this choice of words, in another way as well. Although the new nation would need capitalists, mercantilists and entrepreneurs—men of property—Jefferson also imagined, correctly, that for many Americans the pursuit of their freedoms wouldn't involve engaging in commerce or farming or in the accumulation of material possessions at all. Perhaps the ministry—or a career in the army—was what he wanted the Declaration to guarantee. Or maybe a chance at the writer's life. In *The Story of American Freedom*, Columbia University history professor Eric Foner explains it this way: "When Jefferson substituted 'the pursuit of happiness' for 'property' in the familiar Lockean triad that opened the Declaration of Independence, he tied the new nation's star to an open-ended, democratic process whereby individuals develop their own potential and seek to realize their own life goals."

Foner's explanation has the ring of truth to it. Jefferson may not have ever explained exactly what he had in mind when he tinkered so wonderfully with Locke's original formulation—and with George Mason's lengthier wording—but this is precisely its genius. Americans can grow into the phrase as they, and their nation, change. And like so much else that Jefferson did, such as orchestrating the Louisiana Purchase, his words and deeds shaped the very character of the nation he did so much to create. In their 1943 article published in the now-defunct scholarly *Ethics* magazine, Frank P. Bourgin and Charles E. Merriam wrote of Jefferson's interests in land-use planning, education, agriculture, economics, political science and central planning while postulating that Jefferson "not only set forth the *ends*, but also planned constructively the *means* of attaining life, liberty, the pursuit of happiness, and the consent of the governed."

Walter Berns, a more contemporary political scientist, lends his weight to this view of Jefferson. In *The New Pursuit of Happiness*, published in 1987, Berns suggests that when the Founders specifically delegated to Congress the authority to promote science and the "useful arts," they were consciously joining science and industry, and they helped create the nation in which Jefferson's pursuit of happiness came to be understood, as Tocqueville expressed it, as pursuing "the good things of life."

Thus, in writing quixotically about "happiness," as well as in nudging a nation westward to wild, untamed lands, Jefferson helped American generations achieve their destiny—without knowing himself exactly what that destiny might be. Perhaps this was Jefferson's true genius. The future of an individual—or of a nation—is an open-ended question that shouldn't be, can't be, determined by kings, customs or decrees. That's what freedom is.

On his first July 4 as president, Bill Clinton put it this way in remarks at Independence Hall in Philadelphia: "Thomas Jefferson wrote that blistering Declaration of Independence knowing that his ideals challenged his country to change."

After he left office, in an e-mail to me, Clinton expounded on this theme.

> He gave us the Declaration of Independence, the Louisiana Purchase, the Lewis and Clark expedition. He created the first effective political party, which dominated American political life for his two terms and a generation afterward. Most important, he gave us an understanding of how America works, how we have become the longest lasting great democracy in history: always holding to fixed principles—life, liberty, the pursuit of happiness—but always willing to change to meet the challenges of each new time. As he said,

"life belongs to the living." Thomas Jefferson understood that no politician, no government, no piece of paper could do for the American people what they would have to do for themselves, that the people of this country would always have to be not only the protectors of their own liberty, but the agents of their own transformation and change.

The last letter Jefferson wrote, just ten days before his death, contains a passage in which Jefferson takes pride, seemingly on behalf of all the Founders, in the fact that the American Revolution had exposed this "palpable truth" to the world: *". . . that the mass of mankind has not been born with saddles on their backs, nor a favored few booted and spurred, ready to ride them legitimately, by the grace of God."*[24]

This has become an oft-quoted line, invariably attributed to Jefferson. But at the time he wrote it, it would have been recognizable to many of Jefferson's contemporaries as a faithful recitation of the dying words of an English rebel named Richard Rumbold, who was hanged in 1685. Executed in Edinburgh for his role in a failed insurrection and the unsuccessful ambush of King Charles II and his brother James, Rumbold had this to say on the gallows, according to English historian Thomas Babington Macaulay: "He was a friend, he said, to limited monarchy. But he never would believe that Providence had sent a few men into the world ready-booted and spurred to ride."

Rumbold's execution and his dying words are reminiscent to Americans of the brave death of defiant American patriot Nathan Hale, also hanged by the British, on September 22, 1776. But there is another connection. Rumbold had been a Leveller, and therefore was also a link to men who inspired John Locke, as well as Jefferson and Adams and the other Founders. Late in life, as Jefferson and Adams grew old together, communicating through letters, they looked out on the world and wondered how much of it would be backlit by the fires they had helped light. Jefferson seemed to be assuring his friend of the universality of the longing for freedom.

In 1821, Adams had expressed dismay with the endless wars and machinations of the European monarchs. The Greeks' war for independence against Turkey had erupted that year. Russia encouraged the Greeks, while Great Britain and Austria tried to persuade the Tsar that supporting revolutions might set a bad precedent. This reactionary stance was not momentous—Greek independence was won the following January—but it was discouraging to Adams, who feared that the great western powers of Europe had learned nothing from the American Revolution. Jefferson counseled his friend to think otherwise.

"Yet I will not believe our labors are lost," he wrote Adams in a letter from Monticello dated September 12, 1821. "I shall not die without a hope that light and liberty are on a steady advance. We have seen indeed once within the records of history a compleat eclipse of the human mind continuing for centuries. And this too by swarms of the same Northern barbarians, conquering and taking possession of the countries and governments of the civilized world. Should this again be attempted . . . the art of printing alone, and the vast dissemination of books, will remain the mind where it is, and raise the conquering ruffians to the level of the conquered, instead of degrading these to that of their conquerors. And even should the cloud of barbarism and despotism again obscure the science and liberties of Europe, this country remains to preserve and restore light and liberty to them. In short, the flames kindled on the 4th of July 1776 have spread over too much of the globe to be extinguished by the feeble engines of despotism. On the contrary they will consume those engines and all who work with them."

This Jefferson copied from no one.

3

Everywhere in Chains

While bivouacked at Valley Forge, the troops of the Continental Army frequently played a form of baseball. General Washington liked to watch the games, which the soldiers called "fives." But this was difficult. The general, preserving a formality between himself and his troops, refused their entreaties to join in. For their part, the men displayed their respect for Washington by stopping the game whenever they became aware he was observing them.[1] But Washington's passion for what would become the national pastime would not be quenched. A French officer attached to the American army named Francois, Marquis de Barbe-Marbois wrote in letters back to France that Washington sometimes "throws and catches a ball for whole hours with his aides-de-camp."

But war is not a game, and in a democracy almost all of the men sent to fight it are happiest when it ends. So too was it with General Washington's army. On the 19th day of April in 1783, Congress proclaimed an end to the hostilities with Great Britain. The day before, as word went through the officer corps that official victory was imminent, the General issued an uncharacteristic order: that an extra ration of liquor to be issued "to every man tomorrow, to drink Perpetual Peace, Independence and Happiness to the United States of America."[2]

But the inherent and abiding contradiction in the success of the American Revolution was there from the beginning and everyone knew it; Southerners as well as New Englanders, blacks as well as whites, slaves as well—no, better—than free men. Out of a population of 3.9 million, some 700,000 of those residing in the American colonies were living in human bondage. How were these people, who had not realized liberty in the War for Independence, to pursue their happiness? How could they pursue anything? Even keeping their families together was beyond their control.

> Now my dear son I pray you to come and see your dear old Mother—Or send me twenty dollar and I will come and see you in Philadelphia—And if you cant come to see your old Mother pray send me a letter and tell me where you live what family you have and what you do for a living—I am a poor old servant I long for freedom . . . I love you Cato . . . (you) are my only son.

So wrote, in 1805, a slave woman named Hannah Grover, who added in her postscript that she loved her son "with all my heart."[3] She had last seen him in 1785.

Such heartbreaking emotions were a daily reality for more than one-sixth of the inhabitants of the new nation. The magnitude of this daily, ongoing tragedy was not lost on the men who had founded the United States. Jefferson's own writings on this subject are well known even today. "I tremble for my country when I reflect that God is just," he wrote in 1782 in *Notes on Virginia* as he contemplated the effects of slavery. Jefferson added, in a less famous passage: "With what execration should the statesman be loaded who, permitting one half the citizens . . . to trample on the rights of the other, transforms those into despots, and these into enemies, destroys the morals of the one part, and the *amore patriae* (love of country) of the other."

But neither Jefferson nor George Mason, the Founder who wouldn't sign the Constitution because it lacked a Bill of Rights, relinquished their own slaves. And Mason was even blunter than Jefferson about how the institution he called "that slow poison" shamed and warped whites even as it was enchaining blacks.

> [Slavery] is daily contaminating the Minds & Morals of our People. Every Gentlemen here is born a petty Tyrant. Practiced in Acts of Despotism & Cruelty, we become callous to the Dictates of Humanity, & all the finer feelings of the Soul. Taught to regard a part of our own Species in the most abject & contemptible Degree below us, we lose that Idea of the dignity of Man which the Hand of Nature had implanted in us, for great & useful purposes. Habituated from our Infancy to trample upon the Rights of Human Nature, every generous, every liberal Sentiment, if not extinguished, is enfee-

bled in our Minds. And in such an infernal School are to be educated
our future Legislators & Rulers.

John Locke had pointed out plainly that slavery was one of the vestiges of the old, monarchal world. He compared the institution to a state
of war. But in America it was only in the northern colonies that the Declaration of Independence's implications for slavery were understood
clearly at the time that document was written. When the Framers met in
Philadelphia in 1776, slavery was present in every northern colony. But
in that region of the new nation, the spirit of Revolution was followed
to its logical conclusion. Bernard Bailyn, the Pulitzer Prize–winning Harvard historian and author of *The Ideological Origins of the American
Revolution*, attributed the end of Northern slavery to the "Contagion of
Liberty."[4] In the year after the Declaration, Vermont formed as a state
and abolition was part of its Constitution. In 1804, when New Jersey
adopted an emancipation statute, it became the last Northern state to do
so. But even by then, the institution was deeply embedded in the Southern economy, and more ominously, in the Southern identity.

To modern observers, slavery seems so monumentally immoral—
and the defense of it so grotesquely blind—that we have trouble compre-
hending it. Yet it must be emphasized that there were men and women
alive at that time who felt the way we do now—and who said so. The
first article ever penned by Thomas Paine was a powerful screed against
slavery. It was published March 8, 1775, in the *Pennsylvania Journal
and the Weekly Advertiser*.[5] The Quakers petitioned the federal government to end the practice of slavery as early as 1783, as soon as there was
a government to petition. They put their objections in language that was
both theological and evocative of the secular spirit of independence:

"We conceive it our indispensable duty to revive the lamentable
grievance of that oppressed people," they wrote. They demanded, but in
polite language, "the serious attention of those who are entrusted with
the powers of Government, as Guardians of the common rights of Mankind and advocates for liberty."

In 1784, Yale-educated Samuel Hopkins, a Congregational minister with a church in Newport, R.I., persuaded the members of his church
to exclude members who held slaves. In *A Dialogue Concerning the
Slavery of Africans*, he wrote, "The Declaration of Independence says
'*all* men are created equal and they are endowed by their Creator with
certain unalienable rights.' Oh, the shocking, the intolerable inconsis-

tence!" In 1787, Benjamin Franklin was elected president of the Pennsylvania Society for Promoting the Abolition of Slavery. The same year, Pennsylvania sent Franklin to the Constitutional Convention, where he shared his views, but signed anyway when they were not adopted. A Quaker-led petition calling on Congress to abolish slavery carrying Franklin's signature was submitted to the House and the Senate in 1790, the year of Franklin's death.

Over the next forty years, so many such petitions would make their way to Congress that in 1836 Southern members of the House of Representatives succeeded in passing a gag rule that automatically tabled them. John Quincy Adams, after serving one term as president and returning to the House of Representatives in 1831, would rail against this rule—he got it repealed after eight years—while inveighing against slavery itself until he died in 1848 from a stroke suffered on the floor of the House.

Quincy Adams, who in his diary characterized slavery "a foul stain" upon the nation, regularly tried to explain to South Carolina Sen. John C. Calhoun that the institution was in every way incompatible with America's founding documents and with the spirit of Independence. Calhoun's reply? "He said he did not think it would produce a dissolution of the Union," Adams wrote, "but if it should the South would be from necessity compelled to form an alliance, offensive and defensive with Great Britain."[6]

Adams persisted, asking Calhoun how enslaving men—and spreading the institution of slavery to new territories—could possibly, in the Senator's mind, be consistent with such documents as the Declaration of Independence or the Constitution of the United States. Adams specifically mentioned the latter document's preamble, and its vow to establish justice.[7] Calhoun's answer to this line of entreaty was as chilling as his threats of disunion. "Calhoun . . . said that the principles which I had avowed were just and noble: but that in the Southern country, whenever they were mentioned, they were always understood as applying only to white men. Domestic labor was confined to blacks, and such was the prejudice, that if he, who was the most popular man in his district, were to keep a white servant in his house, his character and reputation would be irretrievably ruined."

In other words, the ominous predictions of George Mason that the institution of slavery would produce a region of "petty tyrants" in whose minds "generous" or "liberal" sentiment would be extinguished had already come true. ("I am an aristocrat," maintained Virginia plantation owner John Randolph, who represented the Old Dominion in both the House and the Senate. "I love liberty. I hate equality.") The pursuit of happiness was not altogether forgotten as a concept by the citizens of the South, or by its leaders. It just wasn't applied to blacks. In time, revisionist Southern apologists would insist that slaves were happier on well-run plantations with enlightened owners than they would have been on their own. George Washington, who knew better, seems to have done what in a later time would be known as "compartmentalizing" the issue. He talked about liberty; he talked about slavery. He just didn't talk much about liberty for slaves.

In his first inaugural address, Washington had used the word "happiness," just as he had done at Valley Forge:

> I dwell on this prospect with every satisfaction which an ardent love for my Country can inspire: since there is no truth more thoroughly established, than that there exists in the economy and course of nature, an indissoluble union between virtue and happiness, between duty and advantage, between the genuine maxims of an honest and magnanimous policy, and the solid rewards of public prosperity and felicity: Since we ought to be no less persuaded that the propitious smiles of Heaven, can never be expected on a nation that disregards the eternal rules of order and right, which Heaven itself has ordained: And since the preservation of the sacred fire of liberty, and the destiny of the Republican model of Government, are justly considered as deeply, perhaps as finally staked, on the experiment entrusted to the hands of the American people.

This was no intended irony here, just an oversight of historic proportions. The sacred fire of liberty was not to be entrusted to blacks or Indians or, for that matter, white women. In Virginia, the lack of women's rights and the institution of slavery intersected in a way that complicated and vexed the lives of even the most powerful families, George and Martha Washington's particularly.

Washington's thinking about slavery changed during the Revolutionary period. In this time, he resolved to stop buying or selling more slaves, and in his will, Washington ordered that his slaves be freed upon his death. But when he died, few of them were truly made free: over the generations, his slaves had intermarried with the slaves owned by Martha Washington, slaves she inherited on the death of her first husband.

Virginia law forbade the widow of a man who died without a will from either freeing or selling her slaves. The upshot was that when George Washington died, many of the slaves he had ordered freed were married to slaves owned by Martha Washington—slaves she could legally neither sell nor liberate. By the end of her life, she was so paranoid that a slave would kill her—there was certainly motive enough—that she took to locking herself in her room at night.[8] Not unlike the guard in Alexander Solzhenitsyn's classic *One Day in the Life of Ivan Denisovich*, the putative jailer was herself a prisoner of the system that imprisoned others. This was yet another of the invidious facets of having slavery entrenched in the legal system: George Washington, the Father of a Country, vanquisher of the British Army, couldn't manage to dismantle the system of slavery on his own plantation.

To abolitionists, including John Quincy Adams, such conditions only reinforced their revulsion of this peculiar and perverse institution. Phrases like "eternal rules of order and right" and "life, liberty and pursuit of happiness" hovered in the air as tangible rebukes to the incongruity of any American depriving another American of his freedom, let alone condoning one race of people holding another in perpetual bondage. But just as the Founders of the Declaration had done in Philadelphia in 1776 and the Framers of the Constitution had done in 1787, so too did Congress continue to skirt the issue—primarily to avoid armed conflict. The first great "compromise" reached at the Constitutional Convention allowed the slave trade to continue for another twenty years in exchange for an agreement that navigational laws only require a simple majority. This long-forgotten and now trivial-seeming concession is all the New Englanders got from the Southerners. It was a cheap price for a guilty conscience.

In 1819 through 1821, with a series of legislative actions that came to be known as the Missouri Compromise, Congress again forestalled dealing with this great moral question. The deal, brokered by Henry Clay, consisted of three main provisions: Maine would break off from Missouri and enter the union as a free state; Missouri would be admitted as a slave state; a line on the map, the 36–30 parallel (Missouri's southern border), would be extended westward and to the lands of the Louisiana purchase with the understanding that slavery would not be allowed north of that line.[9]

But what was the alternative? War, most likely. Or disunion. John Calhoun wasn't—forgive the pun—whistling Dixie when he matter-of-factly spoke of secession some four decades before Abraham Lincoln's election sparked the South's attack on Fort Sumter. Although importing slaves was abolished in 1808, the slave population grew rapidly, and by the 1830s slavery was deeply embedded in the political, economic and cultural structures of the Southern states. So much so that by February 1, 1836, when congressman James Henry Hammond, a preening bigot from South Carolina, stood in the well of the House of Representatives and capped off a vitriolic and threatening racist diatribe by declaring smugly—citing economic arguments—that "slavery can never be abolished" even millions of non-Southern, non-slave-owning Americans would have agreed.[10] In *Arguing About Slavery,* the definitive book chronicling the great congressional debate of the 1830s over this question, University of Virginia scholar William Lee Miller succinctly provides the bleak historic context in which Hammond's hate speech was considered commonplace political discourse:

> In place of a king the nation had had as its first chief executive and symbol a hero-president who was a slaveholder . . . a Virginia congressman, in the midst of the debate, will point triumphantly to George Washington's picture hanging in front of the House of Representatives itself. There he is! A slaveholder! Five of the first seven presidents were slaveholders; for thirty-two of the nation's first thirty-six years, forty of its first forty-eight, fifty of its first sixty-four, the nation's president was a slaveholder. The powerful office of Speaker of the House was held by a slaveholder for twenty-eight of the nation's first thirty-five years. The president pro tem of the Senate was virtually always a slaveholder. The majority of cabinet members and—very important—of justices on the Supreme Court were slaveholders. The slaveholding Chief Justice Roger Taney, appointed by the slaveholding President Andrew Jackson to succeed the slaveholding John Marshall, would serve all the way through the decades before the war into the years of the Civil War itself; it would be a radical change of the kind the slaveholders feared when, in 1863, President Lincoln would appoint the anti-slavery politician Salmon P. Chase of Ohio to succeed Taney. But by then, even *having* a President Lincoln had been the occasion for the slaveholders to rebel, to secede, and to resort to arms.

All the presidents before Lincoln had worked to avoid civil war. The unintended result was that while the rest of the nation was changing rapidly in the first part of the nineteenth century, the South was not. In his examination of the Jacksonian period, Arthur M. Schlesinger Jr. noted that the utopian American idealized by Jefferson had begun to disappear even in Jefferson's day. The new nation was growing rapidly, and its cities were growing fastest of all. Jefferson mistrusted industrialization: he'd seen it at work in France and believed it led to widespread underemployment, misery, perhaps even starvation for the masses. "Those who labor in the earth are the chosen people of God, if ever He had a chosen people," Jefferson had written in *Notes on Virginia*. "While we have land to labor then, let us never wish to see our citizens occupied at a work-bench, or twirling a distaff." The Sage of Monticello was an early, if ineffectual, opponent of globalization as well. He actually thought it more desirable to send raw materials to Europe for their manufacture, rather than import labor to the American colonies.

"But actuality was betraying the dream," Schlesinger noted in *The Age of Jackson*. "The America of Jefferson had begun to disappear before Jefferson himself had retired from the presidential chair. That paradise of small farms, each man secure on his own freehold, resting under his own vine and fig trees was already darkened by the shadow of impending change." Not only was the Jefferson ideal of the educated gentleman farmer overseeing a plantation dependent on a doomed and corrupt social arrangement (slavery), but industrious German immigrants were proving on slaveless farms all over Pennsylvania, Maryland and the upper Shenandoah Valley that it was thoroughly inefficient besides.

The 1828 election of Andrew Jackson signified the change sweeping the nation. Jackson probably should have won in 1824, when he outpolled three other candidates in the popular vote and the electoral college vote as well, losing only when Henry Clay threw his support to John Quincy Adams. Four years later, the momentum could not be turned back. Increased suffrage meant that for the first time more than one million Americans cast direct votes for the presidency. This was three times as many as in 1824, and Jackson won his rematch with Adams in a landslide. Jackson was no Populist by any true modern definition, but he certainly had popular appeal, and his candidacy altered the nature of presidential politicking forever. Despite the selection of Washington as the first president, being a war hero had not been a particular political advantage. That changed with Jackson as an increase in the voting pool had the effect, then as now, of reducing the advantages of an intellectual while helping the candidacy of a man who captured the popular imagination—a man of action. And "Old Hickory" surely was that. Most of the nation knew the legend: Andy Jackson served as a courier in the Continental Army even though he was only thirteen years old. When captured, the teenaged recruit refused the order of a British officer to polish the officer's boots, an insolence repaid by a slashing blow across the face with a saber. Jackson carried the scars of the blow on his hand and his face the rest of his life, but it did not quell his valor. In the War of 1812, he had shown mettle as an officer while fighting Indian uprisings. In 1815, he was the general responsible for the Americans' decisive victory over the British in a series of battles for New Orleans. Jackson's army was a diverse group that included sailors, soldiers and militiamen from Tennessee as well as Indians and freed slaves from Louisiana, some of them of mixed race.

But it was not to matter: For Jackson, like Monroe, Madison, Jefferson and Washington before him, was a slave owner. The Jacksonian movement, concerned as it was with the explosive issues of central banking and hard money, would today be described as political campaigns that invoked "class warfare." But they were between whites, these fierce policy debates. One of the reasons it was never more than that—that it was never a national debate over life, liberty and happiness for *all* of America's citizens—was that Andrew Jackson had seen war up close and knew what dealing with the larger question would mean. He said as much in his second inaugural address. It came in March of 1833. Jackson pointedly used the word "happiness" but not as a call for Emancipation. Rather he used it as a way of warning against dissolution of the union—and of the civil war that would surely follow.

> Without union our independence and liberty would never have been achieved; without union they never can be maintained. Divided into twenty-four, or even a smaller number, of separate communities, we shall see our internal trade burdened with numberless restraints and exactions; communication between distant points and sections obstructed or cut off; our sons made soldiers to deluge with blood the fields they now till in peace; the mass of our people borne down and impoverished by taxes to support armies and navies, and military leaders at the head of their victorious legions becoming our lawgivers and judges. The loss of liberty, of all good government, of peace, plenty, and happiness, must inevitably follow a dissolution of the Union.

This is always the rub isn't it? War is a terrible experience. It's expensive and frightening, many people die—and for what? What could possibly be worth such a price? Well, John Quincy Adams, the former president defeated by Jackson and then beginning his second term as a Massachusetts representative in the U.S. House of Representatives, knew of a cause that was worth risking war over. In his mind, it was even worth disunion. Adams had known it since 1820 when he acquiesced to the Missouri Compromise.

Many years later, in our time, a president who was also the son of a president would be criticized by those opposed to his martial impulses on the grounds that he had never been anywhere in the world. George W. Bush, it was said by his critics, was not well traveled enough to know how Americans were perceived internationally. This was decidedly not John Q. Adams' shortcoming. He had made his name as a diplomat, serving as George Washington's envoy to The Hague and later to Berlin. Quincy served briefly in the Senate, but was virtually recalled for voting for Jefferson's Embargo Act, a tariff that wreaked economic hardship on New England's shipping industry. President Madison appointed Adams the United States' first ambassador to Russia; later he was an envoy in London and served as the chief of the American diplomatic mission that negotiated peace with Great Britain. James Monroe summoned him back to Washington in 1817; at the time of the Missouri compromise John Quincy Adams was serving as Secretary of State. Even then, Adams had harbored private misgivings about the wisdom of deferring the inevitable apocalypse over slavery. Reading his diary almost two centuries later, it seems doubtful that, had he been in Congress in 1820, Adams would have been able to bring himself to vote for that invidious compromise. Here is more of Adams' recounting of his conversations with John Calhoun.

> I told Calhoun I could not see things in the same light. It is, in truth, all perverted sentiment—mistaking labor for slavery and dominion for freedom. The discussion of this Missouri question has betrayed the secret of their souls. In the abstract they admit that slavery is an evil, they disclaim all participation in the introduction of it, and cast it all upon the shoulders of our old Grand[m]am Britain. But when probed to the quick upon it, they show at the bottom of their souls pride and vainglory in their condition of masterdom. They fancy themselves more generous and noble-hearted than the plain freemen

who labor for subsistence. They look down upon the simplicity of a Yankee's manners, because he has no habits of overbearing like their(s) and cannot treat negroes like dogs. It is among the evils of slavery that it taints the very sources of moral principle. It establishes false estimates of virtue and vice: for what can be more false and heartless than this doctrine which makes the first and holiest rights of humanity to depend upon the color of the skin?

I have favored this Missouri compromise, believing it to be all that could be effected under the present Constitution, and from extreme unwillingness to put the Union at hazard. But perhaps it would have been wiser as well as a bolder course, to have persisted in a restriction upon Missouri, till it should have terminated in a convention of the States to revise and amend the Constitution. This would have produced a new Union of thirteen or fourteen States unpolluted with slavery, with a great and glorious object to effect, namely, that of rallying to their standard the other States by the universal emancipation of their slaves. If the Union must be dissolved, slavery is precisely the question upon which it ought to break.

No one, even John Quincy Adams, had to persuade the moral clarity of this vision to the slaves. These millions knew first hand the evils and stunning hypocrisy of a nation that professed Christianity but ruled by force over a society of chained laborers, whose families were broken apart at auction, for whom learning to read was a crime punishable by the lash and for whom inciting others to flee—to seek the very liberty promised in the Declaration and the Constitution—was a capital crime. And from among their ranks there rose the greatest abolitionist voice of all, a man whose logic gathered force during his orations like a runaway locomotive. There were many powerful voices of abolition in the North as the 1830s turned into the 1840s and the 1850s, as well as a fiery abolitionist newspaper (William Lloyd Garrison's *The Liberator*) but none more commanding—or authoritative—than that of Frederick Douglass.

Douglass had been born a slave in 1818 on a plantation on Maryland's Eastern Shore to a black field hand and a white father, whose identity is uncertain but who was perhaps the plantation's sadistic owner, Aaron Anthony. Douglass, then named Frederick Bailey, was sent as a boy to Baltimore, where he lived in the house of Anthony's daughter and her husband, who was a sea captain. Later, Douglass would leave Northern audiences spellbound with his descriptions of his harrowing experiences as a slave, but none were more poignant than the descriptions of the sights and sounds this observant slave boy witnessed on the docks in the Baltimore harbor neighborhood of Fells Point. "[I] have watched from the wharves, the slave ships in the Basin, anchored from the shore, with their cargoes of human flesh, waiting for favorable winds to waft them down the Chesapeake," he said.

At the head of Pratt Street, in what today is Baltimore's fashionable Inner Harbor shopping district and tourist destination, was a teeming slave market, owned by an entrepreneurial slaver named Austin Wold-folk. "His agents were sent into every town and county in Maryland, announcing their arrival, through the papers, and on flaming 'hand-bills,' headed CASH FOR NEGROES," Douglass recalled. "These men were generally well dressed men, and very captivating in their manners. Ever ready to drink, to treat, and to gamble. The fate of many a slave has depended upon the turn of a single card; and many a child has been snatched from the arms of its mother by bargains arranged in a state of brutal drunkenness."

Douglass taught himself to read at any early age, and this bright, strapping teenager mixed easily with the society of free blacks that was establishing itself in Baltimore. In his autobiography, Douglass tells of devouring articles in *The Columbian Orator*, a widely used contemporary primer containing famous speeches and essays. One of them, "Master and Slave," purports to be a discussion between a slave and a slave owner in which the slave is so persuasive that the master frees him.[11] After he became literate, Douglass was sent back to plantation life for a while, then returned to Baltimore a second time. He was hired out for wages by his master, who promised to free Douglass at age twenty-five. He could not wait—nor did he trust his master—and at age twenty he escaped, heading north by train to Delaware, by ship to Philadelphia and then on to New York City where he entered the welcoming bosom of the Underground Railroad and the abolitionist movement. There he formed a friendship with Garrison, an alliance foreordained to become a rivalry. But Douglass never minimized the galvanizing effect Garrison and his newspaper had on the newly liberated slave.[12]

Leaving aside the personal slights that often mar the relationships between great men living at the same time, Douglass and Garrison would eventually part company because they developed sharply divergent views about Thomas Jefferson, George Washington and the other patriots of 1776—and about the efficacy of the nation's founding language. Garrison, like many leading abolitionists of his day, dismissed the

Declaration and the Constitution as tainted documents that formed the legal justifications for slavery.[13] Were they not prepared by slave owners, and ratified by a slave-owning society? In reading the documents in this way, Garrison was at one with his southern enemies, who themselves cited the Constitution as a *justification* for slavery. Not surprisingly, then, Garrison also called for secession—but by the Northern states. On July 4, 1854, Garrison celebrated Independence Day in Massachusetts by burning a copy of the Constitution, which he dismissed as "a covenant with death and an agreement with Hell!"

Initially, Douglass agreed with this line of reasoning. But after discussing this issue with an Ohio abolitionist congressman named Joshua Giddings—Douglass had actually debated Giddings—Douglass tempered his views. Giddings, "the Lion of Ashtabula," had arrived in Congress in December of 1838. He immediately lent John Quincy Adams a hand in opposing the gag rule, and the two became allies. (Adams, the son of one of the most prominent Founding Fathers, certainly did not consider the Constitution or the Declaration to blame for Southern intransigence on slavery. Nor did most of the abolitionists in Congress.) In time, this became Douglass' view, too. In 1852, two years before Garrison burned a copy of the Constitution in Framingham, Douglass was in Rochester, giving voice to the 3.3 million slaves then living in the United States in a patriotic speech extolling, rather than condemning, the Founders and their documents.

He spoke, Douglass said, in a spirit that drew "encouragement from the Declaration of Independence, the great principles it contains, and the genius of American Institutions . . ." His address, brilliant, methodical, at times mocking, should have deeply shamed every white American who had spent Independence Day setting off firecrackers, reciting the lines of the Declaration, or simply basking in their liberty. Douglass' speech was called, simply enough, *What to a Slave is the Fourth of July?* It began with a recitation of the sacrifices and wisdom displayed by the men of 1776, a formula not unlike a thousand others taking place all over the United States at annual Independence Day festivities:

> Fellow-citizens, I shall not presume to dwell at length on the associations that cluster about this day. The simple story of it is that, 76 years ago, the people of this country were British subjects . . . But, your fathers, who had not adopted the fashionable idea of this day,

of the infallibility of government, and the absolute character of its acts, presumed to differ from the home government in respect to the wisdom and the justice of some of those burdens and restraints. They went so far in their excitement as to pronounce the measures of government unjust, unreasonable, and oppressive, and altogether such as ought not to be quietly submitted to. I scarcely need say, fellow-citizens, that my opinion of those measures fully accords with that of your fathers. . . . Pride and patriotism, not less than gratitude, prompt you to celebrate and to hold it in perpetual remembrance. I have said that the Declaration of Independence is the ring-bolt to the chain of your nation's destiny; so, indeed, I regard it. The principles contained in that instrument are saving principles. Stand by those principles, be true to them on all occasions, in all places, against all foes, and at whatever cost. . . . The whole scene, as I look back to it, was simple, dignified and sublime.

Fellow Citizens, I am not wanting in respect for the fathers of this republic. The signers of the Declaration of Independence were brave men. They were great men too—great enough to give fame to a great age. It does not often happen to a nation to raise, at one time, such a number of truly great men. The point from which I am compelled to view them is not, certainly, the most favorable; and yet I cannot contemplate their great deeds with less than admiration. They were statesmen, patriots and heroes, and for the good they did, and the principles they contended for, I will unite with you to honor their memory. . . . Your fathers staked their lives, their fortunes, and their sacred honor, on the cause of their country.

But then Douglass abruptly switched gears. Speaking pointedly about the current time, he said that the glory of Revolution belonged to a previous generation. In a stern rebuke to those who blamed the Constitution for a system of institutionalized inequity, Douglass launched into a spirited defense of the Constitution. Southerners maintained that the Constitutional Convention did not outlaw slavery; Douglass' rebuttal was that the Constitution did not legalize it either. In so doing, Douglass was foreshadowing the arguments Lincoln would make two years later in a seminal speech at the State Capitol in Illinois.[14] "Washington could not die till he had broken the chains of his slaves," Douglass said, noting with bitter sarcasm that at that moment his memorial was being constructed with, in part, slave labor. What traits, then, characterized the current generation, the generation of Douglass' listeners? Lethargy, laziness and lassitude, he said. He went on to imply that a primary motivation for the ostentatious displays of patriotic fervor that swept the nation every Fourth of July was, precisely, because the current generation was so mediocre.

"You have no right to wear out and waste the hard-earned fame of your fathers to cover your indolence," Douglass said, beginning to pick up steam. "Sydney Smith tells us that men seldom eulogize the wisdom and virtues of their fathers, but to excuse some folly or wickedness of their own."[15] Douglass then proceeded to tell his audience exactly what wickedness he had in mind, as if anyone needed telling.

> Fellow-citizens; above your national, tumultuous joy, I hear the mournful wail of millions whose chains, heavy and grievous yesterday, are, to-day, rendered more intolerable by the jubilee shouts that reach them. . . . My subject, then fellow-citizens, is AMERICAN SLAVERY. Whether we turn to the declarations of the past, or to the professions of the present, the conduct of the nation seems equally hideous and revolting. America is false to the past, false to the present, and solemnly binds herself to be false to the future . . .
>
> Would you have me argue that man is entitled to liberty? That he is the rightful owner of his own body? You have already declared it. . . . How should I look today, in the presence of Americans, dividing, and subdividing a discourse, to show that men have a natural right to freedom? . . . To do so would be to make myself ridiculous, and lo, offer an insult to your understanding. There is not a man beneath the canopy of heaven, that does not know that slavery is wrong for him. What am I to argue that it is wrong to make men brutes, to rob them of their liberty, to work them without wages, to keep them ignorant of their relations to their fellow men, to beat them with sticks, to flay their flesh with the lash, to load their limbs with irons, to hunt them with dogs, to sell them at auction, to sunder their families, to knock out their teeth, to burn their flesh, to starve them into obedience and submission to their masters? . . . At a time like this, scorching irony, not convincing argument, is needed. O! had I the ability, and could I reach the nation's ear, I would, to-day, pour out a fiery stream of biting ridicule, blasting reproach, withering sarcasm, and stern rebuke. For it is not light that is needed, but fire; it is not the gentle shower, but thunder. We need the storm, the whirlwind, and the earthquake. The feeling of the nation must be quickened; the conscience of the nation must be roused; the propriety of the nation must be startled; the hypocrisy of the nation must be exposed; and its crimes against God and man must be proclaimed and denounced.

> What, to the American slave, is your 4th of July? I answer: a day that reveals to him, more than all other days in the year, the gross injustice and cruelty to which he is the constant victim. To him, your celebration is a sham; your boasted liberty, an unholy license; your national greatness, swelling vanity; your sounds of rejoicing are empty and heartless; your denunciations of tyrants, brass fronted impudence; your shouts of liberty and equality, hollow mockery; your prayers and hymns, your sermons and thanksgivings, with all your religious parade, and solemnity, are, to him, mere bombast, fraud, deception, impiety, and hypocrisy—a thin veil to cover up crimes which would disgrace a nation of savages. . . . You declare, before the world, and are understood by the world to declare, that you "hold these truths to be self evident, that all men are created equal; and are endowed by their Creator with certain inalienable rights; and that, among these are, life, liberty, and the pursuit of happiness"; and yet, you hold securely, in a bondage which, according to your own Thomas Jefferson, "is worse than ages of that which your fathers rose in rebellion to oppose," a seventh part of the inhabitants of your country . . .

And so did a freed slave who had bucked insuperable odds to personally prove the possibilities of what would later become known as the American Dream throw down the gauntlet to a nation that prided itself on nothing more than its freedom. He did so at the very hour that the nation was congratulating itself by remembering the celebrated words of the men at Philadelphia, patriots all, who wrote so glowingly about the rights to life, liberty and the pursuit of happiness. The men who wrote the Declaration had been brave and they had been visionary, but in the end they hadn't possessed enough courage or enough foresight to extend that promise to the people brought on slave ships from Africa, against their will, and in chains, to a New World.

At the time Frederick Douglass spoke in upstate New York on July 5, 1852, there were more black slaves in the United States of America than there had been people of both races living in the thirteen colonies that broke away from England. It was way past time to free them, too, or quit pretending that the promise of the Declaration really applied to "all men." On this point, perversely, the abolitionists had come to a tacit understanding with the southern firebrands—if only in their mutual understanding that this issue must ultimately be settled by force.

George Washington, in his 1796 farewell address to the nation upon leaving the presidency, had alluded obliquely to the differences between North and South, but had urged Americans who were citizens "by birth or choice" that they shared a "common country," one that had earned the right to benefit from their common affections. "In this sense . . . your union ought to be considered as a main prop of your liberty, and that the love of the one ought to endear to you the preservation of the other," he had said.

But what about those who had found themselves in America neither by "birth" nor by "choice"—when would the government extend the prop of liberty to them? Two years before Douglass' electrifying speech, in 1850, Congress had passed yet another grand "compromise" on slavery. This one, signed into law by President Millard Fillmore, admitted California as a free state, but did not prohibit the former territories of Mexico from entering the union as slave states. Under the terms of this deal, slavery was finally abolished in Washington, D.C., where it had offended the sensibilities of Northern congressmen for decades. But that was only accomplished by Northern acceptance of the Fugitive Slave Act, which required that runaway slaves be returned to their masters even if they had made it to safe havens in the North—including places where slavery was considered an abomination.

Later, Abraham Lincoln would note that both sides pray to the same God. Both sides also invoked the Founding Fathers and the United States Constitution as proof for the rightness of their cause. Both North and South cited the Declaration of Independence, as well, specifically citing Thomas Jefferson and the phrase "life, liberty and the pursuit of happiness." But both sides could not prevail. And what Frederick Douglass saw clearly—what the southern demagogues had been saying for thirty years—was now plain to all: However much the American presidents—from Washington to Monroe to Jackson to Fillmore—desired peace, the "common sense" of the matter was that freeing these three million souls from human bondage was going to require a war.

Frederick Douglass had warned of the impending thunder, along with the storm, the whirlwind and the earthquake. He was prescient, for all of them were coming.

4

Unfinished Work

An oft-invoked adage when the subject is war and peace holds that victors write the history. It's an unfortunate saying for several reasons, not
least of which is that it is a snide observation, employed to convey almost the opposite of what it appears to mean. It is used as a way of
asserting that victors, having won the battlefield, can write whatever
they want—and that what they want to write is usually a justification of
what they did. But this can be done by anyone who sits down to write
history, even those who sat out the war—or who didn't believe in it. It
was just such authors whom President Richard M. Nixon had in mind
when he complained, "among those who say the nations of the West are
on the wrong side of history in the fight against communism are people
who actually write history."

But there is something else wrong with the saying that victors write
history. It isn't strictly true. Both sides write history, the winners and the
losers. The most chilling record left behind of the battle of Agincourt
was not penned by Shakespeare or anyone in the camp of Henry V; it
was written by a French knight who fought there amid the wholesale
destruction of his friends and comrades-in-arms.[1] And in the case of the
American Civil War, the victors-as-historians justification is used by
apologists of the Confederacy to explain away the sordid underlying
cause of the Southern rebellion.

"The history of the Civil War has been sorely distorted because the
victors write the history," a man named Ronald T. Clemmons is telling
me. Clemmons is the "communications general" in a volunteer organization called the Military Order of the Stars and Bars. He accepted this
position after serving for years as executive director of his local chapter
of the Sons of Confederate Veterans. We are talking on the phone while

I am in Washington and he is at his home in Murfreesboro, Tenn. The date is February 9, 2003; I'm checking 1997 quotes of his from a Richmond newspaper to see if Clemmons' views have mellowed with the passing of time.[2] But, as our conversation is taking place some 138 years after Robert E. Lee's surrender at Appomattox, I'm thinking that Mr. Clemmons won't have tempered his views much in five-plus years. My assumption is correct.

"If you believe what you read—written by Northerners—the main factor was slavery," he said. "But the Confederate soldier was not fighting for slavery. Ninety percent of them had no slaves. They said they were fighting because someone had invaded their homeland. We think the war was actually fought over whether we would have a large central government removed from people versus a government more state-oriented. Big government won over states' rights."

Clemmons is a working-class person (and a decent-seeming fellow), with no formal training as a historian. But Edwin M. Yoder Jr. of Virginia is a man of letters, and he makes the same claims—while adding a few more. In a positive review of the last book historian Stephen E. Ambrose produced before his death, Yoder makes only "a single . . . quibble" with the book.[3] Writing "with a memorial nod to my Confederate officer-ancestors," Yoder takes issue with Ambrose's passing observation that, "The South had fought to keep African-Americans in slavery."

Not so fast, says Yoder: "Notwithstanding its congruence with current fashion (of which Ambrose was usually no follower), this is demonstrably untrue," he asserts. "A small minority of Confederates held slaves. Most did not, and many disliked slavery and would have agreed with the midwestern free-soilers that it diminished the value of white men's labor. Some realized that when a faraway Russian czar was even then liberating the serfs, bondage was not long for civilized society. The South clearly fought for other reasons, some worthy, some misguided. It was Lincoln, not the Confederacy, who transformed a war for union into a war against slavery, and for the good reason that European intervention was a lurking danger."

Well, this is certainly an earful. They never rest, these defenders of their rebel great-great grandfathers. They can never be too vigilant. But slavery was always the central cause of that conflict, and should not be glossed over so glibly. Neither can the reason why European powers, notably Great Britain and Spain, were circling like vultures hoping the

United States of America would break apart into so many European principalities. It would have meant that the grand experiment in self-government had proven itself a dud. And, keeping in mind Ulysses S. Grant's characterization of the Southern cause as "one of the worst for which a people ever fought,"[4] it is not casting aspersions on the valor or the sincerity of the rank-and-file Confederate soldier to point out that the motivations behind Southern revisionism were originally cynical, not romantic.

After the Confederacy was vanquished in the war, the South's political leaders, Jefferson Davis included, decided to win the peace. To them, that meant reclaiming power from black Republicans taking seats in their legislatures and reinstating a system of apartheid based on white power and white supremacy. They couldn't call it that, of course, as Union troops still occupied their state capitals, so they gave it another name. They called it "states rights." To prove this, as Jefferson would say, let us submit facts to a candid world:

The records of the great debates in the years prior to the war reveal that the burgeoning regional schism between North and South was always about a single issue—slavery, specifically whether slavery could be extended into new states. Initially, the first wave of pro-slavery arguments used by southern orators against northern abolitionists was economic. Leaving aside the question of the survival of the plantation system, the slaves themselves represented an investment so colossal that it dwarfed the ability of the federal government—and surely the government had no legal authority to simply appropriate a man's property—to ever pay it. In 1836, when Rep. James Henry Hammond claimed that this reality alone was enough to prove that "slavery can never be abolished" the price tag he put on the value of the slaves was $900 million.[5] This was in a nation in which the federal government's annual receipts totaled less than $24 million. But the economic arguments were met by moral arguments from the Northern men. Did not the God that gave man life, give him liberty as well? And what is money compared to the principle of freedom for all of God's people—and for honoring the spirit of 1776? Lincoln put it this way in a political speech in Illinois in which he called for the repeal of the Missouri Compromise.[6]

> This *declared* indifference, but as I must think, covert *real* zeal for the spread of slavery I cannot but hate. I hate it because of the monstrous injustice of slavery itself. I hate it because it deprives our re-

publican example of its just influence in the world—enables the enemies of free institutions, with plausibility, to taunt us as
hypocrites—causes the real friends of freedom to doubt our sincerity, and especially [because] it forces so many really good men
amongst ourselves into an open war with the very fundamental principles of civil liberty—criticizing the Declaration of Independence,
and insisting that there is no right principle of action but *self-
interest.*

In later years, this 1854 speech would be scrutinized and found
wanting by well-meaning campus modernists because Lincoln goes on
to ruminate about shipping the slaves to Liberia (he rejects this as im-
practical—and highly dangerous for the slaves), confesses he does not
quite see blacks as the social equal of whites, and says that, in any event,
he knows white voters even in the North would not consent to immediate emancipation. But Lincoln also calls matter-of-factly in his remarks
for gradual emancipation, and chides the southern states for not already
starting this process, which he clearly suggests is the only possible end
result of slavery. At the time it was delivered, this speech was understood
to be what it truly was, the abolitionists' case for not extending slavery
into a single other state. Neither Russian czars, nor Russian serfs, make
any appearance here, rhetorically or otherwise.[7] Lincoln's formulation,
though he took pains to present it as the embodiment of the democratic
notion and not as a religious notion, was the perfect application of the
Golden Rule. "As I would not be a slave, so I would not be a master,"
Lincoln wrote in 1858. "This expresses my idea of democracy."[8]

The sons of the South responded to this simple logic with a second
line of argumentation that at least went beyond the notion that slaves
were simply property, no more and no less, and that the main issue was
restitution. Blacks, they maintained with great passion, were the natural
inferiors of whites. This obvious fact, and not abolitionist "fanaticism,"
is the true expression of God's law, they insisted. Here is Hammond
again:[9]

Although I am perfectly satisfied that no human process can elevate
the black man to an equality with the white—admitting that it could
be done—are we prepared for the consequence which then must follow? Are the people of the North prepared to . . . place their political
power on an equality with their own? Are we prepared to see them
mingling in our Legislatures? Is any portion of this country prepared

to see them enter these halls and take their seats by our sides, in perfect equality with the white representatives of an Anglo Saxon race—to see them fill that chair—to see them placed at the heads of your Departments; or to see, perhaps some "Othello," or "Toussaint," or "Boyer," gifted with genius and inspired by ambition, grasp the presidential wreath, and wield the destinies of this great republic? From such a picture I turn with irrepressible disgust.

Hammond's satire of black first names notwithstanding, this was mild fare as far as racist diatribes went in the years leading up to secession. Jefferson Davis, in a speech to the Confederate Congress on April 29, 1861, extolled slavery as a benevolent institution by which "a superior race" had managed to transform "brutal savages into docile, intelligent, and civilized agricultural laborers." Before the war began, Davis' vice president, Alexander H. Stephens, told a cheering throng of his fellow Georgians, that the South's new Constitution had "put to rest *forever* all the agitation questions relating to . . . the proper status of the Negro in our form of civilization."

Davis' and Stephens' quotes—and many others—were resurrected by Williams College professor Charles B. Dew, in *Apostles of Disunion: Southern Secession Commissioners and the Causes of the Civil War*, a debunking book that examines the rhetoric used by leading Southern politicians and the Southern "secession commissioners" sent by the states of the Deep South—South Carolina, Mississippi, Georgia and Alabama—to rally support for secession among the states of the South.[10]

Over and over again, these commissioners invoked apocalyptic descriptions of the horrors that would befall white Southerners if they remained in the union. Certainly some of them mention the doctrine of states rights, but the only one they got around to discussing in any detail was the "right" to own other human beings in chattel slavery. The language of the commissioners makes it clear that the South's only real grievance was that it saw the election of Abraham Lincoln as the event that, if left to stand, would doom the institution of slavery. And though Lincoln had professed during the campaign a reluctance to free the Southern slaves—he insisted he had no legal authority to do so—the Southern officeholders made it clear that they believed that even forbidding slavery to spread to other states meant for them inevitable ostracism, isolation and the eventual economic and social ruin of the Old South. In fact, the governors of the Southern states frame the very act of appointing the commissioners as an action that will help preserve slavery.

Alabama Gov. Andrew B. Moore, in a proclamation naming his state's commissioners, expressed the rationale for his action—the rationale for secession—quite plainly: "As the slaveholding States have a common interest in the institution of slavery, and must be common sufferers in its overthrow, I deemed it proper, and it appeared to be the general sentiment of the people, that Alabama should consult and advise with the other slaveholding States, so far as practicable, as to what is best to be done to protect their interest and honor in the impending crisis."[11]

William L. Harris, a Mississippi-appointed secession commissioner, sounded the same themes. In his sales pitch for disunion, delivered to the Georgia state legislature, Judge Harris went through the litany of "outrages" perpetuated in a spirit of "fanaticism" by the Northern men, culminating in the election of Lincoln and the "Black Republicans."[12] All of those aggravations, in Harris' recitation of them, concerned slavery:

> Today our government stands *totally revolutionized* in its main features, and our Constitution broken and overturned. The new administration, which has effected this revolution, only awaits the 4th of March for the inauguration of the new government, the new principles, and the new policy, upon the success of which they have proclaimed freedom for the slave, but eternal degradation for you and for us. . . .
>
> Our fathers made this a government for the white man, rejecting the Negro as an ignorant, inferior, barbarian race, incapable of self-government, and not, therefore, entitled to be associated with the white man upon terms of civil, political, or social equality. The new administration comes into power, under the solemn pledge to overturn and strike down this great feature of our Union . . . and to substitute in its stead their theory of the universal equality of the black and white races. . . .
>
> Mississippi is firmly convinced that there is but one alternative: This *new union* with Lincoln Black Republicans and free Negroes, without slavery, or, slavery under our old constitutional bond of union without Lincoln Black Republicans, or free Negroes, either, to molest us.

This was pretty standard fare for all the secession commissioners. At Florida's secession convention on January 7, 1861, South Carolina secession commissioner Leonidas W. Spratt spoke in even starker racial terms:

> Within this government two societies have become developed. The one is the society of one race, the other of two races. The one is based on free labor, the other slave labor. The one is braced together but by the two great relations in life—the relation between husband and wife and parent and child; the other by the three relations of husband and wife, parent and child, and master and slave. The one embodies the social principle that equality is the right of man; the other, the social principle that equality is not the right of man, but the right of equals only. . . . There is and must be an irrepressible conflict between them, and it were best to realize the truth.

The speech by the Confederacy's vice president is particularly revealing. Alexander Stephens delivered it on March 21, 1861, in Savannah, to a cheering crowd. In it, he makes direct reference to the Founders, and to the Declaration of Independence and to the Constitution. He acknowledges that the spirit of these documents implies freedom for all men, black or white. But Stephens insists that the Founders, Jefferson in particular, were *wrong* about blacks, and thus *wrong* about slavery. The Confederate Constitution, he told the crowd, had corrected this historic oversight, the oversight that had led directly to secession.

> The new Constitution has put at rest *forever* all the agitating questions relating to our peculiar institutions—African slavery, as it exists among us—the proper *status* of the Negro in our form of civilization. *This was the immediate cause of the late rupture and present revolution.* Jefferson, in his forecast, had anticipated this, as "the rock upon which the old Union would split." He was right. What was conjecture with him, is now a realized fact. But whether he fully comprehended the great truth upon which that rock *stood* and *stands,* may be doubted. The prevailing ideas entertained by him and most of the leading statesmen at the time of the formation of the old Constitution were, that the enslavement of the African was in violation of the laws of nature; that it was wrong in principle, socially, morally and politically. It was an evil they knew not well how to deal with; but the general opinion of the men of that day was, that, somehow or other, in the order of Providence, the institu-

tion would be evanescent and pass away. This idea, though not incorporated in the Constitution, was the prevailing idea at the time. . . . *Those ideas, however, were fundamentally wrong. They rested upon the assumption of the equality of races. This was an error.* It was a sandy foundation, and the idea of a Government built upon it—when the "storm came and the wind blew, it *fell.*"

Our new Government is founded upon exactly the opposite ideas; its foundations are laid, its cornerstone rests, upon the great truth that the Negro is not equal to the white man; that slavery, subordination to the superior race, is his natural and moral condition. This, our new Government, is the first, in the history of the world, based upon this great physical, philosophical, and moral truth . . .

All fanaticism springs from an aberration of the mind; from a defect in reasoning. It is [characteristic] of insanity. One of the most striking characteristics of insanity, in many instances, is, forming correct conclusions from fancied or erroneous premises; so with the *anti-slavery* fanatics: their conclusions are right if their premises are. They assume that the Negro is equal, and hence conclude that he is entitled to equal privileges and rights, with the white man. . . . They were attempting to make things equal which the Creator had made unequal.

One biographer of Jefferson Davis, Hudson Strode, asserted that Davis was vexed by Stephens' "rabble-rousing" address in Savannah. But if that is so, it could only have been for tactical reasons: the views expressed by Stephens on race are Davis' as well. How could they be otherwise? What other justification could freedom-loving men have for keeping another race in bondage, except that they weren't really fully human at all? Such arguments of racial superiority certainly weren't new—Hammond was advocating them on the House floor twenty-five years before secession. But when openly debated in the light of day these arguments tended to fall of their own weight. Hence gag rules, and the Southern practice of referring to abolitionists, always, as not only "fanatics," but "ignorant fanatics." But the common sense of the matter was that too much evidence was accumulating in the other direction.

The case *against* slavery began with the alarming frequency with which white masters sought the sexual favors of slave girls. Why would members of "a superior race" (Jefferson Davis' phrase) seek companionship of the most intimate nature with "brutal savages" (Jefferson Davis' other phrase)? Another point, made often by abolitionists, was that freemen who had been slaves were already proving their mettle as skilled laborers in a host of complicated fields. And why, if Africans were intellectually so feeble, did white slaveholders in the South use the lash to prevent them from learning to read; and why did tradesman—in the North as well as the South—so often resort to organized violence to keep skilled black artisans from competing with them?

In his July 5, 1852, Rochester speech, Frederick Douglass attacked this notion of black inferiority with fierce sarcasm. He impeached the Southerners' claim of black inferiority with the South's own legal codes and morés.

> What point in the anti-slavery creed would you have me argue? . . .
> Must I undertake to prove that the slave is a man? That point is
> conceded already. Nobody doubts it. The slaveholders themselves
> acknowledge it in the enactment of laws for their government. They
> acknowledge it when they punish disobedience on the part of the
> slave. There are seventy-two crimes in the State of Virginia, which,
> if committed by a black man, (no matter how ignorant he be), sub-
> ject him to the punishment of death; while only two of the same
> crimes will subject a white man to the like punishment. What is this
> but the acknowledgement that the slave is a moral, intellectual and
> responsible being? The manhood of the slave is conceded. It is ad-
> mitted in the fact that Southern statute books are covered with en-
> actments forbidding, under severe fines and penalties, the teaching
> of the slave to read or to write. When you can point to any such
> laws, in reference to the beasts of the field, then I may consent to
> argue the manhood of the slave . . .

Two years later, in 1854, Lincoln, then a local politician and law-yer in Springfield, Ill., approached the issue in a similar way. He attempted to use the internal illogic of the thing against the institution being so fiercely defended by the Southern men. He tried, with a lighter touch than Douglass (then again, Lincoln had never been a slave so he could afford a lighter touch), to fashion a dialectic that would demonstrate the unsustainable nature of the Southerners' position. Lincoln wrote:

> If A. can prove, however conclusively, that he may, of right, enslave
> B.—why may not B. snatch the same argument, and prove equally,
> that he may enslave A?

You say A. is white, and B. is black.

It is color, then; the lighter, having the right to enslave the darker?

Take care. By this rule, you are to be slave to the first man you meet, with a fairer skin than your own.

You do not mean color exactly?—You mean the whites are intellectually the superiors of the blacks, and, therefore have the right to enslave them?

Take care again. By this rule, you are to be slave to the first man you meet, with an intellect superior to your own.

But, say you, it is a question of interest; and, if you can make it your interest, you have the right to enslave another.

Very well. And if he can make it his interest, he has the right to enslave you.

But by the 1850s, the South was past the point of being amenable to gentle needling—or even logic. The answer to why such thoughtful discourse engendered only spluttering rage in the hearts of the southern men was that they discerned mockery in it, as well as arrogance, and a dangerous level of unawareness besides. The reason for this was that well before the onset of the Civil War, the South had come up with a third rationale in its triad of reasons—the first two being economic interests and the presumed inferiority of the black man—that justified slavery and explained why it could never be dispensed with. This third reason was a more visceral one, and, as a result, more ominous. It went to the crux of why so many southern whites who did not own slaves were willing to volunteer and fight and to die under the banner of the Confederacy.

This reason was that they perceived their own personal safety, and that of their wives and children, to be on the line—along with that of all whites living in the South. This is what they had been told so many times and for so long by their political leaders that they could not help but believe it: That the end of degradation for blacks was the beginning of degradation for them. Their imaginations warped by the brutality of the "peculiar institution," Southern whites could no longer imagine any other outcome other than a bloody one. George Mason's glum observation about the effects of this pernicious institution on the minds of the whites in a slaveholding society was now complete.

James Henry Hammond had warned of the horrific possible effects—on whites—of Emancipation on the floor of the House as early as 1836. And as Christmas season of 1860 turned into the springtime of 1861, the secession commissioners were spreading their gospel of fear in every slave state capital. Stephen F. Hale, secession commissioner from Alabama, in a letter to Kentucky Gov. Beriah Magoffin, began his appeal by invoking the Declaration of Independence, noting how the men of 1776 had said plainly that when a government becomes a barrier to the inalienable rights of the people, it is the right and the duty of the people "to alter or abolish it."[13]

Hale then went on to the Constitution, and his understanding of the obligations of each state to respect the "stipulations and covenants" of the other states, before coming to the heart of the matter, which was slavery.

> It is upon this gigantic interest, this peculiar institution of the South, that the Northern States and their people have been waging an unrelenting and fanatical war for the last quarter of a century; an institution with which is bound up not only the wealth and prosperity of the Southern people, but their very existence as a political community. This war has been waged in every way that human ingenuity, urged on by fanaticism, could suggest. They attack us through their literature, in their schools, from the hustings, in their legislative halls, through the public press, and even their courts of justice forget the purity of their judicial ermine to strike down the rights of the Southern slaveholder and override every barrier which the Constitution has erected for his protection. . . .
>
> The more daring and restless fanatics have . . . put in practice the terrible lessons taught by the timid by making an armed incursion upon the sovereign State of Virginia, slaughtering her citizens for the purpose of exciting a servile insurrection among her slave population, and arming them for the destruction of their own masters. During the past summer the abolition incendiary has lit up the prairies of Texas, fired the dwellings of the inhabitants, burned down whole towns, and laid poison for her citizens, thus literally executing the terrible denunciations of fanaticism against the slaveholder . . .

Hale was tapping into something basic here. John Brown's bloody raid at Harper's Ferry had engendered fear in the South, but even more so, it had sparked an orgy of fear-mongering among Southern politicians and a fierce backlash in slaveholding states. Brown and his followers could be dismissed, in Hale's phrase, as only "a few half-crazy fanatics," but the celebration of Brown's memory in the North did not go down well south of the Mason-Dixon line.[14] The true nature of the "Black Republican Party," Hale asserted, could be discerned by "the sympathy manifested all over the North, where, in many places the tragic death of John Brown, the leader of the raid upon Virginia, who died upon the gallows a condemned felon, is celebrated with public honors, and his name canonized as a martyr to liberty."

It was in this context, Hale urged the Commonwealth of Kentucky, that Kentuckians must view Lincoln's election. It was accomplished by voters who privately cheered on John Brown and who, in their heart of hearts, would like nothing better than to see the kind of slave uprising that in Haiti resulted in the gruesome slaughter of Haiti's white French population.[15]

> Therefore it is that the election of Mr. Lincoln cannot be regarded otherwise than a solemn declaration, on the part of a great majority of the Northern people, of hostility to the South, her property, and her institutions; nothing less than an open declaration of war, for the triumph of this new theory of government destroys the property of the South, lays waste her fields, and inaugurates all the horrors of a Santo Domingo [-like] insurrection, consigning her citizens to assassinations and her wives and daughters to pollution and violation to gratify the lust of half-civilized Africans. Especially is this true in the cotton-growing States, where, in many localities, the slave outnumbers the white population ten to one. . . .
>
> If we fall, the light of our civilization goes down in blood, our wives and our little ones will be driven from their homes by the light of our own [burning] dwellings, the dark pall of barbarism must soon gather over our sunny land, and the scenes of West India emancipation, with its attendant horrors and crimes . . . [will] be reenacted in [our] own land upon a much more gigantic scale.

This was the message, uttered many times in every Southern state capital, reprinted in hundreds of Southern newspapers, and repeated by word-of-mouth to thousands upon thousands of Southern whites: Emancipation for the Negro predestined for the whites burned homes, gang rapes, blood in the fields. What people would willingly submit to such a fate? Not us, cried the secession commissioners and office-holders of the new Confederacy. "Sink or swim, live or die, survive or perish—

the part of Mississippi is chosen *she will never submit* to the principles and policy of this Black Republican Administration," was the way Judge Harris ended his appeal to the Georgia Legislature.

Other secession commissioners sounded the same theme. Jacob Thompson, a former North Carolina congressmen serving as Secretary of the Interior in the administration of James Buchanan, returned to his native state that December in a newfound role of secession agitator. There, he warned lawmakers in Raleigh that the incoming "Black Republican" administration was about to bring to power "a majority trained from infancy to hate our people and their institutions." He added that the federal government in Washington, the one he was still officially a part of, was about to be "perverted into an engine for the destruction of our domestic institutions and the subjugation of our people."

Alexander Hamilton Handy, Mississippi's secession commissioner to Maryland, warned state's leaders not only that "slavery was ordained by God," but—more to the immediate point—that Southerners would never give it up, because to do so meant "the beautiful cotton fields" of their homelands would be rendered into "barren wastes." Secession was necessary as a preemptive measure, he said, because the new administration would soon be sending down government agents—postmasters and other officials, he said—whose real purpose would be to "excite the slave to cut the throat of his master."

The distinction of painting the fright-scenario in the most offensive language might belong to John C. Calhoun's son Andrew, chosen to be South Carolina's secession representative to Alabama. Besides having a famous father, Andrew Calhoun was a prosperous slave-owning planter himself who was well known in South Carolina. Before leaving for Alabama, where he had once lived, Calhoun honed his arguments on an audience of his fellow South Carolinians in a fiery speech delivered on November 13, 1860, seven days after Lincoln's election.[16] Lincoln and his Republicans, Calhoun said, sought to "seduce the poor, ignorant, and stupid nature of the Negro in the midst of his home and happiness." Calhoun, too, summoned the specter of Haiti, reminding the crowd scornfully how the cry of the French Revolution, "Liberty, Equality, Fraternity!" had fired up the slaves on that hapless island. The same thing could happen in the cotton states, he said:

> Well, the [Haitian] Negro heard the ill-omened words and he, born
> in Africa, the slave whose head was always in danger, perhaps to

repair some skull-built wall of a kinky-headed chief, who, hunted down, captured, famished in his native land could only view his change as a blessed one—he, too, arose, with all the fury of the beast, and scenes were then enacted over a comparatively few planters that the white fiends [of the North] would delight to see re-enacted with us.

By the time he addressed Alabama's secession convention on January 8, 1861, Calhoun had tempered his rhetoric some. But in Montgomery he was most decidedly speaking to the choir. Even before he addressed the convention, it adopted a resolution that began:

WHEREAS, the election of Abraham Lincoln, a Black Republican, to the Presidency of the United States, by a purely sectional vote, and by a party whose leading and publicly avowed object is the destruction of the institution of slavery as it exists in the slaveholding States, is an accomplished fact; and whereas, the success of said party, and the power which it now has, and soon will acquire, greatly endanger the peace, interests, security and honor of the slaveholding States, and make it necessary that prompt and effective measures should be adopted to avoid the evils which must result from a Republican administration of the Federal Government; and as the interest and destiny of the slaveholding States are the same, they must naturally sympathize with each other; they, therefore, so far as may be practicable, should consult and advise together as to what is best to be done to protect their mutual interest and honor.

This was not atypical: Georgia's Declaration of Secession begins this way:

The people of Georgia having dissolved their political connection with the Government of the United States of America, present to their confederates and the world the causes which have led to the separation. For the last ten years we have had numerous and serious causes of complaint against our non-slaveholding confederate States with reference to the subject of African slavery. They have endeavored to weaken our security, to disturb our domestic peace and tranquility, and persistently refused to comply with their express constitutional obligations to us in reference to that property . . .

Thus did the secession commissioners do their dirty work, and do it well. Here is the beginning of Mississippi's explanation for why it left the United States:

Our position is thoroughly identified with the institution of slavery—the greatest material interest of the world. Its labor supplies the product, which constitutes by far the largest and most important portions of commerce of the earth. These products are peculiar to the climate verging on the tropical regions, and by an imperious law of nature, none but the black race can bear exposure to the tropical sun. These products have become necessities of the world, and a blow at slavery is a blow at commerce and civilization. That blow has been long aimed at the institution, and was at the point of reaching its consummation. There was no choice left us but submission to the mandates of abolition, or a dissolution of the Union, whose principles had been subverted to work out our ruin. . . .

South Carolina's Declaration does go on for a while about how the principles of the Founding Fathers have been violated, but cites only one issue in support of how South Carolina has been disadvantaged: "A geographical line has been drawn across the Union, and all the States north of that line have united in the election of a man to the high office of President of the United States, whose opinions and purposes are hostile to slavery," it reads. "[Lincoln] is to be entrusted with the administration of the common Government, because he has declared that that 'Government cannot endure permanently half slave, half free,' and that the public mind must rest in the belief that slavery is in the course of ultimate extinction . . ."

*　　*　　*

It was not surprising, given the inflammatory speech of its political elites leading up to secession, that when war finally came that the sentiments on race expressed by Confederate fighting men were little different than those of their leaders. "It is insulting to the English common sense of race [to say that we] are battling for an abstract right common to all humanity," South Carolina low-country planter—and Confederate volunteer—Charles Woodward Hutson said in a September 14, 1861, letter to his mother. "Every reflecting child will glance at the darkey who waits on him & laugh at the idea of such an 'abstract right.'"[17]

"A stand must be made for African slavery," wrote William Grimball, a South Carolina artillery officer, "or it is forever lost."[18]

"Life, liberty and property are at stake," wrote Hannibal Paine, a volunteer for the Tennessee 26th, referring to slavery with the last item on his Lockean list. "Any man in the South would rather die battling for civil and political liberty than submit to the base usurpations of a northern tyrant."[19]

All three of these letters were included by Princeton University historian James M. McPherson in his Lincoln Prize–winning book, *For Cause and Comrades: Why Men Fought in the Civil War*. McPherson also points out that it was in response to such sentiments about the South's love of "liberty" that Lincoln observed sarcastically, "the *perfect* liberty they sigh for" is "the liberty of making slaves of other people." Samuel Johnson had noticed this internal contradiction among the southern gentlemen as early as 1775, dryly observing, "How is it that we hear the loudest yelps for liberty among the drivers of Negroes?"

As to the nature of the issue that caused the rift between North and South, neither Lincoln nor his adversaries had any difference of opinion. "One section of our country believes slavery is *right* and ought to be extended, while the other believes it is *wrong* and ought not to be extended," Lincoln added in his March 4, 1861, address. "This is the only substantial dispute."

By the time Lincoln had made his way to Washington, secession was a fact. Jefferson Davis was sworn in as President of the Confederacy before Lincoln took the oath as the sixteenth president of the United States. But if the South understood the war to be about slavery, and Lincoln did as well, this left a third party to be heard from: the Northern people themselves, the population that would furnish the Union troops that would invade the South. Did these men march and fight, and die, to free the slaves? Or did they muster under their nation's flag for the somewhat theoretical cause of the "perpetual" union Lincoln also discussed in his first inauguration? Or was it a more reflexive sense of patriotism, not unlike that exhibited by the upper classes in the South—or, for that matter, the kind one would find even today in the United States? (Ulysses S. Grant was a Democrat whose wife had owned slaves and he had served in the Army with some of the leading secessionist military leaders. Yet his first reaction in February 1861 on hearing about the formation of the Confederate States of America and its selection of fellow West Pointer Jefferson Davis as president was to offer the opinion that "Davis and the whole gang of them ought to be hung.")[20]

One Federal soldier, looking back on his four years of service in the Union army, touched on all of these reasons in two short sentences. "I have been successful in my Army life simply because I have always been ready and willing to do my duty," wrote Elisha Hunt Rhodes at the end of the Civil War. "I thank God that I have had an opportunity of serving my country, freeing the slaves and restoring the Union."[21] Rhodes entered the 2nd Rhode Island Volunteers as a nineteen-year-old private in the infantry. He left the unit when it disbanded in April 1865, a seasoned twenty-three-year-old colonel with a wisdom earned at killing fields with famous names, Bull Run, Gettysburg, Fredericksburg, the Wilderness, Cold Harbor.

Rhodes survived all those horrors, married the year after the war ended, had children, became a brigadier general in the Rhode Island Militia, and lived until January 14, 1917, when he was seventy-five years old. His service was celebrated long after his death by documentary filmmaker Ken Burns, who drew on his diary for his *Civil War* series. Burns made another fighting man from the 2nd Rhode Island volunteers, Major Sullivan Ballou, famous, too. But Ballou was not as fortunate as Rhodes. Ballou's claim to fame was a single letter he wrote his wife Sarah, a moving and eloquent missive that conveyed not only a deep love for her and their children, but also his eerie (and accurate) premonition of his own impending demise on the battlefields of Manassas.

"Sarah, my love for you is deathless, it seems to bind me to you with mighty cables that nothing but Omnipotence could break," Ballou wrote. "And yet my love of Country comes over me like a strong wind and bears me irresistibly on with all these chains to the battlefield."[22]

But other Union soldiers wrote home to tell their pride about *breaking* chains, specifically the chains of the slaves. On March 24, 1863, while the 2nd Michigan Infantry was on the road to Richmond, an officer named Hiram Underwood labored for hours to liberate slaves—called "contrabands" in the parlance of the Union army—across the James River to safety, and eventual freedom. What was noteworthy about it to Charles B. Haydon, the 2nd Michigan private who put it in his diary, was that Underwood was known in the regiment for ambivalence for Emancipation.

"Major Underwood has always been very bitter on the Abolitionists but tonight he worked more than 3 hours in water up to his waist to help 20 contrabands across the river & on their way to their Paradise at Fort Monroe," Haydon wrote. "He said they looked so frightened that he had to help them."[23]

It is conventional wisdom that in the early part of the Civil War Lincoln was highly vexed by commanders, such as generals George B. McClellan and Henry W. Halleck, who repeatedly proved themselves unwilling to fight. What is not as well remembered is that when it came to wanting to liberate the slaves, Lincoln lagged *behind* some of his generals. It is true that the President had other political considerations to contend with, not the least of which was keeping the border states from seceding, but it is also true that the Civil War was only a month old when Maj. Gen. Benjamin F. Butler started the practice of accepting fugitive slaves from Maryland and Virginia into his safe keeping at Fort Monroe near Washington. Using impeccable logic, Butler told the Virginia slave owner who demanded their return under the Fugitive Slave Act that, as Virginia had seceded from the Union, federal laws no longer applied in the state. Butler declared them "contraband property," and promptly hired them to build fortifications, just as he would do in New Orleans, the following year.[24] In August 1861, Gen. John C. Fremont declared free all the slaves of non-Union Missouri slave owners. Fremont was the first presidential candidate the Republican Party had fielded; nevertheless, this was an order Lincoln countermanded himself.[25]

But Lincoln's private desires weren't that different than Fremont's; and the President finally pushed McClellan aside after the self-important general had presented Lincoln with a letter fervently urging that slave owners be recompensed for contrabands who had been pressed into service, that the Union army should never be used to interfere "with the relations of servitude" and that if the federal government exhibited "radical views" on slavery the whole military campaign would fall apart. In his 1862 message to Congress (today it's called the annual State of the Union address) Lincoln revealed that he had reached the exact opposite conclusion. "Without slavery the rebellion could never have existed," he said. "Without slavery it could not continue." And so McClellan's letter gave the president tangible proof—if any was still needed—that McClellan was part of the problem, not the solution.[26]

Meanwhile, their military incursions into Dixie were giving the Northern fighting men their first up-close look at slavery, and many didn't like what they were seeing. Charles Haddon reports going to church in Alexandria, Va.—to George Washington's church—and seeing an estimated two thousand Negroes in that town, along with many "wicked secessionists," who glared at the men from the Michigan 5th. The whole scene, Haddon reported, made him want to "slash" some of the Southern whites with his sword.

Robert Gould Shaw, a captain in the 2nd Massachusetts, recalled a white girl in Maryland yelling hatefully, "I like a *nigger* better than a Massachusetts soldier."

"I thought I hated slavery as much as possible when I came here," Alexander Caldwell, a private in the 83rd Pennsylvania, wrote to his brother after hearing a Virginia slave describe how her husband was brutally whipped. "But here, where I can see some of its workings, I am more than ever convinced of the cruelty and inhumanity of the system."

The same was true of Northern civilians exposed to the slave-state way of thinking as a part of their proximity to invading Confederate troops. One Pennsylvania farm wife, Rachel Cormany, expressed her sympathy for the plight of the black refugees in her diary. Cormany had moved with her husband from Canada to Pennsylvania—just in time for him to get drafted and for her to find herself and her baby on the path of Lee's army on its way to Gettysburg. The way the Army of Northern Virginia treated the blacks—including freed blacks—who were attempting to escape ahead of the Confederates shocked her:

> [The rebels] were hunting up the contrabands & driving them off by droves. O! How it grated on our hearts to have to sit quietly & look at such brutal deeds—I saw no men among the contrabands—all women & children. Some of the colored people who were raised here were taken along—as I sat on the front step as they were driven by just like we would drive cattle. Some laughed & seemed not to care—but nearly all hung their heads. One woman was pleading wonderfully with her driver for her children—but all the sympathy she received from him was a rough "March along"—at which she would quicken her pace again. It is a query what they want with those little babies—whole families were taken. Of course when the mother was taken she would take her children. I suppose the men left thinking the women & children would not be disturbed . . .[27]

When Ken Burns' Civil War documentary first aired, many viewers marveled at the lovely use of the English language by some of these Victorian-era witnesses, especially Sullivan Ballou. But his letter is treasured precisely because it is so rare. Few Civil War soldiers exhibited an ability to produce stirring prose either in their diaries or their letters home. I read hundreds of such diaries and letters in researching this chapter; most of them are deadly dull and concerned primarily with the trivia of both camp and home life. But not all of them.

"Relatively few Union volunteers mentioned the slavery issue when they enlisted," writes James McPherson, someone who has read many, many more letters than I have. "But those who did were outspoken in their determination to destroy the 'slave power' and to cleanse the restored Union of an evil they considered a mockery of American ideals of liberty."[28]

Bruce Catton, another respected Civil War historian, found that attitudes in the North varied somewhat by geography. He noted that, as in John Adams' time, Massachusetts and the states surrounding the Commonwealth produced the most progressive Northern soldiers. "In general, the Western troops were less disturbed [by slavery] than the New Englanders," Catton wrote. "To the Westerners, this war was being fought to restore the Union; to the New Englanders, the abolition of human slavery was mixed up in it too, and freedom was an all-embracing idea that included black men as well as white. Sentiment back home was strongly abolitionist, and it was felt in camp."[29]

Still, such feelings were not confined to the men from New England. In researching *For Cause and Comrades*, the meticulous McPherson read and catalogued the letters and diaries of 1,076 Civil War soldiers—and he found plenty of abolitionist sentiment from soldiers in blue who came from all over the union. It was an Iowa volunteer, Jacob Ritner, who wrote his wife in July of 1864:

> This is a most horrible war, is it not, dear, to take me away from you for so long a time and to make it necessary to endure such dangers and labors as we both have felt on account of it. But you must not think that I regret that I entered the army. . . . No, my dear, if only through this baptism of blood, our nation, freed and purified from the blighting curse of slavery, shall lift her radiant forehead from the dust, and crowned with the wisdom of freedom go on her glorious way rejoicing.

And it was Ohio man Tully McCrea, an artillery officer who roomed with George Custer at West Point, who told his sweetheart in June 1861 that the war "will not be ended until the subject of slavery is finally and forever settled. It has been a great curse to this country."

But there *was* something distinctive about the New England men, especially those from the home state of the Adams clan—Samuel, John, Abigail, and John Quincy. "Slavery has brought death into our own households already in its wicked rebellion," wrote John Worthington

Ames, a Harvard man and Massachusetts infantry captain, to his mother in 1861. "There is but one-way and that is emancipation. . . . I want to sing 'John Brown' in the streets of Charleston, and ram red-hot abolitionism down their unwilling throats at the point of the bayonet."[30]

How deep abolition ran in the veins of those in the Massachusetts units was a lesson that Brigadier General Charles P. Stone learned the hard way. Stone, a West Point man, issued orders that the troops were "not to incite and encourage insubordination among the colored servants in the neighborhood of the camps." A junior officer in the 20th Massachusetts, following this order to the letter, rousted a couple of runaway slaves that had sought refuge within the lines of the regiment—and returned them to their owner. This didn't go down well with the men, some of whom wrote home about it. When word of this episode reached the ears of abolitionist Massachusetts Gov. John A. Andrew, he fired off an indignant letter dressing down the colonel in charge of the regiment. The colonel passed it along to General Stone, who penned an angry letter of his own. The spat escalated to the point where Stone found himself being denounced by name on the floor of the U.S. Senate by Massachusetts' abolitionist Charles Sumner.[31]

What of Capt. Ames' reference to John Brown; was that typical? Well, it wasn't atypical. Spirited debates broke out in Union camps over the wisdom of Emancipation, especially early in the war. Many of those soldiers were Democrats; some deserted after the Emancipation Proclamation when enlistments declined. But as more Union men came in contact with slaves, their attitudes against slavery hardened.

"Since I [came] here I have learned and seen more of what the horrors of Slavery was than I ever knew before," Col. Marcus M. Spiegel of the 120th Ohio wrote home to his wife after arriving in Louisiana. "I am [in] favor of doing away with the . . . accursed institution. I am [now] a strong abolitionist."

Whatever their politics had been before the war—Spiegel had spoken against Emancipation only a year earlier, in 1863—as the Northern men took territory in the South, fugitive slaves flocked to their camps, making the Union units *de facto* emancipators.[32] One of them, William Tell Barnitz, a volunteer in the 158th Pennsylvania infantry, wrote to his hometown newspaper from North Carolina in March 1863 extolling the virtues of the 8,000 fugitive slaves who are under protection of the Union army. Many of them were children learning to read and write for the first time in schools that have been opened for them by "philanthropists from the north." Many others are men who were being incorporated into the army itself.

"It humbles one to see the efforts these youth put forth to attain knowledge, and it is a grand omen for the amelioration of the race," Barnitz wrote. "As soldiers they evince the same traits, attentive, active, quick to learn, ambitious, and above all, courageous. . . . the Union is safe!"[33]

Pvt. Samuel S. Dunton, of the 114th New York State Volunteer Infantry, writes home from Louisiana about being "heartily sick of this war" and about the hardships of war and the climate of the Deep South. But he, too, alludes, to a larger purpose for his sacrifice. "Had I thought at the time I enlisted that I should be sent so far away from my wife and child, my patriotism would have lost some of its ardor," Dunton wrote on February 20, 1863, "but think there is a better country coming."[34]

No one needed to tell that to the "contrabands" who found themselves under the protection of—and working for—various Union regiments. A Maryland fugitive slave named John Boston wrote gleefully to his wife, Elizabeth, January 12, 1862. The spelling isn't as good, but the sentiment is equal to Sullivan Ballou's:

> My Dear Wife it is with grate joy I take this time to let you know Whare I am i am now in Safety in the 14th Regiment of Brooklyn this Day i can Adress you thank god as a free man I had a little truble in giting away But as the lord led the Children of Isrel to the land of Canon So he led me to a land Whare fredom Will rain in spite Of earth and hell Dear you must make your Self content i am free from al the Slavers Lash . . . am With a very nice man and have All that hart Can Wish But My Dear I Cant express my grate desire that i Have to See you i trust the time Will Come When We Shal meet again And if We dont met on earth We Will Meet in heven Whare Jesas ranes . . .
>
> Your Affectionate Husban Kiss Daniel For me
>
> John Boston
>
> Give my love to Father and Mother[35]

As the momentum of the war turned against them, Southern leaders confronted an obvious, and obviously difficult, dilemma: should they muster slaves into the Confederate Army? As early as December of 1861, Mary Chesnut had seen the solution—and she had seen it clearly.

"Our only chance is to be ahead of [the Union]," she had written. "Free our Negroes and put them in the army." Such an action would have begged the rationale for secession itself, however, and though this debate raged through the South for two years, it was not acted upon until quite late in the game. The sea change came in 1865, by which time Richmond was surrounded and cut off, and Lee and Jefferson Davis had both given the plan their blessing. On March 24, 1865, Richmond's besieged populace watched as two companies of freed black soldiers marched up Main Street with three new companies of whites. They were to be incorporated into Lee's much-revered Army of Northern Virginia. Except that, weeks later, Lee surrendered that legendary fighting force at Appomattox. "Having gone to war to preserve slavery, the South [was] now willing to sacrifice it to gain independence," noted David Chambers, who wrote the script of the History Channel documentary *April 1865*.[36]

After the war was over, blacks who had served in the Union Army didn't need to be told why they were fighting—or quibble with the varied motivations of the Union's commander-in-chief. In April 1865, Lincoln also visited Richmond, the burned shell that had been the capital of the Confederacy, and walked the city's streets holding the hand of young son Tad. The president was greeted as a savior by the black populace of Richmond. "As if upon the wings of lightning," noted black correspondent Thomas Morris Chester, the news spread that the liberator "had come." The crowd surged to see Lincoln, shouting, "Glory to God! Glory! Glory! Glory!"

Gabor Boritt, director of the Civil War Institute at Gettysburg College, remarking on the scene, added, "At one point an old man with tears in his eyes stopped before Lincoln, raised his hat and bowed. The president removed his own hat and bowed silently in return. . . . As another reporter noted: 'It was a bow which upset [the] forms, laws, customs and ceremonies of centuries.'"[37]

Nor did the 200,000 fugitive slaves, former slaves and freedmen who enlisted in the Union army have to be convinced that they were fighting for freedom—and a better America. Frederick Douglass had urged Lincoln to use black troops since Fort Sumter. But Douglass faced reluctance on all sides, including from some freedmen, who dubbed the conflict "the white man's war." Douglass scorned this line of argument as an excuse for cowardice, and exhorted blacks to join the colored regiments that began forming up in 1862.

"Liberty won by white men would lack half its lustre," Douglass wrote. "Who would be free themselves must strike the blow. Better even to die free than to live slaves."[38] Douglass served as an official recruiter for the Union army; among those he recruited were two of his own sons, Charles and Lewis, both of whom enlisted in the famed 54th Massachusetts, the regiment led by Robert G. Shaw, a captain in the Massachusetts 2nd who had survived his wounds at Antietam and who was tapped personally by Massachusetts' Gov. Andrews for his historic mission. Shaw made a major and then a colonel for agreeing to command black troops. The Massachusetts 54th was one of the first to see sustained combat.

Shaw's description of July 4, 1863—the last Independence Day he would ever see—is as poignant a picture of the Fourth of July that has ever been penned by an American soldier. Writing to his mother, a dedicated abolitionist, he wrote:

> Mr. Lynch [the black Baptist preacher giving the speech] was very eloquent. Can you imagine anything more wonderful than a coloured-Abolitionist meeting on a South Carolina plantation? Here were collected all the freed slaves on this Island listening to the most ultra abolition speeches that could be made; while two years ago, their masters were still here, the lords of the soil & of them. Now they all own a little themselves, go to school, to church, and work for wages. It is the most extraordinary change. Such things oblige a man to believe that God isn't very far off.
>
> A little black boy read the Declaration of Independence, and then, they all sang some of their hymns. The effect was grand. I would have given anything to have had you there. I thought of you all the time. The day was beautiful and the crowd was collected in the churchyard under some magnificent old oaks, covered with the long, hanging, grey moss, which grows on the trees here. The gay dresses & turbans of the women made the sight very brilliant.

Less than two weeks later, the 54th, along with two brigades of white troops, was thrown into a suicidal and ineffectual attempt to capture Fort Wagner on the South Carolina coast. More than 1,500 Union soldiers were killed or wounded. Of the 600 soldiers in the 54th Massachusetts, 281 were casualties, 54 killed or mortally wounded, 48 never accounted for and presumed dead. Shaw was among them. Sword in hand, he was fatally shot while atop a parapet of the impregnable Confederate works. His last words were "Onward 54th!"[39]

But if the battle at Fort Wagner was a military failure and a human disaster, what happened on the South Carolina beach galvanized abolitionists and made an impression on the Union Army's officer corps. The question in the minds of some white military men about whether the colored troops would fight—and fight gallantly—had been answered in the affirmative, as no less a personage than General Grant took note. Frederick Douglass' son Lewis, a twenty-two-year-old sergeant major who survived the carnage at Fort Wagner, wrote a letter to his fiancée two days after the battle was over. "Remember if I die, I die in a good cause. I wish we had a hundred thousand colored troops. We would put an end to this war."

Lewis Douglass would get his wish: By the time Lee surrendered at Appomattox, one in every eight Union soldiers was a black man. Union recruiting posters aimed at blacks had carried not just the prose of Lewis' famous father, but also the lines of a song that had swept through the North, the *Battle Hymn of the Republic.*

In an age when prerecorded music follows Americans into their cars, their elevators, even their bathrooms, it is hard to imagine how large a role spontaneous singing played in the everyday lives of people in the nineteenth century. Songs and music were also a significant form of political expression. Robert E. Lee once expressed his pleasure at being serenaded by a North Carolina regimental band, by saying, "I don't believe we can have an army without music."[40] But that statement may be more revealing than Lee intended, for the songs clearly roused the troops—and revealed much about them as well. The 54th Massachusetts, for example, had its own regimental song. It went like this:

> *So rally boys, let us never mind the past;*
> *We had a hard road to travel, but our day is coming fast;*
> *For God is for the right, and we have no need to fear.*
> *The Union must be saved by the colored volunteer.*

There were hundreds of such ditties sung by both sides in the Civil War.[41] But two of them—one from each side—have lasted through the ages. And in the realm of music, perhaps the victor *does* get to write the history: In modern America, the cheerful strains of *Dixie* have all but been banned, even at college football games in the Deep South, while the *Battle Hymn of the Republic* is the song America still turns to in its hour of need. On September 14, 2001, three days after the United States was attacked at the World Trade Center and the Pentagon, President Bush, along with four former presidents and their wives, sat together for a ceremony at Washington's National Cathedral. After Bush spoke, the first families joined the congregation in singing *Battle Hymn of the Republic,* an anthem someone hearing for the first time would find decidedly martial in character, and unabashedly Christian. But it is much more than that. It is an abolition song, a freedom song.

The hymn has a convoluted and murky provenance, but the tune seems to have been written in the mid-1850s by a Philadelphia insurance salesman and part-time songwriter named William Steffe. He wrote it, he asserted later, at the behest of the Good Will Engine Co. as a welcoming song for a visiting contingent from the Liberty Fire Co. of Baltimore.[42] The original first line was "Say, Bummers, Will You Meet Us?" But it was too infectious a melody to stay consigned to commercial purposes, and by 1858, the song began showing up in printed versions with a more religious set of lyrics. It began: "Say, brothers, will you meet us, on Canaan's happy shore?" and included the "Glory, Glory, Hallelujah" refrain. It was probably not played as an anthem, but at a quicker tempo, probably allegro or even presto. It was a popular enough tune that, by the first months of the war, Union regimental bands were regularly playing it and Union soldiers singing it—as they prepared for war. By then it had become an abolition song that began, "John Brown's body lies a-mouldering in the grave," sung three times with the end of the first stanza being, ". . . His soul goes marching on!"

It regularly picked up new verses as the war progressed, and before the war was a year old it seems to have become the Union army's unofficial song. In March of 1862, Edward Dicey of *The Spectator,* a British newspaper, crossed the Potomac River to view the Union troops assembling for their spring campaign in the peninsula. They headed back toward evening, but were halted at the Chain Bridge for hours while some 16,000 Union troops crossed it into Virginia. "With colors flying and bands playing, regiment after regiment filed past us," he wrote. "The men were singing, shouting, cheering. . . . They chanted 'John Brown's Hymn' . . . and the heavy tramp of a thousand feet beat time to that strange weird melody."

A few months before, in November 1861, Julia Ward Howe, a white abolitionist, had also been invited to view a Union encampment near Washington. She, too, heard the troops singing the song with the hypnotically "weird melody," and on her way back from the front,

Ward and those in her carriage began serenading the soldiers they passed on the road. When the men heard Howe and her party sing the John Brown's body song, they whooped it up delightedly, shouting, "Good for you!" Her minister, Unitarian theologian (and fellow abolitionist) James Freeman Clarke turned to Howe and asked her if she would write some more inspiring lyrics "for that stirring tune."

Howe obliged that very night. She said later that the words came to her in her sleep. The poem appeared in the February editions of *The Atlantic Monthly*, its title having been suggested by the Boston-based magazine's editor James T. Fields, who paid Howe the standard fee of four dollars, but did not give her a byline.[43] The poem, set to the tune known then as the John Brown song, was more religious, but it was still an abolition song. The new inspiration invoked by Howe, however, was not the untamed Kansas abolitionist hanged in Charles Town, Va., for his raid on nearby Harper's Ferry, but a man nailed to the cross 1,860 years earlier just outside the city gates of Jerusalem:

> In the beauty of the lilies, Christ was born across the sea,
> With a glory in his bosom that transfigures you and me:
> As he died to make men holy, let us die to make men free,
>   While God is marching on.

The effect of this poem wasn't immediate; some Union troopers liked the old version—the John Brown version—better anyway. *The Atlantic* was then, as now, a literary magazine, but in a nation that was mobilizing en masse, some of its readers were soldiers. Among them were Charles Haydon, who describes a scene in which one of the magazine's articles is read aloud inside the tent housing several soldiers.[44] Another *Atlantic* reader was Charles Cardwell McCabe, a recruiter and Methodist chaplain for the 122nd Ohio Volunteers. Upon seeing Howe's poem, McCabe memorized it on the spot and after he heard it sung to the John Brown tune, he began singing it regularly himself in his rich baritone voice. After being captured by Confederate forces and sent to Libby Prison in Richmond, McCabe led Union prisoners in singing the song to celebrate the Union victory at Gettysburg. They sang until their guards hushed them. In early 1864, McCabe related this story in the Capitol to an audience that included President Lincoln. "I made a brief address and wound up as requested, by singing the 'Battle Hymn,'" McCabe wrote in a letter to his wife. "When we came to the chorus the audience rose. Oh, how they sang! I happened to strike exactly the right key and the band helped us. I kept time for them with my hand and the mighty audience sang in exact time. Some shouted out loud at the last verse, and above all the uproar Mr. Lincoln's voice was heard: 'Sing it again!' "[45]

By the time Abraham Lincoln heard McCabe sing the Battle Hymn, he had already concluded that preserving the Union was necessary to ensure freedom, not just for the four million in bondage on American soil, but also for future generations, for tens of millions of people as yet unborn, white as well as black, all over the world. In 1861, Lincoln had characterized secession as "the essence of anarchy," and maintained that if the Confederacy were to prevail "it will go far to prove the incapability of the people to govern themselves."[46] That same year, in a July 4th speech to Congress, Lincoln had termed the Civil War "a people's contest" that would provide an answer to the question of "whether discontented individuals, too few in number to control administration . . . can arbitrarily, without any pretense, break up their Government, and thus practically put an end to free government upon earth."

Lincoln cited the Declaration in that speech. In doing so, and in harking back repeatedly to Jefferson and the language of the Declaration, Lincoln was making the tacit claim that Jefferson's ownership of slaves was of less consequence than the implications of Jefferson's formulations about the origins and nature of freedom. Lincoln did this most notably at Gettysburg, where on November 19, 1863, he delivered his most famous address. In that spare 272-word speech, Lincoln specifically dates the birth of the American nation to the writing of the Declaration of Independence, not the Constitution. This assertion caused heartburn over the years for any number of historians. Garry Wills, who is not among those distressed by Lincoln's formulation, has pointed out that Lincoln mentioned neither slavery at Gettysburg, nor, specifically, the Union. In *Lincoln at Gettysburg: The Words That Remade America*, Wills asserts that the "great task" the soldiers died for on the consecrated Pennsylvania battlefield is not only Emancipation, but the very preservation of self-government. In other words, the "unfinished work" Lincoln alludes to is fulfilling the true promise of the Declaration—even if the men who wrote it did not fully do so themselves.

"This explains, at the level of tactics, the usefulness of the Declaration of Independence for Lincoln," Wills writes. "That revered document was antimonarchical in the common perception, and, so far as that took the reader, unchallengeable. But because it indicted King George III in terms of the equality of men, the Declaration committed Americans to claims even more at odds with slavery than kingship—since kings do not, necessarily, claim to own their subjects. Put the claims of the Declaration as mildly as possible, and it still cannot be reconciled with slavery."

Thus, when Lincoln calls up the image of "a new nation, conceived in liberty and dedicated to the proposition that all men are created equal"—and this is the first time an American president has ever suggested such a thing—he was, first of all, really talking about *all* people, even those and their descendants who had arrived from Africa in chains.[47] But this was not a new idea for Lincoln. Fifteen years earlier, in his celebrated debates with Stephen Douglas, Lincoln was quite explicit:

> I think the authors of that notable instrument [the Declaration] intended to include *all* men, but they did not intend to declare all men equal *in all respects*. They did not mean to say all were equal in color, size, intellect, moral development, or social capacity. They defined, with tolerable distinctness, in what respects they did consider all men created equal—equal in "certain inalienable rights, among which are life, liberty, and the pursuit of happiness." This they said, and this they meant. [October 15, 1858, at Alton, Illinois]

> I, as well as Judge Douglas, am in favor of the race to which I belong having the [socially] superior position. I have never said anything to the contrary, but I hold that, notwithstanding all this, there is no reason in the world why the Negro is not entitled to all the natural rights enunciated in the Declaration of Independence: the right to life, liberty, and the pursuit of happiness! [August 21, 1858, in Ottawa, Illinois]

But by the middle of the Civil War, it was clear that Lincoln had greatly expanded his already expansive vision of the potential pool of human beings who would benefit by keeping the United States of America together. Who did he have in mind? Merely everyone in the world. And much of the world was watching back, thinking the same thing.

In England, John Stuart Mill said that the armed struggle in North America was "destined to be a turning point, for good and evil, of the course of human affairs." A victory for the slave-holding secessionists,

Mills added, "would be a victory for the powers of evil which would give courage to the enemies of progress and damp the spirits of its friends all over the civilized world while it would create a formidable military power, grounded on the worst and most anti-social form of the tyranny of men over men, and, by destroying for a long time the prestige of the great democratic republic, would give to all the privileged classes of Europe a false confidence, probably only to be extinguished in blood."[48]

In the 29th Jefferson Lecture in the Humanities, delivered at the Kennedy Center on March 27, 2000, James McPherson amplified on the point that what we now called "the world community" believed it had a stake in the outcome of the American Civil War, too. French republicans, he said, some in exile, expressed solicitude for Lincoln and the cause of Union as "defenders of right and humanity." But, as McPherson explained, that view was hardly unanimous across the oceans:

> Some European monarchists and conservatives did indeed make no secret of their hope that the Union would fall into the dustbin of history. The powerful *Times* of London considered the likely downfall of "the American colossus" a good "riddance of a nightmare. . . . Excepting a few gentlemen of republican tendencies, we all expect, we nearly all wish, success to the Confederate cause." The Earl of Shrewsbury expressed his cheerful belief "that the dissolution of the Union is inevitable, and that men before me will live to see an aristocracy established in America." In Spain the royalist journal *Pensamiento Espanol* found it scarcely surprising that Americans were butchering each other, for the United States, it declared editorially, "was populated by the dregs of all the nations of the world. . . . Such is the real history of the one and only state in the world which has succeeded in constituting itself according to the flaming theories of democracy. The example is too horrible to stir any desire for emulation." The minister to the United States from the Czar of all Russia echoed this opinion in 1863. "The republican form of government, so much talked about by the Europeans and so much praised by the Americans, is breaking down," he wrote. "What can be expected from a country where men of humble origin are elevated to the highest positions?" He meant Lincoln, of course.

Thus, the causes of ending slavery and the cause of union and the cause of American democracy all came to be seen in both the North and

South, and on both sides of the Atlantic, as a single cause. The president of this experimental nation had proclaimed the United States of America to be "the last, best, hope of earth" adding that, "in giving freedom to the slave," the North would "assure freedom to the free." And as the war grinded on, the men in Mr. Lincoln's army came to believe it, too.

Josiah B. Chaney, a sergeant of the 2nd Company, Minnesota Sharpshooters, explained to his wife Melissa, home in St. Paul with their daughters Aprilla and Delia, why he was re-enlisting after being wounded: "My grandfather fought and risked his life to bequeath to his posterity . . . the glorious Institutions" now under attack from "this infernal rebellion," he wrote on October 13, 1862. "It is not for you and I, or us & our dear little ones, alone that I was and am willing to risk the fortunes of the battlefield, but also for the sake of the country's millions who are to come after us."[49]

Chaney was hardly alone, either in his forward-looking sense of patriotism, nor in having to justify those feelings to a wife left at home with small children to raise—along with the fears that her husband might never return. "Remember that thousands went forth and poured out their life's blood in the Revolution to establish this government," wrote Ephraim S. Holloway, a lieutenant in the 41st Ohio to his wife Margaret, "and twould be a disgrace to the whole American people if she had not noble sons enough who had the spirit of seventy-six in their hearts."[50]

Lincoln would have appreciated that sentiment, especially the reference to 1776. In 1864, soldiers from another unit of the Buckeye State dropped by the White House on their way home to pay their respects to the commander-in-chief. Lincoln went to the balcony above what is now called the South Lawn to say a few remarks to the men from the 166th Ohio regiment. "I almost always feel inclined, when I happen to say anything to soldiers, to impress upon them . . . the importance of success in this contest," Lincoln told them. "It is not merely for today, but for all time to come that we should perpetuate for our children's children this great and free government, which we have enjoyed all our lives."

Lincoln continued:

> I beg you to remember this, not merely for my sake, but for yours. I happen to temporarily occupy this big White House. I am a living witness that any one of your children may look to come here as my father's child has. It is in order that each of you may have through

95

this free government which we have enjoyed, an open field and a fair chance for your industry, enterprise, and intelligence; that you may all have equal privileges in the race of life, with all its desirable human aspiration. It is for this the struggle should be maintained; that we may not lose our birthright. . . . The nation is worth fighting for, to secure such an inestimable jewel.

When Lincoln told these men that their nation was worth fighting for, they understood far better than Lincoln—for they had seen death at close quarters—that this often meant the very possibility of *dying* for their nation as well. Lincoln himself would be one of the last casualties of the war, killed by a secessionist and pro-slavery zealot who stood behind the White House and listened on April 11, 1865, as Lincoln—in what was to be his last public address—threw his support behind limited suffrage for blacks in the South by endorsing a plan for Louisiana that granted blacks the franchise.

Four years earlier in a speech not much remembered today Lincoln himself had all but foretold his own death, while accurately describing the cause—applying Jefferson's words to an entire nation—for which he would lay it down. That speech came at Independence Hall, as President-elect Lincoln made his way by train toward Washington to assume the presidency of a fragmenting nation. The threats on Lincoln's life were considered serious enough that he entered the capital in disguise. For doing that he was criticized, just as George W. Bush was criticized on September 11, 2001, for initially heading west on Air Force One, all the way to Nebraska, instead of heading directly to the capital. But just as Bush's immediate concerns about security were forgotten as he found his voice as president of a nation under attack, so were Lincoln's. If the second President Bush's resoluteness was of some surprise to many Americans, Lincoln's was not. It was a voice that had been a long time in developing, and that derived its power from an intellect and a character that was a revelation to his contemporaries, as it has served as an inspiration to Lincoln's successors. To hear him tell it, on February 22— George Washington's birthday—in the year 1861, Lincoln was himself drawing his strength of ideas from the men of '76, who'd met in that hallowed place to formulate, announce and justify a Revolution in the affairs of men.

. . . All the political sentiments I entertain have been drawn, so far as I have been able to draw them, from the sentiments which originated and were given to the world from this hall. I have never had a feeling, politically, that did not spring from the sentiments embodied in the . . . Declaration of Independence, which gave liberty, not alone to the people of this country, but I hope, to the world for all future time. . . .

Now, my friends, can the country be saved upon that basis? If it can, I will consider myself one of the happiest men in the world if I can help to save it. If it cannot be saved upon that principle, it will be truly awful. But if this country cannot be saved without giving up that principle, I was about to say I would rather be assassinated on this spot than surrender it. . . .

My friends, this is wholly an unexpected speech, and I did not expect to be called upon to say a word when I came here. I supposed it was merely to do something toward raising the flag. I may, therefore, have said something indiscreet. I have said nothing but what I am willing to live by and, if it be the pleasure of Almighty God, die by."

5

Peace Now!

If it was incongruous with the spirit of 1776 to deny blacks the right to life, liberty and the pursuit of happiness—and Abraham Lincoln believed that this was so—it took the Civil War to bind the American union together, end chattel slavery and answer the question being mockingly posed by European potentates about whether a nation founded on the principle of self-government could long endure. But it was a war that took such a frighteningly high toll in human life that it scarred the nation's psyche forever.

As an Illinois lawyer and budding Republican politician called upon to respond to the appalling judgment of the U.S. Supreme Court in the Dred Scott decision, Abe Lincoln had asserted that the Declaration of Independence was a pledge "augmenting the happiness and value to life to all people of all colors everywhere." But only as commander-in-chief of the vast Federal army he deployed to apply that principle did Lincoln discover just how expensive a promissory note the Founders had bequeathed him.

Even before 1865, American presidents tended to equate civic happiness with peace. It is only natural in a democracy, in which the citizenry votes for the representatives who send their own sons off to war, that this should be so. When James Monroe took the oath of office as America's fifth president on March 4, 1817, some level of armed conflict had disturbed the tranquility of the former colonies for the better part of four decades. And when Monroe used the word "happiness" in his inaugural address he essentially defined that term as meaning the absence of being in a state of war.[1]

But the Civil War had a way of making everything that had come before it seem insignificant. In a nation of 34 million people, nearly 3.9

million had seen military service. (More than 2.8 million had donned a Federal uniform, and slightly more than one million had taken up arms for the Confederacy.) Of the Union troops, 110,070 had perished in combat, and another 249,458 had died from other causes, mostly disease. The number of wounded Union soldiers—and many of them were perilously disfigured—was 275,175. The South suffered 74,524 killed in combat, another 124,000 from other causes—and 137,000 wounded. When the numbers of missing who were presumed dead are added up, the figure for those who lost their lives in the Civil War is most often estimated at 620,000 men. When that number is added to the 412,000 on both sides who were wounded, it comes to more than a million men, killed or maimed in a country one-tenth the population of America today. It was a numbing cost, in a young nation that had nothing to compare it to. Civil War soldiers—on both sides—invoked the Spirit of '76 in their letters home, but the stark truth of the matter was that George Washington lost fewer men in eight years than Grant did in one day at Shiloh, or Lee in one afternoon at Gettysburg.

From 1865 onward, Americans would always be wary of war, no matter how noble the cause, no matter how unspeakable the enemy, no matter how high the stakes. In the years before the Civil War, people on both sides, North and South, would employ the concept of "liberty" to explain why they were fighting. *After* that war, with its hundreds of thousands of widows and orphaned children and broken bodies, Americans would pay more attention to the first word of Jefferson's trilogy—"life"—when judging whether a cause was worth going into combat over. *The pursuit of happiness* would emerge as argument both for and against war. Just as Lincoln noted that both sides in the Civil War prayed to the same God, since his time so do those on both sides in America's long, ongoing conversation about war and peace fall back on the Declaration's credo for their justification. The arguments of both sides are almost always powerful.

"The seeds of the Declaration of Independence are yet maturing," was the way John Quincy Adams put it in 1820 while referring to the inexorable march toward Emancipation. But this well-read man of the world knew enough to add that the harvest of the crop produced by those seeds would be "the terrible sublime," as it always is when brother fights against brother.[2]

Woodrow Wilson, who would win reelection to the presidency as the candidate who kept America out of World War I, recalled that his first memory as a boy was learning that his country was arming for conflict against itself. "My earliest recollection," Wilson said long afterward, "is of standing at my father's gateway in Augusta, Georgia, when I was four years old, and hearing someone pass and say that Mr. Lincoln was elected and there was to be war."[3]

Wilson's father, Joseph Ruggles Wilson, a minister and a Southern sympathizer, served as a chaplain in the Confederate Army. His son resolved that when he grew up he would avoid war. In Wilson's second year as president, Europe exploded. Wilson wanted no part of it. In 1914, with a nod to the rhetoric, if not the fighting spirit of Thomas Paine, Wilson sent peace envoys to the continent while telling Americans it was their patriotic duty to remain neutral "during these days that try men's souls." Wilson almost made it sound like it was every American's duty to think happy thoughts.

> The effect of the war upon the United States will depend upon what American citizens say and do. . . . Every man who really loves America will act and speak in the true spirit of neutrality, which is the spirit of impartiality and fairness and friendliness to all concerned. The spirit of the nation in this critical matter will be determined largely by what individuals and society and those gathered in public meetings do and say, upon what newspapers and magazines contain, upon what ministers utter in their pulpits, and men proclaim as their opinions upon the street.[4]

But positive thinking did not stop the Kaiser's deadly U-boats, nor induce the French or the Russians, who had escalated a regional conflict into total war, to end the slaughter in Europe by sitting down at the bargaining table with Germany. In 1916, President Wilson won reelection on the slogan, "He kept us out of war." But it was an empty promise. Wilson's second inauguration, which came exactly one hundred years after James Monroe congratulated himself on coming to power in a time of tranquility, was a somber affair in which Wilson prepared Americans to accept the great paradox of a people who want to pursue their own happiness in peace, which is that sometimes they get dragged into war no matter what their initial intentions. At his 1917 swearing in, Wilson spoke grimly of an "armed" neutrality, even as he invoked the prosecutorial cadences, aggrieved tones and even some of the precise language of Philadelphia and 1776:

It has been impossible to avoid [events in Europe]. They have affected the life of the whole world. They have shaken men everywhere with a passion and an apprehension they never knew before. . . . We are a composite and cosmopolitan people. We are of the blood of all the nations that are at war. . . . The war inevitably set its mark from the first alike upon our minds, our industries, our commerce, our politics and our social action. To be indifferent to it, or independent of it, was out of the question. . . .

We shall be the more American if we but remain true to the principles in which we have been bred. They are not the principles of a province or of a single continent. We have known and boasted all along that they were the principles of a liberated mankind. These, therefore, are the things we shall stand for, whether in war or in peace: That all nations are equally interested in the peace of the world and in the political stability of free peoples, and equally responsible for their maintenance; that the essential principle of peace is the actual equality of nations in all matters of right or privilege; that peace cannot securely or justly rest upon an armed balance of power; that governments derive all their just powers from the consent of the governed and that no other powers should be supported by the common thought, purpose or power of the family of nations; that the seas should be equally free and safe for the use of all peoples, under rules set up by common agreement and consent . . . I need not argue these principles to you, my fellow countrymen; they are your own part and parcel of your own thinking and your own motives in affairs. They spring up native amongst us.

Less than four weeks later, on April 2, 1917, Wilson asked Congress for a formal declaration of war. "We have no quarrel with the German people," Wilson said in a formulation that sounds remarkably familiar today, having been employed almost word-for-word by both presidents named Bush about the Iraqi people. "We have no feeling toward them but one of sympathy and friendship," Wilson added. "It was not upon their impulse that their government acted in entering this war; it was not with their previous knowledge or approval."

Wilson continued, in language that also foreshadowed George W. Bush's words on the eve of the second Persian Gulf War. Once again, Wilson borrowed phrases from the Declaration:

The world must be made safe for democracy. Its peace must be planted upon the tested foundations of political liberty. We have no selfish ends to serve. We desire no conquest, no dominion. We seek no indemnities for ourselves, no material compensation for the sacrifices we shall freely make. We are but one of the champions of the rights of mankind. We shall be satisfied when those rights have been made as secure as the faith and the freedom of nations can make them.

But the right is more precious than peace, and we shall fight for the things which we have always carried nearest our hearts—for democracy, for the right of those who submit to authority to have a voice in their own governments, for the rights and liberties of small nations. . . . To such a task we can dedicate our lives and our fortunes, everything that we are and everything that we have, with the pride of those who know that the day has come when America is privileged to spend her blood and her might for the principles that gave her birth and happiness and the peace which she has treasured. God helping her, she can do no other.

To this day, there is debate whether America needed to involve itself in the First World War at all. Conversely, some critics maintain that if United States troops had been committed earlier, peace would have come earlier, too, thus sparing the lives of many European soldiers, while simultaneously leading to a more just peace for Germany as well as creating a more fertile soil in that nation for the planting of a true democracy.

But if Wilson was late in coming to the decision that war was the path that he must take, this hesitation may have stemmed from Wilson's own ambivalence about the Declaration of Independence itself. In his book, *The New Freedom,* Wilson wrote that "some citizens of this country have never got beyond the Declaration of Independence, signed in Philadelphia, July 4, 1776."

Two contemporary conservative academics, Thomas G. West and Douglas A. Jeffrey, believe that Wilson's principal qualms about that document stem from its very intellectual underpinnings, namely, the concept of natural law. Wilson's misgivings about natural rights are reflective of Wilson's brand of Progressivism, that it is to say, the brand espoused then, as now, by elite professors and exclusive universities. Wilson's words, they believe, represent an early—and influential—descent into the moral relativism that has become the bane of America's national life in the minds of social conservatives.

"Wilson—pretending to agree with the Declaration, but in fact rejecting it—wrote that the Declaration's unalienable rights to life, liberty and the pursuit of happiness mean that 'each generation of men [may determine] what they will do with their lives, what they will prefer as the form and object of their liberty, in what they will seek their happiness,'" West and Jeffrey write. Wilson, they assert, characterized the Declaration as being "outdated bunkum."[5]

Wilson never used such a phrase, of course, and in fairness to him, it must be pointed out that the purpose of his book *The New Freedom: A Call for the Emancipation of the General Energies of a People,* is not to disparage Jefferson or the other Founders, but rather to get Americans to apply their birthright to the problems of the future. This is especially true of the section in which Wilson discusses the Declaration of Independence. The book was based on Wilson's campaign speeches of 1912; sections of it might strike a reader today as the long version of the catchy rhetoric Bill Clinton would apply in the 1996 campaign while asking Americans to imagine "the bridge to the twenty-first century." (I covered that campaign, and I believe that Clinton—and Wilson's—oratory accurately evokes an optimistic spirit consistent with that of the Framers of democracy.) Here is more of Wilson:

Progress! Did you ever reflect that that word is almost a new one? No word comes more often or more naturally to the lips of modern man, as if the thing it stands for were almost synonymous with life itself, and yet men through many thousand years never talked or thought of progress. They thought in the other direction. Their stories of heroisms and glory were tales of the past. The ancestor wore the heavier armor and carried the larger spear. "There were giants in those days." Now all that has altered. We think of the future, not the past, as the more glorious time in comparison with which the present is nothing. Progress, development,—those are modern words. The modern idea is to leave the past and press onward to something new.

But what is progress going to do with the past, and with the present? How is it going to treat them? With ignominy, or respect? Should it break with them altogether, or rise out of them, with its roots still deep in the older time? What attitude shall progressives take toward the existing order, toward those institutions of conservatism, the Constitution, the laws, and the courts?

. . . All that progressives ask or desire is permission—in an era when "development," "evolution," is the scientific word—to interpret the Constitution according to the Darwinian principle; all they ask is recognition of the fact that a nation is a living thing and not a machine.

Some citizens of this country have never got beyond the Declaration of Independence, signed in Philadelphia, July 4th, 1776. Their bosoms swell against George III, but they have no consciousness of the war for freedom that is going on today.

The Declaration of Independence did not mention the questions of our day. It is of no consequence to us unless we can translate its general terms into examples of the present day and substitute them in some vital way for the examples it itself gives, so concrete, so intimately involved in the circumstances of the day in which it was conceived and written. It is an eminently practical document, meant for the use of practical men; not a thesis for philosophers, but a whip for tyrants; not a theory of government, but a program of action. Unless we can translate it into the questions of our own day, we are not worthy of it; we are not the sons of the sires who acted in response to its challenge.

What form does the contest between tyranny and freedom take today? What is the special form of tyranny we now fight? How does it endanger the rights of the people, and what do we mean to do in order to make our contest against it effectual? What are to be the items of our new declaration of independence?

Is this a direct challenge to the very idea of natural rights, and thus on the idea of standards of right and wrong that are fixed in place from one century to the next? I think not, although it is easy to see in Wilson's words the early stirrings of a debate that flourishes even today over the idea that there are objective truths in the universe that men have only to discover or, instead, merely socially desirable "values" that alter and evolve over time. Leaving aside the most obvious alternative—that this is a false choice and that there are both universal truths about mankind as well as evolving standards of ethical behavior—one problem is that this is an academic debate that has spilled over from the academic into the political world. Because the denizens of the two realms don't always speak the same language, it might have been best had this debate remained confined to the philosophy or political science departments of the universities. But one reason it didn't is that Woodrow Wilson was that rarest of creatures: The high-ranking member of academia who transfigured himself into a highly successful politician.[6]

But if West and Jeffrey might be a bit too hard on Wilson, they are astute in discerning that the operative dichotomy as far as the Declaration of Independence is concerned is not so much liberals vs. conservatives as it is academia against the rest of the world. Modern campus liberals dismiss claims of natural rights—and, by implication, the superiority of one culture over another—reflexively and very nearly out of hand. But so do many modern campus conservatives.

The Declaration's natural law argument is so patently and obviously wrong, according to influential professors such as brilliant Stanford University philosophy professor Richard Rorty, that it goes without saying. (In fact, most of the criticism directed at Rorty has come from neo-Marxist professors dismayed by his call for progressives to construct a "pageant of historical progress," in which they spin stories, even if they must be fanciful ones. Even this mild form of a pro-American narrative is too much for some on the academic Left.) But Rorty is on completely solid ground inside academia when he writes of the "contingency of language," by which he means that the meaning of all language is contingent upon the individual using it—or hearing it. Rorty also argues for the "repudiation of the very idea of anything . . . having an intrinsic nature to be expressed or represented. There is no distinction between a "true" meaning of words and a false one. "Truth," he says, "is not out there." And the Declaration of Independence's natural rights argument is simply a "language game."

Perhaps this is what is to be expected (at least by political conservatives) from a university professor who describes himself as "a romantic bourgeois liberal." But what is a beleaguered Jeffersonian to make of the University of Notre Dame's Alasdair MacIntyre, who made the intellectual journey all the way from Marxism to a right-to-life, St. Thomas Aquinas–inspired brand of Catholicism, only to write:

> There are no self-evident truths . . . I mean, those rights which are alleged to belong to human beings as such and which are cited as a reason for holding that people ought not to be interfered with in their pursuit of life, liberty and happiness . . . there are no such rights, and belief in them is one with belief in witches and unicorns.[7]

"On both the right and the left, this rejection of natural rights is almost universal among intellectuals," write West and Jeffrey. But if Rorty comes across as just one more liberal postmodern moral relativist, albeit an unusually practical one, and MacIntyre as a cranky malcontent, this is because we are viewing them through the prism of elective politics. This is not how they should be seen, even if such dismissive thinking of natural law partially explains the reflexive antiwar stance that has been endemic on college campuses in the past half-century. Actually, Rorty and MacIntyre are two of the most gifted philosophers to come along in a century, and they are widely acclaimed as such even in the vicious, backstabbing world of academia. As writers and thinkers and college professors, their job is to engage in precisely such provocative musings and, in the process, to inspire their students to think critically. Their job is *not* to fashion U.S. foreign policy. No less an academic light than Woodrow Wilson himself understood the difference. Wilson may have come out of the very environment that produced such a sour assessment of the sweetest fruits of the Enlightenment, but he was also a pol, with all that that implies, and he knew better than to ever directly impugn Thomas Jefferson or the fighting spirit of the Founding Fathers.

And although there was no real public opinion polling in his day, it is safe to say that Wilson was certainly in sync with the voters in 1914, when he eschewed war, and probably so in 1917, when he embraced it. By that time, Americans had absorbed a steady diet of war coverage from a mass media, which, except for the German-language press, was emphatically pro-British in its outlook. The coverage eventually reached the point of caricature, with the Kaiser routinely being portrayed in ways that, by comparison, made Saddam Hussein look like an amateur. But if much of this news was clearly biased, and if the stories alleging German atrocities were invented, the sinking of the British cargo and passenger ship Lusitania, with the loss of twelve hundred people, was real enough—and it horrified Americans.

President Wilson had implored the Kaiser to put an end to submarine warfare, and he had, but only for a little while. But believing, tragically and incorrectly, that Wilson was not negotiating in good faith, the German leader announced on January 17, 1917, that he was resuming unrestricted submarine attacks. The Kaiser apparently assumed that unleashing his killer subs would force Britain to sue for peace. This was as unwise as some of Saddam's tactical judgments; what the Kaiser's decision really accomplished was to put the United States and Germany on a collision course. Then, foreseeing possible American entry into the war, a German foreign minister sent an ill-advised cable to Mexico City, proposing that the Mexicans join them in war against the United States (and persuade Japan to do the same), in return for which Mexico would be allowed to "re-conquer" Texas, New Mexico and Arizona. This, the mother-of-all miscalculations, made war a foregone conclusion in the minds of many Americans, who learned of it when the cable was intercepted by the British, who leaked it to American newspapers on March 1.[8]

The response was a spike upward in the war fever already gripping the nation. A sample of the reaction in the United States can be found in the March 30, 1917, editions of the *North American Review*, an influential literary and political magazine.

> Just as Thomas Jefferson experienced difficulty in compressing a multitude of complaints against a German king of Britain into a modest "Declaration of Independence," so will President Wilson, when the time comes, find himself overwhelmed by a sense of the grievances which this country has endured at the will of the madman of Prussia. We shall await with grimmest zest his recital of treaties broken, of wrongs to be done, of lies told, of treacheries bared, of insults borne, of murders committed, of all the most shameful shocking, mean and low practices against civilization, humanity and common decency recorded even in the history of barbarism, in the face of forbearance for the sake of peace unprecedented in the chronicles of governing Powers. . . .
>
> [W]e owe it to our forefathers who founded the Republic and to our fathers who saved the Union to prove ourselves not merely worthy of the happiness which flows from prosperity but eager and fearless in support of free life and full liberty the world over, to the end that the noble example set by them may not be degraded in gluttonous realization by us; because as a practical matter if spies and traitors infest our land now is the time to smoke them out; if a few scattering undersea waifs can break down our defenses and damage our cities, let them do their utmost that we may discover what might be anticipated from a fleet and prepare accordingly . . . because simply and finally, in such a case, war is curative, not destructive, a blessing not a curse.

But there were eloquent voices on the other side of the political equation, as well, even after the Kaiser's disastrous diplomatic and public relations blunders. And these voices, too, invoked the spirit of the Declaration—and of America's continued happiness—to make their case that war is ever to be avoided and that entering *this* war, in particu-

lar, was a wretched mistake. The most roaring of them all belonged to
Senator Robert M. La Follette, a volatile Republican from Wisconsin
with populist leanings and a highly confrontational debating style.

In a memorable speech on the Senate floor two days after Wilson's
call to arms, La Follette read telegrams from German-American towns
in Wisconsin where straw votes had revealed widespread opposition to
"the European war." La Follette railed against the "irresponsible and
war-crazed press" that had led an unsuspecting nation of working-class
people into a war in which they had no stake.

> The poor, sir, who are the ones called upon to rot in the trenches,
> have no organized power, have no press to voice their will upon this
> question of peace or war; but, oh, Mr. President, at some time they
> will be heard. I hope and I believe they will be heard in an orderly
> and a peaceful way. I think they may be heard from before long. I
> think, sir, if we take this step, when the people today who are stag-
> gering under the burden of supporting families at the present prices
> of the necessaries of life find those prices multiplied, when they are
> raised 100 percent, or 200 percent, as they will be quickly, aye, sir,
> when beyond that those who pay taxes come to have their taxes
> doubled and again doubled to pay the interest on the nontaxable
> bonds held by [J. P.] Morgan and his combinations, which have
> been issued to meet this war, there will come an awakening; they
> will have their day and they will be heard. It will be as certain and
> as inevitable as the return of the tides, and as resistless, too. . . .

This argument is a timeless one. As recently as January 1991, when
the Persian Gulf War was about to be fought, liberal Democrats in the
House and Senate opposed the Iraq war resolution on the grounds that
the young American troops who would pay the ultimate price came from
the nation's poorest families, not the families of those making the decision in the Capitol and the White House.

"I'm convinced in my own mind that if the sons and daughters of
all of us, of the President, the Vice President, the Cabinet were all over
there in the Persian Gulf right now, right up on the front line and were
going to be part of that first assault wave that would go on into Kuwait,
I think we'd be taking more time," Michigan Democratic congressman
Donald W. Riegle Jr. told his colleagues in 1991. "I think we'd be working harder on the sanctions policy. I think we'd be trying to squeeze Saddam Hussein in every other way that we could, short of a shooting war."

This view was most palpable among the Black Congressional Caucus, which voted 23–1 in opposition to the first President Bush's gulf war resolution. Their sentiments were captured best by Rep. Major R. Owens, an African-American Democrat who represented a district in Brooklyn, N.Y.

> Nearly one-third of our soldiers in Operation Desert Shield are African-American, many of them with families in districts like mine, the 12th Congressional District of Brooklyn. My district is the 10th poorest district in the nation. My district is the second—has the second-largest number of African-Americans. Young African-American men and women are three times more likely to be in the armed forces and involved in this impending war in the sand as young whites are. There is a reason for this. When people can't get jobs they find the Army and the Navy and the other military units as an opportunity to be utilized. There are many very bright young people who never looked for a job but who are recruited from high school and told that you can go to college after you go through the military and get those advantages. And there are many—there are a few others who are officers, quite a number are officers—are African-American men and women who went to military academies or they used the benefits of the R.O.T.C. as the only way they could make it. For this reason you have this disproportionate number.[9]

The liberals lost that vote in 1991, but the results were close enough that it immediately became clear that Bush's own credibility was on the line. In the House, the president prevailed on a vote of 250–183. In the Senate, the margin was only 52–47. The lessons of Vietnam were invoked quite readily in 1991; and the vote was a stark contrast from the Gulf of Tonkin resolution, which passed in 1964 with only two senators, and no House members, voting no.[10]

In Bob La Follette's day, openly opposing war in Congress required a great deal of courage, as only six senators voted against Wilson's war resolution. Moreover, La Follette actually may have delayed America's entry into the war, if only for a few weeks, with a parliamentary maneuver that earned him considerable scorn and vituperation. On March 3, with only hours remaining in the 64th Congress, La Follette led a filibuster to kill a House-passed measure to arm merchant ships for their own protection. Not since the Civil War had tempers in the chamber been as out of control. Sen. Henry Cabot Lodge, aged sixty-seven, punched a constituent who came to complain about war.[11] When the senator presiding over the debate recognized only those in opposition to La Follette, the Wisconsin firebrand erupted in anger, screaming from the Senate floor, restrained from throwing a spittoon only by Democratic senators who crowded around him. Theodore Roosevelt, borrowing a page from Grant's reaction to Jefferson Davis, called La Follette "a skunk who ought to be hung."[12] And after La Follette's four-hour April 4 harangue against Wilson's war declaration, the vitriol directed against him only grew. One of his Senate colleagues, John Sharp Williams of Mississippi, called La Follette "pro-German, anti-American, anti-Wilson, anti-Congress, a knave and a fool." And that was hardly all of it: Williams' denunciation goes some seven columns in the congressional record. "There are some things worse than war, and there are some things worse than death," Williams said in reference to La Follette. "One of them . . . is to have self-contempt because you are a pusillanimous, degenerate coward."

A *New York World* cartoon showed La Follette being pinned with the Iron Cross, presumably by the Kaiser himself, and after La Follette was quoted in a Minnesota speech as seeming to trivialize the sinking of the Lusitania, a new round of attacks began. La Follette's subsequent October 6, 1917, speech on the Senate floor is today considered a classic defense of free expression.[13] At the time, however, it prompted a Senate investigation of La Follette on possible charges of treason.

Such behavior—by both La Follette and his adversaries—seem to belong to the quaint eccentricities of another century. In truth, the arguments he waged against war with Germany are timeless. So much so that in his speeches, if "Iraq" were substituted for "Germany," the arguments would sound entirely contemporary.

*   *   *

At the outset of the post-9/11 war on terrorism, the American Civil Liberties Union actually initiated contact with U.S. embassies of Arab states and nations with large Muslim populations and solicited complaints about heavy-handed treatment of its citizens. With three thousand civilians dead, this tactic struck many Americans as misplaced sympathy. Perhaps it was, but in so doing, the ACLU leadership was as true as it could be to the organization's roots, for the ACLU was originally an anti-war group. The anti-war movement in 1915 was led by German-Americans, pacifists, suffragists, civil libertarians, socialists, isolationists and liberal members of the Protestant clergy. (If one were to trade German-Americans with Arab-Americans at the front of this list, and add to it the *New York Times,* the U.S. Catholic Bishops and a few other institutions—and replace the word "suffragists" for "feminists"—nearly the same coalition exists today.)

The present-day ACLU began as the National Civil Liberties Bureau. Among its founders were Roger Nash Baldwin, a Socialist and a pacifist who had spent time in federal prison for resisting the draft in World War I and who went on to become the ACLU's first president. The National Civil Liberties Bureau, in turn, was the outgrowth of the American Union Against Militarism, a peace organization formed in an attempt to lobby against U.S. entry into the First World War. Modern political conservatives tend to loathe the ACLU, which they characterize as aspiring to undermine core American values. But the charter documents of the rights group express fealty to the charter documents of the United States. The ACLU's founders specifically invoked the best work done by the nation's founders, the Declaration of Independence and the Constitution. Eight decades later, the organization still proudly employs this language:

On May 22, 2002, ACLU executive director Anthony D. Romero put it this way while discussing the impact of 9/11 on the United States:

> It is hard to disagree that our country has not changed in some significant way now that it is no longer immune to the furies of foreign events. But I would also remind us all of the transformative nature of 1776, 1787 and 1791—the Declaration of Independence, the signing of the Constitution, and the ratification of the Bill of Rights. For Americans, these must remain the key transformative events, shaping how we see the world and what we understand our role to be. In this spirit of our founder Roger Baldwin, let us go forward to make this country a better place for all people who yearn for freedom and dignity.
>
> It is, after all, our values—not our fears—that bind us together.[14]

It is difficult to argue with such lofty sentiments. And if the pacifist coalitions of today are similar to those of 1915, so are the most powerful arguments for peace. Bob La Follette (and Robert Baldwin and Jane Addams and many others) protested America's entry into World War I on the basis that there was little popular support for it among rank-and-file

Americans; that war is immoral because innocents die and that negotiations are preferable to fighting; that going to war would cost a lot of money that would be underwritten by the tax dollars paid by working people; that war was being undertaken to benefit the industrialists; that America had ills here at home she had not yet addressed; that America shouldn't presume to be "the world's policeman"—and couldn't be even if it tried; that congressional input into the decision to go to war was only sought, as a practical matter, after the fact; that it was up to the people living under a despot, not the U.S. government, to decide for themselves what kind of government they want. And, finally, La Follette complained about a new theory for going to war: support of the president for its own sake.

"Quite another doctrine has recently been promulgated by certain newspapers, which unfortunately seems to have found considerable support elsewhere, and that is the doctrine of 'standing back of the President' without inquiring whether the President is right or wrong," La Follette said on the Senate floor.

Such sentiments could have been uttered in 2002 or 2003—and were. In a televised debate on October 11, 2002, Minnesota Democratic Sen. Paul Wellstone was pointedly criticized by his Republican opponent, Norm Coleman, for declining to "stand together with the president."[15] Another Democratic Senator Mark Dayton of Ohio said that although calls to his office were running ten to one against the war resolution, senators still felt the pressure to "support the president." When it was his time to speak on the war resolution, Dayton pulled out a copy of the Constitution and read it to his colleagues before voting no.

"It is totally wrong for the administration to beat the drums of war," added Massachusetts Democratic Sen. Edward M. Kennedy, who spent the first few months of 2003 urging his colleagues to request a second debate and a second resolution authorizing force. "If we rush to pull the trigger against Iraq, we will invite catastrophe and condemnation."

The most passionate voice in Congress against the second war in Iraq came from Rep. Dennis J. Kucinich, a Democratic member from Ohio. Kucinich is a backbencher, but he took a back seat to nobody in using the words of the Declaration to argue against a second American invasion of Iraq. "There is no reason for war against Iraq!" Kucinich shouted in a keynote speech at the "Fighting Bob La Follette Fest" in Baraboo, Wisconsin, in September 2002. "Stop the drumbeat! Stop the war talk! Pull back from the abyss of unilateral action and preemptive strikes. It is time, instead, to explore more peaceful, consistent rhythms of the language of peace, of cooperation, mutuality, of recognition that all people—all people—have a right to life, liberty, and pursuit of happiness."

"Fighting Denny" Kucinich only spoke for twenty minutes or so—and La Follette used to go for three hours at a time—but "Fighting Bob" would have been proud of Kucinich's spunk. He also would have approved of Kucinich's improbable announcement in early 2003 that he was exploring a presidential run. La Follette himself ran for the White House in 1924 as a Progressive—and made a decent showing, too, garnering nearly 5 million popular votes out of the 29 million that were cast. More Dennis Kucinich in Babaroo:

> These self-evident truths of inherent equality of all, the rights of all, and the connection of all are the highest creative forces recognized in our Declaration of Independence, written into our Bill of Rights, and actively present in the soul of every American and freedom-loving person. This is the time today, to reconnect with the highest purposes of our nation.
>
> This was a gift. This was the gift of our founders: A new nation with the ability to adapt to the future of our dreams. Now is the time to restore that gift through traveling with faith and with courage, to follow the upward spiral path to the unseen heights of human endeavor; to create an evolutionary politics of creativity, of vision, of heart, of compassion, of joy; to create a new nation and a new world using the power of love, of community, of participation, to transform our politics, and yes, to transform ourselves.

On February 15, 2003, at a peace rally in New York, Kucinich again invoked the Declaration's pronouncement on the pursuit of happiness as an argument against war.

> Two hundred and fourteen years ago the First Congress standing upon the holy ground of a new Constitution met in this city. Their permit came from the Declaration of Independence. The same High Power [that] entrusted them entrusts us with the Declaration, the Constitution, and the Bill of Rights. We call upon the Spirit of the Founders to guide us as we create a new world where all may live in peace.

The United States, brought forth by the power of human unity, seeks to be reborn. We invoke the Spirit of Freedom. We hear the cadence of courage echo across the ages: "Life, Liberty, pursuit of Happiness." Once again, the hour has come for us to stand for unity, even as our government tells us we must follow it into war. Once again the hour has come for us to be strong of heart. The direction of human unity is forward. We are on the march. It is our government which must follow, or be swept aside.

Anti-war presidential candidates and members of Congress have flung similar arguments against the White House in every major American conflict since the Civil War. Franklin D. Roosevelt had to contend with doubting senators from both major parties as he tried to position the United States to enter World War II. The most prominent isolationists were Senate Foreign Relations committee chairman Arthur H. Vandenberg, a Michigan Republican; Burton K. Wheeler, a Montana Democrat and Gerald Nye, a progressive Republican from North Dakota. Nye was the father of the Neutrality Act, which forbade the sale of arms to "belligerent states"—nations at war.

Even after Germany's September 1, 1939, invasion of Poland, an act that brought Britain into the conflict, the isolationists refused to accept FDR's conclusion that war was inevitable. Nye was fond of spouting La Follette–like conspiracy theories about how American mercantilists had been determinant in pushing America into World War I—and were bent on doing so in World War II as well.[16] Wheeler's main view, and echoes of it can be heard today when the subject is Iraq, was that the world is an awful place and the United States can't protect everyone. American troops, he insisted, could not forestall what he termed "international anarchy." The phrase "body bags," heard so frequently in the congressional debate for the 1991 Persian Gulf War resolution, was not in vogue, but on January 12, 1941, Wheeler warned his Senate colleagues that being dragged into another European bloodbath would result in the "plowing under of every fourth American boy." As late as 1940, some congressmen were circulating a draft of legislation that would require a national referendum for the United States to declare war.

These men certainly believed they were reflecting the will of their constituents, and had reason to believe so. A Gallup Poll taken in November 1939—as the Wehrmacht raced through Eastern Europe—

showed that 96 percent of Americans opposed U.S. entry into the war. When the question was rephrased to postulate that even if this meant the fall of France and Britain, 79 percent of Americans still didn't want to go in; moreover, some 68 percent of respondents told Gallup they believed it was a mistake for the United States to have entered the *previous* world war. Gallup didn't give up easily, though. How about whether the United States should "do everything possible" to help England and France—even at the risk of getting into war ourselves? Even to this question, some 66 percent of respondents still said no. (In July of 1940, as the Battle of Britain raged, Americans stuck to their guns, or rather, to their butter. Eighty-five percent still said they wanted to stay out of the war. In May of 1941, 79 percent still did not want to intervene.)

Polling, then in its infancy, wasn't as scientific as it is now. But these numbers were a pretty good barometer of the public mood.

"Roosevelt was the first to even have [polling data] available to him," notes David Kennedy, Stanford University history professor and author of *Freedom From Fear: The American People in Depression and War*. "But FDR had already had a long and successful political career in the absence of that information and was not habituated to relying on it. . . . The country was decidedly isolationist. He undertook to change public opinion. There was no mystery to the isolationist tendencies of the American public. You didn't need polls to tell you that."[17]

America's two political parties have, in the past century, taken turns at being dominated by isolationist notions. Apocalyptic warnings about the horrors of war have emanated from the Right and the Left. Even after France was occupied by the Nazis, along with Norway, Poland, Belgium, Holland and Czechoslovakia—and London was being bombed nightly—conservative Charles A. Lindbergh was giving speeches urging his countrymen to stay out of the war.

"We in this country have a right to think of the welfare of America first," the famous aviator said in an April 23, 1941, New York speech. "When England asks us to enter this war, she is considering her own future and that of her Empire. In making our reply, I believe we should consider the future of the United States and that of the Western Hemisphere."

This is precisely what La Follette had said, and Lindbergh (with much more reason) was also denounced as putting his pro-German sympathies ahead of any commitment to democracy. But voices from the Left were heard warning against the perils of entering World War II as well. Robert M. Hutchins, the liberal president of the University of Chicago, echoed the World War I pacifists—and foreshadowed America's twenty-first-century liberals—by suggesting that because the United States had not lived up to its own creeds in the Declaration, it lacked the moral authority to try and set things right elsewhere on the globe.

"If we stay out of war, we may perhaps some day understand and practice freedom of speech, freedom of worship, freedom from want, and freedom from fear," Hutchins said in a January 23, 1941, speech. "We may even be able to comprehend and support justice, democracy, the moral order, and the supremacy of human rights. Today we have barely begun to grasp the meaning of the words."

This was not, even then, a new idea. In 1900, Socialist leader Eugene V. Debs (who would also be jailed by the Wilson administration) wrote a scathing attack on both political parties. Using the language of the Declaration, Debs charged the Democrats and the Republicans with being equally exploitive of the working man. Fusing Marxist ideology with American historical analogies, he used the phrases "wage working slaves" and "wage-slavery." Writing in the *International Socialist Review* in September 1900, Debs wrote:

> The working class must get rid of the whole brood of masters and exploiters, and put themselves in possession and control of the means of production, that they may have steady employment without consulting a capitalist employer, large or small, and that they may get the wealth their labor produces, all of it, and enjoy with their families the fruits of their industry in comfortable and happy homes, abundant and wholesome food, proper clothing and all other things necessary to "life, liberty and the pursuit of happiness." It is therefore a question not of "reform,' the mask of fraud, but of revolution. The capitalist system must be overthrown, class-rule abolished and wage-slavery supplanted by the cooperative industry.

In the Red Scare days after the end of the Second World War, the Left also employed the language of the Declaration of Independence. At his 1949 sedition trial, Communist Party USA president Eugene Dennis invoked not the only the spirit of the Declaration, but its letter and its author.[18] After describing Marxism-Leninism in his opening statement to the court as an evolving system of beliefs that will enable all people "to make a better and happier lives for themselves," Dennis added, "You will see that our Communist Party Constitution acknowledges not only that we learn from Marx and Lenin but that we owe much to and learn from the teachings of men like Thomas Jefferson, Abraham Lincoln, Frederick Douglass . . . and Eugene V. Debs."

Two years earlier, in answer to a criminal charge of contempt stemming from a refusal to testify before the House Committee on Un-American Activities, Dennis made this speech before U.S. District Court Judge David A. Pine:[19]

> Those who conceived this nation in liberty could not foresee that a vast empire of monopoly capital would one day come into being . . . nor could they foretell that the economic royalists would attempt to enslave America's working men and women with a Taft-Hartley law and other measures. But the Founding Fathers wisely sought to provide all future generations with the means to defend themselves against whatever form of tyranny the uncharted future might hold. Those who dedicated this nation to the proposition that all men are created equal could not envision the race hatred and terror rule of fascism, be it of foreign or native origin. Those who brought forth a new nation on this continent could not conceive of a [joint] Truman-G.O.P. doctrine proclaiming America the enemy of the newer democracies and the ally of decaying monarchs and fascist quislings. But the Founding Fathers did foresee that their posterity would have need to struggle against new enemies and new instruments of oppression. Those who endowed our people with the spirit that cherished liberty as the heritage of all men, in all lands everywhere, also sought to arm us against whatever threats to liberty the future might bring. For these wise purposes, those who shaped the Declaration of Independence and our Constitution proclaimed certain rights to be inalienable. They reserved to the people, and for all time, the right to exercise their sovereign power and democratic will to pursue happiness and progress.

In the days after the First World War and throughout the remaining years of the twentieth century, socially progressive presidential candidates and other prominent national Democrats would use the language and the spirit of the Declaration of Independence as an argument against war, and in support of a host of other causes. The Democrat who set the tone was America's most popular twentieth-century president.

"Liberty requires opportunity to make a living—a living decent according to the standard of the time, a living which gives man not only enough to live by, but something to live for," Franklin Roosevelt said in his June 27, 1936, acceptance speech of the Democratic nomination. "For too many of us the political equality we once had won was meaningless in the face of economic inequality. A small group had concentrated into their own hands an almost complete control over other people's property, other people's money, other people's labor—other people's lives. For too many of us life was no longer free; liberty no longer real; men could no longer follow the pursuit of happiness."

It was a speech that Gene Debs could have appreciated. Roosevelt began his second inaugural address, on January 20, 1937, in the same spirit: "When four years ago . . . we dedicated ourselves to the fulfillment of a vision—to speed the time when there would be for all the people that security and peace essential to the pursuit of happiness." And in 1939, FDR sought to make the same doctrine universal to everyone in this hemisphere. In radio remarks commemorating the opening of the Pan American Hernando de Soto Exposition, Roosevelt said, "The spirit of Pan Americanism happily is coming more and more to dominate the thoughts and aspirations and the actions of all of the diverse peoples and cultures which comprise the three Americas. It is the certain and unfailing safeguard of our inalienable right to life, liberty and the pursuit of happiness. Although the peoples of the New World are of many origins, they are united in a common aspiration to defend and maintain the self-governing way of life. That way of life is instinctive in all the peoples of the Western Hemisphere."

Eleanor Roosevelt, who wrote prolifically (and who wrote her own material), made similar references in the years before her husband became a war president. "The attainment of life and liberty required most of our energy in the past, so the pursuit of happiness and the consideration of the lives of human beings remained in the background," Mrs. Roosevelt wrote in 1936. "Now is the time to recognize the possibilities which lie before us in the taking up and developing of this part of our forefathers' vision. Therefore, I hope that the parents in this country will take enough interest in the new reorganization plans to realize that the interest of youth which lie close to their hearts can best be served by a federal department which will include such things as I have suggested and which touch primarily the homes and youth of America."[20]

The men, Democrat and Republican, who followed Roosevelt into the Oval Office in the decades that spanned the end of World War II and the long Cold War with the Soviet Union often used the language of the

Declaration to marshal Americans into accepting war. But in these same years, a host of would-be Democratic presidents echoed Eleanor's arguments—that happiness is an unmet domestic policy challenge as well—and continue to do so to this day.

George McGovern, who used the Founders as an argument for ending U.S. involvement in the Vietnam War when he was the Democratic presidential nominee in 1972, went on later in his life to employ Jefferson's words in support of everything from expending more government resources fighting alcohol and drug addiction to calling on Congress to refrain from shutting down the government during the budget wars between Newt Gingrich and President Clinton in 1995 and 1996. Writing in *The Nation*, a liberal magazine, McGovern quoted not only Jefferson, and Abraham Lincoln, but also Gladstone, who had pronounced the U.S. Constitution "the most remarkable work" on governing known to man.

"The Constitution was preceded and undergirded by the Declaration of Independence, which set forth on the eve of the American Revolution the basic rights of life, liberty and the pursuit of happiness," McGovern wrote. "When you denigrate the U.S. government you are denigrating the best government with the best employees on the face of the earth. Of course our system is sometimes flawed and is staffed by people who make mistakes; all human institutions are faulty. But one of the reasons we have an immigration problem is that millions of people abroad believe that the U.S. government and the U.S. economy are better than theirs. How ironic that those who run it have deigned to shut it down! In this New Year, let's not forget that we are citizens of what Lincoln called 'the last, best hope of earth.'"

McGovern's writings about alcoholism, inspired by the tragic struggle waged by his daughter, are even more emotive—and also evocative of the Declaration. "Alcoholism is like a thief in the night," he wrote in his 1996 book *Terry: My Daughter's Life-And-Death Struggle with Alcoholism*. "It can steal up on you and seize your life, liberty, and pursuit of happiness before you comprehend what has happened."[21]

Four years before McGovern was nominated, Minnesota Sen. Eugene McCarthy ran for president as an anti–Vietnam War candidate. McCarthy's strong showing in the 1968 New Hampshire Democratic primary against Lyndon Johnson, coupled with the looming entry of Robert F. Kennedy (RFK also ended up running as a peace candidate), prompted Johnson's withdrawal from the race. McCarthy's campaign brochure that year was modeled on the Declaration of Independence. By the late 1970s, Democratic candidates all over the United States would routinely attend myriad annual "Jackson-Jefferson Day" dinners. There was, to be sure, a central incongruity at work here. Jefferson and Jackson were two presidents whose words—and in Jackson's case deeds—were undeniably warlike; and by the 1970s the Democratic activists attending such fundraising dinners tended to be peaceniks. But that is part of the beauty, and appeal, of Jefferson's prose: It doesn't just lend itself to one narrow viewpoint.

In 1984, Colorado Sen. Gary Hart, McGovern's former campaign manager, let it be known that even more than John F. Kennedy (whose cadences and gestures he consciously mimicked) Thomas Jefferson was his idol. Asked by *Washington Post* reporter David Maraniss what it meant in the late part of the twentieth century to run for president as a Jeffersonian Democrat, Hart replied, "I mean by that that I stand for a set of principles that have a respect for individuality, to seeing what can be done in this industrial age to restore the integrity of the individual in mass society. I also mean that the principle of avoiding concentrated power has to be respected. Big government can be benign or repressive. It was in fact a big government under Richard Nixon that was taking away our individual liberties. Many of the agencies that had protected our welfare were turned around on the people."

In 1992, former California Gov. Edmund G. "Jerry" Brown Jr. used Jefferson's phrase as a call to increase the minimum wage. "I want to see a government that is fully committed to a living, family wage for every American," Brown said in a March 16, 1992, debate in Chicago with the other Democratic candidates. "We're rich enough, and our tradition is life, liberty and the pursuit of happiness for every person." Two weeks later, in a speech to the AFL-CIO Brown used the phrase as a more general call for social activism.

"[What's needed] is the political will to recognize the Cold War is over, that America is being pulled apart, and that millions and millions are in despair and hopelessness because they can't support their families," Brown said. "I come from a Catholic social tradition that says every person is worthy of their hire, they're worthy of earning a living family wage. . . . and what is missing is a commitment to social and economic justice. What I'm inviting you to do is to galvanize a moral force in this country that acknowledges and rededicates this nation to the ideals on which we are founded, and when our forebears said that all of us have an inalienable right to life, and to liberty, and the pursuit of happiness, they meant something."

In April of that year, in a debate that featured the last two Democrats standing, Brown and Gov. Bill Clinton of Arkansas, Brown seemed to use the "pursuit of happiness" as a call for campaign finance reform.[22] Clinton himself waited until his inaugural address to employ Jefferson's phrase. When the time came, he did so as a way of calling for the government to change with the times and "invest" more in its people.

"When our founders boldly declared America's independence to the world and our purposes to the Almighty, they knew that America, to endure, would have to change. Not change for change's sake, but change to preserve America's ideals—life, liberty, the pursuit of happiness," Clinton said. "Though we march to the music of our time, our mission is timeless. Each generation of Americans must define what it means to be an American."

Thus did Clinton deftly bridge the gap between those who believe the Locke and Jefferson and Rousseau conception of natural rights cannot be improved on and those, like Woodrow Wilson, eager to apply the words of the Declaration to new problems, new times, and in a new way.

New Jersey Sen. Bill Bradley, running in the Democratic presidential primaries in 2000 against Al Gore, used the language of the Declaration to call for universal medical coverage. "Health care is not a luxury," Bradley said. "Americans have the right to life, liberty and the pursuit of happiness. But Thomas Jefferson, who proclaimed those rights in our Declaration of Independence, also said, 'Without health, there is no happiness.' We can't abolish sickness or deny mortality, but we can help care for the sick, ease the pain of the dying and ensure children have a healthy start in life. We can commit ourselves to the proposition that, when it comes to health care, everyone will have the American dream at last."

Bradley dropped out early, leaving the Democratic field to Al Gore, but progressive icon Ralph Nader stuck around to the bitter end of the 2000 campaign. Wearing the mantle of the Green Party (and, in the process, probably costing Gore the presidency), Nader routinely closed out his stump speech by saying: "I believe in the pursuit of happiness. But the pursuit of happiness is inextricably tied to the pursuit of justice. So, in public life, I pursue justice." This was a variation on a theme that Nader had been playing for thirty years. In the July 9, 1971, issue of *Life* magazine, Nader had written that "a new kind of patriotism" was needed in America. "There is no reason," he wrote, "why patriotism has to be so heavily associated, in the minds of the young as well as adults, with military exploits, jets and missiles." There was much more of this. In what can now be seen as a kind of blueprint that the activist Left would embrace for the three decades following the Vietnam War, Nader laid out the progressive's vision. He touched on all the major points of the now-familiar liberal coalition, along with one more that was, and remains, his pet issue—protection for whistleblowers:

> If it is unpatriotic to tear down the flag (which is a symbol of the country), why isn't it more unpatriotic to desecrate the country it-self—to pollute, despoil and ravage the air, land and water? Such environmental degradation makes the "pursuit of happiness" rag-ged indeed. Why isn't it unpatriotic to engage in the colossal waste that characterizes so many defense contracts? Why isn't it unpatri-otic to draw our country into a mistaken war and then keep extend-ing the involvement, with untold casualties to soldiers and inno-cents, while not telling Americans the truth? Why isn't the deplorable treatment of returning veterans by government and in-dustry evaluated by the same standards, as is their dispatch to war? Why isn't the systematic contravention of the U.S. Constitution and the Declaration of Independence in our treatment of minority groups, the poor, the young, the old and other disadvantaged or helpless people crassly unpatriotic? Isn't all such behavior contra-dicting the innate worth and the dignity of the individual in America? Is it not time to end the tragic twisting of patriotism whereby those who work to expose and correct deep injustices, and who take intolerable risks while doing it, are accused of running down America by the very forces doing just that? Our country and its ideals are something for us to uphold as individuals and together, not something to drape, as a deceptive cloak, around activities that mar or destroy these ideals.

Nader, of course, never made it to the White House and almost certainly never will, except possibly as a visitor. Most progressive candi-dates, these men who used the phrasings of a war document and applied them to the language of peace, did not make it to the Oval Office, either. But one of them did, a southern governor—not Bill Clinton—who is often maligned for his supposedly lackluster performance as president. And days before leaving office, in what may have been his finest speech, Jimmy Carter articulated a poignant definition of what life, liberty and the pursuit of happiness meant to a peace-loving and progressive American in the late twentieth century.

"America did not invent human rights," Carter said. "In a very real sense, it's the other way around. Human rights invented America." He continued:

> Ours was the first nation in the history of the world to be founded explicitly on such an idea. . . . Our American values are not luxuries but necessities—not the salt in our bread but the bread itself. Our common vision of a free and just society is our greatest source of cohesion at home and strength abroad—greater even than the bounty of our material blessings. Remember these words: 'We hold these truths to be self-evident, that all men are created equal; that they are endowed by their creator with certain inalienable rights; that among these are life, liberty and the pursuit of happiness.'
>
> This vision still grips the imagination of the world. But we know that democracy is always an unfinished creation. Each generation must renew its foundations. Each generation must rediscover the meaning of this hallowed vision in the light of its own modern challenges. For this generation, ours, 'life' is nuclear survival; 'liberty' is human rights; 'the pursuit of happiness' is a planet whose resources are devoted to the physical and spiritual nourishment of its inhabitants.[23]

In 1984, while speaking at the Democratic National Convention in San Francisco, Carter took another stab at modernizing Jefferson's words: "For this generation, our generation, 'life' is nuclear survival, 'liberty' is human rights, 'the pursuit of happiness' is equal opportunity to enjoy the fruits of a productive society," the former president said.

I was present on the convention floor in San Francisco's Moscone Center, when Carter uttered these words, and was struck by Carter's simple eloquence. I remembered it after the attacks of September 11, 2001, while I was pursuing my project of asking the former presidents to write down their thoughts on the meaning of the pursuit of happiness. So I went to Plains, Ga., a town I had not visited since Carter first ran for president in 1976, to hear the former president deliver his regular Sunday school bible lecture before regular services at Maranatha Baptist Church. The date was September 30, 2001. The Sunday before, Carter told the Maranatha congregants that his planned trip to Bangladesh to monitor elections had been scrapped because of the 9/11 attacks, and he used the first portion of his talk to tell the congregation what he knew about Islamic rage in the Arab world. Carter even read the chilling words of Osama bin Laden's two previous *fatwas* against Americans.

As President George W. Bush has been doing, Carter went on to defend most Muslims, explaining that Osama's violent fantasies are no more reflective of mainstream Islam than the Ku Klux Klan's views are representative of established Christianity. But he went on to make a broader point; namely that it is no accident that such hatred emanates from a part of the world that excoriates people because of their race or religious faiths—and which grants women no rights. Relating this point to that week's lesson, Carter said, "Luke is the (gospel) . . . that point(s) out that facet of Jesus' ministry—the exaltation of women, the equality with which Jesus treated women," Carter said.

The following Sunday, the day before his seventy-seventh birthday, Carter taught again. That day's Sunday school lesson dealt with the New Testament story—related in the book of John—about the raising of Lazarus. Carter teaches this class two or three Sundays a month, and he usually begins it by relating where he's been in his world travels since the last class. This morning, he described spending five days fly fishing and whale-watching on Kodiak Island. That sounded pretty much like pursuing happiness, if not paradise, to some of us in the audience, at least until Carter began describing the huge Kodiak grizzlies that inhabit the island. But when he turned to the Lazarus story, the part of it Carter stressed was the faith Jesus required of Lazarus' sisters, Mary and Martha, when Jesus didn't go to Lazarus' side immediately when it was known Lazarus was sick. To illustrate the point that mortals cannot know God's will, Carter drew on an analogy from his own life, his bitter loss in the 1966 Georgia gubernatorial race to segregationist Lester Maddox. "I was disillusioned with the people of Georgia, myself—and with God," Carter said. He then said that upon hearing this his sister Ruth, a famous evangelist in her own right, came to visit her brother and told him that he should see this defeat as an opportunity to strengthen his faith.

Carter, a former Navy officer, let it be known without actually saying the word in church that his response to his sister was, "Bullshit!" In time, however, he says he realized she was right, and went to Lock Haven, Pa., to do some missionary work before returning home, running for governor successfully in 1970 and then for the presidency in 1976. But on this day, the accomplishments Carter emphasized were the souls he saved in Lock Haven, and how those converts started a church that lasted long after the Baptist boys all went back home. Afterward, with no elections to monitor, Carter lingered awhile after the service was over, allowing every worshipper or tourist who had come to hear him speak to shake his hand or have his or her picture taken with him and his wife. After everyone had left, and it was just he, the pastor, and the Secret Service agents left, I approached him.

"Mr. President, I am a reporter from Washington who covers the White House. I'd like to ask you about an essay we are doing on the pursuit of happiness. . . ."

"I don't do that at church," he snapped.

"I understand sir," I replied, "but I've come a long way to ask you a single question. It's about something you said about the 'pursuit of happiness' in 1981. It was quite eloquent, but in light of the September 11 attacks on this country, I'd like to know if you believe this definition is still current."

"Well, if it's about something I wrote," he said, his tone softening, "I guess there's no harm in answering one question."

He then asked me to wait under a shade tree while the last of the tourists cleared out. A few minutes later, he came over, and I showed him the passage he had delivered twenty years earlier about "life" being nuclear survival; "liberty" being human rights and "the pursuit of happiness" being a planet whose resources are devoted to the physical and spiritual nourishment of its inhabitants.

"Do you still believe this is true?"

"What I wrote, that's still true, yes," he replied. He paused, then added quietly, "But there's always a new threat, isn't there?"

"Yes, Mr. President," I replied. "But can I ask you about happiness? Mother Theresa says that the first obligation of a Christian is to be happy, to show the world that belief in Jesus makes a person happy."

"She did? [pause] Well, it depends on where you find your happiness. As I tried to say in today's lesson, the truth preserved in the teachings of Christ—what the bible says—is that your happiness is not based on worldly successes and failures. . . . You think you have a successful and happy life, but if you lead a Christian life, it surpasses all understanding. I found that out in my own life—that apparent failures can actually lead to true happiness, a different kind of happiness."

Carter is a rarity in modern American politics, an evangelical Christian who is conservative theologically, but generally liberal in political affairs. His overt religiosity—as well as his Southern-ness—made him suspect among Democratic Party activists, even though his record on race was impeccable. Many of those self-same activists backed Ted Kennedy in the presidential primaries of 1980, notwithstanding the fact that Carter was already in the White House. In Carter's mind, the Kennedy challenge made it easier for Ronald Reagan to win in November. Neither movement conservatives (who revere Reagan and treat his ascension to power as something akin to an act of God) nor the liberal establishment (which recoils from acknowledging its role in helping Reagan get elected) has ever faced up to the obvious truth of Carter's claim, just as Carter has never accepted blame for undermining his own presidency by alienating all of official Washington. Even now, Carter has never quite worked his way back into the good graces of his party, despite his impressive array of humanitarian works around the globe and his tireless work in international politics for democracy and the social betterment of the poor and disenfranchised. Partly, this is because his freelance approach to diplomacy is perceived by sitting presidents of either party as meddlesome—and sometimes unhelpful. In addition, in the years since Carter left office, an impression had taken root inside the White House—whether Republican presidents or Democrats occupied it—that America's thirty-ninth president was on a kind of unseemly quest to win the Nobel Peace Prize. It is certainly human of Carter to desire this award, not only for the million dollars and the prestige that accompany it, but also because the Norwegian Nobel Committee all but conceded publicly that they should have given it to Carter for the Camp David accords in 1981, and didn't owing to a clerical error.

For my money, Carter's humanitarian efforts alone should have been enough to win him a Nobel Prize. But that wasn't why he was given it. He was awarded the prize, at least in part, in an attempt to embarrass George W. Bush prior to the war in Iraq. "In a situation currently marked by threats of the use of power," the committee said in its commendation, "Carter has stood by the principles that conflicts must as far as possible be resolved through mediation and international cooperation based on international law, respect for human rights, and economic development."

This citation made it sound as though Carter was getting the award for his kibitzing against the U.S. government's push to force Saddam

Hussein to knuckle under to real weapons inspections, or face invasion. Exactly right, replied Gunnar Berge, the obscure Oslo bureaucrat who chaired the Nobel committee. "It should be interpreted as criticism of the line that the current administration has taken," Berge told reporters. "It's a kick in the leg to all that follow the same line as the United States."[24]

But in the buildup to the second Iraq war, such comments were commonplace among liberals in the United States, too. Some came from members of Congress. In a March 3, 2002, address to a Washington conference of the United Methodist Church, Senator Kennedy accused Bush of having "squandered" much of the good will of the world community with his "single-minded rush to war with Iraq."

"Our nation was founded on the unalienable right of all of our citizens to life, liberty and the pursuit of happiness," Kennedy added. "And we share a strong commitment to the belief that each of us can make a difference in shaping the world we live in, and all of us must try."

When the second Persian Gulf war actually began, Kennedy swiftly and ungrudgingly rallied around U.S. policy, U.S. troops and the U.S. president. But until that moment, he had been using Jefferson's language in the same way that prominent progressives and Democratic presidents had used it for a century—even presidents who ultimately ended up taking their nation to war.

In 1935, when the Depression, not Japan or a rearming Germany, was the threat on the horizon, FDR cited the "equal rights to enjoy life, liberty and the pursuit of happiness," as underlying "the Herculean task of the United States government to [ensure] that its citizens have the necessities of life."[25] It probably should also be noted that Roosevelt made these remarks as part of an explanation justifying his 1935 veto of a $2.2 billion bonus bill for World War I combat veterans.

This is not an uncommon practice. It is normal for presidents—even great presidents—to put Jefferson's phrase to rather parochial uses. It's one of the luxuries of peacetime. FDR also employed "pursuit of happiness" to laud Theodore Roosevelt at the 1936 dedication of TR's memorial, to lament the Depression-era hardships of Americans at the one hundredth anniversary celebration of the state of Arkansas and to gratuitously slam Republicans. In a November 1, 1940, campaign speech in Brooklyn during his third reelection campaign, a worried FDR asserted: "Most Republican leaders in our own country for the last seven years have bitterly fought and blocked the forward surge of average men and women in their pursuit of happiness. . . ."

Roosevelt has not been alone among presidents in using "pursuit of happiness" in a partisan way. Forty-some years later, Ronald Reagan repeatedly cited Jefferson's language as a rationale for his right-to-life views on the issue of abortion. "With me, abortion is not a problem of religion," Reagan said in an October 7, 1984, debate with Walter Mondale. "It's a problem of the Constitution. I believe that until and unless someone can establish that the unborn child is not a living human being, then that child is already protected by the Constitution, which guarantees life, liberty and the pursuit of happiness to all of us."[26]

The 1940 Brooklyn rally was the last time FDR used the phrase "pursuit of happiness" without America being at war, and war would change everything. The United States had entered the First World War, the "war to end all wars," very late in the game, but 53,513 Americans were still killed in combat in Europe, with another 63,195 dead from other causes, most of them influenza. Another 204,000 were wounded. Although these figures paled by comparison with the frightful losses suffered by Russia, Germany, Britain, France, Turkey and other nations, it was enough. The United States virtually disarmed itself after that war.

And when Europe exploded again in 1939, the prevailing mood in the United States was symbolized by the fact that the United States was still governed by the Neutrality Act, which had been passed in 1935 and amended twice, as a legal barrier to any internationalist-minded chief executive who might be occupying the White House. The United States happened to have just such a president in Roosevelt, but he was constrained by public opinion and by powerful isolationists in Congress from both parties. If the gruesome carnage of the Civil War had shaped American attitudes toward war, World War I had only reinforced the pacifist impulses of a self-governing nation that understandably balked at the idea of committing itself and its sons to armed combat in far off lands. This is as it should be, and underscores the natural tension among the inheritors of such high-minded fighting words as the Declaration of Independence.

In 1939 and 1940, the same Gallup Polls that showed a huge majority in the United States wanting to stay out of the Second World War also showed signs that, deep down, Americans knew this was going to be a difficult war to avoid, and that perhaps it would be morally wrong to do so. In a September 22, 1939, Gallup Poll, 62 percent of respondents said they favored repeal of the mandatory arms embargo. The following summer, as the Battle of Britain raged, there was a run on American flags. Sometimes, in public, crowds would break into songs such as *America the Beautiful*, which is not a fighting song exactly, but which is a song about a land worth fighting for. It is not about *fighting for pie*—or even the amber waves of grain, purple mountain majesties and gleaming, alabaster cities. The song, and the poll numbers, reflected a love of home, a love of country, not a love of war. But if the price of peace was the end of democracy for freedom-loving people outside America's borders, what then? Roosevelt understood these conflicting impulses perfectly. He felt them himself. On October 30, 1940, a week before the election and two days before his Brooklyn political speech in which he used the phrase "pursuit of happiness" so lightly, Roosevelt attended a raucous rally at Boston Garden.

"While I am talking to you mothers and fathers, I give you one more assurance," FDR told the cheering crowd. "I have said this before, but I'll say it again and again and again: Your boys are not going to be sent into any foreign wars."

His Republican opponent, fellow internationalist Wendell L. Willkie knew this promise was, if not an outright lie, at least a vow that was unlikely to be kept—and not what FDR himself believed would happen. But it was what the electorate wanted to hear, and Roosevelt was savvy enough to let them hear it, if only for one more year. According to Willkie's biographer, Steve Neal, the Republican presidential candidate exploded when he heard Roosevelt's speech on the radio.

"That hypocritical son of a bitch!" Willkie shouted to his brother. "This is going to beat me!"

And perhaps it did, or at least it helped. But war was coming anyway.

6

Happy Warriors

In the aftermath of September 11, 2001, it was commonly said—even by people who were alive and could remember—that the only event to compare it to was the terrible Sunday morning on December 7, 1941, when Japanese war planes attacked Pearl Harbor, destroying much of the Pacific fleet and killing 2,403 people, almost all of them sailors in the U.S. Navy.

Until 9/11, as the second attack came to be known, Pearl Harbor was the last time the United States was attacked on its own soil—although Hawaii, not yet a state, was more removed from the average American's consciousness than either the Pentagon or the World Trade Center. Both sneak attacks, six decades apart, generated intense feelings of national unity, epitomized by a lull in political partisanship and a surge in flag-waving outpourings of patriotism. The *United We Stand* slogans and posters that emerged, practically overnight, in September of 2001 were, in fact, borrowed directly from the lexicon of World War II. And though the contemporary press accounts didn't dwell on this concept the way we do today, any American alive in 1941 who was above the age of reason remembers where and when he was when he heard the shocking news of Pearl Harbor.

There were differences in the two attacks as well, which were reflected in the divergent rhetorical responses of Franklin D. Roosevelt and George W. Bush. President Roosevelt did not need to convince Americans they were suddenly involved in the middle of a great worldwide struggle. They already knew. But both leaders faced the same tricky rhetorical task. On the one hand, they needed to stoke Americans' fighting spirit while preparing them for a long arduous war against a deadly and committed foe. Yet at the same time, the two presidents also had to shore up Americans' belief that they were up to the daunting challenge in front of them by sounding supremely self-confident that victory was inevitable. A shaken nation looked to them for reassurance.

In each attack, Americans' level of alarm differed by region. People in Washington and New York felt under siege after 9/11. In New York City, a hole had been carved in the skyline, as well as in 3,000 families. Washington had its own horrors. The bombing at the Pentagon, although overshadowed by the Trade Towers, claimed more lives than did the Oklahoma City bombing of 1995. Then the U.S. Capitol was hit by a terrorist anthrax attack of unknown origin that stopped the mail, required the evacuation of Congress and claimed five innocent lives. That trauma was followed by a seemingly unrelated attack by snipers who shot thirteen people in the Washington area, killing ten of them, and making virtually everyone in a hundred square miles a hostage for weeks.

In 1941, Americans living on the West Coast were instantly—and understandably—more alarmed in the weeks following Pearl Harbor. This wasn't just a war in Europe or even the far reaches of the Hawaiian Islands. This was a war in the ocean next to them, the ocean they considered their front yard, and which was supposed to protect them. But after the attack on the American fleet at Pearl, that ocean seemed a menace. It could hide anything. Tensions increased when it became apparent that the Japanese sent a small fleet of submarines east after the attacks, toward California, to hunt merchant shipping. One Japanese sub sank the tanker *Emidio* off the coast of Eureka, killing five seamen. Nine more lives were lost in the coming weeks as other ships were torpedoed and disabled, some within sight of land. And on February 23, 1942, while Roosevelt was delivering a fireside chat, one Japanese submarine surfaced off the coast of Goleta, and fired torpedoes at the oil wells near Santa Barbara.[1] The night of the attack on Pearl Harbor, air raid sirens prompted temporary blackouts in San Francisco, although almost certainly due to a false alarm. In Seattle, a mob of one thousand people vandalized storefront windows—for the purpose of enforcing a blackout. In the coming days, school children as far inland as Reno were instructed at school-wide assemblies on what to do in the event of a bomb attack. The annual New Year's Day Rose Bowl game was moved from its traditional home in Pasadena to North Carolina.

Air raid sirens filled the air in New York City the night of December 7. Fearful of German subs, Coney Island was blacked out. Moviegoers emerging from the showing of *Dumbo* in Times Square found themselves staring at bulletins proclaiming the attack on Pearl Harbor. A crowd gathered; spontaneous shouts broke out: "We're into it, boys!"

In Washington, hundreds of people drifted downtown to stand outside the White House and the State Department. They stood five deep outside the White House gates, watching the comings and goings as top congressional and administrative leaders came in to confer with Roosevelt. A few of the citizens sang "God Bless America." Others just stared silently at the dimly lit White House. The following morning, commuters crossing the capital would notice an armored truck on M Street, guarding Key Bridge. Machine-gun nests—and soldiers to man them—materialized overnight in the boxwood orchards located behind the Lincoln Memorial, standing sentry on the banks of the Potomac River for the first time since Lincoln himself was president.

But ordinary life coexisted with the war, just as it did in this country after the attacks of 9/11. In 1941, few sporting events were cancelled, and the baseball owners meeting in Chicago scheduled for December 8 went ahead as planned.[2] And the mood was strangely upbeat. In Dallas, twenty-five hundred people at the Majestic Theater had finished watching *Sergeant York*, a Gary Cooper movie about a World War I hero, when news of the Japanese attack was announced. There was a pause—and then, suddenly, a thunderous applause.

"More then than now, life went on as before," noted David Brooks, the author and social critic who documented this phenomenon by delving into the popular press in the weeks and months after Pearl Harbor. "Americans at the start of World War II did not appear emotionally wounded the way they did after the attack on the World Trade Center. There are no articles in which people described where they were when they heard the news or how they felt. There are not accounts of people crying or hugging each other for support. Instead, the dominant mood is one of relentless cheerfulness."

One of the reasons such stories didn't exist is that our culture—and the news media—have changed. It would have struck 1940s reporters as frivolous to ask policy-makers—or everyday Americans—what they "felt" when they heard of the Japanese attack. It was understood that what almost everyone felt was anger. Moreover, even if asked, the average American of that generation would have been more reluctant to volunteer his or her deepest and most personal fears to a journalist. But if some of the stylistic conventions of today are obvious excesses, others are a clear improvement. Although it might have been unthinkable for the American media in the 1940s to devote article after article on today's tiresome "Why do they hate us?" formula, it's also true that the nation's public institutions now steer clear of the casual racism that dominated World War II coverage of the Japanese.

Another difference is technology. The newsreels we've all seen of the USS *Arizona* burning uncontrollably and then sinking with one thousand sailors still aboard were not available in real-time back then; most people heard the news on the radio, heard it word-of-mouth, or read about it in the extra editions of afternoon newspapers printed all over the country. The whole world watched the Twin Towers fall, knowing that many, many American civilians were trapped inside. They watched the mass murder live, and in color.

Finally, there was another factor at play in 1941 that helps explain Americans' almost heady reaction to Pearl Harbor, and it was this: The rest of the world was already at war, and in their hearts millions of Americans—though not all—were relieved that they would no longer be shirking their rightful role in the great struggle between democracy and fascism. This mood became clear in the months and years ahead. At the 1943 Oscars ceremony, after the "Star Spangled Banner" was played, movie stars Alan Ladd and Tyrone Power marched onto the stage in their private's uniforms.

But some Americans had not waited to be drafted. Jimmy Stewart, perhaps the most bankable star in Hollywood, had enlisted in the Army on March 22, 1941. At thirty-two years of age and carrying only 130 pounds on his 6-foot 4-inch frame, Stewart was initially rejected as too old and too light. But as he explained later, men named Stewart had left the small hardware store run by his family in Indiana, Pa., in every American war since 1861. And Stewart figured, as did Roosevelt, that war was indeed coming. Stewart had made *Mr. Smith Goes to Washington* in 1939 and *The Philadelphia Story* (for which he'd won the Oscar for Best Actor) in 1940, so when he informed his local draft board that he wanted *in*, and not out, of military service they were willing to do anything he asked. "After they got over their surprise," Stewart explained later, "they told me it was simple: 'We just won't weigh you, and we'll put down any weight you want!' And that's what they did. And I was in."

So when Pearl Harbor was bombed, Jimmy Stewart was already in the service, pulling guard duty as a corporal at Moffett Field outside San Francisco, waiting for his commission as a second lieutenant and aviator to come through.³ It did so on January 19, 1942, and within six months Stewart was made a flight instructor on the B-17. He then lobbied for a combat role and was given one: He flew twenty highly dangerous daylight-bombing missions over Germany before becoming a wing commander. His wartime decorations included the Distinguished Flying Cross with Oak Leaf Cluster, four Air Medals, and the French Croix de Guerre. He impressed everyone who served with him, and became one of only a handful of men in American military history to rise from private to full colonel in only four years. Stewart, in other words, was even more impressive than his title character in *Mr. Smith Goes to Washington*, a title character, incidentally, whose name was inspired by Thomas Jefferson.⁴

It's tempting to think that there weren't too many Jimmy Stewarts in his or any other generation, but Franklin Roosevelt was banking on something else: namely, that what made Jimmy Stewart a celluloid hero—that he was a kind of American everyman—was in fact true, and that the seamless transition from citizen to citizen-soldier would be the norm in the United States. And FDR, who had guessed right, used his bully pulpit accordingly. In his brief December 8 speech to Congress—it ran to fewer than five hundred words—FDR broke with tradition by not dwelling on the constitutional arguments, let alone the moral rationale, for war. In fact, Roosevelt didn't mention them. In his bill of particulars against Japan, he discussed no event that was more than twenty-four hours old. FDR wasn't trying to talk his countrymen into going to war. Americans knew that war had already come to them, fulfilling as prophesy Leon Trotsky's famous taunt, "You may not be interested in war, but war is interested in you." No, Roosevelt was trying to rally them. He spoke of "inevitable triumph," and added, "No matter how long it may take us to overcome this premeditated invasion, the American people in their righteous might will win through to absolute victory."

The president didn't sugarcoat things, however. In a radio address the following day, December 9, he conceded, "so far the news has been all bad," while adding: "It will not only be a long war, it will be a hard war." Isolationists had believed that America could avoid war by not firing the first shot. Pearl Harbor proved to almost all of them that this had been wishful thinking.⁵ "The issue of our time," President Roosevelt said a week later in a December 15 radio address to the nation, "the issue of the war in which we are engaged, is the issue forced upon the decent, self-respecting peoples of the earth by the aggressive dogmas of this attempted revival of barbarism; this proposed return to tyranny; this effort to impose again upon the peoples of the world doctrines of absolute obedience, of dictatorial rule, of the suppression of truth, of the oppression of conscience, which the free Nations of the earth have long ago rejected."

No matter what he'd said in the waning days of the 1940 presidential campaign, Roosevelt had been trying to condition his fellow Americans to this reality for a long time. In his October 5, 1937, "quarantine speech" in Chicago, FDR attempted to arouse the nation to the dangers of Nazi and Japanese aggression, and he used Americans' "happiness" relative to the rest of the world to do it.[6]

When the media correctly characterized Roosevelt's Chicago speech as a change in policy, the isolationists pounced—and the president was hit in the face with the political realities that would require him to ease his rhetoric back a notch. "It's a terrible thing," he observed to White House aide Sam Rosenman, "to look over your shoulder when you are trying to lead—and find no one there."

Roosevelt was getting at the crux of the dilemma faced by all U.S. heads of state. American presidential *candidates*, responding to the public's institutional knowledge about the frightening human cost of warfare, almost invariably vow to avoid armed conflict. But American *presidents* are often haunted by the simple question on the other side of the equation: If the United States doesn't free those who are "everywhere in chains," what nation will?

This dilemma is particularly difficult when it is American citizens themselves who are in chains—and Lincoln wasn't the only one to confront such a thing. In 1979, a terrifying new age of terrorism, hostage-taking and worldwide sectarian guerrilla war forced modern presidents to face it, too. The fact that it was on a vastly smaller scale doesn't seem to have made it any easier. Jimmy Carter's presidency was never the same after November 4, 1979, when militant Iranian "students," sanctioned by Ayatollah Khomeini, seized the American embassy in Tehran, and made hostages of fifty-two of the U.S. government personnel inside the compound. Iran would keep these prisoners for 444 days, despite the ensuing death of the shah, a bungled military rescue effort that left eight U.S. servicemen dead, the invasion of Iran by Iraq and an American presidential election that resulted in the termination of the Carter presidency.

To this day, Carter believes he was not given enough credit—either by the electorate or the Reaganites—for getting those fifty-two hostages home safely. He is probably be right, but there is an aspect of the ordeal that Carter himself may not appreciate: Although Reagan did not esteem Carter's political skills, his 1980 campaign tactics or his policies as president, when it came to the Iranian hostage crisis, Reagan's contempt was directed solely at the regime in Teheran, not at his rival in the White House. Unbeknownst to Carter, on Inauguration Day, Reagan had instructed top aide Michael K. Deaver that if the hostages were out of Iranian airspace while Reagan was still giving his inaugural address, Deaver was to hand a note to Reagan telling him so.

"If they are released, I'm going to interrupt the speech," Reagan told Deaver privately. "I'm going to bring President Carter up here."[7]

Islamicist-inspired terrorism would put its mark on Reagan's presidency as well. The suicide bombing of the Marine barracks in Lebanon with a death toll of 241 was the most tragic example, but in his autobiography, Reagan indicates that he was utterly haunted by the American hostages being held in Beirut. His own words suggest that it's scarcely an exaggeration to say that Reagan's literal application of Jefferson's words in the Declaration's preamble led to the arms-for-hostage swap that was at the heart of the Iran-contra scandal, a controversy that dogged the last two years of the Reagan presidency. Reagan wrote:

> Long before I entered the Oval Office, I had adopted a very simple philosophy regarding what we as a nation should do if an American were held captive abroad: whenever one of our citizens, even the least among us, through no fault of his or her own, was denied the right to life, liberty and the pursuit of happiness, it was up to the rest of us to do everything we could to restore those rights, wherever it took us, anywhere in the world. It was a policy I followed for eight years as President. Following the example set by Iran, the barbarian Hizballah—the Shi'ite Party of God in Lebanon—had turned the systematic kidnapping and torture of innocent Americans into an instrument of war. No problem was more frustrating for me than trying to get the hostages home. Almost every morning at my national security briefings, I began by asking, "Any progress on getting the hostages out of Lebanon?"[8]

Certainly as American presidents, Carter and Reagan had a special obligation to American prisoners of war—as did Lyndon Johnson and Richard Nixon during the Vietnam War, when hundreds of Americans were held as POWs, and as did Harry Truman and Dwight Eisenhower during the Korean War, when even more Americans were taken prisoner. But the questions implied by the Declaration are much broader. Jefferson claimed these rights to be "inalienable," that they derived not from governments, but from God. The thinkers of the Enlightenment called them Natural Rights, and so the natural question is whether the brave words of 1776 are a promise that applies only to Americans. How could such a thing possibly be so? The answer is that it can't be, that they are for everyone. That's what the Civil War was about, but that was just the beginning. Doesn't Jefferson's promise imply that it includes women as well? Certainly, immigrants to this country must be included. In Franklin Roosevelt's day, one might have asked, what obligations does America have to the Dutch or the French? How about the Jews who were victims of SS-orchestrated genocide? Or German citizens who themselves wanted no part of Nazism? The Japanese?

Today, we ask about freedom for Iraqis and Saudis and Kurds and the Arabs of old Palestine. And it is fitting and necessary that we do so. Who is entitled to liberty—and whose blood is spilt bringing it to them—is the ultimate question posed by the Declaration of Independence. As the war in Iraq was wrapping up, George W. Bush went to Dearborn, Michigan, to address this very question. In an April 28, 2003, speech to an audience comprised mostly of Arab-Americans, many of them from Iraq, Bush said:

> Many Iraqi Americans know the horrors of Saddam Hussein's regime firsthand. You also know the joys of freedom you have found here in America. You are living proof the Iraqi people love freedom and living proof the Iraqi people can flourish in democracy. People who live in Iraq deserve the same freedom that you and I enjoy here in America. And after years of tyranny and torture, that freedom has finally arrived. Whether you're Sunni or Shia or Kurd or Chaldean or Assyrian or Turkoman or Christian or Jew or Muslim—no matter what your faith—freedom is God's gift to every person in every nation.

But if the truth of those words is obvious—"self-evident" to use Jefferson's expression—it must also be said that the obligation behind such a sentiment is daunting; the responsibilities for backing it up seem infinite. It is a big world out there, with no shortage of tyrants, and it is little wonder that so many American conservatives in Roosevelt's time, and the majority of liberals in our time, have concluded that the job is too big for one nation. But, again, such mental reservations beg the crucial question, which in the mind of all American presidents, often comes down to this: If not the people (and the armies) of the United States of America, who will extend this great gift of freedom to those who don't have it?

This was the demanding dilemma that Americans were facing in the aftermath of 9/11, but they were confronting it before that date as well. President Bush (Forty-One) and President Clinton were forced to decide how much ethnic rape and ethnic murder in the former Yugoslavia they could abide without interceding. When CNN cameramen brought the reality into Clinton's own White House living room—the reality being that the so-called U.N. "safe havens" had become designated killing fields where Serb paramilitaries knew to find helpless Bosnian Muslims—Clinton dispatched U.S. ground troops and NATO planes to stop it. When the pattern repeated itself in Kosovo, Clinton didn't wait three years. He bombed Belgrade into quick submission. This may have gone unnoticed by the likes of Osama bin Laden and the mouthpieces for the corrupt state-owned media in much of the Arab world, but it did not go unnoticed by the people it saved. On September 12, 2001, the people of Kosovo—ethnic Albanians who are predominately Muslim—marched ten thousand strong in their city of Pristina, carrying American flags and signs of support.

"America, we share your sorrow," these signs said.

Five thousand Kosovars lined up to donate blood, and schoolchildren painted handwritten messages of condolence. Ethnic Albanians on both sides of the border were among those lighting candles that night at a vigil for America's three thousand dead. Two years later, Albania would join the other former Soviet-dominated nations in support of the United States' action in Iraq.

Removing the Taliban from Afghanistan was a reaction most American presidents would have made. Invading Iraq was a different sort of response, and one that will be debated for decades to come. But one of the several rationales offered for that war—its potentially liberating effect on the Iraqis themselves—is not something that would be minimized by Bush's predecessors in the Oval Office. It was Franklin Roosevelt's fellow internationalist, Wendell Willkie, who expressed the great dilemma in timeless language. "Freedom is an indivisible word," Willkie maintained in his 1943 book *One World*. "If we want to enjoy it, and fight for it, we must be prepared to extend it to everyone, whether they are rich or poor, whether they agree with us or not, no matter what their race or the color of their skin."

"Extend" is an interesting word. Extending freedom often means just what Willkie suggested, fighting. Or to put it more bluntly, it often means conquering a totalitarian regime by armed force. It entails killing the armed troops of other nations, and often some of their civilians as well, and it means sacrificing the blood of American citizen-soldiers. Not everyone has the stomach for it, even when those in the country being liberated greet the American soldiers with kisses and praise.

In the days leading up to the second war in the Persian Gulf—and even while it was going on—those opposed to George W. Bush's military plans invariably prefaced their objections by saying that "of course" they would like to see the brutal Saddam Hussein removed from power in Baghdad. But then they would go ahead and list their qualms and their doubts about the only plan ever devised that had any hope of actually accomplishing that task. Some Democrats, showing perhaps too much fealty to the necessities of partisan politicking, continued to adhere to this internally contradictory construct even *after* Saddam's government had fallen. On May 3, 2003, in the first debate among the 2004 Democratic presidential hopefuls, former Vermont Gov. Howard Dean asserted that Bush had waged "the wrong war at the wrong time," while also blithely pronouncing himself "delighted to see Saddam Hussein gone."

This is the kind of curious logic that frustrates American presidents. (This is true even when the criticism comes from *former* presidents, a particular specialty of Jimmy Carter's, and, to a lesser extent—at least so far—of Bill Clinton's.) Sitting presidents tend to ask, and not rhetorically, how a place like Syria or Iran would ever actually acquire democracy without the assistance of the U.S. Marines. Long before Carter traveled to Oslo to claim his Nobel Peace Prize, Theodore Roosevelt was awarded that honor for helping mediate a peace in the Russo-Japan War. But the man who bequeathed the slogan "speak softly and carry a big stick" to the English language was no peacenik. In his acceptance speech of the peace prize itself, Teddy Roosevelt offered a clarifying call for freedom, not peace. Roosevelt's words in that May 9, 1910, speech could apply to France in the 1930s (or France today), while serving as a reminder for future presidents:

We must ever bear in mind that the great end in view is righteousness, justice as between man and man, nation and nation, the chance
to lead our lives on a somewhat higher level, with a broader spirit
of brotherly goodwill one for another. Peace is generally good in itself, but it is never the highest good unless it comes as the handmaid
of righteousness; and it becomes a very evil thing if it serves merely
as a mask for cowardice and sloth, or as an instrument to further
the ends of despotism or anarchy. We despise and abhor the bully,
the brawler, the oppressor, whether in private or public life, but we
despise no less the coward and the voluptuary. No man is worth
calling a man who will not fight rather than submit to infamy or see
those that are dear to him suffer wrong. No nation deserves to exist
if it permits itself to lose the stern and virile virtues; and this without
regard to whether the loss is due to the growth of a heartless and
all-absorbing commercialism, to prolonged indulgence in luxury
and soft, effortless ease, or to the deification of a warped and
twisted sentimentality.

It was pacifists who engendered Roosevelt's utmost loathing. His
view, in the main, was that the wavering of statesmen who claimed to
want peace but who weren't willing to wage war to enforce it did not,
in the end, prevent war. He believed they actually made war more
likely—and on less favorable terms, timing, and terrain.

"We wish peace, but we wish the peace of justice, the peace of righteousness," Roosevelt said in his 1905 inaugural address. "We wish it
because we think it is right and not because we are afraid. No weak nation that acts manfully and justly should ever have cause to fear us, and
no strong power should ever be able to single us out as a subject for
insolent aggression."

Seven years later, Roosevelt amplified on this sentiment, and in less
general terms, in a private letter to British Foreign Secretary Edward
Grey, whose flawed diplomacy contributed to the outbreak of World
War I. "President Wilson is certainly not desirous of war with anybody.
But he is very obstinate, and he takes the professorial view of interna-
tional matters," Roosevelt wrote on January 22, 1915, to Sir Grey.[9]

"I need not point out to you that it is often pacificists [*sic*] who
halting and stumbling and not knowing whither they are going finally
drift helplessly into a war, which they have rendered inevitable, without
the slightest idea that they were doing so," Roosevelt added in his 1915
letter. "A century ago this was what happened to the United States under

Presidents Jefferson and Madison—although at that time the attitude of both England and France rendered war with one of them, and ought to have rendered war with both of them, inevitable on our part. . . ."

Roosevelt was not an angry man; combat of all kinds seemed to put a smile on his face. In war or in peace, it would be difficult to find a single American citizen in history, let alone an American president, who lived out the creed implied by "life, liberty, and the pursuit of happiness" more than Theodore Roosevelt. His élan was present whether he was serving as a fearless cavalry officer in the "Rough Riders" in the Spanish-American War, hunting big game in Africa, tramping across (and preserving) hundreds of millions of acres of priceless lands in the American West, romping in delighted physical play with his five children in the White House, busting the big trusts that were stifling U.S. commerce or running for president a second time around in 1912 as a Progressive, a party that became known as the Bull Moose party when Roosevelt told reporters he felt as fit as a bull moose. While Roosevelt was campaigning that year in Milwaukee, a would-be assassin shot him in the chest. He was not seriously hurt, but the incident prompted Roosevelt to utter his own epitaph: "No man has had a happier life than I have led," Roosevelt asserted. "A happier life in every way." (The remark was impromptu as well as premature, for Roosevelt would not die until 1919, but no one doubted the truth of it.) In fact, Roosevelt went ahead and delivered the speech he was planning to make, even holding up a copy of it for the audience so they could see the bullet hole in his prepared text.[10]

Speaking at the fiftieth anniversary of Mount Rushmore National Memorial in 1991, the first President Bush said of Roosevelt: "He won renown as a warrior." Then, glancing at the mountain on which Roosevelt shares equal billing with Jefferson (and Washington and Lincoln), Bush added, "These heroes were fighters."

I have often heard it lamented, even by those who ought to know better, that it's a shame no one like Theodore Roosevelt walks among us today. To me, this is a misplaced regret for the simple reason that Americans have had just such a happy warrior among them for more than a generation. His name is John McCain.

Even while he was still a midshipman at the United States Naval Academy in Annapolis, John Sidney McCain III was already well known inside the Navy officer corps. It was not because was he a good student—he was actually a poor one—or because he was the informal leader of a group of rebellious middies known as "The Bad Bunch." It was because McCain was the scion of not one, but two, famous admirals. His grandfather, John S. McCain, was on the deck of the USS *Missouri* during the Japanese surrender that brought World War II to a close. His father, John S. McCain Jr., was the officer in operational control of the bombing of North Vietnam.

It was in fact that very bombing campaign that helped make John S. McCain III famous while he was still a lieutenant commander in the Navy. Flying his twenty-third mission in Vietnam on October 26, 1967, young McCain's A-4 Skyhawk was hit by anti-aircraft fire that tore off one of its wings. McCain ejected suddenly, breaking his kneecap and both arms when he slammed against the plane. He landed roughly in the middle of Truc Bach (White Bamboo) Lake, tangled in his parachute, and was fished out of the lake by local peasants, who proceeded to beat him savagely. McCain's shoulder was crushed by someone who smashed him with the butt of a rifle. He was bayoneted in the groin and in the left ankle, then thrown onto the back of a truck and driven to the infamous Hoa Ho Prison, a 2½ acre compound surrounded by 20-feet walls, built by the French in 1901. Located in the middle of Hanoi, the foreboding prison was dubbed the "Hanoi Hilton" by another downed American flier, Navy Lt. Cmdr. Robert Shumaker. The name stuck.

In the ensuing years, McCain's story has become a genuine American legend: How he refused, adhering faithfully to the Code of Military Conduct, to be released earlier than other POWs who'd been captured before him—deducing, correctly, that the North Vietnamese wanted to use him for propaganda purposes. How that refusal resulted in especially horrific treatment from his sadistic guards, treatment that included daily beatings and long stretches in solitary confinement during his five and a half years in captivity. How his physical wounds never really healed, but how he persevered anyway, leaving the Navy for a successful career in politics. McCain won a seat in Congress while running as a Republican in an Arizona district, and later won a Senate seat.

From that perch, McCain provided indispensable cover for the White House when President Clinton, who had avoided military service during the war, wanted to normalize relations between the United States and Vietnam. On this issue, McCain had as much credibility as anyone in American public life. McCain had always been brave, loyal to his country and, not to put too fine a point on it, stubborn as hell. But it was in Hanoi, in a rat-infested prison cell, wracked by dysentery, lack of food, debilitating and untreated injuries, facing continued torture where

McCain says he figured out what it really meant to be an American. Fighting in a war that would never be venerated the way World War II was, McCain's explanation of what Americanism means to him is perhaps even more poignant than that of John Hersey's Guadalcanal Marines. This passage is from the first volume of McCain's autobiography, *Faith of My Fathers*:

> In prison, I fell in love with my country. I had loved her before then, but like most young people, my affection was little more than a simple appreciation for the comforts and privileges most Americans enjoyed and took for granted. It wasn't until I had lost America for a time that I realized how much I loved her. I loved what I missed most from my life at home: my family and friends; the sights and sounds of my country; the hustle and purposefulness of Americans; their fervid independence; sports; music; information—all the attractive qualities of American life. But though I longed for the things at home I cherished the most, I still shared the ideals of Americans. And since those ideals were all that I possessed of my country, they became all the more important to me.
>
> It was what freedom conferred on America that I loved the most—the distinction of being the last, best hope of humanity; the advocate for all who believed in the Rights of Man. Freedom is America's honor, and all honor comes with obligations . . .[11]

In 1999, this happy warrior bucked the Republican Party establishment and decided to run for president. In the first primary election of the 2000 campaign, in New Hampshire, McCain handily defeated the favored party candidate, George W. Bush. McCain's underfinanced, but highly charismatic campaign frightened the frontrunner into spending a great deal of money—and good will—to meet the challenge of this incorrigible maverick. But while McCain's candidacy was still viable, he attempted to put Republican audiences in touch with their inner Abe Lincolns and Teddy Roosevelts—often while citing the doctrine of life, liberty and the pursuit of happiness. During a debate in Iowa among the Republican presidential hopefuls in December of 1999, McCain, along with five other candidates, was asked what "political philosopher or thinker" he most identified with. "Obviously all of our Founding Fathers were probably the most remarkable group of men ever assembled in history," McCain replied. "But my modern-day role model and hero is Theodore Roosevelt."[12]

From the beginning of his presidential campaign, starting with his September 27, 1999, announcement speech, McCain harked back to themes of sacrifice reminiscent of an earlier age. Most specifically, they sounded more akin to the sensibilities of another former junior Navy officer, John F. Kennedy, than to those of most contemporary American politicians. At the rousing end of his announcement address, delivered in Nashua, N.H., McCain said:

> When my time is over, I want only the satisfaction of knowing I was true to the faith of our fathers; true to the faith of a young Czech student who ten years ago stood before a million of his countrymen while a hundred thousand Soviet troops occupied his country and read a manifesto that declared a new day for the people of Czechoslovakia. But he began the new day with borrowed words when, trembling with emotion, he proclaimed: "We hold these truths to be self-evident, that all men are created equal, that they are endowed by their creator with certain unalienable rights, that among these are life, liberty and the pursuit of happiness." I want to be president to protect, until my life's end, our magnificent dream of freedom, God's great blessing to the world.

Sometimes McCain's fervor got the better of him. In South Carolina, he responded to a whispering campaign against him making the rounds in circles of the Religious Right (and one he believed was orchestrated by the Bush camp) with an ill-advised frontal attack on prominent conservative evangelists Jerry Falwell, Pat Robertson and Bob Jones.

"We are the party of Ronald Reagan not Pat Robertson," McCain said on February 28, 2000. "We are the party of Theodore Roosevelt not the party of special interests. We are the party of Abraham Lincoln not Bob Jones. Join us."

The rift that developed between McCain and Bush in the roughly fought South Carolina primary never really healed. The two men's staffs, not friendly to begin with, loathed each other from that moment forward. Bush and McCain themselves were civil toward one another after that, but that was about as far as it went. Nonetheless, it will also be remembered that when it came to war in Iraq McCain was one of Bush's most staunch and influential political allies in the days before the second Gulf War. He supported Bush in public and private, speaking in favor of the administration's war resolution both on the nation's airwaves and on the floor of the Senate. He privately asked Secretary of

State Colin L. Powell how he could help build support in Congress for the war resolution and wrote influential op-ed pieces in an attempt to rally the public.

"Americans fight and die in Iraq today not for empire, not for oil, not for a religion, not to shock and awe the world with our astonishing power. They fight for love—for love of freedom, our own and all humanity's," McCain wrote in the *Washington Post* on March 23, 2003. "When the guns are silent, their political leaders must take every care to advance the aspirations that have given their sacrifice its nobility, and our country its real glory."

In the *New York Times*, McCain wrote that "only an obdurate refusal to face unpleasant facts" could allow anyone to believe that the United States had "rushed" to war. "Our armed forces will fight for peace in Iraq—a peace built on more secure foundations than are found today in the Middle East. Even more important, they will fight for the two human conditions of even greater value than peace: liberty and justice," McCain wrote. "Some of our soldiers will perish in this just cause. May God bless them and may humanity honor their sacrifice."

The senator's impulses to extend liberty around the globe—by force, if necessary—were in evidence before the Bush administration set its sights on Iraq. In the spring of 2002, while giving the commencement address at Wake Forest University, McCain offered the following rebuttal to those who think Americans' freedom and wealth makes them easy pickings for fascists or violent religious zealots:

> For all the terrible suffering they caused, the attacks of September 11 did have one good effect. Americans remembered how blessed we are, and how we are united with all people whose aspirations to freedom and justice are threatened with violence and cruelty. We instinctively grasped that the terrorists who organized the attacks mistook materialism as the only value of liberty. They believed liberty was corrupting, that the right of individuals to pursue happiness made societies weak. They held us in contempt.
>
> Spared by prosperity from the hard uses of life, bred by liberty only for comfort and easy pleasure, they thought us no match for the violent, cruel struggle they planned for us. They badly misjudged us.

McCain did not come by these views recently or in the heat of political battle. Months before the attacks on the World Trade Center and the Pentagon, I asked him to write an essay on the pursuit of happiness as part of the project of interviewing former presidents.[13]

"Today, America is engaged in a great struggle against a depraved enemy, bent on taking our freedom from us," he wrote. "The sacrifices entailed in our defense will not be shared equally by all Americans. But all Americans must share a resolve to see this war through to a just end. . . . There is no greater cause, and we are all called to share in it. You will know a happiness far more sublime than pleasure, and no one will ever take it from you."

In the 2000 campaign, even the hard-boiled political reporters traveling with McCain on the bus the candidate dubbed the "Straight Talk Express" found it difficult to resist the charm of a man with the confidence to challenge Americans in this way. But the truly unexpected factor in the McCain campaign was the makeup of the voters attracted most strongly to his message. Vietnam veterans, to be sure, rallied to his side. But against all known conventional wisdom, it was young people who were disproportionately represented in the surging, enthusiastic crowds that came to hear him speak. This was counterintuitive for a candidate who insisted that America needed a system of compulsory national service. Perhaps it shouldn't have been. In sounding Kennedyesque themes of sacrifice John McCain was taking his audiences back to the ethos of the war his own grandfather had fought, a war almost all Americans are proud of, and doing so at a time when its veterans were dying out and the nation was giving them one last, affectionate hurrah, whether it was by watching HBO's *Band of Brothers* or buying *The Greatest Generation*, Tom Brokaw's best-selling valentine to the heroes of World War II. This was a war that left America as the acknowledged savior of the free world, not only in the fighting, but also during the peace that followed. It left the populaces of the nations that fought the United States with far better futures *after* they were conquered than they ever had before. The results of the Second World War brought stability to Italy, and thriving democracies in Germany and Japan, two nations with martial pasts that hadn't been pacified from the outside in a thousand years.

The great currents of history seem inevitable when we look back on them. But those who lived through it realize that there was nothing inevitable at all about the outcome of the Second World War. Certainly, the Japanese could never conquer the United States, but that wasn't really their plan. The goal was to gain from a war of attrition a negotiated settlement that institutionalized Japanese power in the Pacific. If Britain, with its powerful Navy, had fallen, that might well have happened. And Britain almost did fall.

On May 10, 1940, with the Nazis already occupying Austria, Poland and Czechoslovakia, the German invasion of the Low Countries and Norway began. That day, Hitler sent forty-five German divisions through the Ardennes forest, which French military commanders considered impenetrable. But it was not, and when the German forces, led by seven Panzer divisions, emerged on the other side of the woods, what lay before them was France itself—exposed and virtually undefended. Meanwhile the "blitzkrieg" had overwhelmed Holland and Belgium, meaning that when the Germans reached the English Channel near Abbeville, a quarter of a million English soldiers in Belgium—the cream of the British army—were cut off and surrounded, along with another one hundred thousand French troops.

The disaster led to a change in government in London. The English people turned to Winston Churchill, who had been warning his countrymen about Hitler for years. Churchill immediately ordered a strategic retreat, which consisted of an emergency evacuation at Dunkirk. In nine days of frantic ferrying across the channel in the face of withering fire from Luftwaffe fighters and bombers, 200,000 seasoned British soldiers and another 140,000 French troops were rescued. It happened because Churchill was decisive, because the British managed to scrape together a flotilla of 825 ships, and because the Germans inexplicably stopped their advance at Calais. None of that had to happen. It just did.

Nevertheless, the fall of all of continental Europe meant the likelihood that England would fall was quite real. Certainly Joseph P. Kennedy, the United States ambassador in London, thought so. "The jig is up," Kennedy wrote in a letter to FDR.

"Roosevelt's generals gave him 3-to-1 odds that the Wehrmacht, fresh from parading down the Champs-Elysees, would be goose-stepping through London's Trafalgar Square by August," noted former Harvard professor and Roosevelt scholar Frank Freidel, author of *A Rendezvous with Destiny*. "Kennedy, the ambassador in London, was certain that Hitler would win a dictated peace and, with it, the British Navy. Once Germany took over the French and British fleets, the experts warned, it could be in Latin America in six months. What's more, Japan was poised to occupy Indochina, a possession of the defeated French."

These were the kinds of scenarios Churchill had in mind when he warned, "If we go down, Hitler has a very good chance of conquering the world." But in Washington, Roosevelt had been waiting for a sign that the British wouldn't capitulate the way the French had. Stanford historian David M. Kennedy believes that Churchill himself *was* that sign. When Hitler went before the Reichstag to mock Churchill's pledge to keep the war going from Canada, if necessary, Churchill did not even deign to respond. Instead, he dispatched Lord Halifax, who had previously hoped for a negotiated peace with Germany, to speak for him—and for the English people. "We shall not stop fighting," Lord Halifax said simply, "until freedom is secure."

This is the kind of talk Roosevelt wanted to hear. Like Wilson before him, FDR believed he had given peace a chance. It only had postponed the inevitable. And, now, as he led his nation into a two-ocean war against two martial dictatorships that had swept away everything in their paths, FDR went back to his Jeffersonian roots to explain why the United States had to fight—and what it was fighting against.

"The truths which were self-evident to Thomas Jefferson, which have been self-evident to the six generations of Americans who followed him—were to [the Nazis] hateful," Roosevelt told the nation eight days after the Pearl Harbor attack. "The rights to life, liberty and the pursuit of happiness which seemed to the Founders of the Republic, and which seem to us, inalienable, were, to Hitler and his fellows, empty words which they proposed to cancel forever."[14]

In his 1942 State of the Union address, Roosevelt, in a speech studied by George W. Bush's communications staff sixty years later, said, "In fulfilling my duty to report upon the state of the Union, I am proud to say to you that the spirit of the American people was never higher than it is today—the Union was never more closely knit together—this country was never more deeply determined to face the solemn tasks before it. The response of the American people has been instantaneous. It will be sustained until our security is assured." He continued, in language that sounds quite familiar today, to discuss America's enemies—and America's resolve:

> They know that victory for us means victory for freedom. They know that victory for us means victory for the institution of democracy—the ideal of the family, the simple principles of common decency and humanity. . . .
>
> If any of our enemies from Europe or from Asia attempt long-

range raids by "suicide" squadrons of bombing planes, they will do so only in the hope of terrorizing our people and disrupting our morale. Our people are not afraid of that. We know that we may have to pay a heavy price for freedom. We will pay this price with a will. Whatever the price, it is a thousand times worth it. No matter what our enemies in their desperation may attempt to do to us—we will say, as the people of London have said, "We can take it." And what's more, we can give it back—and we will give it back—with compound interest.

But the news would get worse before it would get better, and Roosevelt devoted his entire February 23, 1942, fireside chat radio broadcast to dispelling rumors that the British were broken and that the Russians and the Chinese are about to capitulate to Germany and Japan, respectively. "With a pointed reminder of the Continental Army's travails at Valley Forge, [FDR] also felt it necessary to disabuse his countrymen of the demoralizing notion that they were 'soft and decadent, that they cannot and will not unite and work and fight,'" noted David Kennedy.

At this point, it is worthwhile to remember that the Declaration of Independence was written with the expectation that it be read aloud—and read to would-be soldiers. Among those introduced to the galvanizing document in this way were George Washington's own troops, ensconced in New York where they awaited the arrival of the British fleet, carrying what were believed to be the best combat troops on Earth. John Hancock, the president of the Continental Congress, sent Washington a copy of the Declaration; Washington ordered it read to his men. It apparently had the desired effect: That night, July 9, 1776, the American troops tore down a leaden statue of King George III that stood at the foot of Broadway on the Bowling Green and melted it down for bullets.

Roosevelt, too, used the language of the Declaration of Independence in a way that served as a reminder that it was a document written on behalf of a people who have announced they are marching into battle for their freedom. In January 1942, twenty-six nations became a signatory to a treaty forming the basis of the United Nations. Today, it is easy to dismiss the United Nations as bumbling and ineffectual, but on New Year's Day of 1943, Roosevelt paid homage to the original intent of the organization by issuing a statement noting that the coalition of signatory nations [had]

. . . signed an act of faith that military aggression, treaty violation, and calculated savagery should be remorselessly overwhelmed by their combined might and the sacred principles of life, liberty, and the pursuit of happiness be restored as cherished ideals of mankind.

Roosevelt issued a similar statement on Labor Day that year, in a remark intended for domestic consumption. "[W]e are determined that this World War, too, shall result in victory so that life, liberty and the pursuit of happiness shall be the lot of man when he wills it and that he be not the downtrodden serf of brutal Axis masters," the president said. "To make time and thus save lives and suffering, our American workers, employers, and farmers will need not only to maintain their production pace but to increase it. . . . That increased production effort will be forthcoming. It will be given gladly for love of country and for liberty, as it has been given since Pearl Harbor, to set up a record that never has been equaled. We well may be proud of that achievement for it has done much to make possible the successes of the armed forces of the United Nations. Its continuation will spell the defeat of our enemies—the preservation of our way of life."

Our way of life is still a common phrase in American civic life, and it means roughly the same thing that it did in Roosevelt's time. But the pre–World War II American landscape was much different than it is today. A decade of active federal intervention in the marketplace and ambitious government-funded social programs had barely dented the numbing effects of the Great Depression. World War II would do that, although at the time Roosevelt spoke, no one could be certain that war would actually end the Depression. But we know now that it *had* ended it. Had, in fact, launched the United States on an economic arc toward a half-century of basically uninterrupted and unprecedented prosperity.

Until the Second World War broke out, Roosevelt had been leading a nation in which 25 percent of able-bodied adults couldn't find work—at a time when most households had only one wage earner. The number of unemployed in some cities was 50 percent. In the countryside, crops rotted in the fields, as it cost more to harvest them than they were worth. A bushel of wheat that sold in Chicago for $2.94 plunged to $1 in 1929 and thirty cents by 1932. Half a million homeowners, many of them farmers, defaulted on their mortgages. Thousands of banks failed. The gross national product had halved, the stock market lost 75 percent of its value, whole sections of the rural part of the country were depopulated, the nation realized negative immigration as new migrants—some who'd been here ten and twenty years—returned to Mexico, Poland and other lands of their origin. Many Mexicans were, in fact, deported against their will, foreshadowing the incarceration of the Japanese and Japanese-Americans on the West Coast after Pearl Harbor. It's hard to overestimate the hardships faced by American families. The marriage rate declined, as did the birthrate. This was the nation that Roosevelt tried to lead by the force of his personality; this was the nation that had been attacked by Imperial Japan.

During all that time, and in the horrific war that followed, Roosevelt was unrelentingly upbeat, usually positively cheerful, in public. "Even through the grainy newsreels, we can see what the people at the time saw," Doris Kearns Goodwin wrote in a 1999 essay. "The radiant smile, the eyes flashing with good humor, the cigarette holder held at a jaunty angle, the good-natured toss of the head, the buoyant optimism, the serene confidence with which he met economic catastrophe and international crisis."

Orson Welles put it this way: "Desperately we needed his courage and his skill and wisdom and great heart. He moved ahead of us showing a way into the future."

Many years after the fact, Princeton University literary professor Samuel Hynes would recall in *The Growing Seasons*, his lovely memoir of a boyhood spent in Minneapolis during the Depression, how simply catching a glimpse of Roosevelt waving from his motorcar would change him from a Republican (like his father) to the Democrat he remains to this day. "In the back seat sits a big man with a full, smiling face, and a thrusting chin," Hynes remembered. "He wears glasses without earpieces pinched on the bridge of his nose, and a gray hat with the brim rolled over all the way round. He turns from one curb to the other, smiling and waving, and the people in the crowd cheer and cheer. Then the procession is gone, north toward Lake Street. I have seen the President of the United States, my first Great Man. I am 12 years old, and I have just become a Democrat."

Hynes' autobiography is a tale of resilience—his own and that of those around him—an attitude made all the more admirable by the death of his mother when he was five years old. But in another book set in the Depression, *And a Time For Hope*, historian James R. McGovern documents how widespread such hopefulness was in the nation during the Depression and the war that followed. "Roosevelt galvanized the country," McGovern told me when I discussed presidential leadership with him in the wake of 9/11. "And this is one of the reasons that Americans tended to be optimistic even during the worst years of the Depression—much more than is commonly remembered."

Roosevelt's effect on people was pretty much the same in private—because *he* was pretty much the same. This man with all the weight of the free world on his broad shoulders, a man who'd lived since his thirty-ninth year with paralysis and in a marriage without physical intimacy, impressed his own White House aides with his capacity for unwinding at the end of another harrowing day as commander-in-chief. Of a normal evening, the president would host in-house happy hours—Roosevelt would mix the martinis himself—with the unspoken proviso that Harry Hopkins (who actually lived in the White House) and the other regulars were not to discuss the war. Trading funny political stories, telling jokes, gossiping about politics—such banter kept Roosevelt sunny and sane. According to Doris Goodwin, only Eleanor Roosevelt was exempted from the no-weighty-subjects taboo. Even the always-serious Eleanor realized that her husband's end of the day cocktail hour was a small price to pay for a man who was personally responsible for keeping Americans believing in themselves—and who was holding up his end of the bargain. World War II and the associated Nazi atrocities would ultimately claim something like sixty million lives worldwide, half of them noncombatants, and included among that number were nearly 432,000 American servicemen (along with another 600,000 wounded). But there was life to be lived as well, and Roosevelt set the example. When Hopkins married in 1942, Roosevelt had the ceremony in the White House. Later that year, when some Americans complained to the White House asking that Thanksgiving be cancelled as a holiday, FDR responded by holding the first-ever Thanksgiving Day religious services in the East Room, an affair attended by members of Congress, the cabinet, the Supreme Court and the extended "White House family."[15]

During the war years, Roosevelt also managed to dedicate the Jefferson Memorial, speak at the White House Correspondents' Association annual dinner, renew a friendship with his old flame Lucy Mercer Rutherfurd, watch murder mystery movies, spend hundreds of hours on his beloved stamp collections and take Churchill fishing at a Maryland trout stream near Shrangri-la (now Camp David).[16] As commander-in-chief, FDR campaigned for Democrats, raised money for the March of Dimes research into infant paralysis and personally ordered that the annual Army-Navy football game be played, rather than cancelled. (The game was held in Annapolis, but wartime travel restrictions prevented the West Point cadets not on the football team from attending; the Navy commandant ordered third and fourth-class midshipmen to do the unimaginable, which was to root for the rival cadets. The young middies did so, lustily singing the Army fight songs.) Roosevelt continued during the war to use the radio for his "fireside chats"—and he practically invented the press conference. He swam daily, often playfully dunking or spraying in the face those he enticed to swim with him.

"The President loved jokes and laughter and good company," the *New York Herald Tribune* reported after his death. "He delighted in a friendly game of poker with plenty of wild cards. The more hilarious it got, the better. At ball games he would boo an umpire with the best of them. . . . He liked to 'razz' people, dragging out a story at the victim's expense. A few blushers only spurred him on."

All this he did, of course, while fighting polio, the Great Depression, Hitler and the Japanese. No wonder that Churchill had marveled at "this shining personality."

FDR truly was the original Happy Warrior, a name that, fittingly enough, entered the American political lexicon on Roosevelt's own lips. The year was 1924, Franklin Roosevelt had appeared on crutches at the Democratic National Convention to place into nomination the name of New York Gov. Alfred E. Smith, introducing him as "the Happy Warrior." The words weren't originally Roosevelt's; they were poet William Wordsworth's (it was a Smith campaign hack, not FDR, who put them into the speech), but as events unfolded, the description fit Roosevelt himself better than they did Al Smith, who was rendered miserable when he lost even his home state in the landslide presidential election of 1928, the year he actually was nominated. It was Roosevelt who ran successfully for the presidency with a campaign song, "Happy Days are Here Again!"[17]

And so it was that a song celebrating happiness would forever be associated in Americans' consciousness with Franklin Roosevelt. In January 1945, on the occasion of Roosevelt's sixty-third birthday—it would be his last one—the president asked Eleanor to read a statement on his behalf. In it, FDR equated the war against totalitarianism with the war on childhood disease—and invoked the doctrine of the pursuit of happiness as the organizing principle in the fight against each:

> We will never tolerate a force that destroys the life, the happiness, the free future of our children, any more than we will tolerate the

continuance on earth of the brutalities and barbarities of the Nazis or of the Japanese warlords. We combat this evil enemy of disease at home just as unremittingly as we fight our evil enemies abroad. . . .

We must give our scientists and research workers the necessary equipment to find this invidious enemy, to corner and destroy him. The task is not an easy one. The mystery shrouding the infantile paralysis virus is not readily penetrated. But we will persist—and we will triumph. There is no yardstick long enough to measure the happiness our children give us. Whatever we can contribute to promote our children's health is an investment in our country's future. It is an assertion of our American birthright to life, liberty, and the pursuit of happiness.

The wartime action having nothing to do with war for which Roosevelt is best remembered is probably his interceding to make sure that Americans were able to enjoy major league baseball. The military draft would require most able-bodied males to be inducted into the armed forces, including some of the recognizable names in major league baseball, and the draft came at the end of the 1941 season—one of the most memorable in history. That year Ted Williams hit .406 (the last player to hit .400), while Joe DiMaggio hit safely in fifty-six consecutive games, a record that has *never* been equaled. Within two years, Williams was flying combat missions as a Navy pilot while DiMaggio had quietly traded in his $43,500 annual salary for the $50-a-month the government was then paying Army enlisted men.[18] And so it went. The draft took effect on September 16, 1940, and by the 1943 season stars such as Williams and DiMaggio had been replaced by the likes of Pete Gray, the valiant, but one-armed outfielder, and pitcher Johnny Gee, who didn't have much of an arm, but who, at six feet nine inches, was too tall to be drafted.

But the public wanted professional baseball anyway—and Roosevelt wanted them to have it. Five weeks after Pearl Harbor, baseball commissioner Kennesaw Mountain Landis, a former Tennessee judge, (and no fan of the New Deal) sent the president a handwritten letter inquiring if keeping baseball operating was conducive to the war effort. "My dear Judge," Roosevelt replied the next day, January 15, 1942, "I honestly feel that it would be best for the country to keep baseball going. There will be fewer people unemployed and everybody will work longer hours and harder than ever before. . . ."

And that means that they ought to have a chance for recreation and for taking their minds off their work even more than before.

Baseball provides a recreation which does not last over two hours or two hours and a half, and which can be got for very little cost. And, incidentally, I hope that night games can be extended because it gives an opportunity to the day shift to see a game occasionally.

As to the players themselves, I know you would agree with me that individual players who are of active military or naval age should go, without question, into the services. Even if the actual quality of the teams is lowered by the greater use of older players, this will not dampen the popularity of the sport. Of course, if an individual player has some particular aptitude in a trade or profession, he ought to serve the Government. That, however, is a matter which I know you can handle with complete justice.

Here is another way of looking at it—if 300 teams use 5,000 or 6,000 players, these players are a definite recreational asset to at least 20,000,000 of their fellow citizens—and that in my judgment is thoroughly worthwhile.

Sixty-one years later, a similar issue arose, and the reason George W. Bush didn't even have to intercede is because Roosevelt had long ago answered the question as to whether war can coexist with games and fun and simple happiness. On the eve of the United States' invasion of Iraq, a few prominent voices called for the canceling of the NCAA basketball tournament known as "March madness," a tournament that has, in some respects, replaced baseball's World Series as the most riveting and unifying sports event in America. "The NCAA tournament is one of the great sporting events of the year, but this tournament should have been canceled," argued William C. Rhoden, the thoughtful sports columnist for the *New York Times*. Rhoden's words were echoed by University of Utah head coach Rick Majerus, one of the most decent men associated with college basketball. "My father was one of seven brothers, and all of them were in the service," Majerus said. "My father was in Okinawa. I had an uncle die in Normandy. I had classmates die in Vietnam. One-third of the people we have over there are reservists."

These were noble sentiments, but they did not get far. "We will go forward with our plans to play the games, if and when war breaks out," NCAA president Myles Brand announced. "We were not going to let a tyrant determine how we were going to lead our lives."

Apparently, the troops in the field agreed, and they found much of the concern for them misplaced. "I watched basketball yesterday, not war. It felt a little weird at first," wrote Michael Wilbon, the popular sports columnist for the *Washington Post* in a March 21, 2003, column headlined "In Time of War, a Peaceful Pursuit." But then Wilbon related the content of several e-mails he had received from servicemen stationed overseas—all of whom wanted the games to continue.

"As someone who is forward deployed to the Arabian Gulf . . . there is no greater support the NCAA could provide than holding March Madness as scheduled," wrote Lt. Cmdr. John D. Rickards Jr., a damage control assistant aboard the USS *Abraham Lincoln* and a self-identified Oklahoma fan. "Sports are a great escape for many and a connection to home for all."

Added Sean Higgins from Arlington, another Navy careerist, "In the days before satellite TV and e-mail, the most important news coming off the teletypes were the sports scores. No matter what time of the day somebody was stopping by the communication center and asking if the scores had come out yet. We serve for the American way of life, and anybody who thinks that athletic events should be cancelled . . . obviously has no idea what it is like to be in the military, away from home, or why most of us serve."

The commander-in-chief certainly agreed. He mentioned to the author that even while the fighting in Iraq was going on, he liked to unwind at the end of the day by watching major league baseball games at night in the White House residence. "I've got a satellite dish, set on the right station," he told me at a journalists' black-tie dinner one night, while sneaking a look at his watch. "The (Texas) Rangers are playing the Yankees tonight. I'd kind of like to get home by the seventh inning or so."[19]

In pursuing happiness this way—in the midst of war—Bush brought Roosevelt to my mind. In fact, Bush discussed Roosevelt with me that night, lauding FDR as a successful wartime president, while asking questions about how Roosevelt relaxed at the White House with friends. The two presidents are very different, of course, but I rather think Roosevelt would have appreciated Bush's determination to keep running, lifting weights, spending time at his ranch and doing all the things that make him happy—and I do mean *all* the things—during a war. While it might be hard to imagine FDR characterizing 1941 the way Bush did the year 2001 ("All in all," he told reporters in Crawford at Christmas time, "it's been a fabulous year for Laura and me."), Roosevelt surely would have loved it when Bush was asked by those same reporters how he was spending his time over the holiday. "Well, I was up this morning at 5 A.M.," Bush said with a lusty smile. "Spent a little quality time with the first lady."

And so American life went on after the attacks, at all levels.

It will be interesting to look back and recall that during the war in Iraq some of those who provided the diversions that made others happy were themselves conflicted about their proper role. Michael Jordan, the world's most famous gym rat, shrugged off any notion that players shouldn't pursue their happiness on the basketball court. "We're entertainers," he said. "We're supposed to play." But not everyone was certain that that was enough. Professional football player Pat Tillman left his team and enlisted in the Army after 9/11, giving up a $1 million annual salary in the bargain. But as the nation inched closer to war in Iraq, one obscure, small-college basketball player, Toni Smith of Manhattanville College, began turning her back on the flag in protest during the playing of the national anthem, offending many fans and dividing her own team. Two professional players on the National Basketball Association's Dallas Maverick's team made antiwar statements, even as bombs were falling on Iraq. It started when Steve Nash, the team's star guard, showed up at the NBA all-star game wearing a t-shirt that said, "No War. Shoot for Peace." It was a fairly innocuous enough sentiment—although his explanation that war shouldn't be used "as a means of conflict resolution" was beyond parody—but because Nash is from Canada, he generated a bit of heat. Then teammate Nick Van Exel piped up that President Bush was giving Americans "a bad name."

This became a bit much for David Robinson, of the rival San Antonio Spurs, who is not only the league's top philanthropist and one of its officially designated Fifty Greatest players of all time but, more importantly, a Naval Academy graduate.

"I get a little bit upset," Robinson said on ESPN. "The time for debate is really beforehand. Obviously history will speak on whether this was the right thing or the wrong thing, but right now [the troops] are out there. Support 'em. There's plenty of time for commentary later. If it's an embarrassment to them, maybe they should be in a different country, because this is America and we're supposed to be proud of the guys we elected and put in office."

Who was right? Well, to me the answer is . . . all of these people. The players who were just happy to be playing, the protestors, the counter-protestors. No less a light than the commander-in-chief himself said as much. Iraqis hadn't been freed from Saddam Hussein for forty-eight hours when various factions began demonstrating—against the Americans who had liberated them. The picture of Shiites on a mass pilgrimage that Saddam had outlawed waving their fists at the Marines who made it possible was a bit hard to stomach, especially if you knew any of the Marines who were killed or wounded over there. But the Shiite protests didn't seem to bother President Bush. Asked about those protesting Iraqis on April 20, 2003, after emerging from Easter Sunday services at Fort Hood, Tex., Bush responded this way:

> I'm not worried. Freedom is beautiful, and when people are free, they express their opinions. You know, they couldn't express their opinions before we came. Now they can. I've always said democracy is going to be hard. It's not easy to go from being enslaved to being free. But it's going to happen, because the basic instinct of mankind is to be free. They want to be free. And so, sure, there's going to be people expressing their opinions, and we welcome that, just like here in America people can express their opinion.

A couple of weeks earlier, the wisdom of Bush's insight had been lost on the management of the National Baseball Hall of Fame in Cooperstown, N.Y. The Hall had been planning a fifteenth-anniversary celebration of the classic baseball movie *Bull Durham*, until Dale Petroskey, president of the Hall, canceled it on the grounds he didn't want to give a forum to two of the movies stars, Tim Robbins and Susan Sarandon, who are highly partisan Democratic Party activists and who've been outspokenly opposed to Bush and the war in Iraq. Dale Petroskey is a friend of mine, and Robbins, in particular, is an intemperate person who has been known to physically threaten reporters who irritate him. But in this instance, for the reasons cited by Bush himself, Dale was wrong and Robbins was right.

Those U.S. Marines and members of the Third Army Infantry Division were in Iraq fighting to extend democracy to a land that hasn't had it. And robust political discourse—and peaceful political dissent—here at home serve to showcase America's strength, not her weakness. On Sunday April 13, 2003, at an ill-defined Washington protest march against the World Bank (or Israel or war in Iraq or globalization or the presence of too many Taco Bell restaurants—it was hard to tell) the marchers pointed accusingly at passers-by frequenting the merchants on U Street. They chanted:

"While you're shopping, bombs are dropping!"

As stark as this sounded, it was literally true. But in ways the protestors did not intend, it was also precisely the point—and one Alexis de Tocqueville would have approved of.

There is another thing to say about dissent. The First Amendment is not a nicety the Founding Fathers cooked up as a way of showing that they were tolerant men. Freedom of speech is infinitely more than that. It is the process by which a democratic people hash out the truth—or try to—and the method they use to determine the direction they want their nation to go.

Today's dissent, as Frederick Douglass showed us, is tomorrow's consensus. Likewise, today's enemies may be tomorrow's friends, and vice-versa. Franklin Roosevelt died on April 12, 1945, having helped save democracy and its promise of a government that guarantees the opportunity to life, liberty and the pursuit of happiness. Five months later, a fifty-five-year-old revolutionary trained in Paris, London and the Soviet Union borrowed Jefferson's language in a call for the liberation of his country from the undemocratic vestiges of colonialism. His name was Ho Chi Minh.

7

More Unfinished Work

As President Roosevelt changed hats, in his words, from "Doctor New Deal" to "Doctor Win-the-War," it became evident to him—and his nation of citizen-soldiers—that what had motivated America's enemies to attack their neighbors was a brand of racism so primal that it had mutated into a political rationale for invasion, imperialism and slaughter. Racialism was the animating principle of Nazism, and it was at the heart of the Fascist movement, whether espoused by Tojo, Mussolini—or Hitler himself. But if the mad Austrian corporal took his half-baked theories of racial superiority to their sick extremes, it also became uncomfortably apparent that there was a profound disconnect on this issue inside the bosom of America.

In the years 1941–1945, Franklin Roosevelt not only presided over a military that was segregated by race, he was forced by the exigencies of wartime unity to tolerate the ugly customs of Jim Crow in munitions plants, airplane factories and shipyards located in the old South. These traditions did not go down easy with black soldiers, sailors and defense workers, and they did not go down easy with many of the nation's whites who were seeing southern-style segregation up close for the first time. They caused special consternation inside the White House—particularly with the First Lady.

On her three-week trip to review the American troops stationed in England, Eleanor Roosevelt took note of the differences she found on the other side of the Atlantic. One of them was that Great Britain was ahead of the United States in mobilizing its female workforce into formerly all-male professions, even to the point of setting up vast day care facilities for them. Another was that the morale of the black soldiers, most of whom were from the South, was quite high. Mrs. Roosevelt attributed this fact, as did the soldiers themselves, to the most obvious factor—that they experienced less racial prejudice in England than in their home states. Doris Kearns Goodwin postulates that Mrs. Roosevelt brought this issue up with her husband immediately upon returning from her trip on November 17, 1942. Her evidence is fairly convincing: The same afternoon Eleanor debriefed the president on her trip, FDR sent a confidential memo to Attorney General Francis Biddle asking him to analyze the Constitutional ramifications of using the power of the federal government to dismantle the apparatus upon which the South's organized system of apartheid depended, namely the myriad barriers that had been erected to prevent blacks from voting. These obstacles varied from literacy tests to fees charged to blacks (and included out-and-out intimidation) and came to be known collectively by the shorthand phrase "poll tax."

"Would it be possible," FDR inquired, "for the Attorney General to bring an action against, let us say, the State of Mississippi, to remove the present poll tax restrictions? I understand that these restrictions are such that poor persons are, in many cases, prevented from voting."

A year-and-a-half earlier, in June of 1941, Roosevelt had issued an executive order banning employment discrimination in the federal government and defense industries. As part of that order, FDR had established the President's Commission on Fair Employment Practice to adjudicate complaints of discrimination. But Dr. Win-the-War was up against forces more potent than a temporary five-member commission with little enforcement authority could handle. Those forces not only included Nazi Germany and Imperial Japan, but the white power structure entrenched in the American South. In the spring of 1942, eleven Negroes were hospitalized and an entire defense plant nearly shut down for days when skilled white workers at a shipyard in Mobile, Ala., went on the rampage over the issue of working side-by-side with black welders. Roosevelt found himself lobbying his own fair employment practices commission to acquiesce to the compromise solution that brought peace to the plant, which was to set up separate (and presumably unequal) ship-welding facilities for Negro welders.

Roosevelt felt even more helpless after a Detroit-area race riot left twenty-five blacks and nine whites dead, hundreds more injured and nearly four thousand federal troops patrolling the city. As discouraging as this was to FDR, it was even more so for his wife. In *No Ordinary Time*, Goodwin relates a vignette that captures the anguish felt at that time by racially progressive people who understood clearly that the principles Americans were fighting for were utterly incompatible with the easy, institutionalized racism that was the virtual law in much of the United States:

> The story was told of . . . white youths [who] had begun to close in on a Negro. Three white sailors stepped in and broke it up.
>
> "He's not doing you any harm," one of the sailors said. "Let him alone."
>
> "What's it to you?" snapped one of the gang.
>
> "Plenty," replied the sailor. "There was a colored guy in our outfit and he saved a couple of lives. Besides, you guys are stirring up something that we're trying to stop."

There were thousands of such stories being told by American servicemen during World War II. Putting 12 million men in uniform and shipping them all over the world, including to places in the United States they had never seen, entailed exposing many of the GIs to staggering injustices. This went for whites and blacks alike. A black corporal named Rupert Trimmingham opened the eyes of the Army—and the nation—to the truly pernicious effects Jim Crow was having on the morale of black troops with an April 1944 letter to *Yank* magazine, a U.S. Army publication. The corporal's letter begins with a simple question: "What is the Negro soldier fighting for?"—an eerie echo of Frederick Douglass' 1852 speech "What to the Slave is the Fourth of July?" Trimmingham continued: "On whose team are we playing?" He then relates the travails he and eight other black GIs experienced while making their way through the South en route from Camp Claiborne, La., to an Army hospital in Arizona. This incident took place in Texas . . .

> We could not purchase a cup of coffee at any of the lunchrooms around here. The only place we could be served was at the railroad station but, of course, we had to go in [through] the kitchen. As you know, Old Man Jim Crow rules. But that's not all; at 11:30 A.M. about two dozen German prisoners of war, with two American guards, came to the station. They entered the lunchroom, sat at the tables, had their meals served, talked, smoked, in fact had quite a swell time. I stood on the outside looking on, and I could not help but ask myself why are they treated better than we are? Why are we pushed around like cattle? If we are fighting for the same thing, if

we are to die for our country, then why does the Government allow such things to go on? Some of the boys are saying that you will not print this letter. I'm saying that you will.[1]

The situation was so perverse that many Americans simply refused to face it. Many years later, while he was between jobs as governor of California and president of the United States, Ronald Reagan would tell audiences that segregation in the armed forces ended in World War II after a black mess steward aboard a Navy ship in Pearl Harbor "cradled a machine gun in his arms" after a white gunner had fallen. The black sailor then proceeded to fire the gun at the Japanese planes strafing the ships in harbor. If only this were so. Reagan's heart was in the right place insofar as this story is concerned, but when a California reporter interviewing Reagan in 1975 pointed out to him that the U.S. armed forces weren't integrated until 1948 when Harry Truman did it by executive order, Reagan ignored this detail. "I can remember the scene," Reagan replied, as if recalling it from a movie. "It was very powerful."[2]

Reagan's command of history may have been faulty, but his memory of having seen this event reenacted on celluloid probably was not. There almost certainly *was* such a scene in one of the many World War II training films that Hollywood churned out of its studios in Culver City where Reagan spent most of his wartime service in uniform. That's because there was, indeed, a black mess steward in the U.S. Navy who manned a machine gun at Pearl Harbor. His name was Dorie Miller, and he was a twenty-one-year-old ship's cook on the USS *West Virginia*. Miller was the first black man ever awarded the Navy Cross, an award given for heroism "performed in the presence of great danger or at great personal risk."[3]

As president, Reagan would sign a bill of redress complete with an official national apology and monetary reparations to the 120,000 Americans of Japanese ancestry interred in relocation camps during the war. Reagan's successor, the first President Bush, would also apologize on behalf of the country for the internment of the Japanese, which he characterized as incompatible with the ideals of the Declaration of Independence. The setting for Bush's remarks was powerful. It came at the ceremony commemorating the fiftieth anniversary of the attack on Pearl Harbor at the National Cemetery of the Pacific, known as Punchbowl. Although most of the service was devoted to the American sailors who lost their lives on December 7, 1941, Bush paused to draw attention to the unfairness of those infamous relocation camps.

"These and other natural-born American citizens faced wartime internment, and they committed no crime," Bush said in that 1991 ceremony. "They were sent to internment camps simply because their ancestors were Japanese. Other Asian-Americans suffered discrimination, and even violence, because they were mistaken for Japanese. And they, too, were innocent victims, who committed no offense."

The American survivors of Pearl Harbor treated Bush that day as one of their own, as they should have. Encouraged by his own father, Prescott Bush—who had connections in the Roosevelt administration—to go to Yale after prep school, Bush had instead enlisted in the Navy. He spent the war as one of the youngest Navy pilots in the Pacific theater, and was shot down over water in 1944. But the first President Bush did not dwell on that. He used the occasion to commemorate the American dead and the other veterans of that war, to speak out against racism in a broader way and to celebrate America's long period of reconciliation with Japan. "Americans did not wage war against nations or races," Bush said. "We fought for freedom and human dignity against the nightmare of totalitarianism. The world must never forget that the dictatorships we fought—the Hitler and Tojo regimes—committed war crimes and atrocities. Our servicemen struggled and sacrificed not only in defense of our free way of life but also in the hope that the blessings of liberty someday might extend to all peoples."

Some of those people Bush was talking about lived here in the United States.

"It is pretty grim to have a black boy in uniform get an orientation lecture in the morning on wiping out Nazi bigotry and that same evening be told he can buy a soft drink only in the colored post exchange," was the way NAACP official Roy Wilkins put it. And so, a half-century before Bush spoke in Hawaii, the vast upheaval of World War II—and the starkness of what America was fighting against—provided a long-overdue impetus to the civil rights movement in the United States. The leaders of that noble cause joined in common purpose with the elected leaders of this nation, setting about the great task of reawakening a people who had been too long asleep on the issue of race. Between the end of the Second World War and the passage of the Voting Rights Act two decades later, the movement fielded an extraordinary array of leaders, a second crop of Founding Brothers. The group included Wilkins, A. Philip Randolph, Bayard Rustin, Walter Francis White, Thurgood Marshall, Eleanor Roosevelt herself and, of course, the preternaturally charismatic Martin Luther King Jr.[4]

On May 16, 2003, White House National Security Adviser Condoleezza Rice had these progressive patriots in mind when she gave the commencement address at Mississippi College School of Law. "The civil rights struggle was America's chance to resolve the contradictions inherent in its birth," she told the graduating law students. "And at its roots, it was a legal struggle, pitting the natural law that underpins our Constitution and Declaration of Independence against unjust laws on the books that fell far short of that ideal." Rice, a black woman who as a girl lost a childhood friend in the infamous 1963 Klan bombing of the Sixteenth Street Baptist Church in Birmingham, Ala., continued:

> The Founding Fathers didn't mean me when they wrote the Bill of Rights. But by their terms, those rights were universal in theory, and you can trace the history of the civil rights era in the court filings of lawyers arguing that they should be universal in fact. The civil rights struggle was in a very real way America's second Founding.

In the years after World War II, the architects of this second Founding would cajole, beg, bully and, ultimately, work hand-in-hand with the warrior presidents who followed Roosevelt into office: Harry Truman, the World War I artillery captain who served as commander-in-chief at the end of the Second World War; Dwight D. Eisenhower, the five-star general who had crushed Hitler's armies; John F. Kennedy, a Harvard man who talked his way into the Navy despite a bad back and ended up winning the Navy and Marine Corps medal for valor (along with a Purple Heart) for rescuing his PT-109 crew by leading them on a three-mile swim to an island—with Kennedy towing one of them by a rope held in his teeth. Just as Lincoln and Frederick Douglass had done, these presidents—and the civil rights leaders who coaxed them along—used Thomas Jefferson's words to appeal to the pride and sense of fair play of a people who had conquered evil and racism abroad, and who now had to tackle it in their own home and in their own hearts.

But if World War II set the stage for the revival of the Spirit of 1776 and the extension of the ideals of the Continental Congress' work in Philadelphia, some of the heaviest lifting was done by two politicians with national ambitions who'd done their best to stay out of the fighting. Congressman Lyndon B. Johnson enlisted in the Navy, and then used his connections to spend the months after Pearl Harbor partying in Hollywood. When Texas newspapers wrote that their blustery House member had reneged on his promise to go into combat, LBJ arranged a single ride aboard an airplane that was nominally in the war zone. Hubert H. Humphrey did even less for the war effort. HHH took a teaching deferment in 1941 that allowed him to stay out of uniform altogether, and spent the war politicking even more overtly than Johnson: Humphrey ran for mayor of Minneapolis in 1943, losing, and then again successfully in 1945. But they would make their contributions to freedom in other ways, starting in their own political party.

From the end of the Civil War until the end of the Second World War, the Democratic Party put together successful national tickets by patching together disparate voting blocs that included big-city Catholics, union voters, Northern liberals and the solid South, which is to say the vast white segregationist vote. The implications of this coalition on the Democrats' policies were not trivial. Liberal Democrats today often get misty-eyed when talking about Woodrow Wilson, but it was Wilson, a Virginian by birth and Georgian by upbringing, who segregated the federal government and screened *Birth of a Nation*, D. W. Griffith's unashamedly pro–Ku Klux Klan movie, at the White House. Franklin Roosevelt campaigned as a racial liberal in New York, but would take a train down South and tell redneck farmers, "I'm one of you!" FDR carried every Southern state every time he ran. That wasn't necessarily something to be proud of.

The 13th Amendment abolishing slavery had been passed by Congress and ratified by the states in 1865, two years after the Emancipation Proclamation. The 14th Amendment guaranteed the free slaves "equal protection" of the laws, and the 15th Amendment granted them the right to vote. The Southern states voted for all three of these amendments, but in practice, the only one they accepted was the 13th. The 14th and 15th Amendments—and all the rights and political power that flow from them—were essentially nullified by a mosaic of customs, statutes and practices called the Black Codes, and later, the Jim Crow laws.

"This bargain that the South made with the nation as a whole— Thirteenth Amendment yes, Fourteenth and Fifteenth no—was durable to the point of seeming unchangeable," notes Nicholas Lemann, in describing the situation up to and through World War II. "The South was an essential element in the Democratic Party's coalition, after all; and the country as a whole was, at best, unused to thinking of segregation as a problem."

But the great upheaval of World War II shook the foundations that supported even these bedrock assumptions. The Detroit riots, lamented Eleanor Roosevelt, were not just sad, they were a national disgrace that put Americans "on a par with Nazism which we fight." As the war ended and the returning soldiers and sailors—including more than a million black men—returned to their homes, Mrs. Roosevelt's sharp observation would be made by many others, including the black soldiers themselves.

Something had to give—and it did.

*   *   *

On July 18, 1946, President Truman received a letter from a prominent black man named R. R. Wright Sr., the son of Georgia slaves, who had become an Army major during the Spanish-American War. Wright was later recommissioned as an instructor of recruits during World War I when young soldiers were mustered into service at Georgia State College (now Savannah State University), of which he was the president. Wright enclosed for the president's perusal a story in a local newspaper about a returning black GI, Isaac Woodward Jr., who just three hours after he returned home to South Carolina—and still in uniform—was pulled off a bus by local policemen who beat him and, the story asserted, deliberately gouged his eyes out.

"I am taking the liberty to write to you, because I myself am a veteran," Wright tells the president respectfully. "I love the South. I was born there. I worked there 50 years as a teacher of young men, some of whom fought in all our wars from the Spanish-American War down to the last war. . . ." But, he suggests, things must change:

> Now Mr. President, I think it is a terrible disgrace to our beloved South and to the United States, that a returned veteran who has risked his life for the purpose of maintaining freedom in our country, is not permitted to travel in his own native country subject to decent treatment by the law officers of the land, without being beaten unmercifully and deprived of his eyes. I could hardly keep from shedding tears as I read this report. . . .
>
>   It seems to me that we are compelled to call upon the Chief Executive to instruct or request the Attorney General to look into

this case so that justice may be meted to those unfaithful officers whose duty it was to keep the peace and protect the citizens of our country. Mr. President, I am not able to put this matter before you, even as I feel it. To "gouge out the eyesight" of a man who had used his eyes to safeguard the freedom of his country is surely a disgrace unheard of in any other country of the world.

The White House response to Maj. Wright came a week later, on July 25, 1946, from Truman aide David K. Niles. The War Department had no jurisdiction, Niles explained, because Isaac Woodward had already been discharged from the service. But in a preview of how the federal government—and presidents—would eventually break the Klan, Niles informed Wright that the matter had been referred to the Justice Department's civil rights division. Later that summer, NAACP officials met with Truman personally to discuss this case as well as another, even more horrifying, episode of vigilantism in Georgia. On September 20, Truman wrote a memo to his Attorney General Tom Clark.[5] With marvelous understatement, Truman casually propelled the federal government into the middle of the modern civil rights movement:

Dear Tom:

I had as callers yesterday some members of the National Association for the Advancement of Colored People and they told me about an incident which happened in South Carolina where a negro sergeant who had been discharged from the army just three hours was taken off a bus and not only seriously beaten, but his eyes deliberately put out, and that the mayor of this town had bragged about committing this outrage.

I have been very much alarmed at the increased racial feeling all over the country and I am wondering if it wouldn't be well to appoint a commission to analyze the situation and have a remedy to present to Congress—something similar to the Wickersham Commission on Prohibition.

I know you have been looking into the Tennessee and Georgia lynchings, and have also been investigating the one in Louisiana, but I think it is going to take something more than handling each individual case after it happens—it is going to require the inauguration of some sort of policy to prevent such happenings.

Although he died in 1992 in near-total obscurity, Isaac Woodward was the Rodney King of his generation.[6] As in the King case, legend attached itself to the basic facts of the case from the start. Contrary to the representations made to Truman, there was no evidence that Woodward's blinding was deliberate—or that the perpetrators boasted about it.[7] The earliest news accounts, in fact, had it occurring in Aiken, S.C., not in Batesburg where it actually happened. Woodward was removed at nighttime from a southbound Greyhound bus for boisterousness after a white bus driver said he saw him drinking. Two Batesburg, S.C., policemen, including the chief (not the mayor), escorted Woodward off the bus and apparently were manhandling him when Woodward grabbed the blackjack from the chief's hand. The other officer drew his gun; the chief retrieved his blackjack and whacked Woodward in the face with it hard enough to rupture both his eyeballs. The next morning, after a court appearance—he was fined the $44 he had with him—Woodward was taken back to the jail for medical treatment. Later, the police took him to the VA hospital in Columbia. He stayed there for two months, emerging sightless in April. It took awhile for word of this event to make its way North. What distinguished it from garden-variety police brutality were two facts: Woodward was a World War II veteran and his sight never returned.

But the incident struck a chord because it epitomized the rough treatment routinely visited upon blacks in the South. At trial (the police officers were acquitted) Greyhound Bus driver A. C. Blackwell said that Woodward asked at a stop if he could "take a piss." Blackwell said he told the twenty-seven-year-old Woodward, "Boy, go on back and sit down and keep quiet and don't be talking so loud."

"God damn it," answered Woodward, fresh from his fifteen-month stint in the Pacific. "I'm a man just like you."

That was the crux of the argument. And in targeting lynching and its first cousin, white-on-black official brutality against blacks who resisted staying "in their place," the White House was taking aim at the heart of the beast. The Constitution-nullifying, apartheid system that had been reconstructed in the South after the Civil War that effectively disenfranchised blacks depended ultimately on blacks' servility. Black servility, in turn, depended on organized, officially sanctioned white terrorism. From 1880 until the end of World War II, some 4,700 Americans were lynched, 3,450 were black—almost all of them in the South.[8] Tens of thousands—or more likely hundreds of thousands—had, like Isaac Woodward, been beaten, maimed or brutalized in other ways. As has been documented in recent years, some of these lynchings in the early part of this century were social events attended by hundreds, even thousands of whites, some of whom took photographs and even made postcards featuring the murdered victims. After viewing one such photograph in 1935, poet, songwriter and civil rights activist James Weldon Johnson described lynching as a "problem of saving black America's body and white America's soul."

Ten years before Truman's memo to his attorney general, Eleanor Roosevelt sent Walter White a letter that must have been a painful one for her to write. It was in March of 1936, an election year, a fact Eleanor alludes to with some embarrassment. Mrs. Roosevelt responds to White's despair that her husband will not push anti-lynching legislation with some gloom of her own. "The President feels that lynching is a question of education for the states, rallying good citizens, and creating public opinion so that the localities themselves will wipe it out," Mrs. Roosevelt wrote. "I am deeply troubled by the whole situation as it seems to me a terrible thing to stand by and let it continue. . . ."

Fifty years later, another prominent civil rights leader, A. Philip Randolph, was still perplexed that FDR wasn't more supportive on anti-lynching efforts. "President Roosevelt was a strong man," Randolph later recalled. "But on this issue of civil rights we were never able to get him to take a basic position on it."

As early as World War I, Randolph, then a New York actor, pamphleteer and socialist agitator—today we would use the term "activist"—had urged blacks not to enlist in the army because they did not enjoy full civil rights in their own country. He was arrested, but not prosecuted, and, if anything, emboldened by the experience. In 1925, Randolph organized black railway workers, and after a grueling twelve-year stalemate, settled a contract with the Pullman Company that guaranteed black workers overtime pay. This fight made Randolph into a nationally prominent labor leader and one of the most influential civil rights figures in the nation.

By the time World War II came around, Randolph was a power within the Democratic Party, at least in the North. The year 1919 was a time of resurgence by the Ku Klux Klan. Seventy-six blacks lost their lives to mob violence in southern states that year, including nine returning veterans of the war. One of them, Private William Little of Blakely, Ga., was apparently lynched precisely *because* he was wearing his uniform. The accounts of the time state that a few days after being mustered out he took a train home and was beaten by local whites for wearing his uniform around town. The mob made him remove it. A couple of days later, he was caught wearing it again—Little protested that he had no other clothes—and was beaten to death and left at the end of town.

On the eve of World War II, Randolph threatened to march on Washington and issued a call to blacks to resist the 1941 draft. It was Roosevelt's effort to defuse this march before it took place that was the impetus behind his executive order ending discrimination in the federal government and the defense industries. After the war, as Congress dealt with the issue of reconstituting the peacetime army and recalibrating Selective Service regulations, Randolph renewed his pressure. Negroes, he warned Truman in a 1948 letter, would refuse to serve if segregation in the armed forces continued. Several Truman biographers have asserted that Truman was angered by Randolph's threats. Perhaps he was, but Randolph had been saying similar things in speeches since before Truman entered politics; and Randolph had made the identical point in congressional testimony before he sent Truman the letter. During a White House meeting attended by twenty civil rights leaders and White House aides, Randolph also bluntly vowed that he would encourage blacks not to serve in a segregated Army. Accounts from both sides—Truman aides and Randolph himself—describe a tense scene.

"Mr. President," Randolph recalled saying, "the Negroes are in the mood not to bear arms for the country unless Jim Crow in the armed forces is abolished."

This offended Truman's patriotic sensibilities.

"Mr. Randolph," the president replied evenly, "I wish you hadn't made that statement."

But Randolph and the other civil rights leaders were undeterred. Charles Houston, recently put in charge of the litigation arm of the NAACP (Thurgood Marshall was his deputy), took a stab at explaining the black perspective to the president:

"When Negroes came back from the First World War and they marched down Fifth Avenue behind the James Reese Europe Band singing, "Over There, Over There" and so forth, the Negroes applauded them to the highest heaven," Houston said. "But it wasn't long before these very men were being lynched and abused by their own white countrymen. And this is a deep sore in the heart of the Negro and something has got to be done about it."

This line of argumentation appealed to the old artillery captain—so much so that the civil rights leaders were taken aback.

"Well, that's right, our boys who fight for our country are entitled to just treatment," Truman answered. "I *will* do something about it."[9]

Earlier, in his 1946 letter to Tom Clark, Truman had revealed that the fact that recently discharged servicemen were among the blacks being lynched and abused made the injustice of the situation much more clear-cut for him. The Georgia and Tennessee cases he referred to in that letter also involved black veterans.

The first occurred on February 25, 1946, when a black man named James Stephenson accompanied his mother, Gladys, into an appliance store in Columbia, Tenn., to complain that her radio had not been repaired properly. Billy Fleming, a white store employee, apparently found the Stephensons' attitude insufficiently deferential, and he followed them out into the street. If Fleming was looking for a fight, he got more than he bargained for. Although he was only nineteen years old, James Stephenson was a boxer in the U.S. Navy, from which he had recently been discharged after serving in the war. Fleming soon found himself back inside the store, having been knocked through a plate-glass window. Other whites joined the fracas, and Stephenson and his mother were arrested. They admitted fighting, were fined $50 apiece and, because they didn't have the cash, were taken to the county lockup. In the two decades before the war, three local black men had been murdered after being held in similar circumstances. One was shot in the courtroom after his acquittal, another was abducted and lynched shortly after being released from jail and a third was actually forcibly removed from the jail by a mob, which lynched him from the balcony of the courthouse itself.

In 1946, Columbia's blacks, which numbered 25 percent of the town, decided they were going to let nothing happen to Stephenson. As rumors swept the black community that a lynching was planned, black men armed themselves and fanned into the darkened street corners and alleys of the town. Black businessmen paid their bail, and the Stephensons were released; James was spirited out of town to Nashville. Nevertheless, the town erupted. Four white police officers who ventured into the black area to calm the gathering mob were shot and wounded. Tennessee Gov. James McCord sent in the Tennessee State Guard and troopers from the state highway patrol who rampaged through the black part of town, arresting over a hundred blacks, and eventually killing two of them. At the black-owned Morton Funeral Home, the patrolmen did $2,000 worth of vandalism, even writing the letters "KKK" in white powder across a closed blue coffin, an image that went around the country via a wire-service photograph.

Later that year, in Georgia, a gruesome lynching also made national news. Roger Malcolm, a black man from Walton County, Ga., was jailed after being charged with stabbing his white employer. On July 15, a mob demanded Malcolm's release from jail, apparently so they could lynch him. The sheriff initially refused, but eleven days later, he released Malcolm into the custody of Loy Harrison, a white landowner, who had allegedly posted Malcolm's bail so he could work on Harrison's farm. When Harrison drove to the jail, he had Malcolm's wife, Dorothy, and her brother, George W. Dorsey, and his wife, Mae Murray Dorsey, with him.

On the way back to town, Harrison's car was stopped by a mob of two dozen whites, who waved them over at gunpoint at a bridge over the Apalachee River, near a spot called Moore's Ford. Harrison reported that Roger Malcolm and George Dorsey were ordered from the car and led down a side road. Their wives began to scream, and the leader of the mob shouted, "Get those damned women, too!" The women, shrieking in horror, were then dragged out of the car. They were all shot many times. Harrison, whom the FBI suspected of being involved in planning the murders, was unharmed. He said he couldn't identify anybody, however, and no one was ever charged in the case. All four victims were in their twenties, and Dorothy Malcolm was seven months pregnant. One reason the case engendered such national revulsion and attention all the way to the White House, was that George Dorsey—his full name was George Washington Dorsey—was a decorated World War II veteran.

This was the context in which Truman, in December 1946, appointed a distinguished biracial panel to serve on a Commission on Civil Rights, headed by Charles E. Wilson, the president of General Electric. The announcement of the formation of this commission came in a December 5 executive order. It was accompanied by a White House press release called "Freedom From Fear," an allusion to one of the "four freedoms" articulated in a famous speech given by Franklin Roosevelt in 1941. The Truman White House was appropriating FDR's phrase for a highly specific purpose; the freedom from fear Truman was talking about was the freedom from lynching. Here are excerpts from that written presidential statement issued along with the executive order:

> Freedom From Fear is more realized in our country than in any
> other country on the face of the earth. Yet all parts of our popula-

tion are not equally free from fear. And from time to time, and in some places, the freedom has been gravely threatened. It was so after the last war when organized groups fanned hatred and intolerance, until, at times, mob action struck fear into the hearts of men and women because of their racial origin or religious belief.

Today, Freedom From Fear, and the democratic institutions which sustain it, are under attack. In some places, from time to time the local enforcement of law and order has broken down, and individuals, sometimes ex-servicemen and even women—have been killed, maimed, and intimidated.

The preservation of civil liberties is a duty of every government—state, Federal and local. . . . Yet, in its discharge of the obligations placed on it by the Constitution, the Federal government is hampered by Civil Rights statutes. The protection of our democratic institutions, and the enjoyment by the people of their rights under the Constitution require that these weak and inadequate statutes should be expanded and improved.

I have, therefore, issued today an Executive Order creating the Presidents Committee on Civil Rights and I am asking this committee to prepare for me a written report. The substance of this report will be recommendations with respect to adoption or establishment of legislation or otherwise of more adequate and effective means and procedures for the protection of the civil rights of the people of the United States. . . .

Eleven months later, on October 29, 1947, the Commission submitted a 178-page report, "To Secure These Rights," which is nothing less than a blueprint for where the civil rights movement—at least its legislative arm—would be headed for the next generation. The commission called for national anti-lynching laws, federal legislation doing away with the poll tax, making Roosevelt's Fair Employment Practices Committee (FEPC) permanent, integrating the armed forces and making the civil rights division of the Justice Department the driving executive branch office responsible for enforcement of these laws.

Truman hadn't waited for the report to begin speaking out. He drew attention to this issue twice in January of 1947, once when he was meeting with his hand-picked commission ("go to it!" he told them), and again in his 1947 State of the Union address. And in two speeches in a six-day span in the summer of 1947, Harry Truman swung the full power of the presidency behind civil rights. Truman brought other big guns along, at least rhetorically, for support. They included Jefferson, Lincoln and two Roosevelts—Franklin and Eleanor. The first of these Truman addresses came on June 29, 1947, on the steps of the Lincoln Memorial, where sixteen years later Martin Luther King would deliver his "I Have a Dream" speech. The occasion of Truman's address was the NAACP convention. This product of a nineteenth-century pro-Confederacy Missouri household warned his own ailing mother in advance that she wouldn't like his speech. Truman told her why, too: because he'd be quoting Abraham Lincoln. But he did it anyway.

"I should like to talk to you briefly about civil rights and human freedom," Truman said at the beginning of his Lincoln Memorial talk. "It is my deep conviction that we have reached a turning point in the long history of our country's efforts to guarantee freedom and equality to all our citizens." He continued, using the kind of blunt language on race no president had used since the man whose statue he was standing beside had occupied the white House:

> Recent events in the United States and abroad have made us realize that it is more important today than ever before to ensure that all Americans enjoy these rights. When I say all Americans I mean all Americans.
>
> The civil rights laws written in the early years of our Republic, and the traditions which have been built upon them, are precious to us. Those laws were drawn up with the memory still fresh in men's minds of the tyranny of an absentee government. They were written to protect the citizen against any possible tyrannical act by the new government in this country. . . .
>
> But we cannot be content with a civil liberties program which emphasizes only the need of protection against the possibility of tyranny by the Government. We cannot stop there. We must keep moving forward, with new concepts of civil rights to safeguard our heritage. The extension of civil rights today means, not protection of the people against the Government, but protection of the people by the Government.
>
> Our immediate task is to remove the last remnants of the barriers which stand between millions of our citizens and their birthright. There is no justifiable reason for discrimination because of ancestry, or religion, or race, or color. . . .
>
> The way ahead is not easy. We shall need all the wisdom, imagination and courage we can muster. . . . When past difficulties

faced our Nation we met the challenge with inspiring charters of human rights—the Declaration of Independence, the Constitution, the Bill of Rights, and the Emancipation Proclamation.

Walter White later said that when he heard Truman utter these words he thought of the Gettysburg address. Less than a week later, on Independence Day, Truman gave another speech expounding on his vision of what the Founders words required of Americans. This time, he was looking outward, to the rest of the world. But the message was similar. The Declaration was a call to universal human rights; and neither peace at home, nor peace abroad was possible without respect for those rights. If July 4 was a fitting day to give the speech, so was the venue. Truman went to Monticello to pay his respects to the man whose vision he was trying to implement, not needing to remind his audience that Jefferson hadn't managed to do it himself. Again, Truman made the connection between human rights in the United States for blacks and human rights throughout the world in and among the community of nations.

The Declaration of Independence was an expression of democratic philosophy that sustained American patriots during the Revolution and has ever since inspired men to fight to the death for their "unalienable rights." The standard phrase used by writers of Jefferson's day to describe man's essential rights was "life, liberty and property." But to Jefferson, human rights were more important than property rights, and the phrase, as he wrote it in the Declaration of Independence, became "Life, Liberty and the pursuit of Happiness."

The laws and the traditions of the colonies in 1776 were designed to support a monarchial system rather than a democratic society. To Thomas Jefferson the American Revolution was far more than a struggle for independence. It was a struggle for democracy. . . .

A second requisite of peace among nations is common respect for basic human rights. Jefferson knew the relationship between respect for these rights and peaceful democracy. We see today with equal clarity the relationship between respect for human rights and the maintenance of world peace. So long as the basic rights of men are denied in any substantial portion of the earth, men everywhere must live in fear of their own rights and their own security.

We have learned much in the last fifteen years from Germany, Italy, and Japan about the intimate relationship of dictatorship, aggression, and the loss of human rights. The problem of protecting human rights has been recognized in the Charter of the United Nations, and a Commission is studying the subject at this time. No country has yet reached the absolute in protecting human rights. In all countries, certainly including our own, there is much to be accomplished.

On October 29, 1947, Truman noted the receipt of his civil rights commission's report with a brief, but forceful statement. "I created this committee with a feeling of urgency," Truman began. "No sooner were we finished with the war than racial and religious intolerance began to appear and threaten the very things we had just fought for." Forgiving Truman his rhetorical tic—that racial and religious intolerance "began to appear" after the war—his statement is breathtaking. In twenty-six simple words, the plainspoken Missourian had connected the commission's work (in a report he had not yet read) to the work of the Founding Fathers, to the work performed by democracy's troops in World War II and to Americanism itself.

"In times past, where our American freedoms were threatened, groups of our citizens banded together and set out on paper the principles they felt would preserve freedom and the kinds of actions that would defend freedom," Truman added. "The Declaration of Independence was that kind of document, and I notice that the title of this report is taken from the Declaration of Independence. I hope this Committee has given us as broad a document as that—an American charter of human freedom in our time."

But if civil rights leaders in the United States were finding in Harry Truman an unlikely, but worthy, successor to Lincoln, southern Democrats were thinking along the same lines. It was not a realization that warmed their hearts. In 1948, Harry Truman reiterated his support for civil rights in his State of the Union address (January); sent civil rights legislation to Congress (February); integrated the armed forces of the United States by executive order (July) and agreed to a civil rights plank in the platform of the Democratic National Convention (also in July) held, fittingly, in Philadelphia. Truman reminded Americans that the war they had waged was a costly and consuming worldwide struggle against racism, and that racial discrimination itself was explicitly incompatible with American ideals. That the doctrine of white supremacy was, in a word, unpatriotic. And he did all this in an election year in which the electoral college votes of southern states were necessary to return him to the White House.

Meanwhile, almost all prominent southern Democrats warned that they would resist integration—the Democratic Party be damned. Letters with ugly racial slurs aimed at the president poured into the White House. Arkansas Gov. Ben Laney denounced Truman's civil rights message as "distasteful, unthinkable, and ridiculous." Led by Georgia Sen. Richard Russell, nineteen of the twenty-two U.S. Senators from the South vowed to "use every resource at our command" to block it. Truman's executive order, Russell said, constituted an "unconditional surrender . . . to the treasonable civil disobedience campaign organized by Negroes." Meanwhile, liberals, led by Hubert Humphrey, a thirty-seven-year-old firebrand, were coming at Truman from the other direction. The civil rights plank the White House had signed off on was slightly stronger than the 1944 plank, but the Humphrey forces wanted more. They introduced an amendment, consisting of the following provisions:

> We highly commend President Harry S. Truman for his courageous stand on the issue of civil rights.
>
> We call upon the Congress to support our President in guaranteeing these basic and fundamental American Principles:
>
> (1) the right to full and equal political participation;
>
> (2) the right to equal opportunity of employment;
>
> (3) the right to security of person;
>
> (4) and the right of equal treatment in the service and defense of our nation.

The president had been trying to avoid a walkout of southern delegations, and watching the convention on television, Truman didn't think Humphrey was doing him any favors. But the young mayor from Minneapolis certainly breathed life into what had been shaping up as a moribund convention by delegates who all seemed to expect that Truman would lose in November. In one of the great dramatic oratorical moments in American history, Humphrey rose to address the convention delegates in Philadelphia, to defend his amendment against the charge that it tried to do too much, too soon. Humphrey invoked the names of Jefferson, Roosevelt, Truman and the language of Lincoln (although he didn't attribute Lincoln's words, the Great Emancipator being a Republican).

"To those who say, my friends, to those who say, that we are rushing this issue of civil rights, I say to them we are 172 years late!" Humphrey thundered. "To those who say this civil-rights program is an infringement on states' rights, I say this: the time has arrived in America for the Democratic Party to get out of the shadow of states' rights and walk forthrightly into the bright sunshine of human rights!"

"This is the issue of the twentieth century," Humphrey added. "Let us not forget—let us do forget—the evil passions, the blindness of the past. In these times of world economic, political, and spiritual crisis, we cannot—we must not—turn from the path so plainly before us. That path has already led us through many valleys of the shadow of death. Now is the time to recall those who were left on that path of American freedom."

Pandemonium erupted in the hall. The Illinois and California delegations leapt to their feet and danced in the aisles, marching past glum southern delegates sitting on their hands. The amendment passed, and the southerners honored their threat, walking out of the convention, and reconvening in Birmingham, Ala., as the Democratic States Rights Party, known forevermore as the "Dixiecrats."

Their nominee for president was Gov. Strom Thurmond of South Carolina, who until then was building a reputation at home as something of a racial moderate.[10] Thurmond was careful then, and later, not to engage in overtly racialist appeals. But he didn't have to—it was all out there. Local newspaper clippings at the time reveal that this enthusiastic little rebel howdy-do in Birmingham featured the revival (by Ole Miss frat boys) of the "stars and bars" flag as a symbol for resistance; passionate nostalgia for the hallowed heroes of the Old Confederacy and a visceral enthusiasm for white supremacy that would have done the 1861 Secession Commissioners proud.

"It was a responsive, excited, sometimes hysterical crowd—and the convention orators made the most of it," the *Birmingham News* noted on its front page on Sunday, July 18, 1948. "The magic names were Robert E. Lee and Jefferson Davis. They never failed to bring swelling roars from the audience."

Meanwhile, Tuscaloosa Democrat Thomas Maxwell, who had previously called for "shipping the Negroes back to Africa," tried to whip up the crowd. Bull Connor, an Alabama delegate, brought the audience to its feet by introducing those who'd walked out of the Philadelphia convention while the band broke into "Dixie" and other Confederate Civil War fighting songs. Over in another corner of the convention, according to contemporary newspaper accounts, rabid William H. Murray, seventy-nine-year-old former governor of Oklahoma, was reading passages from his book, *The Negro's Place in Call of Race*, to college students from Ole Miss.

In the end, none of this hurt Truman who won his stunning, and narrow, come-from-behind victory over Thomas Dewey by polling one million more popular votes than Dewey and Thurmond combined, and earning 303 electoral college votes in the process, 114 more than Dewey—despite losing 39 electoral votes to the Dixiecrat ticket, which carried Alabama, Mississippi, South Carolina and Louisiana. In 1947, White House aide Clark Clifford had written Truman a heretical memo suggesting that civil rights could be a net plus for the Democratic ticket, that the loss of white segregationists' votes would more than be offset by northern liberals and blacks (where they could vote). The 1948 election returns proved Clifford's prophetic memo to be true. The alignment of the two major political parties had been upended in the first national election after the war. Just eleven years later, in 1957, former FDR assistants James H. Rowe and Thomas G. Corcoran warned Senate Majority Leader Lyndon Johnson (of Texas!) that if he failed to move through the Senate an Eisenhower-backed civil rights bill he could forget his presidential ambitions in 1960.[11]

Congress did pass—and Eisenhower did sign—a voting rights act in 1957, followed by another civil rights bill in 1960. And Eisenhower, the highest-ranking military officer during World War II, often cited the Founders' desires as part of his rationale for civil rights. Interestingly, when Ike brought up the context of war, it was usually the Cold War he was discussing, not World War II. In his 1956 State of the Union address, Eisenhower mentioned both civil rights and the right to pursue happiness. But he mentioned the latter by way of a contrast with communism. Likewise, when Eisenhower committed federal troops to uphold a federal court order integrating Central High School in Little Rock, Ark., he lamented that the mob in Little Rock had made America look ugly and hypocritical to the rest of the world.

"At a time when we face grave situations abroad because of the hatred that communism bears toward a system of government based on human rights, it would be difficult to exaggerate the harm that is being done to the prestige and influence, and indeed to the safety, of our nation and the world," Eisenhower said in a nationally televised address on September 24, 1957. "Our enemies are gloating over this incident and using it everywhere to misrepresent our whole nation. We are portrayed as a violator of those standards of conduct which the peoples of the world united to proclaim in the charter of the United Nations."

If Ike was responding to a new global challenge, that of communism, John F. Kennedy would also employ Jefferson's words to the same effect. But if World War II began to form less of the narrative foundation during the late fifties and early sixties for the civil rights movement, the Declaration of Independence itself did not fade in importance. The words written in 1776 in Philadelphia would be employed by Humphrey, Johnson, Kennedy and, most dramatically, by Martin Luther King Jr.

Kennedy's crucible on civil rights came in 1963 when he faced down Alabama Gov. George C. Wallace over integrating the University of Alabama. Earlier that year, he had signaled his intention to send to Congress another, more sweeping, civil rights bill. In that message to Congress, JFK began with a recitation of the many ways in which discrimination was holding back black Americans.

"No American who believes in the basic truth that 'all men are created equal, that they are endowed by their Creator with certain unalienable Rights,' can fully excuse, explain or defend the picture these statistics portray," Kennedy's message said. "Race discrimination hampers our economic growth by preventing the maximum development and utilization of our manpower. It hampers our world leadership by contradicting at home the message we preach abroad. It mars the atmosphere of a united and classless society in which this nation rose to greatness. It increases the costs of public welfare, crime, delinquency and disorder. Above all, it is wrong."

In a prime time radio and television address on June 11, Kennedy repeated much of what was in his message to Congress:

> One hundred years of delay have passed since President Lincoln freed the slaves, yet their heirs, their grandsons, are not fully free. They are not yet freed from the bonds of injustice. They are not yet freed from social and economic oppression. And this nation, for all its hopes and all its boasts, will not be fully free until all its citizens are free.

Later that year, six civil rights groups banded together to organize a historic march on Washington.[12] Martin Luther King's electrifying "I

Have a Dream" speech is what most people remember from that swelter-
ing August day at the Lincoln Memorial, as well they should. But King
had used some of the speech's most evocative imagery in earlier sermons.
Moreover, King wasn't the only one who discussed the Declaration of
Independence. The speakers who preceded him invoked the Declaration,
the Emancipation Proclamation and the 13th, 14th, and 15th Amendments. In the process, they demonstrated conclusively that the ancient
debate between William Lloyd Garrison and Frederick Douglass had
been settled in Douglass'—and Lincoln's—favor. America didn't need a
new Declaration of Independence or a new Constitution, a new history—or even new songs of freedom. The ones it had in place served the
cause of civil rights just fine.

"My country 'tis of thee, sweet land of liberty, of thee I sing," King
intoned. "Land where my fathers died, land of the Pilgrims' pride . . ."

King used this construction as early as 1957, along with the "Let
freedom ring . . . from every hill and molehill in Mississippi!" construct
that was the crescendo of his "I Have a Dream" speech. And earlier in
1963, in his "Letter from Birmingham Jail," King had quoted Lincoln
and Jefferson, and asserted that what Negroes were doing was nothing
short of fighting for their birthrights as Americans. "Abused and scorned
though we may be, our destiny is tied up with America's destiny," he
wrote. "Before the pilgrims landed at Plymouth, we were here. Before
the pen of Jefferson etched the majestic words of the Declaration of Independence across the pages of history, we were here. . . . If the inex-
pressible cruelties of slavery could not stop us, the opposition we now
face will surely fail."

On August 28, 1963, on the Mall in Washington, he amplified on
this point in words that galvanized a nation:

> In a sense we have come to our nation's capital to cash a check.
> When the architects of our great republic wrote the magnificent
> words of the Constitution and the Declaration of Independence,
> they were signing a promissory note to which every American was
> to fall heir.
>
> This note was a promise that all men, yes, black men as well
> as white men, would be guaranteed to the inalienable rights of life,
> liberty, and the pursuit of happiness.
>
> It is obvious today that America has defaulted on this promis-
> sory note insofar as her citizens of color are concerned. Instead of

honoring this sacred obligation, America has given the Negro people a bad check, a check that has come back marked "insufficient
funds."

But we refuse to believe that the bank of justice is bankrupt.
We refuse to believe that there are insufficient funds in the great
vaults of opportunity of this nation. So we have come to cash this
check, a check that will give us upon demand the riches of freedom
and security of justice.

The following year, Martin Luther King won the Nobel Peace
Prize, although when those who lived through these events think back
on them what they tend to dwell on is that John F. Kennedy's assassination presaged Martin's own death five years later. But King and Ralph
Abernathy and the other leaders of the civil rights movement had faced
death threats, and seen death and assumed that they might die for their
cause. But the cause went on anyway, and in March of 1965, Lyndon
Johnson sent his historic Voting Rights bill to Congress with these
words: "This was the first nation in the history of the world to be
founded with a purpose. The great phrases of that purpose still sound in
every American heart, North and South: 'All men are created equal'—
'Government by consent of the governed'—'Give me liberty or give me
death!' Well, those are not just clever words, or those are not just empty
theories. In their name Americans have fought and died for two centuries, and tonight around the world they stand there as guardians of our
liberty, risking their lives."

Buried in Lyndon Johnson's largely forgotten eloquence is an implication that the words of Jefferson and the other Founders, however
powerful and original, are so familiar to Americans that they are taken
for granted. It was certainly true, even as early as 1965, that the "guardians of liberty" Johnson was referring to—the soldiers in Korea, Germany, and most especially Vietnam—were not being given their due by
their countrymen. But in addition to complacency, there is another inherent tension in how human beings relate the words of the Declaration
of Independence to their lives: the words in it are so original, and so
powerful, that no U.S. president, no administration, no generation, has
anything like a copyright on them. The words of the Preamble can be
used on both sides of a question, whether that question is the Vietnam
War or reproductive rights or war in Iraq, and it can be used by people,
any people, who think they are being left behind. This was a problem, if

you want to call it that, from the very beginning. "Remember the Ladies," Abigail Adams counseled her husband in 1776, as he made his way to Philadelphia. He didn't do so, even though she chided him in as charming and gentle a way as possible:

> Do not put such unlimited power into the hands of the Husbands. Remember all Men would be tyrants if they could. If perticuliar care and attention is not paid to the Laidies we are determined to foment a Rebelion, and will not hold ourselves bound by any Laws in which we have no voice, or Representation.
>
> That your Sex are Naturally Tyrannical is a Truth so thoroughly established as to admit of no dispute, but such of you as wish to be happy willingly give up the harsh title of Master for the more tender and endearing one of Friend. Why then, not put it out of the power of the vicious and the Lawless to use us with cruelty and indignity with impunity. Men of Sense in all Ages abhor those customs which treat us only as the vassals of your Sex. Regard us then as Beings placed by providence under your protection and in immitation of the Supreem Being make use of that power only for our happiness.[13]

Adams responded in the same playful tenor as his wife. "We are obliged to go fair, and softly, and in Practice you know We are the subjects," he replied. "We have only the Name of Masters, and rather than give up this, which would compleatly subject Us to the Despotism of the Peticoat, I hope General Washington, and all our brave Heroes would fight."

Adams deflected his wife's restrained entreaties for women's suffrage with good-natured humor, which was in keeping with the wholesome and reciprocal love that characterized their marriage. Each truly was the others' "endearing Friend." But there is a serious point here, which Adams—with uncharacteristic obtuseness—actually refers to without seeming to fully comprehend.

"As to your extraordinary Code of Laws, I cannot but laugh," his letter to Abigail began. "We have been told that our Struggle has loosened the bands of Government every where. That Children and Apprentices were disobedient—that schools and Colledges were grown turbulent—that Indians slighted their Guardians and Negroes grew insolent to their Masters. But your Letter was the first Intimation that another

Tribe more numerous and powerfull than all the rest were grown discontented."

Well, yes, this is the long and short of it. Jefferson's words are so potent, they are a kind of nightingale's song to the human ear. Anyone who has been denied freedom and who hears that song wants to sing it himself—or herself—forever. In 1848, American abolitionist Lucretia Mott was denied permission to speak at the world antislavery conference in London, because she was a woman, even though she was an official delegate. This seems almost perversely comical, like a guy in a wheelchair trying to trip a blind man. But Mott wasn't a woman to take such a slight passively. The same year, she teamed with fellow abolitionist Elizabeth Cady Stanton to draft a feminist manifesto. It begins with a Jeffersonian preamble and segues deftly into a bill of particulars that makes King George look benign by comparison to other men:

> When, in the course of human events, it becomes necessary for one portion of the family of man to assume among the people of the earth a position different from that which they have hitherto occupied, but one to which the laws of nature and of nature's God entitle them, a decent respect to the opinions of mankind requires that they should declare the causes that impel them to such a course.
>
> We hold these truths to be self-evident: that all men and women are created equal; that they are endowed by their Creator with certain inalienable rights; that among these are life, liberty, and the pursuit of happiness; that to secure these rights governments are instituted, deriving their just powers from the consent of the governed. Whenever any form of government becomes destructive of these ends, it is the right of those who suffer from it to refuse allegiance to it, and to insist upon the institution of a new government, laying its foundation on such principles, and organizing its powers in such form, as to them shall seem most likely to effect their safety and happiness. . . . The history of mankind is a history of repeated injuries and usurpations on the part of man toward woman, having in direct object the establishment of an absolute tyranny over her. To prove this, let facts be submitted to a candid world.
>
> He has never permitted her to exercise her inalienable right to the elective franchise.
>
> He has compelled her to submit to laws, in the formation of which she had no voice.
>
> He has withheld from her rights which are given to the most ignorant and degraded men—both natives and foreigners.

> Having deprived her of this first right of a citizen, the elective franchise, thereby leaving her without representation in the halls of legislation, he has oppressed her on all sides. . . .

It was another seventy-two years before the 19th Amendment guaranteed women the right to vote. Other rights for women were still longer in coming, but in the end, the Declaration of Independence was used to good effect, namely, to trump the failings of the Constitution. But these lessons come hard, and must be learned again and again. And they are not always as clear-cut as in the case of women's rights.

On May 1, 2003, an influential centrist Democrat named Will Marshall wrote an op-ed piece for the *Washington Post* praising 2004 Democratic presidential contenders Joseph Lieberman, Richard Gephardt, John Edwards, and John F. Kerry for their votes in favor of the congressional resolution authorizing the invasion of Iraq. Dubbing them "Blair Democrats" after British Prime Minister Tony Blair, Marshall said approvingly that in demonstrating a willingness to "use force in the national interest" the trio was moving the Democratic Party "away from McGovernism and back to its internationalist roots."

This was, of course, a reference—and not a flattering one—to George S. McGovern, the Democrats' 1972 presidential standard-bearer who won the party's nomination and who subsequently campaigned on a platform of ending American involvement in the Vietnam War. It would seem a fair example. Although the pacifist thread in American liberalism certainly predates McGovern's candidacy for president, the current leftist brew of multinationalism mixed with a dash of isolationism dates to the Vietnam era, as do many of the modern Democratic Party structures that determine party policies and party nominees. Moreover, in early 2003 McGovern—at the age of eighty—was agitating against George W. Bush's invasion plans for Iraq, employing the arguments of the lessons of Vietnam himself. Still, Will Marshall ran into a slight problem: the *Washington Post* is McGovern's hometown paper, and he didn't like being the foil of Marshall's column. McGovern promptly penned a blistering response that ran in the *Post* on May 12.

"I first used force in the national interest during World War II, when I flew 35 combat missions in Europe," McGovern wrote by way of rebuttal. "American involvement in that war was clearly in our national interest, and that is why I volunteered at the age of 19 to be part of it. It is true that I opposed the American war in Vietnam, but not because I had ceased to be an internationalist. That war was a disastrous folly, as all literate people now acknowledge. . . ."

Both men have a point. Marshall's was that his party has become so reflexively antiwar that even the attacks of September 11, 2001, awakened only about half of the Democratic Party's establishment. This fact was underscored in the early debates among the Democratic presidential hopefuls of 2004, where the "peace" candidates were the ones who received the loudest applause from the liberal activists who participate early in the process. Marshall is not alone in believing that this dynamic has potentially perilous implications for his party. On the other hand, McGovern is hardly out of line in raising skeptical questions about congressional resolutions giving the president carte blanche to wage war whenever he chooses. McGovern also noted that the difference between "pre-emptive war" and "aggression invasion" is a thin line, adding that measuring a nation's commitment to "internationalism" by how many troops its sends abroad is a dubious standard. "By that test, Adolf Hitler would be the greatest internationalist of the 20th century," he quipped.

Finally, McGovern employed Jefferson to make his point. "I have always thought America to be the greatest country on earth," McGovern wrote. "One of the reasons I think so is because of our great founding fathers, including Thomas Jefferson, who spoke of 'a decent respect to the opinions of mankind.' Is there any doubt that the opinion of mankind was overwhelmingly against our wars in Vietnam and Iraq?"

John F. Kennedy, Lyndon Johnson and Richard Nixon—two Democrats and a Republican—always cast the Vietnam War as a fight for freedom. The people of South Vietnam wanted to live free they said, unfettered by a brutal and totalitarian Communist dictatorship. For their part, officials of North Vietnam, and their Soviet allies, stressed the right of the Vietnamese people to live independent of colonial domination. In a sense the two sides were talking past each other, and doing so deliberately, for the cause had been joined on the battlefield. But in hindsight, it's certainly possible to imagine that the Communists, whether in Hanoi or Moscow, believed they could influence American attitudes by appealing to what they found most salient about the spirit of 1776—revolution against a foreign power. The first year Kennedy was president, Leonid Brezhnev and Nikita Khrushchev sent him a message of greeting on the Fourth of July. "Personally and on behalf of the Soviet people we send to the American people, and to you personally, our sincere congratulations on the occasion of this important date in the life of the American people, namely, the 185th anniversary of achieving their independence," the telegram said. Surely, the United States' adversaries underestimated Americans' commitment to freedom around the world. But they never underestimated the power of the words that America's Founders sent forth into that world with the proclamation of their independence.

Harry Truman had been president less than six months when Ho Chi Minh declared his nation's independence from France—and from a U.N.-brokered deal to partition Vietnam. In a September 2, 1945, speech crafted with a wary eye toward the United States, Ho Chi Minh, a devoted Communist, told his people, "All men are created equal. They are endowed by their Creator with certain inalienable rights, among these are Life, Liberty, and the pursuit of Happiness. This immortal statement was made in the Declaration of Independence of the United States of America in 1776. In a broader sense, this means: 'All the peoples on the earth are equal from birth, all the peoples have a right to live, to be happy and free.'"

8

Pursuit of Knowledge

In 1972, John McCain and his fellow prisoners of war learned, quite by accident, that Apollo 11 had reached its glorious destination. This was two years after Neil Armstrong had taken his giant step for mankind, but the captured Americans only found out about it when "Hanoi Hannah," the official Voice of Vietnam, repeated in her daily broadcast piped into the prison camp a snippet of a speech by George McGovern: The Democratic presidential nominee had criticized the United States for putting a man on the moon but failing to end the Vietnam War. The McGovern sound bite was intended to demoralize the POWs, but, because it contained the nugget about the moon landing, it had the opposite effect.

"It was wonderful," McCain recalled later. "We were happy as hell."[1]

McCain's spontaneous reaction to the sheer joy of discovery would have pleased the Founding Fathers, especially Jefferson, who in a nostalgic letter to Adams late in life applied the word "Argonauts" to himself, Adams and the other patriots of 1776. Jefferson couldn't have known that two centuries later NASA astronauts would undertake voyages every bit as dangerous as Jason and his intrepid explorers of Greek mythology. Or could he? In 1793, when he saw a hot air balloon that was fancied by its owner only as entertainment, Jefferson's mind immediately anticipated the possibilities for air travel. He wrote to his daughter Martha that he coveted one of those dirigibles "to travel in, as instead of 10 days I should be within 5 hours of home." In 1802, at the dawn of the steam locomotive, Jefferson took notice of the new machine and wrote a letter to James Sylvanus McLean anticipating the automobile. He was a hundred years ahead of himself.

Such futuristic contemplations were characteristic of Jefferson's scientific bent, just as his reference to the Argonauts would have been a typical literary reference for him (and for Adams as well). Neither man believed their education in the classics was incidental to their success in the great enterprise of Revolution. It is a conceit we freely grant them today, as evidenced by a Library of Congress wing containing a display called American Treasures. The specific treasures housed there are rotated by the curators from time to time, but one part of the exhibit—the part that commemorates Jefferson's gift to the library of his own vast collection of books—is permanent.

"For Jefferson," the text of the exhibit reads, "the pursuit of happiness and the pursuit of knowledge were synonymous." In this he was not alone.

Jefferson is remembered by educators for founding the University of Virginia and for saying that a nation that expects to be ignorant and free "expects what never was and never will be." But many of the Founders performed similar deeds and expressed similar sentiments. The first three presidents, in particular, demonstrated repeatedly that they believed the pursuit of happiness was inexorably tied to the pursuit of learning.

George Washington helped found the Alexandria Academy, the first free school in Virginia, gave a friend the sizeable sum of one hundred pounds so the friend's son could attend college, and deeded $20,000 in property to the founding of what would become Washington & Lee College in Virginia. In a 1790 letter to the Hebrew Congregation of Newport, Rhode Island—a letter that is famous today because in it Washington extols religious freedom—the first president also cites "wisdom" as the necessary component for Americans "to become a great and happy people."

And in his first State of the Union address, Washington reports to Congress: "Nor am I less persuaded, that you will agree with me in opinion, that there is nothing which can better deserve your patronage, than the promotion of Science and Literature. Knowledge is in every country the surest basis of publick happiness."

Earlier, John Adams had written into the Constitution of the Commonwealth of Massachusetts a provision calling on the state to educate all its citizens. Jefferson's chestnut about the incompatibility of ignorance and freedom was codified in the Adams-written Massachusetts Constitution this way:

Wisdom, and knowledge, as well as virtue, diffused generally among the body of the people being necessary for the preservation of their rights and liberties; and as these depend on spreading the opportunities and advantages of education in the various parts of the country, and among the different orders of the people, it shall be the duty of legislatures and magistrates, in all future periods of this commonwealth, to cherish the interests of literature and the sciences, and all seminaries of them; especially the university at Cambridge, public schools and grammar schools in the towns; to encourage private societies and public institutions, rewards and immunities, for the promotion of agriculture, arts, sciences, commerce, trades, manufactures, and a natural history of the country; to countenance and inculcate the principles of humanity and general benevolence, public and private charity, industry and frugality, honesty and punctuality in their dealings; sincerity, good humor, and all social affections, and generous sentiments among the people.

For the most part, Adams' fellow Argonauts concurred with his encompassing description of what education could do for a free people. Jefferson, it is no surprise to learn, competed with Adams over who had the idea first. In an October 28, 1813, letter to Adams, Jefferson takes pains to inform his New England pen pal that in the first session of the Virginia legislature after the passage of the Declaration of Independence he authored a resolution calling for the "general diffusion of learning." If this proposal had passed into law in Virginia, Jefferson adds, "our work [in Williamsburg] would have been compleat."

In this instance, Jefferson's recollections are mostly accurate. The record shows that he had indeed long agitated for such measures, and continued to do so after Independence. In a 1787 letter to James Madison from Paris, Jefferson registered his objections to the new Constitution (chiefly they were two: that there is no Bill of Rights and that Jefferson thinks presidents should be term-limited), while closing with an upbeat assessment for the new Republic and a passionate call for general education of the populace: "Above all things," Jefferson wrote his fellow Virginian, "I hope the education of the common people will be attended to; convinced that on their good sense we may rely with the most security for the preservation of a due degree of liberty."

To family friend Mann Page Jr., Jefferson wrote (in 1795) that "if anything could ever induce me to sleep another night out of my own house," it would have been for the very cause that Page had summoned

Jefferson: "the education of our youth." And as late as 1821, Jefferson was still agitating for a university system to complement the College of William and Mary in his native state. "Nobody can doubt my zeal for the general instruction of the people," he wrote from Monticello to General James Breckenridge. "Who first started that idea? I may surely say, myself. Turn to the bill in the revised code, which I drew more than forty years ago, and before which the idea of a plan for the education of the people, generally, had never been suggested in this State. . . . If we cannot do every thing at once, let us do one at a time."[2]

Four years later, in a letter to William Green Munford, Jefferson wrote, "[S]cience can never be retrograde; what is once acquired of real knowledge can never be lost. To preserve the freedom of the human mind then and freedom of the press, every spirit should be ready to devote itself to martyrdom; for as long as we may think as we will, and speak as we think, the condition of man will proceed in improvement."

Then, as now, there were less momentous feelings associated with the quest of knowledge; to some, it simply brought its practitioners pure joy. "In general, happiness was understood to mean being at peace with the world in the biblical sense, under one's own 'vine and fig tree,'" said David McCullough, in *The Course of Human Events,* his Jefferson Lecture in the Humanities. "But what did they, the Founders, mean by the expression, *pursuit of happiness?*"

McCullough proceeds in the prestigious lecture, delivered May 15, 2003, to answer this question:

> It didn't mean long vacations or material possessions or ease. As much as anything it meant the life of the mind and spirit. It meant education and the love of learning, the freedom to think for oneself. Jefferson defined happiness as "tranquility and occupation." For Jefferson, as we know, occupation meant mainly his intellectual pursuits. . . . For Washington, happiness derived both from learning and employing the benefits of learning to further the welfare of others. John Adams, in a letter to his son John Quincy when the boy was a student at the University of Leiden, stressed that he should carry a book with him wherever he went. And that while a knowledge of Greek and Latin were essential, he must never neglect the great works of literature in his own language, and particularly those of the English poets. It was his *happiness* that mattered, Adams told him. "You will never be alone with a poet in your pocket."

There is also a component to the pursuit of knowledge that entails action instead of scholarship. Here, too, Jefferson was vigorous. As president, he launched his personal secretary, Meriwether Lewis, along with Captain William Clark and thirty-three other men, on their arduous expedition to explore the lands of the Louisiana Purchase. Jefferson's own written directives to Lewis instruct him to search for navigable waters to the Pacific Ocean. As the explorers discovered, the Rocky Mountains dispelled the dream of a "Northwest Passage," but Jefferson's own obsessions about this epic journey centered on his pure intellectual curiosity more than upon the commercial possibilities of intracontinental water travel.

Jefferson's intellectual curiosity was eclectic, and he made no clear differentiation between "basic" research—science for its own sake—and "applied" research. He insisted that Lewis master the latest scientific methods and theories before beginning the journey. Consequently, Lewis traveled throughout the Eastern seaboard learning the latest in botany, zoology and paleontology before setting out on May 14, 1804. The very name of the expedition, *Corps of Discovery*, which was chosen by Jefferson, conveys the excitement its patron experienced in anticipation of learning new things. Lewis and Clark were explorers; Monticello was Mission Control.

It is a model that has persisted through the centuries, although George W. Bush doesn't personally devise the experiments to be performed on the space shuttle. "Jefferson's instructions to find out about this and to measure that, and to describe this, in some ways is the same set of instructions we give the astronauts," Robert Archibald, president of the National Council of the Lewis & Clark Bicentennial, noted in a 2003 interview with *Newhouse Newspapers*. Jefferson specifically directed Captain Lewis to delve into dozens of areas of inquiry, ranging from the possessions and domestic arrangements of the Indians they encountered to the plants, animals and minerals they were able to classify. "The story of the *Corps of Discovery* began with a rigorous formulation of questions," observes Michael Umphrey, director of the Montana Heritage Project. "But the big question, of course, was, 'What was out there?'"

It is the cosmic question American presidents have posed from the beginning of the Republic, in peacetime and in wartime, for reasons that range from the infinitely sublime to the decidedly practical. U.S. presidents have spoken for more than two centuries about the pursuit of knowledge as though it were an American birthright—and its own reward. This is true if the presidents were intellectuals, such as Adams, Jefferson, John Quincy Adams, Madison, Monroe, Teddy Roosevelt, Woodrow Wilson, Calvin Coolidge and Bill Clinton. And it is true if they were men of action: Jackson, Grant, Teddy Roosevelt (he's on both lists), Eisenhower, Ford, Reagan and both Bushes. If pressed to explain why taxpayers' money should be spent on explorations into the unknown, or in adding to mankind's store of knowledge about the past, or in the pursuit of pure science, the nation's chief executives fall back on the Jeffersonian truism that America's success as a free people is ultimately dependent on the presence of an informed electorate. And they invariably use this definition in a most expansive way.

"We come here today . . . to continue the guarantee of progress in the future by continuing knowledge of progress in the past," said Calvin Coolidge while addressing the University of Pennsylvania at the July 7, 1921, convocation of the American Classical League. "We come to proclaim our allegiance to those ideals which have made the predominant civilization of the Earth. We come because we believe that thought is the master of things. We come because we realize that the only road to freedom lies through a knowledge of the truth." He went on:

> It is impossible for society to break with its past. It is the product of all which has gone before. We could not cut ourselves off from all influence which existed prior to the Declaration of Independence and expect any success by undertaking to ignore all that happened before that date. The development of society is a gradual accomplishment. Culture is the product of a continuing effort. The education of the race is never accomplished. It must be gone over with each individual and it must continue from the beginning to the ending of life.

While Coolidge was advocating the intrinsic value of acquiring knowledge for its own sake, he was simultaneously postulating that such knowledge cannot do otherwise than help advance the cause of the promise of life, liberty and the pursuit of happiness. Often citing the Declaration, this is the justification presidents have offered—and which Americans accept—for the risking of lives and the spending of vast sums of money to expand the intellectual horizons of the human race and the physical horizons of the galaxy. In so doing, the nation's leaders tap into a deep national faith in the positive power of new technology. This faith constitutes nothing less than a quiet confidence that "American know-how" will come to the nation's rescue. It will save troops on Midway Island—and in Baghdad—and it will protect us at home, defending what presidents invariably call "our way of life."

If one parses these presidential remarks carefully, America's chief executives are offering two competing visions about the value of education and the pursuit of higher learning. The first rationale is that acquiring knowledge for its own sake is its own, enriching experience. The second is that the pursuit of knowledge is a necessary component of making the United States a supreme military and economic power. These explanations are quite different, but if presidents are aware of this dichotomy, they have been untroubled by it. In fact, these vastly differing impulses about learning often coexist inside the head of the same president at the same time. Ronald Reagan envisioned outer space as an ideal locale for laser-guided weapons that could shoot down intercontinental ballistic missiles. Yet Reagan also ruminated enthusiastically in National Security Council meetings that discovering alien life elsewhere in the galaxy might someday convince human beings of the trivial nature of their differences here on Earth. And he made these observations in the very context of discussing his proposal for a space-based, antimissile system. Bill Clinton, who kept the funding for that program alive for all eight years he was in office, expressed the exact same sentiments.

Through it all runs a thread: U.S. presidents have felt, and acted on, a notion that Americans have something like a divine responsibility to keep exploring, no matter the danger and no matter the cost. Over the years many voices have been raised, such as George McGovern's, questioning the advisability of looking at the stars when there is so much to do right at our feet. But this argument has never moved presidents.

* * *

In the twenty-first century, the phrase "the world's only super-power" has become a kind of synonym for the United States. And let there be no mistake; this is a status attained by wealth, technological superiority and by a willingness to expend that riches and that technology on advanced weaponry. This was not always a national ethic. America's entry into World War I may have been inevitable after the Germans' sinking of the Lusitania, but it's important to remember that that event occurred on May 15, 1915. The United States didn't enter the war for nearly two years.

"What President Wilson did in 1915 was send a letter of complaint to the German government," observed G. Calvin Mackenzie, a government professor at Colby College in Maine.[3] The reason, Mackenzie pointed out, is that Wilson could do little else. The president couldn't convene an emergency meeting of the National Security Council because the executive office of the presidency didn't yet exist. He couldn't give a broadcast to the nation, because radio hadn't been invented. He couldn't scramble aircraft carriers or fighter planes for the same reasons or even battleships of contemporary vintage because the United States hadn't bothered to build them. Wilson presided over a nation, still affected in its martial attitudes by the carnage of the Civil War, which had simply not seen fit to arm itself for modern warfare. While the *Guns of August* of 1914 were firing on the other side of the Atlantic, the United States basically owned the guns of the 1800s. America had no tanks, no gas masks, few modern rifles, no modern naval vessels—and a standing army of only 130,000 men. The few troopers with combat experience had gained that experience in the Indian Wars on the plains of the American West.

"This was a nineteenth-century army," Mackenzie notes.

After World War I ended, America decommissioned itself again, but the lesson that it was perilous to be caught flat-footed on the issue of modern weapons technology had taken root in Washington. On April 3, 1939—five months before the Nazis invaded Poland—Roosevelt signed the National Defense Act of 1940, which authorized the administration to spend $300 million building up the Army Air Corps' strength to 6,000 planes. This was prudent legislation; at the time the Army Air Corps fielded only 52 heavy bombers and some 160 fighters. But Roosevelt and Congress quietly transformed the United States into a stunning military power. Total appropriations for defense grew from $500 million in 1939 to $26 billion in 1941. Also, by the time of the Pearl Harbor attack a conscription measure was already law. It wasn't going to take two years—or even two months—to gear up for war this time.

In his January 6, 1942, State of the Union address, Roosevelt told his countrymen that the United States would produce 45,000 bombers, dive-bombers and fighter planes that year—and 100,000 combat aircraft in 1943. "In this year, 1942, we shall produce 45,000 tanks; and to continue that increase so that next year, 1943, we shall produce 75,000 tanks," Roosevelt said. And so it went, with FDR ticking off his fantastic wish list of American manufacturing power—for antiaircraft guns, merchant shipping, everything that could be needed for war. "And I rather hope that these figures which I have given will become common knowledge in Germany and Japan," he added brazenly.

But it wasn't only the raw tonnage of this war materiel that ultimately brought World War II to a decisive close. It was also the technology—the knowledge—behind the arsenal as well. Initially, and with Roosevelt's urgings, this know-how was employed in assembly-line techniques that allowed the United States to produce more planes, tanks and guns—and do so faster—than any other nation in the world. As the war raged on, American inventiveness and creativity would also be channeled into upgrading the killing power of the machines themselves. In at least seven addresses to the American people during World War II, Roosevelt lauded American technology—the word FDR used was "ingenuity"—as the key to Allied success.[4] The first time came in a May 26, 1940, radio address before the United States was even in the war. "Every day's fighting in Europe, on land, on sea and in the air, discloses constant changes in methods of warfare. We are constantly improving and redesigning, testing new weapons, learning the lessons of the immediate war and seeking to produce in accordance with the latest that the brains of science can conceive," Roosevelt said. "We are calling upon the resources, the efficiency and the ingenuity of the American manufacturers of war material of all kinds—airplanes, tanks, guns, ships and all the hundreds of products that go into this materiel."

In a radio address on October 5, 1944, Roosevelt said, "We have seen our civilization in deadly peril. Successfully we have met the challenge, due to the steadfastness of our allies, to the aid we were able to give to our allies, and to the unprecedented outpouring of American manpower, American productivity, and American ingenuity. . . ." And in his last State of the Union address, Roosevelt explained that technology would save American lives and win the war. "[W]e have constant need for new types of weapons, for we cannot afford to fight the war of today or tomorrow with the weapons of yesterday," FDR said in that January 6, 1945, speech. "Almost every month finds some new development in electronics which must be put into production in order to maintain our technical superiority—and in order to save lives. . . . If we do not keep constantly ahead of our enemies in the development of new weapons, we pay for our backwardness with the life's blood of our sons."

This was a lesson learned from the Germans themselves. At the time the United States entered the war, Nazi Germany was not only the world's preeminent military power, but its most advanced technological power as well. Hitler put submarines, state-of-the-art tanks, long-range rockets and even jet airplanes into the field before the Allies. And they continued to develop deadly new weapons even while fighting a two-front war against the world and while their own nation was subjected to round-the-clock bombing raids.

In 1944, American and British bomber crews returned to their bases in England after flying sorties over Germany asking each other, "What *was* that thing?" They were talking about the Luftwaffe's Messerschmitt-262, the first true jet fighter, which ran on diesel fuel and attained unheard-of speeds in excess of 500 miles-per-hour, all while carrying four 30-mm cannons and two dozen unguided rockets. This lethal aircraft was developed in 1942 and 1943, but primarily because of Hitler's meddling only 300 of the 1,400 such planes built by the Germans made it into combat, most not until the war was effectively over.[5]

The saga of the Messerschmitt-262 demonstrated one of democracy's strengths when it came to harnessing the power of the human mind. While the Nazi dictator was micromanaging his war effort down to the types of guns his planes would carry, the democratically elected Roosevelt exhorted Americans as from Mount Olympus to build more and better armaments, and to do so ever-faster, rarely delving into operational details. In the process FDR instigated a spirited competition between the branches of the services and some dozen aircraft manufacturers to see who could build the most planes, the fastest planes and the deadliest planes. The result was the creation of an airborne armada the likes of which the world had never seen.

Even Americans who are not aviation buffs know something of the glorious history of the legendary P-51 Mustang.[6] But that was just the beginning. Tens of thousands of other fighter planes, the design of which improved virtually on a monthly basis, flooded the skies over Europe and the Pacific. They included Lockheed's P-38 Lightning, the first twin-engine fighter and the killer of more Japanese planes than any fighter; Republic Aviation's P-47 Thunderbolt, which carried eight machine guns and could climb to 42,000 feet; the Vought F4-U Corsair, the favorite of Marine Corps pilots; the Grumman 4-F Wildcat, the plane flown by Navy Lt. Edward H. "Butch" O'Hare when he won the Medal of Honor for shooting down five enemy bombers in a single flight while saving the carrier USS *Lexington*; and the next generation Grumman, the F6F-3 Hellcat, with its amazing 19:1 kill ratio. The Hellcat was the plane Navy pilots were flying when they shot down some 350 Japanese planes—with a loss of only 30 American aircraft—in the great "Marianas Turkey Shoot" of June 19–20, 1944.[7] This arsenal was complimented by some 10,000 Grumman Avengers, which were large, carrier-based torpedo bombers that carried an electrically powered gun turret, four 500-pound bombs, and a crew of three. The Avenger was the plane piloted by a young Navy flier named George Bush when he was downed by antiaircraft fire. Bush bailed out, but his two fellow crew members lost their lives.[8]

Those were the fighters. More lethal still were the bombers. By the end of the war, the United States also had put into service some 12,700 B-17 bombers. These "Flying Fortresses" were complemented by 18,000 bigger and more powerful B-24 "Liberators," and finally by the mighty B-29 "Superfortresses" used to incinerate Tokyo and to drop the atomic bomb—the ultimate technological breakthrough of the war—on Hiroshima and Nagasaki.

It has become fashionable in recent times on college campuses for junior professors to assert confidently that it was no coincidence that the first and only atomic devices ever detonated in war were used against nonwhite people. This is a convenient claim, but a lazy one, for its implications are false. Certainly to the people of Hiroshima and Nagasaki the choice of their cities was cruelly capricious, but the Manhattan Project was begun because European scientists, many of them Jewish, had come out of *Germany* in the 1930s with deeply disturbing reports of Nazi efforts to harness the atom for purposes of war. On August 2, 1939, Franklin Roosevelt received a letter from Albert Einstein alerting him to a new field of physics that opened up the possibility of "the construction of . . . extremely powerful bombs of a new type." Einstein added that German scientists were repeating "some of the American work on uranium . . ." and had commandeered the uranium that had previously been for sale in a Czech mine. Einstein's fears were well founded. By 1941, the Nazi war machine had purview over a heavy-water plant, high-grade uranium compounds, a half-built cyclotron, and had retained a stable of brilliant chemists and engineers. Nuclear weapons were coming. The question was who was going to get them first. J. Robert Oppenheimer, the brilliant Harvard-trained chemist and physicist who headed the Manhattan Project and who later became an advocate of nuclear arms control, had no illusions about what inaction would have meant. "We [scientists] were aware of what it might mean if [the Germans] beat us to the draw in the development of the atomic bombs," he wrote later. Among the American scientists and European ex-pats working in New Mexico and Oak Ridge, Tenn., there was little question about the target of any terrible new weapon they were racing to develop: It was the Third Reich.

By the time the atom bomb was ready for deployment, the decision whether to use it fell to Truman. He appears to have made up his mind without much agony. "The Japanese began the war from the air at Pearl Harbor," Truman told the nation in an August 6, 1945, statement announcing the dropping of the bomb. "They have been repaid many fold."

But that was not the only moral of the story. What America had done, Truman suggested, was nothing less than winning the war of knowledge. And even if that victory was put to awful purpose—if Americans had not won the competition to unlock the power of the atom—those bombs could have been dropped on the United States.

"The battle of the laboratories held fateful risks for us as well as the battles of the air, land and sea, and we have now won the battle of the laboratories as we have won the other battles," Truman added in his statement to the American people. "Beginning in 1940, before Pearl Harbor, scientific knowledge useful in war was pooled between the United States and Great Britain, and many priceless helps to our victories have come from that arrangement. Under that general policy the research on the atomic bomb was begun. With American and British scientists working together we entered the race of discovery against the Germans."

This was, Truman said, a victory not only for the democracies of the world, but a triumph of the democratic system itself:

> But the greatest marvel is not the size of the enterprise, its secrecy, nor its cost, but the achievement of scientific brains in putting together infinitely complex pieces of knowledge held by many men in different fields of science into a workable plan. And hardly less marvelous has been the capacity of industry to design, and of labor to operate, the machines and methods to do things never done before

so that the brain child of many minds came forth in physical shape and performed as it was supposed to do. Both science and industry worked under the direction of the United States Army, which achieved a unique success in managing so diverse a problem in the advancement of knowledge in an amazingly short time. It is doubtful if such another combination could be got together in the world. What has been done is the greatest achievement of organized science in history.

Fifty-eight years later, George W. Bush would make a similar claim—and with the added evidence of more humane bombs. Speaking to returning sailors and airmen aboard the USS *Abraham Lincoln,* Bush said, "Today, we have the greater power to free a nation by breaking a dangerous and aggressive regime. With new tactics and precision weapons, we can achieve military objectives without directing violence against civilians. No device of man can remove the tragedy from war; yet it is a great moral advance when the guilty have far more to fear from war than the innocent."

If Einstein's letter was a wakeup call for America to invest its best minds in the pursuit of knowledge, a second fire bell came ringing into the night a dozen years after the war ended. Until that moment Americans assumed that they lived in the most scientifically advanced nation in the history of the world. But they were jolted out of their complacency by the "beep, beep, beep" sound that came, unbidden, over their radios on the evening of October 4, 1957. The beeps were the sounds of the diminutive, 184-pound Soviet satellite Sputnik orbiting the Earth.[9]

"Never before," wrote Daniel J. Boorstin, "had so small and harmless an object created such consternation." Forty years later, at an anniversary conference on the event, Robert Smith, chairman of the Department of Space History at the National Air and Space Museum, added: "The launch of Sputnik was one of the defining moments in the twentieth century."

The day after it happened, President Eisenhower grilled his aides on why the United States was caught with its scientific smocks down around its knees. Months later, Ike launched NASA. Congress funded NASA—and a whole lot more as well. Senate Majority Leader Lyndon Johnson convened hearings in the Armed Services Committee to review the state of the nation's existing defense and space programs—and found them disorganized and underfunded. After a three-part *New York*

Times series lauded the supposedly superior Soviet educational system, spending on science-related education tripled in this country. Ike's successor in the Oval Office, Jack Kennedy, ran for president in 1960 on the platform of closing the "missile gap." After winning the election, JFK committed the American nation to vanquishing the moon.

"To a remarkable degree, the Soviet announcement changed the course of the Cold War," NASA chief historian Roger D. Launius wrote forty years after the fact. "Two generations after the event, words do not easily convey the American reaction to the Soviet satellite. Without Sputnik, it is all but certain that there would not have been a race to the moon, which became the centerpiece contest of the Cold War."

Perhaps all of this is true. Yet, it's a matter of historical record that the American people—and their presidents—have *always* been deeply enamored of the skies and the stars, and exploration of almost all descriptions. None other than President Theodore Roosevelt was an early patron of Orville and Wilbur Wright. It was during TR's administration that the aeronautical division of the U.S. Army Signal Corps, which would become the Army Air Corps (and, in time, the U.S. Air Force), was formed. And when word finally reached Roosevelt in 1908 that the Wright Brothers were for real and that they had bested the French in a much-watched international competition, Roosevelt himself made certain before he left office that they received a $25,000 contract to build a plane for the army.[10]

Calvin Coolidge was the last president to never fly in an airplane, but he was the first to recognize the vast possibilities for commercial air travel. Coolidge pushed for federal legislation to help organize the industry, emphasized civil aviation in two successive State of the Union addresses, and greeted Charles Lindbergh with a stirring speech upon Lindy's return from Paris after his solo trans-Atlantic flight. ("On behalf of his own people, who have a deep affection for him, and have been thrilled by his splendid achievements, and as President of the United States, I bestow the distinguished Flying Cross, as a symbol of appreciation for what he is and what he has done, upon Col. Charles A. Lindbergh," Coolidge said. He went on to describe Lindbergh as "intelligent, industrious, energetic, dependable, purposeful, alert, quick of reaction, serious, deliberate, stable, efficient, kind, modest, congenial, a man of good moral habits and regular in his business transactions.")

Coolidge was a legendary spendthrift, but he didn't scrimp on spending tax dollars for air travel. He was only the first of many. When

Franklin Roosevelt draped the Medal of Honor around Butch O'Hare's neck on April 21, 1942, FDR asked the pilot "what kind of fighter plane" he needed to defeat the Japanese. "Something that will go upstairs faster," the war hero replied. And it was done.

One reason it was done is that when it comes to conquering the skies there is always an impulse in addition to national defense at work among Americans. This was true even in the frantic days after Sputnik. Yes, Kennedy used the issue—and the dubious "missile gap" scare that Sputnik engendered—to run for office in 1960. But in making his appeal to his countrymen about why Americans should expend the treasure and risk it would take to go to the moon, Kennedy began with practicality but shifted seamlessly to poetry.

In his famous May 25, 1961, speech laying down the marker of landing a man on the moon and bringing him home safely "before the decade is out," Kennedy described the entire endeavor as an extension of the Cold War.

"If we are to win the battle that is now going on around the world between freedom and tyranny, the dramatic achievements in space which occurred in recent weeks should have made clear to us all, as did the Sputnik in 1957, the impact of this adventure on the minds of men everywhere, who are attempting to make a determination of which road they should take," Kennedy said. "We take an additional risk by making it in full view of the world, but as shown by the feat of astronaut [Alan] Shepard, this very risk enhances our stature when we are successful."

The following year, however, speaking at Rice University in Houston, JFK made an appeal based on loftier instincts: "But why, some say, the moon? Why choose this as our goal? And they may well ask, 'why climb the highest mountain?' Why, thirty-five years ago, fly the Atlantic?" Then he answered his own question.

"We *choose* to go to the moon," Kennedy said. "We choose to go to the moon in this decade and do the other things, not because they are easy, but because they are hard, because that goal will serve to organize and measure the best of our energies and skills, because that challenge is one that we are willing to accept, one we are unwilling to postpone, and one which we intend to win, and the others, too."

The president who ushered in the New Frontier ended this speech by recalling the words of famed British explorer George Mallory, who, when asked why he wanted to climb Mount Everest, replied, "Because it is there."

"Well, space is there, and we're going to climb it, and the moon and the planets are there, and new hopes for knowledge and peace are there," JFK added. "And therefore, as we set sail, we ask God's blessing on the most hazardous and dangerous and greatest adventure on which man has ever embarked."

Invoking George Mallory was Kennedy's way of reminding Americans that fulfilling the pull of such basic curiosity, no matter how laudable, is not without risks. Mallory himself had died on Everest, as Kennedy noted. And in this way were Americans warned from the outset that there would be days like January 27, 1967.

That day had started out so well for President Johnson. LBJ had presided over an East Room signing ceremony of a treaty with the Soviet Union and Great Britain barring nuclear weapons from space—a pact that he himself had pushed for.

"This treaty means that the moon and our sister planets will serve only the purposes of peace and not of war," Johnson said that morning. "It means that orbiting man-made satellites will remain free of nuclear weapons. It means that astronaut and cosmonaut will meet someday on the surface of the moon as brothers and not as warriors for competing nationalities or ideologies."

He considered this accord, LBJ confided to his wife Lady Bird, to be one of the greatest accomplishments of his presidency. At that moment, the Apollo 1 crew—astronauts Virgil I. "Gus" Grissom, Edward H. White II and Roger Chaffee—were going through launch pad checks on their doomed spaceship. A little more than two hours later, while Johnson was in the family quarters of the White House listening to a toast from his outgoing commerce secretary, the president was handed a note: "The first Apollo crew was under test at Cape Kennedy and a fire broke out in the capsule and all three were killed . . . Grissom, White, and Chaffee."

Grissom, who had nearly drowned in a splashdown, knew his chosen profession was dangerous. He tried, as Kennedy had done, to acclimate his countrymen to that fact. "If we die, we want people to accept it," Grissom had said publicly. "We're in a risky business, and we hope that if anything happens to us, it will not delay the program. The conquest of space is worth the risk of life."

But brave words did not cushion the impact on Johnson. "The shock," he said later, "hit me like a physical blow."[11] LBJ attended Grissom and Chaffee's January 31 funeral at Arlington National Cemetery, sitting with the widows, but said nothing publicly. The first lady attended White's interment at West Point, and likewise did not speak at the service.

Johnson was uncharacteristically philosophical about outer space, and found the notion of extending the Cold War to the heavens deeply troubling. The night of the Sputnik launch he was hosting a barbeque at his ranch in Texas. As he pondered the news, he went with some of his guests down to the banks of the Pedernales River, where the view of the stars was always impressive.

"Now, somehow, in some new way, the sky seemed almost alien," he recalled later. "I also remember the profound shock of realizing that it might be possible for another nation to achieve technological superiority over this great country of ours."

In time, the Russians would no longer be the animating reason for American space travel—if they truly ever were—and Johnson's soaring rhetoric about cosmonauts and astronauts working together would prove prophetic. But before that day arrived, on January 28, 1986, disaster struck the U.S. space program for a second time. This time the fire came after liftoff and with a schoolteacher, Christa McAuliffe, aboard as one of the seven Argonauts. In the intervening years, the job description of the presidency had changed: Ronald Reagan could not realistically, as LBJ had done, have the White House simply issue a terse, three-sentence statement of condolence and grieve quietly. Cosmic questions were raised by the deaths of those aboard the *Challenger,* and Reagan was expected to address them. He did so, in what is remembered as one of the rhetorical highlights of his presidency.

"Nineteen years ago, almost to the day, we lost three astronauts in a terrible accident on the ground," Reagan said. "But we've never lost an astronaut in flight; we've never had a tragedy like this. And perhaps we've forgotten the courage it took for the crew of the shuttle; but they, the Challenger Seven, were aware of the dangers, but overcame them and did their jobs brilliantly. We mourn seven heroes."

John Kennedy had reminded Americans that Mallory had died in his quest; and Reagan reminded them that the same fate had befallen Sir Francis Drake. "In his lifetime, the great frontiers were the oceans," Reagan said, adding:

> To the families of the seven: We cannot bear, as you do, the full impact of this tragedy. But we feel the loss, and we're thinking about

you so very much. Your loved ones were daring and brave, and they had that special grace, that special spirit that says, "Give me a challenge, and I'll meet it with joy." They had a hunger to explore the universe and discover its truths. They wished to serve, and they did. They served all of us. We've grown used to wonders in this century. It's hard to dazzle us. But for twenty-five years the United States space program has been doing just that. We've grown used to the idea of space, and perhaps we forget that we've only just begun. We're still pioneers. . . .

Borrowing from a World War II–era sonnet, Reagan concluded by saying: "We will never forget them, nor the last time we saw them, this morning, as they prepared for their journey and waved goodbye and 'slipped the surly bonds of Earth' to 'touch the face of God.'"

In his autobiography, Reagan described that day as "one of the hardest I had to spend in the Oval Office." He had called the parents and wives of many American servicemen, but he said a president never gets used to these calls, which he described as weighing on his shoulders "like a ton of iron." Christa McAuliffe had been to the White House with the other teachers vying for the honor of going to space; Reagan himself had announced her as the choice.[12] And yet, President Reagan never wavered on whether this tragedy would induce Americans to turn back from space. Nor have any of the others.

"The cause in which they died will continue," George W. Bush said on February 1, 2003—just hours after learning of the loss of the space shuttle *Columbia* and its crew. "Mankind is led into the darkness beyond our world by the inspiration of discovery and the longing to understand. Our journey into space will go on."

To hear presidents tell it, space exploration is a metaphor for what is best about America. Exploring space signifies both that the United States enjoys freedom of thought and that the nation is rich enough and advanced enough to pursue those thoughts all the way to the stars.

"This cause of exploration and discovery is not an option we choose; it is a desire written in the human heart," was how Bush put it at the Houston memorial service for the crew of the *Columbia*. "We are that part of creation which seeks to understand all creation. We find the best among us, send them forth into unmapped darkness, and pray they will return. They go in peace for all mankind, and all mankind is in their debt."

Notwithstanding such eloquence, practical, earthly reasons remain for the United States not to abandon space travel, and those reasons are the same as they were in John Kennedy's day. The loss of the *Columbia* came between the war in Afghanistan and the war in Iraq. Indeed, the first news reports about the disaster took pains to point out that it couldn't have been terrorism, although there were places in the world where people hoped it was just that. The unspoken point was that surrendering the dream of space exploration carried a potential risk to America's prestige. A second reason, also unremarked upon publicly at the White House, is that Ronald Reagan's dream of an antiballistic missile shield is still very much alive in the military budget process, and it is assumed that some of what is learned in the space program will prove useful to that program.

Once again, exploration is the nexus where a president's altruistic and martial impulses merge. It was Reagan's private musings about the immorality of the Cold War doctrine of mutually assured destruction—along with his viewing of the 1983 antiwar hit movie *War Games*, which deals with a nearly accidental nuclear launch—that led Reagan to propose building his SDI missile defense program.[13]

To underscore the point that protecting, not incinerating, the civilian populations of the world was what SDI was about, Reagan offered to share the technology, as it was developed, with the Soviet Union. Reagan's offer was met with skepticism by liberals in Congress, by the nuclear disarmament establishment, inside the Kremlin and among the news media. Reagan's own national security officials harbored deep doubts about the president's gambit as well, with some privately assuring reporters that Reagan had misspoke when he abruptly proposed giving the Russians access to SDI technology. Reagan insisted publicly that he definitely meant what he said, and that it was his own advisers who didn't quite get the point. But even in private White House meetings Reagan had trouble convincing his own policy aides of his altruism. He tried anyway:

What if aliens from outer space invaded Earth, Reagan would ask his advisers. In that event wouldn't mankind quickly put aside all sectarian, racial and ideological differences and work together? Reagan intended this as metaphor—he wasn't actually thinking of using Star Wars technology on UFOs—but Gen. Colin L. Powell found Reagan's fixation on extraterrestrials unnerving. Powell worked vigilantly to keep this theme out of Reagan's speeches, with only limited success. In 1985 in

Geneva, Reagan tried his interplanetary invasion theory out on Mikhail Gorbachev, who responded by changing the subject. When Reagan returned home, he regaled a high school group in Fallston, Md., by telling them how he'd talked to Gorby about what would happen if Earthlings were attacked "by an alien race."

"Just think how easy his task and mine might be in these meetings that we held, if suddenly there was a threat to this world from some other species from another planet outside in the universe," Reagan told the teenagers. "We'd forget all the little local differences that we have between our countries and we would find out once and for all that we really are all human beings here on earth together." Powell became convinced that Reagan, who was not only a former actor, but a science fiction fan as well, got fixated on the notion of an attack from outer space from another movie, a 1951 sci-fi film called *The Day the Earth Stood Still.* Upon hearing Reagan wax eloquent about the ecumenical benefits to man from an interplanetary threat, the general would roll his eyes and tell his staff, "Here come the little green men again."[14]

If he was watching television on July 15, 1996, Powell must have done a double take when President Clinton, in an interview with Tom Brokaw to help launch MSNBC *Internight,* began taking questions from the audience in a new demonstration of the communicative powers of the Internet. One question came from a moviegoer who'd seen that summer's sci-fi blockbuster *Independence Day* and who wanted to know, "Could we really fight these guys off or what Mr. President?"

An animated Clinton responded that he "loved" the movie, had seen it at the White House with actor Bill Pullman, who plays the role of president in the movie, which features alien invaders who incinerate the White House and the Capitol.

"We'd fight them off," Clinton assured his questioners. "We'd find a way to win." But then he kept going: "The good thing about *Independence Day* is there's an ultimate lesson for that—for the problems right here on Earth," Clinton said. "We whipped that problem by working together with all these countries. And all of a sudden the differences we had with them seemed so small . . . and I wish that we could think about that when we deal with terrorism and when we deal with weapons proliferation."

Three days later, Clinton mentioned *Independence Day* again, this time—as Reagan had done—to an audience of teenagers. "You know you see story after story about how the movie audiences leap up and cheer at the end of the movie when we vanquish the alien invaders," he said. "These people have all of a sudden put aside the differences that seem so trivial once their existence was threatened. . . ."

As he neared the end of his second term in office, Clinton's thoughts seemed to drift toward little green men more and more, particularly in the context of race relations. He brought it up, unprompted, with Bob Deans of Cox Newspapers in an October 2000 interview that dealt primarily with hate crimes and race relations. At one point, Deans asked Clinton a question that he later characterized as being "a philosophical question about harmony and reconciliation." At the end of a lengthy answer, Clinton invoked *Independence Day* to make the point that skin color would seem a small difference indeed if our planet were attacked by aliens. Not sure what to make of this—and nervous about what a headline writer would do with it—Deans never mentioned it in his story. This was just as well with White House assistant press secretary Jake Siewert, who sat in on the interview (and who remembers squirming when the president drifted off into interplanetary invasions).

But Clinton—like Reagan before him—was becoming irrepressible on this point.

The very next night, Clinton mentioned it again, twice, in a talk at a ceremony honoring the best public schools in the nation. "I told somebody the other day," Clinton said apparently referring to Deans. "I said, 'You know I get so angry at all these conflicts around the world and these expressions of hatred here at home based on race or religion or sexual orientation. If we were being attacked by space aliens, like in that movie *Independence Day,* we'd all be looking for a foxhole to get in together and a gun to pick up together.'"

The audience sort of chuckled along with the president. But later in the same talk, Clinton said, almost defensively, "You all laughed when I said this before . . . but you know if we were attacked by space aliens, we wouldn't be playing these kinds of games." This time, realizing Clinton was not talking about the movies or spacemen, but metaphorically, about racism, his audience listened respectfully.

All this was more amusing in the days before Arab extremists commandeered four loaded jetliners on suicide missions and crashed two of them into the Twin Towers and aimed the other two toward Washington. One hit the Pentagon and the other, presumably, was headed for the White House or the Capitol, just like in the movie. In other words, dangerous beings with incomprehensibly alien views *have* tried to attack us, and they came not from outer space, but from the dark corners of our own world. And because their cause is sectarian and nationalist those attacks did not bring the world together, but divided it even more. But if September 11 has focused us less on the stars, history suggests that this is a temporary condition. George W. Bush said as much at the Houston ceremony for the fallen astronauts. One reason for this is that presidents, and the citizens they lead, sense that looking heavenward is a healthy inclination and that all the answers to life's mysteries cannot be found only in the day-to-day doings of the secular world.

The presidency is a job that has been held by exactly forty-two other people, and certainly the eleven who've served in the nuclear age have tended to feel responsible for the entire world. This tends to make them philosophical; and with the stakes so high, this is a good thing.

For Reagan, the overwhelming threat was communism. Clinton considered the great cancer to be racism. Clearly, George W. Bush is focused on terrorism. The desire for otherworldly inspiration is strong. Clinton once ruminated, in an interview with CBS anchorman Dan Rather, that he gazed sometimes from the Truman balcony at the eerily lit Jefferson Memorial and wished Jefferson would come alive so he could ask for advice.[15] Bush, in an interview with another anchorman, NBC's Tom Brokaw, alluded to his habit of getting on "bended knee" to pray for God's guidance.[16]

Some of George W. Bush's critics find his strong religious views unsettling. A more tolerant and historically sound—to say nothing of spiritual—view is that Bush's expressions of faith are common for presidents and that it is reassuring to most Americans when presidents look to the stars, or the future—or the Almighty—for guidance. And there is certainly something that is both faithful to America's past and forward-looking when presidents use the language of Jefferson to lobby for spending more money on education and ingenuity.

Bill Clinton, speaking in a time of peace, invoked the language of the Declaration in calling for more federal spending on education, technology and an innovative future that included space travel. Only a month after his first inauguration, Clinton told a group of workers at a Boeing plant: "My whole goal in this economic program is to try to change the priorities of this country so people can pursue what the founding fathers wanted—life, liberty, the pursuit of happiness—by making change our friend." In his first July 4 as president, Clinton went to Independence Hall in Philadelphia, and said, "Thomas Jefferson wrote that blistering Declaration of Independence knowing that his ideals challenged his country to change."

And in a September 22, 1993, address to a joint session of Congress, Clinton amplified even more on what this phrase meant to him: "Our forebears enshrined the American dream of life, liberty and the pursuit of happiness," he said. "Every generation of Americans has worked to strengthen that legacy, to make our country a place of freedom and opportunity, a place where people who work hard can rise to their full potential, a place where the children could have a better future. From the settling of the frontier to the landing on the moon, ours has been a continuous story with challenges defined, obstacles overcome, new horizons secured. That is what makes America what it is and Americans what we are."

By 1998, with reelection behind him and his famous "bridge to the 21st Century" looming in front of him, Clinton had fine-tuned his definition. At an American Association for the Advancement of Science convention in Philadelphia, Clinton said flatly that the nation's ability to fulfill Jefferson's challenge to pursue happiness depended, foremost, on our willingness to pursue knowledge.

"Our restless quest for knowledge, which has been one of America's defining traits since we got started right here in Philadelphia, will quicken," Clinton said. "And more than ever before, the strength of our economy, the health of our environment, the length and quality of our lives; in short, the success of our continuing pursuit of happiness, will be driven by the pursuit of knowledge."

In hindsight, Clinton's words seem to have been delivered in a period best described as a lull. The space program proceeded without mishap in Clinton's tenure; America was between wars with Iraq, although it didn't know it then. Likewise, the nation was already steeped in the war on terror, although it didn't really understand that, either. But the pursuit of freedom, like that of knowledge, is never without risk. This has always been true. In some important ways, Jefferson was farther away from Lewis and Clark than Richard Nixon was from the astronauts on the moon.

On July 1, 1976, President Gerald R. Ford paid homage to this point—and to Americans' commitment to the stars—at the dedication of the Smithsonian's National Air and Space Museum.

"The story of powered flight is an American saga. The amazing American achievements in air and space tell us something even more important about ourselves on Earth. The hallmark of the American adventure has been a willingness—even an eagerness—to reach for the unknown," Ford said that day. "In the early seventeenth century, a few fragile vessels—like the *Discovery* in 1607 and the *Mayflower* in 1620—sailed across three thousand miles of unfriendly sea. Their passengers and crew knew far less about their destination than the American astronauts knew at lift-off about the lunar landscape, a quarter million miles away."

The occasion was part of a weeklong series of speeches Ford gave on the Bi-Centennial. These speeches constitute a little-known treasure in the American canon, and this was one of the best of them.

"For three and a half centuries, Americans and their ancestors have been explorers and inventors, pilgrims and pioneers, always searching for something new—across the oceans, across the continent, across the solar system, across the frontiers of science, beyond the boundaries of the human mind," Ford said. "The pilgrims feared the perils of the voyage and the misery of the unfamiliar land. But the sentiments that sustained them were recorded by Governor William Bradford '. . . that all great and honorable actions are accompanied with great difficulties, and must be both enterprised and overcome with answerable courage. . . .' Behind them lay the mighty ocean, separating them from the world they knew, and before them lay an untamed wilderness."

Ford continued:

Three and a half centuries later, that wilderness has been transformed. A continent once remote and isolated now supports a mighty nation, a nation built by those who also dared to reach for the unknown. The discovery of this continent was unprecedented. It opened the eyes of mankind, showing them the world was bigger than they had thought.

Our nation's birth was unprecedented as well. A new form of government was begun which would allow for change by future generations, yet secure basic rights to men and women. The chance to earn property was given to those who had never had property, education to those who had never been educated. . . . By the time of the Revolution, there were more colleges and universities in America than in the British Isles. The men who wrote our Declaration of Independence were probably the best-educated rebels and revolutionaries history had ever seen. When Independence was won, the growth of free public education in the United States amazed the world and quickened our pace in science and technology. . . .

But the best of the American adventure lies ahead. Thomas Jefferson said, "I like to dream of the future better than the history of the past." So did his friendly rival, John Adams, who wrote of his dream, ". . . to see rising in America an empire of liberty, and a prospect of two or three hundred millions of freemen, without one noble or one king among them. You say it is impossible. If I should agree with you in this, I would still say—let us try the experiment."

I can only add—let the experiment continue.

9

True Happiness

Hubert H. Humphrey never realized his longtime ambition to become president of the United States, but it did not defeat or demoralize him. For more than thirty years Humphrey was the apostle of an undefined theory that he called "the politics of joy." In his unmistakable high-pitched, singsong Midwestern voice he would ceaselessly remind audiences on the campaign trail—and Hubert loved to speak on the stump—that America was the only place where pursuing your dreams was official government policy. Although Humphrey's career is not well known among young people anymore, when he died in 1978 some sixty thousand souls braved the cold January weather in Washington to trek to the Capitol Rotunda to view his flag-draped casket.

"Today is a day to celebrate the birth of Christ, the birth of Dr. Martin Luther King Jr., and the death of the great warrior," explained one of those mourners, Roy M. Smith, an African-American bus driver from Takoma Park, Md. "I'm sorry to see Hubert Humphrey pass on." At the memorial service, President Carter proclaimed Humphrey "the most beloved of all Americans." Vice President Walter F. Mondale, Humphrey's fellow Minnesotan, added through his tears, "Hubert was criticized for proclaiming the politics of joy, but he knew that joy was essential to us, and is not frivolous. He loved to point out that ours is the only nation to officially declare the 'pursuit of happiness' as a national goal."

It's a splendid goal. And even as American leaders and American citizens have understood the words in the Declaration to be a call for liberation, so, too, has Jefferson's specific admonition to seek happiness become the very essence of the American identity. "The Giver of life," Jefferson himself wrote in a 1782 letter to James Monroe, "gave it for happiness and not for wretchedness." But this raises some profound questions, questions that run deep whether posed by presidents or bus drivers. Questions as basic as: Is such a pursuit really attainable? If so, how does one go about it? What makes men and women truly happy? And do lives of people like Hubert Humphrey—lives of public service—provide evidence about the nature of genuine happiness?

"All men are created equal before fishes," avid outdoorsman Herbert Hoover observed dryly while secretary of commerce during the Roaring Twenties. "The pursuit of happiness," he added, "obviously includes the pursuit of fish."

That's one answer. To Bob Doyle, of the Massachusetts chapter of the National Organization to Reform Marijuana Laws, happiness would consist of a relaxation in the nation's drug laws so he would be free to cultivate a small amount of cannabis for his own personal use. "Pursuit of happiness—it's my right. It's your right. It's our right," Doyle maintains. "Not the right to happiness, of course, but the pursuit thereof. You pursue it your way, I'll pursue it mine. As long as we do no harm to one another, the pursuit is guaranteed."

That's another answer, and it sounds not unlike Ronald Reagan's formulation in a 1967 debate with Robert F. Kennedy. "[E]very American or every person has the right, is born with the right to life, liberty and the pursuit of happiness," Reagan said. "But my pursuit of happiness, if it comes from swinging my arm, I must stop swinging my arm just short of the end of your nose."

Gerald R. Ford considered good humor one of the keys to happiness. "Laughter and liberty go well together," he said on July 2, 1976.[1] He noted that Americans had cracked jokes "as they went into battle." But this good-humored bravery may not be a new idea, or a strictly American theme. In 400 B.C.—or 2,400 years before Maya Angelou made the same point after 9/11—Thucydides urged his fellow Greeks, "Be convinced that to be happy means to be free and to be free means to be brave."

In a wartime speech to the American Historical Association, Arthur M. Schlesinger said that hard work was the key component of Americans' happiness. Schlesinger even suggested (this was in 1942) that Americans were so dedicated to their work—"this worship of work" he called it—that they had never really learned to play. But in a footnote that Schlesinger seems to believe is harbinger that things are about to change, the famed historian noted that in 1940 the American people owned more automobiles than bathtubs. "The pursuit of happiness was transformed into the happiness of pursuit," Schlesinger quipped. "The nation appears to be on the point of solving the riddle of perpetual motion."

He was half-kidding, but in a March 2000 speech at the U.S. Capitol, Republican statesman Bob Dole not only employed his comedic wit to make his point about the pursuit of happiness, but also advanced the proposition that such a pursuit is always aided and abetted by humor itself. "I happen to believe that it is easier to get things done in [Congress] with a sense of humor," said Dole, a successful former Senate majority leader and an unsuccessful vice presidential (1976) and presidential (1996) nominee. "After all, the United States is probably the only country on Earth that puts the pursuit of happiness right after life and liberty among our God-given rights. Laughter and liberty go well together. Indeed, as a weapon against injustice, ridicule can be as effective as moral outrage."

Dole deftly spoofed himself for his singularly ineffectual 1996 campaign slogan aimed at Bill Clinton ("Where's the outrage?"), contrasting it with the more effective wit of former Senator Barry Goldwater, who after being blackballed by an anti-Semitic country club in Phoenix, wisecracked, "Since I'm only half-Jewish, can I join if I only play nine holes?" Dole continued:

> Long before there was an American dream, there was a dream of America. Jefferson captured it in a single, luminous sentence, when he declared, "men may be trusted to govern themselves without a master." Loving liberty as much as they hated tyranny, Jefferson and his contemporaries believed that the greatness of America lay, not in the power of her government, but in the freedom of her people. At the same time, their democratic faith led them to reject bloodlines and bank accounts alike as accurate measures of a man's worth. . . .

And yet, bank accounts are very much part of the equation. Although Americans originally rebelled for the cause of mercantile freedom, Jefferson's suspicion of manufacturing and modern commerce was due, in part, to what he believed was the corrupting influence of capital markets. He worried that America would become a nation of monetary "jugglers" and "gamblers" who manipulated the economy with their "tricks with paper." Adams agreed, responding that he wondered whether human nature itself "could ever bear Prosperity."

There is a profound paradox here, one that cuts to the core of what the American experiment is all about. Those who warn about the corroding effects of wealth are often already rich, or, if not rich, then sufficiently comfortable. This was true of Jefferson and Adams, and of latter-day prophets as well. There is nothing inherently hypocritical about this, or even illogical. The luxury of worrying about the effects of too much money is itself a luxury. University of Illinois psychologist Ed Diener has broken this phenomenon down to a basic proposition. While examining what gives individuals a sense of well-being—what makes them happy— Diener discovered that poverty produces unhappiness, but that the inverse is not necessarily true: wealth does not, by itself, make people happy. This would seem to be common sense, but Diener and numerous other clinical psychologists have reams of actual research to back it up. The correlation between a person's bank balance and their level of happiness is "surprisingly weak," University of Michigan researcher Ronald Inglehart concluded after he helped direct a landmark study on the well-being of some 170,000 people in sixteen nations.

Tocqueville noticed in the early part of the nineteenth century that America's abundance created an unusual cultural dynamic in the new nation, that manifested as a social pressure for ever more material goods. "Men easily attain a certain equality of condition," he noted, "but they can never attain as much as they desire." Today, we would call this the trap of "keeping up with the Joneses," and it is so ingrained as a false god that Madison Avenue has subtle appeals designed to circumvent it. One example is the recent Lexus advertisement proclaiming, "Whoever said money can't buy happiness isn't spending it right."

David G. Myers, a Hope College professor of psychology who has studied happiness, concedes that the Lexus pitch is a clever ad, but goes on to say that research shows it to be palpably and empirically wrong. "Once [people are] comfortable, more money provides diminishing returns," Myers says. "The second piece of pie, or the second $100,000 never tastes as good as the first."

It is certainly true that the Guadalcanal Marines weren't talking about gluttonous amounts of pie or two pies per Marine, but people *do* need the first bite—it is hard to be hungry and be happy at the same time. Eleanor Roosevelt, who attracted her husband's interest while teaching immigrant children calisthenics in a Settlement House in New York City, put it this way: "Happiness may exist under all conditions, given the right kind of people and sufficient economic security for adequate food and shelter."[2]

The obvious conclusion, then, is that the prerequisite to happiness depends, as Eleanor Roosevelt noted, on a modicum of creature comfort. But if the needy aren't happy and if individuals who have attained material ease aren't necessarily happy either—well, then can anybody be happy? Eleanor Roosevelt had an answer to that, as well. "Happiness is not a goal, it is a by-product," she said. "Paradoxically, the one sure way not to be happy is deliberately to map out a way of life in which one would please oneself completely."[3]

That this would be Eleanor's solution is no surprise given her own life's work. She believed, and acted on that belief, that those with the material means to do so can achieve true satisfaction only by going into the world and extending opportunities for others to have them as well. In so doing, she was true to the earliest version of the American Dream.

"To be really American has always meant to see something beyond America," postulates Andrew Delbanco, author of *The Real American Dream: A Meditation on Hope*. And, he adds, beyond oneself as well. "This is what the Puritans meant in insisting that if we fail to contribute to some good beyond ourselves, we condemn ourselves to the hell of loneliness."

Although expressing himself in more secular terms, Columbian University historian Eric Foner agrees that this kind of generosity of spirit is consistent with Jeffersonian principles. Also commenting in 2001 on the concept of "the American Dream," Foner said, "Independence rather than riches was the essence of the American dream for a long time."

Francis Hutcheson, one of those Scottish Presbyterians whom Garry Wills demonstrated had great influence on Jefferson, put it this way: "The surest way to promote private happiness [is to perform] "useful actions."[4] Or, as the more secular American philosopher Mark Twain rendered it, "The best way to cheer yourself up is to try to cheer somebody else up."[5]

This is, of course, an idea much older than America—at least as old as the bible—but it is one in constant need of restoration and restating. All American presidents have demonstrated that they are mindful of this, regardless of political affiliation or the conditions of the world at the moment. "Where there is suffering, there is duty," George W. Bush said in his stylish 2001 inaugural address. "Many in our country do not know the pain of poverty, but we can listen to those who do. And I can pledge our nation to a goal: When we see that wounded traveler on the road to Jericho, we will not pass to the other side."[6]

The same principle is as true of nations as is true of individuals. In *his* first inaugural address, Franklin Roosevelt noted that "only a foolish optimist" would deny the dark reality America faced in the deepest days of the Great Depression. But then the original happy warrior added an uplifting, and spiritual-sounding, series of codicils.

"Yet our distress comes from no failure of substance," FDR told America. "We are stricken by no plague of locusts. Compared with the perils which our forefathers conquered because they believed and were not afraid, we still have much to be thankful for."

In this address, the man who became famous for telling Americans that they had nothing to fear but fear itself was trying to buck up his fellow citizens. But he was doing so by boldly asserting that there were higher laws than the Darwinist imperatives of market capitalism. The specter of locusts wasn't the only biblical imagery that appeared in this speech. "The money changers have fled from their high seats in the temple of our civilization," Roosevelt said with some satisfaction. "We may restore that temple to the ancient truths. The measure of restoration lies in the extent to which we apply social values more noble than mere monetary profit." There was more.

> Happiness lies not in the mere possession of money; it lies in the joy of achievement, in the thrill of creative effort. The joy and moral stimulation of work no longer must be forgotten in the mad chase of evanescent profits. These dark days will be worth all they cost us if they teach us that our true destiny is not to be ministered unto but to minister to ourselves and to our fellow men.

Thus we see that the paradox of a rich nation is the same as that for a rich man. The ability to live in freedom and to pursue happiness is dependent on righteous political systems that guarantee such rights to all the citizens of the Republic. But, as we have established, there are critical times in human history when the preservation of that free society depends—and the extension of those rights to new people depends—on a strong military. That martial force, in turn, depends on the technological know-how, advanced educational system and vibrant economy that make these armed forces so formidable.

Every American fighting man dispatched by FDR to the shores of France during World War II was bolstered by supply lines that moved forty-five pounds of supplies per day, one-fourth of it in the form of petroleum to keep the tanks and artillery moving, David M. Kennedy noted in *Freedom from Fear*. This figure contrasted with the twenty pounds of supplies allotted each British soldier—and even more starkly when compared to German rations and materiel, which as the war grinded into 1945 often averaged less than four pounds per day per soldier. "The imbalance was even greater between American and Japanese combatants in the Pacific theater," Kennedy wrote. "The United States could thus win a war of swift movement, armored and aerial, because the conflict boosted its economy while ruining those of both its allies and foes."

It's a vital factor in peacetime as well. A vibrant private sector is responsible for offering a vast majority of Americans not just necessities such as food and clothing, but also such amenities as higher education, home ownership and comfortable vacations. The rub, for some people, is that there are great profits to be made in this pursuit. But capitalism isn't democracy's embarrassing by-product. It is the engine that makes democracy possible, although with it comes materialism in all its forms, many of them rampant and unseemly.

In *A Christmas Carol*, Ebenezer Scrooge is subjected to a visitation from the ghost of his long-dead business partner, Jacob Marley.

"But you were always a good man of business, Jacob," Scrooge stammers.

"Business!" cries the exasperated spirit. "Mankind was my business. The common welfare was my business; charity, mercy, forbearance, and benevolence were all my business."

In 1925, eighty-two years after Charles Dickens' masterpiece appeared, a similar soliloquy to Marley's—equally misguided—was heard on the other side of the Atlantic. Or so the story goes.

"The business of America is business," President Calvin Coolidge was (and is still) widely quoted as saying. Actually, this is one of the most egregious misquotes in American history, one that is doubly humiliating for the Fourth Estate because it is quite nearly the opposite of what Silent Cal actually said—and because he made these remarks to an audience of journalists.[7]

What Coolidge really said, in a January 17, 1925, speech to the American Society of Newspaper Editors, was: "After all, the chief business of the American people is business. Of course, the accumulation of wealth cannot be justified as the chief end of existence."

Coolidge's entire speech that day was a sophisticated discourse by the president about the implications of the fact that American newspapers serve two purposes—and two masters. Newspapers make their owners money, while proclaiming a duty to inform the public honestly. But after examining the inherent conflict in an institution with such "dual" goals, Coolidge postulates that the latent idealism of reporters and editors trumps the profit motive. "The power of the spirit always prevails over the power of the flesh," Coolidge said in what must rank as one of the most optimistic utterances in presidential history. He went on in this vein awhile longer:

> It is only those who do not understand our people who believe that our national life is entirely absorbed by material motives. We make no concealment of the fact that we want wealth, but there are many other things that we want much more. We want peace and honor, and that charity which is so strong an element of all civilization. . . . The chief ideal of the American people is idealism. I cannot repeat too often that America is a nation of idealists. That is the only motive to which they ever give any strong and lasting reaction. No newspaper can be a success which fails to appeal to that element of our national life.

Such confidence in the idealistic impulses of Americans is not universal, especially in our time. In the present conflict, Islamic terrorists have identified the imperialistic strain in American capitalism (the bogey man *du jour* is "globalism") as one of their grounds for aiming suicide bombers at the United States. Consequently, when they attacked on September 11, 2001, they selected targets that had emotional meaning for Americans—the White House and the Capitol—but also objects with symbolic meaning to them, not just the Pentagon, but also the World Trade Center.

Except for a few dinosaurs hibernating in the far left of the nation's political spectrum, Americans do not feel obliged to apologize to the likes of Osama bin Laden for their economic success—and were far less so inclined *after* 9/11. Nonetheless, there has long been a dilemma in the hearts of a people who consider themselves moral and yet who amass and consume so much of the world's riches. The implicit question is this:

Does the material happiness that most Americans enjoy come at the expense of others? It is not a new question, and it is not a trivial one, and it applies domestically as well as internationally.

"We have always known that heedless self-interest was bad morals; we know now that it is bad economics," Franklin Roosevelt said in his second inaugural address. "Out of the collapse of a prosperity whose builders boasted their practicality has come the conviction that in the long run economic morality pays. We are beginning to wipe out the line that divides the practical from the ideal; and in so doing we are fashioning an instrument of unimagined power for the establishment of a morally better world."

The excesses of capitalism is a recurring theme in America. FDR's words could easily be applied to the Reagan and Clinton years—and even more so to the present time. America had one decade, the 1980s, in which prosperity was built in part on a vast military buildup and unprecedented deficit spending. The affluence of the 1990s also owed too much of its luster to a stock market inflated by dot-com bluster and fraudulent corporate accounting. The turn of the century brought a series of financial scandals on a scale not seen since Warren G. Harding was president—and another cycle of deficit spending. It all brought to mind Winston Churchill's tart observation that democratic capitalism is the worst system in the world—except for all the others.[8]

"Greed is good," says the cold-hearted corporate takeover artist played by Michael Douglas in the Hollywood hit *Wall Street*. The moral of the movie, of course, is just the opposite: that greed is bad.

Douglas' character, Gordon Gekko, is a fictionalized composite of Ivan Boesky, Michael Milken and other Wall Street buccaneers of the era. In his famous line, Douglas is explaining (as did the real-life bond kings) that a ruthless approach to corporate takeovers helps weed inefficient companies out of the marketplace, leaving stronger, better ones in their places and driving up stock prices and productivity at the same time—while making him a very rich man. Gekko's soliloquy is based on an actual speech made by Ivan Boesky. Boesky didn't say greed was "good." He said it was "healthy." And his point was broader than Douglas-Gekko's. Boesky was saying that dynamic capitalism depends on men and women who want to get rich—that this is what drives innovation, and by extension, American prosperity.[9] This point is generally accepted as valid, even if it doesn't exactly put entrepreneurs, millionaires and successful corporate executives in the most flattering light.

In the minds of the zealots who attacked the United States, greed is not America's only sin. Right behind rampant materialism comes its dissolute cousin, moral hedonism. Islamicists insist that they hate America's decadence, which they view as everything from Americans' unnatural commitment to sexual equality to their unhealthy obsession with sex itself. This book is certainly not an exposition of the relative morality of the cultures of East and West, but let us pause to make a couple of stipulations. First, no serious-minded person would assert that western culture has not been debased—and been made more dangerous—by a steady diet of violence in television, movies and misogynist music. Likewise, no rational person can claim that the sexual revolution was accomplished without the collateral damage evident from various social ills ranging from a high divorce rate to epidemics of sexually transmitted diseases. But there is no need for Americans to go too far with the self-flagellation. By any measurable standards Americans are harder working and more church-going than the citizens of any nation in the western world. (Thus, if our enemies were truly attacking us for our values, would they not have had to attack France first?)

But if Americans owe no guilty explanations for their material riches—or even their cultural excesses—that is not the same thing as claiming that the nation's wealth and libertine lifestyles, by themselves, result in genuine contentment. George Washington may have used the word "happiness" three times in his first inaugural address, but he wasn't saying "Just Do It!" For the first president and the Founders, the pursuit of happiness meant more than *personal* freedom. It was tied up in another, more communitarian value of public virtue.

"I dwell on this prospect with every satisfaction which an ardent love for my Country can inspire," Washington said at that historic occasion of taking the oath of office for the first time. "Since there is no truth more thoroughly established, than that there exists in the economy and course of nature, an indissoluble union between virtue and happiness. . . ."

This value is as valid today as it was 225 years ago. But just as there were inherent conflicts in the hearts of (slaveholding) Virginia planters who wanted to do good in the New World, but who farmed with the assistance of men and women in chains, so do ethical conflicts remain in the modern work place. They may not be that stark, but they are real enough. It is as basic as the conflict between high profits and high principles. Exploring this tension, Harvard professor Howard

Gardner led a team of researchers that examined how two groups of professionals (geneticists and journalists) pursue their individual happiness in the workplace. What the researchers discovered was that nearly everyone wants his or her life's work to consist of doing "good work," that is, socially responsible work that contributes to the general good. At the same time they found that many of those they interviewed, particularly the young scientists, admitted to simultaneously harboring less altruistic ambitions.

"I have no doubt that most people want to do good work, but maybe a sharper way to ask the question is whether good work comes out on top in a head-to-head combat with success by any means," Gardner said in a 2002 *New York Times* interview. "The young people we interviewed all wanted to be respectable workers, but if that gets in the way of ambition, they were willing to bracket it."

Nevertheless, the dominant theme that emerged from Gardner's project is that professional happiness is not, generally speaking, accomplished by living a self-aggrandizing life.[10] Gardner is a liberal Democrat, but this is not a partisan issue: Conservative academic Charles Murray, once dubbed "the Tom Paine of the Reagan Revolution," argued in his 1984 book *In Pursuit: Of Happiness and Good Government* that true happiness requires a "lasting and justified satisfaction with one's life as a whole."

In addition, the data unearthed by David Myers and his happy fraternity of clinical psychologists suggest that if Gardner's ambitious young workers catch a break, they will be more inclined to share their good fortune with others. "This is one of psychology's most consistent findings: when we feel happy we are more willing to help others," Myers writes. "In study after study, a mood-boosting experience (finding money, succeeding on a challenging task, recalling a happy event) made people more likely to give money, pick up someone's dropped papers, volunteer time, and so forth." Yale University psychologist Peter Salovey, a pioneer in documenting this occurrence, has a name for it: the "feel-good, do-good phenomenon."

*   *   *

Presidents of the United States have rhetorically reinforced this notion that the pursuit of happiness is a pursuit of something larger than personal gratification. That is what Gerald Ford and George Bush told me when I asked them about happiness. "Public service is a noble calling," Bush Forty-One said simply. It's what Jimmy Carter has written many times since he left office. They and other statesmen, from Humphrey to John McCain, invariably arrive at the same conclusion: That the freedom to pursue happiness may be a requisite ingredient of liberty, but even happiness is not an end in itself. The consistent theme is that when pursued in its highest form true happiness is invariably entwined with the goal of public service, of doing something for others.

Herbert Hoover's lighthearted assertion that Jefferson's words practically guaranteed American boys ready access to their local trout stream was made a year before he became the thirty-first president of the United States. The occasion was a speech to the Izaak Walton League in Chicago, a conservation group of which Hoover was the ceremonial head. "The American is a fisherman," Hoover intoned. "That comprehensive list of human rights, the Declaration of Independence, is firm that all men (and boys) are endowed with certain inalienable rights, including life, liberty, and the pursuit of happiness, which obviously includes the pursuit of fish."

Now, Hoover was a dry-fly fisherman, hence earnest about his pursuit of angling. But Hoover was also an orphan, and what he was truly serious about when it came to pursuing happiness was helping needy children, whether they were among the millions of Europeans facing starvation in the aftermath of two world wars, or whether they were wayward American boys without parents or direction. Ostracized by Franklin Roosevelt, who blamed him (as Democrats would do for half a century) for the Great Depression, Hoover found new meaning in his life in 1936 when he was made chairman of the Boys' Club of America. Because he himself had a harsh childhood, Hoover embraced the then-radical notion that there was no such thing as a rotten kid. "The boy is our most precious possession," he said in the spring of 1937. "He strains our nerves, yet he is a complex of cells teeming with affection. He is a periodic nuisance yet he is a joy forever."

Hoover was no plaster saint. He could be imperious, egotistical, autocratic, sometimes devious—and his reaction to the onset of the Depression was indeed tepid and ineffectual. But it is equally undeniable that for him the pursuit of happiness was nothing less than the lifelong pursuit of public service.

He first made his reputation at the outbreak of World War I when he found himself trapped in London, which was his home at the time and the epicenter of his worldwide mining and engineering business, along with forty thousand other Americans, most of whom lacked money, lodging, (some even lacked luggage)—not to mention a way to get home. Walter Page, U.S. ambassador to Britain, asked Hoover to apply his well-known organizational talents to help the Yanks. Within twenty-four hours, Hoover and nine business partners assembled five hundred volunteers in the ballroom of the Savoy Hotel, where they dispensed $1.5 million in food, clothing, steamer tickets and cash, receiving vouchers in return.[11]

"I did not realize it at the moment," Hoover said later, "but on August 3, 1914, my engineering career was over forever. I was on the slippery road of public life."

The rescue of the marooned Americans in Britain turned out to be Hoover's warm-up act. Across the English Channel neutral Belgium had been overrun by the German army, stranding some eight million Belgians who by October faced malnutrition—with mass starvation looming as a real possibility by Christmas. Again, Ambassador Page asked Hoover for help. He produced an immediate plan for food acquisition and distribution nominally overseen by the United States, which was not a belligerent in the war. On October 22, 1914, the Commission for the Relief of Belgium was launched. Hoover made some forty trips across the channel negotiating so the Germans would consent to allowing the CRB ships through. The organization succeeded in bringing thousands of tons of foodstuffs through Rotterdam, feeding seven million Belgians and two million French people trapped in German-occupied France.[12]

After the war, President Wilson asked Hoover to stay in Europe to continue his efforts. By that time Hoover was already an international hero. The most immediate crisis was in Russia, which had undergone a revolution during the war. At home, some voices were raised in objection. The $20 million approved by Congress was going to feed "Bolsheviks," the complaint went. Hoover replied that children were at risk. "Starvation does not await the outcome of power politics," he said. It is estimated that during and after the war, the CRB fed some 15 million children. Certainly, Hoover was no pariah to Democrats then. The *New York Times* pronounced him one of the greatest of living Americans; many political activists assumed that because Hoover had such a close working relationship with Woodrow Wilson that he was a Democrat. Said New York Gov. Franklin Roosevelt: "[Hoover] is certainly a wonder and I wish we could make him president of the United States. There couldn't be a better one."[13]

In time national events and partisan politics would color FDR's charitable early assessment, and Hoover was made *persona-non-grata* at the White House during Roosevelt's tenure there. But after World War II ended, millions in Europe faced food shortages once again. And once again, a Democratic president sent for Herbert Hoover:

"My dear Mr. President, If you should be in Washington, I would be most happy to talk over the European food situation with you," Truman wrote to the seventy-year-old Hoover. "Also it would be a pleasure for me to become acquainted with you."

This gracious note began an unlikely friendship between the two men that lasted until Truman's death. It was also the start of Hoover's final stint as a one-man breadbasket to the world. Truman would send Hoover all over Europe, and Hoover's subsequent reports to the White House formed the basis for the Marshall Plan.

Hoover outlived Truman, as he had Roosevelt. (For that matter, he outlived John F. Kennedy.) But he never forgot the American kids he had once called his "pavement boys." Under his leadership, the Boys' Clubs of America—now the Boys and Girls Clubs of America—grew to become a national organization with a presence in nearly every city. Hoover's rallying cry was "A thousand clubs for a million boys . . ."

That once-popular phrase is not remembered any more, in part because Hoover's vision was reached and then surpassed. In 1990 the Boys' Clubs of America became the Boys and Girls Clubs of America, as Congress dutifully changed their charter, and today there are more than 3,300 active chapters of the club serving at-risk boys and girls. But Hoover's contribution to his countrymen's lexicon is not unique. Because their every word comes under such meticulous scrutiny U.S. presidents have contributed generously to the vocabulary of the American language. George Washington referred to his own government as an "administration," the first such use recorded by the *Oxford English Dictionary*.[14] Jefferson is credited with formulating the word "belittle" and the phrase "public relations," Lincoln with "relocate" and "point well taken." It was Theodore Roosevelt (and not Dwight Eisenhower) who coined the "military industrial complex."[15]

In 1988 Vice President George H. W. Bush added a couple of others, both of which were working definitions of compassion. They were "kinder and gentler nation" and "thousand points of light." The first phrase has come to be understood as a subtle rebuke aimed at conservative Republicanism in general and Ronald Reagan in particular.[16] The second phrase, despite some initial resistance, retained the meaning Bush intended:

"We're a nation of community, of thousands and tens of thousands of ethnic, religious, social, business, labor union, neighborhood, regional and other organizations, all of them varied, voluntary and unique," Bush said in a nationally televised speech from New Orleans. "This is America: the Knights of Columbus, the Grange, Hadassah, the Disabled American Veterans, the Order of Ahepa, the Business and Professional Women of America, the union hall, the Bible study group, LULAC [League of United Latin American Citizens], Holy Name, a brilliant diversity spreads like stars, like a thousand points of light in a broad and peaceful sky."

A few Democratic Party critics derided the use of Bush's phrase on the grounds they claimed not to know what it meant. This rhetoric resistance was understandable, inasmuch as Bush first used the phrase in a political setting (his acceptance of the 1988 Republican presidential nomination) and in a political context (he criticized Democrats for looking to government to solve all social ills "while Washington sets the rules"). But the simple fact is that Bush's choice of words was so evocative of a noble cause, volunteerism, that it quickly became a virtual synonym for the concept of ordinary Americans giving of themselves for the betterment of those less fortunate or for the greater good.

The notion that, in a democracy, charity starts at the top—with the president of the United States himself—begins, as do most things presidential, with George Washington. Included in the collection of George Washington papers at the Library of Congress are two booklets of his schoolwork done before he was sixteen years old. The first third of one of the notebooks contains legal forms with contracts, deeds, leases and bills of sale that any budding Virginia planter should know. The middle portion includes a Christmas poem and a love poem, "True Happiness," that the editors of the Washington papers are convinced were copies of contemporary verse. The last part consists of Washington's writing out of all 110 of the conventions listed in *The Rules of Civility and Decent Behaviour in Company and Conversation*. The litany includes such basics as not spitting on the fire and refraining from pointing at or turning your back on someone who is speaking to you. The last one reads: "Labour to keep alive in your Breast that Little Spark of Ce[les]tial fire Called Conscience." Today we would call this character education. In the case of young George Washington, it took.

American schoolchildren are introduced to George Washington's principles with an apocryphal story in which young George admits to his father that he chopped down a cherry tree. That's unfortunate. His was not a life that needed burnishing. Washington's true ethical makeup can be deduced by the fact that the Alexandria Academy that he helped establish in 1785 was not only tuition-free, but due to Washington's personal efforts, one that catered to orphans and children of indigent parents. Washington took special interest in the children of the veterans who had served with him in the Revolutionary War. Not just boys. In 1786 Washington directed that up to one-fifth of the charity students attending the school with help from his endowment be "girls who may Fitly share the benefits of the institution."[17]

In 1789, both houses of Congress called on President George Washington to recommend a day of thanksgiving and prayer as a way of acknowledging the opportunity that Americans had been afforded to "establish a form of government for their safety and happiness." Washington duly issued just such a proclamation for a Thanksgiving Day that fell on Thursday, November 26. He wished, he told his countrymen, that they thank God for "the civil and religious liberty with which we are blessed; and the means we have of acquiring and diffusing useful knowledge; and in general for all the great and various favors which he hath been pleased to confer upon us . . . ."

Two hundred years later, on November 22, 1989, President Bush addressed the American people on the eve of Thanksgiving as well. "Like many of you, I'm spending tomorrow with family," Bush said. "And we'll say grace and carve the turkey and thank God for our many blessings—and for our great country. . . . And especially touching is that so many Americans have answered the call for community service, the thousand points of light, by rolling up their sleeves and pitching in for the hopeless, the helpless—each volunteer, a beacon of light for someone who has lost his way."

The power of this phrasing—and of the idea behind it—was understood, and embraced, by Bush's successor in the Oval Office. President Clinton used the expression at a January 24, 1997, East Room ceremony in which he both announced the formation of his own summit on citizen service and paid his respects to the man he defeated in the 1992 campaign. "When President Bush held this office, he understood that so much of what is good in America has to be done and is being done by people who are outside Washington and outside the federal government," Clinton said, as the forty-first president and former first lady Barbara Bush looked on. "And we share his hope that by holding up examples of ordinary Americans engaged in extraordinary service, by holding up those 'thousand points of light,' they will grow by the power of their example into millions of points of light."

Using "millions" instead of "a thousand" was sacrificing poetry for the sake of literalness, and it was a rhetorical switch that Clinton's own successor—Bush's son—made as well. In his first State of the Union after 9/11, George W. Bush asked Americans to commit four thousand hours—the equivalent of two years' work—over the course of their lifetimes "to the service of your neighbors and your nation" while announcing the creation of something called USA Freedom Corps. "This time of adversity offers a unique moment of opportunity, a moment we must seize to change our culture," Bush (Forty-Three) said. "Through the gathering momentum of millions of acts of service and decency and kindness, I know we can overcome evil with greater good."

Two days later, on a trip to Winston-Salem, N.C., George W. Bush told the crowd that fighting evil militarily was one way, but not the only way. "At home you fight evil with acts of goodness," Bush said. "It's the . . . momentum of a million acts of kindness. . . . If people want to fight terror, do something kind for a neighbor. Join the USA Freedom Corps. Love somebody. Mentor a child. Stand up to evil with acts of goodness and kindness."

Just as the first President Bush had attempted to upgrade his party's perceived empathy quotient, so, too did the second President Bush. He ran for office as a "compassionate conservative," and stressed this theme more than any other on the campaign trail. In his inaugural address, Bush said:

> America, at its best, is compassionate. In the quiet of American conscience, we know that deep, persistent poverty is unworthy of our nation's promise. And whatever our views of its cause, we can agree that children at risk are not at fault. Abandonment and abuse are not acts of God, they are failures of love. . . . Where there is suffering, there is duty. Americans in need are not strangers; they are citizens, not problems, but priorities. And all of us are diminished when any are hopeless.

George W. Bush, like his fellow Republicans Hoover and Coolidge, tended to stress private, not governmental, acts of good works. But in his second summer in office Bush was confronted with a calamity at the core of capitalism that required a different kind of response. This crisis was epitomized by the collapse of Enron, the huge Texas-based energy conglomerate, as well as a spate of accounting scandals and fraudulent dealings in the boardrooms of corporations across the country. Bush's long-awaited proposals to crack down on corporate shenanigans were tame enough to disappoint corporate watchdog groups, but if you listened carefully when Bush went to Wall Street to announce them, what he enunciated was an idealistic—and a highly progressive—vision of capitalism.

"All investment is an act of faith, and faith is earned by integrity," he said. "In the long run, there is no capitalism without conscience; there is no wealth without character."

Bush's resolute rhetoric was not bolstered by firm legislative proposals. He offered only the most modest of proposed regulatory reforms of Wall Street. That is not a surprise from a pro-business Republican. Nor is it a surprise that Bush would sound like Roosevelt on this point; the political moment demanded it. What might be a revelation to many, however, is that numerous presidents, Democrats and Republicans, have sounded similar puritanical notes, stern yet idealistic, when discussing the obligations of Americans who benefit from the free market.

Here is Calvin Coolidge on the occasion of the hundred and fiftieth anniversary of the Declaration of Independence. The date was July 4, 1926, one hundred years, to the day, after the deaths of Adams and Jefferson:

> We live in an age of science and of abounding accumulation of material things. These did not create our Declaration. Our Declaration created them. The things of the spirit come first. Unless we cling to that, all our national prosperity, overwhelming though it may appear, will turn to a barren sceptre in our grasp. If we are to maintain the great heritage which has been bequeathed to us, we must be like-minded as the fathers who created it. We must not sink into a pagan materialism. We must cultivate the reverence they had for the things that are holy.

As this quote underscores, and as is evident in the lack of understanding about the origins of the Kennedy family motto, modern commentators suspicious of Bush for his overt religiosity have an ahistorical view of how past presidents communicated. When discussing everything from the reasons America must go to war to the obligations of citizens of the Republic for those less fortunate, presidents have routinely invoked God and the teachings of the bible. This is especially true while they are discussing with their countrymen the concept that the true pursuit of happiness is a mission that entails public service.

Jimmy Carter, even as he settled in his role of ex-president and senior statesman to the world, has never stopped trying to explain the meaning of a purposeful life. In *Everything to Gain: Making the Most of the Rest of Your Life,* he and former first lady Rosalynn Carter equated the pursuit of happiness with the pursuit of hard work in the service of others. Carter writes about restoring an abandoned, utterly dilapidated six-story building on Manhattan's lower east side and turning it, under the auspices of Habitat for Humanity into nineteen apartments for poor families. To get to New York, Carter and his fellow volunteers took a twenty-five-hour bus trip from Plains, Ga.

"It was a long hard day, but we went back to the church in the late afternoon with a sense of fulfillment, for after only one day with fifty of us there we could begin to see that we could make a difference," he wrote. "My wife has never been more beautiful than when her face was covered with black smut from scraping burned ceiling joists, and streaked with sweat from carrying sheets of plywood from the street. . . ."

In a 1998 sequel, *The Virtues of Aging,* Carter amplified on these themes. He went on at some length about his pursuits—fly-fishing, playing tennis, downhill skiing (which he first tried at the age of sixty), sex with his wife (he implies strongly that he was a better lover after the age of seventy than as a newlywed), writing and, finally, volunteering—much volunteering. "Happiness," he said simply, "rests on having a purpose in life and maintaining relationships with others."

Noted presidential scholar Forrest McDonald believes that the assumption that civic virtue is at the heart of things is implicit in the Declaration of Independence itself. McDonald, a professor of history at the University of Alabama, delves into the subtle distinction between the Lockean doctrine of "national-rights" and its slightly less secular cousin "natural law." (If Garry Wills finds influences of the Scottish Enlightenment, McDonald traces Jefferson's inspirations to a Swiss legal philosopher, Emerich de Vattel, but his point is the same: that Jefferson was borrowing from a more communitarian tradition than is commonly supposed.)

"In one key respect, Jefferson used Natural Law instead of natural-rights theory, substituting 'the pursuit of happiness' for 'property' in the trinity of inalienable rights," McDonald writes. "In this change, derived from . . . de Vattel, [Jefferson] emphasized public duty rather than (as the language seems to indicate) personal choice, for natural law theory [holds] that happiness is attainable only by diligent cultivation of civic virtue."

Jefferson himself provided a glimpse into how he personally pursued happiness in an October 28, 1785, letter to Madison. Jefferson wrote from the Fontainebleau, where the king of France repaired each autumn to hunt. It was Jefferson's first trip there, and he determined to take a hike to the top of the nearest mountaintop to survey the sights.

On his way out of town, Jefferson describes meeting "a poor woman," a day laborer who is, at that time, without work and, consequently, without food. Jefferson recalls his "enquires into her vocation, condition and circumstance." He learns that she has two children to feed, and nothing to feed them with. He gives her some money, adding tactfully to her that it is not charity, but payment for her services as a "guide." The woman, overcome by his generosity, bursts into tears and is unable to speak. Whereupon Jefferson uses the silence to formulate a complicated theory about the evil of such iniquity in land ownership, one he naturally shares with Madison. In his mind, walking there in the lush French countryside, Jefferson reformulates all known laws regarding land distribution, inheritance and the right to gainful employment—and, for good measure, invents the progressive income tax.

Jefferson ruminated on all this because his heart was moved by the plight of this poor Frenchwoman. Both Republicans and Democrats claim Jefferson as their own these days, and in this little incident, he was faithful to both traditions: He dispensed *private* charity, freely and with a good heart, and made a difference, if only temporarily, in this woman's life. On the other hand, he wasn't satisfied with that; he also devised—at least in his mind—a multifaceted political solution, using *government* as the instrument of change.

America itself has been doing this now for 225 years, although it must be said that the nation's motives are not always purely altruistic. Even the Peace Corps, which Hubert Humphrey had been pushing for years before John F. Kennedy launched it, was part philanthropy and part public relations. Kennedy said as much when he announced it, and unless anyone doubted it, the initial funds underwriting it came from something called the Mutual Security Act. But JFK had the foresight to know that the volunteers, besides doing something good for their host country and their home country were also doing something for themselves.

"The benefits of the Peace Corps will not be limited to the countries in which it serves," he said in his 1961 statement to Congress announcing the program. "Our own young men and women will be enriched by the experience of living and working in foreign lands. They will have acquired new skills and experience which will aid them in their future careers and add to our own country's supply of trained personnel and teachers. They will return better able to assume the responsibilities of American citizenship and with greater understanding of our global responsibilities."

Even the vastly more expensive and momentous Marshall Plan was initially seen by Truman as the most effective means for the United States to stop the spread of communism. That didn't make it less important, or less noble, and Americans have every right to ask: Who else could have done it? Who else would have? A Gallup Poll done in April 1945, the year Franklin Roosevelt died, found that an amazing 70 percent of Americans said they would be willing to eat about one-fifth less than they ordinarily consumed in order to send more food to war-ravaged Europe. Can that be construed as selfish?

FDR's last birthday came on January 30, 1945. That night, he asked Eleanor to read a statement at a fundraiser of the National Foundation for Infantile Paralysis. Here are some excerpts:

> The success of the 1945 March of Dimes in the campaign against infantile paralysis does not come as a surprise to me. We are a Nation of free people, and free people know how to go over the top—whether it's a Nazi wall, a Japanese island fortress, a production goal, a bond drive, or a stream of silver dimes. The reason for these achievements is no military secret. It is the determination of the many to work as one for the common good. It is such unity which is the essence of our democracy.
>
> Our national concern for the handicapped and the infirm is one of our national characteristics. Indeed, it caused our enemies to laugh at us as soft. "Decadent" was the word they used. But not any more. They are learning—and learning the hard way—that there are many things we are mighty tough about.
>
> We will never tolerate a force that destroys the life, the happi-

ness, the free future of our children, any more than we will tolerate the continuance on earth of the brutalities and barbarities of the Nazis or of the Japanese warlords. We will combat this evil enemy of disease at home just as unremittingly as we fight our evil enemies abroad. . . . The task is not an easy one. The mystery shrouding the infantile paralysis virus is not readily penetrated. But we will persist—and we will triumph.

There is no yardstick long enough to measure the happiness our children give us. Whatever we can contribute to promote our children's health is an investment in our country's future. It is an assertion of our American birthright to life, liberty, and the pursuit of happiness.

10

Freedom Man

In the months and days leading up to the second war in Iraq, George W. Bush, Vice President Dick Cheney and their top White House advisers—along with British Prime Minister Tony Blair and foreign minister Jack Straw—recited to a candid world the litany of reasons justifying the invasion of Iraq:

Saddam Hussein was hell-bent on building an arsenal of chemical, biological, and nuclear weapons; Saddam Hussein was a thug who had thumbed his nose at U.N. resolutions demanding that he get rid of them; Saddam Hussein had already committed acts of war against three of his neighbors—Iran, Kuwait and Israel—and was determined to ethnic-cleanse the Iraqi Kurds from large portions of his own country as well; in the process of committing those outrages, Saddam Hussein had employed chemical weapons against Kurdish civilians and Iranian military units and, during the Persian Gulf War, had fired conventional missiles at Israeli civilian centers; Saddam Hussein was sworn to the destruction of Israel—and, for that matter, the United States; Saddam Hussein was underwriting terrorists in the Middle East; finally, Saddam Hussein was brutalizing and terrorizing the people of Iraq itself, people who themselves have an inalienable right to be free.

The governments of France, Germany, Russia and most of those in the Arab world generally conceded the truth of these assertions, but concluded that war was still unjustified. They urged the United Nations—and undecided nations within that body—to allow U.N.-sanctioned weapons inspections to continue. Tony Blair and the leaders of seventeen other European nations, along with Japanese Prime Minister Junichiro Koizumi, Australian Prime Minister John Howard and others sided with the American president. The invasion took place.

But only one rationale for war, the last one on the list, truly resonated with Americans—or, for that matter, with ordinary Iraqis. And when Bush began emphasizing, perhaps a little late in the debate, that his most ardent resolve was that Iraqis, too, should realize the rights to life, liberty and the pursuit of happiness, most of his countrymen came along with him. This was a reason worth fighting for.

"My fellow citizens, the dangers to our country and the world will be overcome," Bush told the American people in an Oval Office address on March 19, 2003, as the invasion began. "We will pass through this time of peril and carry on the work of peace. We will defend our freedom. We will bring freedom to others, and we will prevail."

Halfway around the world, troopers of the U.S. Army's 3rd Infantry Division gathered under a full moon and listened—it was 4 A.M. Iraq time—to the commander-in-chief. "To all the men and women of the United States Armed Forces now in the Middle East, the peace of a troubled world and the hopes of an oppressed people now depend on you," Bush said, speaking directly to them. "The people you liberate will witness the honorable and decent spirit of the American military."

The Army and Marine commanders in the field did what officers have done since the Revolutionary War: they roused the courage of their citizen-soldiers with a brief explanation of why they were fighting.

"For decades Saddam Hussein has tortured, imprisoned, raped and murdered the Iraqi people," Major Gen. J. N. Mattis told the men of the 1st Marine Division. "The time has come to end his reign of terror. On your young shoulders rest the hopes of mankind. . . . Fight with a happy heart and strong spirit."

In the Army units, the message was the same.

"We are not going up there to fight the Iraqi people," Lt. Col. Stephen Twitty, commanding officer of the 3rd Army Infantry Division, 3rd Battalion, told his troops, a version of remarks delivered all over Kuwait that night. "The Iraqi people are good people. They've just been put in a bad situation."

If the Civil War letters of Union soldiers help shed light on how Northern troops eventually came to see themselves as liberators no matter why they'd gone to war in the first place, so, too, do the first-person words from the American troops in Iraq in 2003 serve to enlighten us as to the motivations of the soldiers themselves. Their words reveal that liberation was very much on their minds even before they crossed over from Kuwait into Iraq. Up and down the Army's famed Long Gray

Line—and in the Marine units as well—the soldiers took Bush's words, and their commanding officers' words, to heart. In e-mails, letters and the interviews they gave to "embedded" journalists, the same three points emerged time and time again: First, without claiming that Saddam was linked to Osama bin Laden, they nevertheless sensed that the impending war stemmed indirectly from the events of 9/11. Secondly, and as a result, they saw their mission as one to defend America itself, and American freedom. Third, they asserted repeatedly in interviews with their hometown newspapers and other embedded American journalists that they were going into Iraq to make life better for the people who lived there.

"This isn't Vietnam," Capt. Tom LaCroix told the men of Charley Company, 1st Battalion of the 7th Marine Regiment: "We're here to liberate this country. You're here to do a good thing. Don't lose sight of that."[1]

And they didn't. "We want regime change, we want to introduce democracy, but above all we want to help the Iraqis help Iraqis," Benjamin Kaye, a twenty-three-year-old sergeant from Buffalo, N.Y., a member of the Army's 402nd Civil Affairs Battalion, to a reporter from his hometown.

"I'm fighting for their freedom," Private First Class Crystal Heyer, of the 190th Military Police Company of the Georgia National Guard, told Phillip Taylor of the *Atlanta Journal and Constitution*, as her unit was being sent overseas. "I'm fighting so they can have a future."

Nathaniel Rogers, a Marine reservist called up to active duty along with his identical twin Mathew, sent an e-mail to his hometown North Carolina newspaper, the *Winston-Salem Journal*, expressing a similar sentiment. "Each Marine out here knows that we are defending freedom and granting freedom to those who want it," he wrote. "You can see it on the faces of the people out here as we go by. They are happy to have us here. They want Saddam out of power and know that we can do that for them."

A dozen years earlier, a Marine Corps captain named Tom Barna left behind his wife and two-year-old son Alex to go fight in the Persian Gulf War. Called back to active duty in October 2002, Barna was a lieutenant colonel in Marine Reserves. He wrote to Alex, now twelve years of age, a letter explaining why:

"Son, my deployment seems a little more personal this time. As you know, it was our nation that was attacked. It was our people who died.

And this fire has been brewing for quite a while. I think all Americans are finally ready to rid the world of men bent on imposing their evil will. This time it's different. . . ."

In a letter he sent his mother from Iraq—his last letter home—Roy Russell Buckley, a twenty-four-year-old reservist from Hobart, Ind., a father of a six-year-old daughter, wrote of the pride he felt at how the Army was helping the Iraqi people. Buckley also expressed distress at their plight. "The kids here are so sad," he wrote. "I give them as much food as possible. I gave my last $20 to a man who looked so bad. I couldn't care less; I can do without the stuff."[2]

The last people in this chain of command were the families of the soldiers. If the interviews they gave are any barometer, a large percentage of these families also took their cue from, if not the president, then their own loved one who was in uniform.

"You figure they got a job to do," Alexandra Tychnowitz, of College Point, Queens, said about her two boys Paul and Stephen, both of whom served in the Army in Iraq. "The Iraqi people are being freed from that nut, and my boys were called to be there."[3]

Betty Jo Smith of Chattanooga, Tenn., discussing her son Jeremy Bowling, a twenty-seven-year-old captain in the Army's 3rd Infantry Division, told her local paper that while she worried about her son, she considered his service in Iraq to be a noble cause. "Absolutely, I worry," she said. "But if God chooses for him to go home to heaven, he would do it defending our nation and fighting for freedom for other people. I have much security in that thought."

Similar sentiments were uttered at funerals, too, funerals of families forced to endure Mrs. Smith's worst fear. When Michael Curtin, an Army corporal from Howell, N.J., was among the four American soldiers killed in a suicide bomber attack north of Najaf, his parents issued the following statement: "He was fighting for our freedom, which we should never take for granted. He was a hero in our eyes." Curtin was twenty-three years old.

"He died doing a good deed and a good job," Donna Bellman said after learning that her son, U.S. Marine Sgt. Michael E. Bitz, was killed in action. "He believed he was helping to liberate people. He believed he was fighting for their freedom, for our freedom."[4]

On April 3, while at Camp Lejeune to pay his respects to the families of the soldiers and Marines fighting in Iraq, Bush proudly related a vignette that he believed summed it all up:

A man in one Iraqi village said this to one of our soldiers: "I want my freedom. I don't want food or water. I just want my freedom." America hears that man! We hear all Iraqis who yearn for liberty, and the people of Iraq have my pledge: our fighting forces will press on until your entire country is free.

It was an inspiring anecdote, and the military families and stateside Marines cheered the president enthusiastically. But in truth, Bush's passion for democracy was running away with him. Less than two months later, reality caught up. In equally impassioned pleas, which also made the front pages of the nation's newspapers, "liberated" Iraqis battered by water shortages, gasoline shortages, food shortages, rampant crime and little employment started answering back.

"America could solve all the problems, serve all the people in days. It knows what the country needs. It doesn't need the opposition parties from abroad. It needs comfort," an Iraqi named Fadhil Murah told *Washington Post* reporter Anthony Shadid. "They came and said, 'I'll give you freedom and democracy.' So what? People should have food first, then democracy."

If Eleanor Roosevelt were still with us, she could have told Bush to expect such reactions; that they are human nature. It is hard to talk politics to a man who is selling the furniture out of his house to feed his four children—as Fadhil Murah was doing. But this was a false choice, for democracy was never supposed to be a trade-off between freedom and prosperity. They are designed to go together. It was this realization that galvanized George Washington, and it was the tenet grasped by Tocqueville. It was this sometimes unforgiving principle that was drummed into Winston Churchill's consciousness when the British electorate rewarded him for saving their beloved islands by retiring him, involuntarily, when World War II was over in favor of someone they thought could get Great Britain's economy moving again.[5]

On the other hand, a healthy financial system doesn't ameliorate the human desire for freedom; nor does it absolve a government that tries to offer prosperity and tyranny at the same time. The pro-democracy demonstration at Tiananmen Square in 1989 came as China began to experience an economic boom and while it was loosening commercial, but not political, restrictions. The rulers of oil-rich sheikdoms of the Middle East have learned to their own horror—and the world's—that all the petrodollars in the world do not bring peace or stability (or even a dependable and lasting prosperity) to a nation without freedom.

Once again, the analogy between nations and individuals is inescapable: Just as a hungry, impoverished person can rarely be happy, neither can an impoverished, failing nation-state console itself with the thought that it has democratic elections. Conversely, just as richness is not enough to make a man happy, neither can wealth alone make a nation free and democratic. This truism, in turn, raises the issue of whether all people of the world *want* freedom. The world events of 2001–2003 suggest strongly that is not merely an academic query: Inside that philosophical question lies the answer to whether war in Iraq, and other wars to come, are justified.

If the rights that Jefferson committed to paper in Philadelphia are truly "unalienable," the idea that flows naturally from this concept is that the human desire for them is universal. For most Americans—and for most American political leaders—this notion is axiomatic. Certainly, President Bush believes this. "Moral truth is the same in every culture, in every time, and in every place," Bush said in a June 2002 commencement address to graduating West Point cadets. This was reminiscent of a July 2, 1976, speech by Gerald R. Ford. "The Declaration is the Polaris of our political order—the fixed star of freedom," Ford said. "It is impervious to change because it states moral truths that are eternal."

Bush has expounded on this outlook several times as president, in both set speeches and extemporaneous comments. "No people on earth yearn to be oppressed, or aspire to servitude, or eagerly await the midnight knock of the secret police," he said in his 2002 State of the Union Address—a line that is a pretty fair modern translation of the Rumbold-Jefferson observation that no man is born wishing for a saddle on his back and spurs in his side. In a 2002 interview with Bob Woodward, author of *Bush at War*, the president amplified on this point:

"There is a value system that cannot be compromised . . . God-given values," he said. "These aren't United States–created values. They are values of freedom and the human condition. . . ." The yearning for freedom, Bush added, is as basic as "mothers loving their children."

As the war in Iraq began, American political leaders of all stripes sounded the same theme. "I am proud of our president, our troops and our allies," House Speaker Dennis Hastert proclaimed as the war in Iraq began. "Yes, we are fighting to preserve our national security. But we are also fighting to preserve the universal ideals of life, liberty and the pursuit of happiness."

Sen. Joseph Lieberman, a Democrat who wants Bush's job, also maintained that Jefferson's promise implied a duty on the part of Americans to export the ideas of liberal democracy into the heart of the Muslim world. In an extraordinary speech at Georgetown University, delivered on January 14, 2002, Lieberman said:

> The United States must steer a new course—one closer to our values and closer to the values that grow from our common humanity. We can and must demonstrate to ordinary people throughout the Islamic world that the United States will take risks to support their freedom, aspirations and quality of life. We must make those values a premise of our alliances and a condition of our aid because the inalienable, God-given rights to life, liberty and the pursuit of happiness that we declared our independence for don't end at America's borders.

Among other things, Lieberman said, this principle obliges the United States to become an effective proponent of women's rights throughout the Muslim world. "For years, the United States has muted our support for the rights of women, for fear of upsetting our relationship with existing regimes," he said. "It's time to become a more outspoken advocate for the right of women everywhere in the world to be educated, to live freely and to rise as far as their talents and hard work will take them. . . ."

Hastert and Lieberman both strongly supported Bush on the war, but even Bush's most prominent antiwar critics agreed with the premise that the promise of the Declaration of Independence extends beyond America's shores. Sen. Edward M. Kennedy of Massachusetts, possibly the most articulate of these critics, prefaced his seminal March 4, 2003, speech against the war in Iraq by noting "our nation was founded on the unalienable right of all of our citizens to life, liberty and the pursuit of happiness," adding that it was each American's obligation to expand that promise to the rest of the world. Kennedy's own legislative efforts during and after the fighting in Iraq have been oriented toward winning minds in the Arab world.

Another viewpoint that cropped up repeatedly among critics of the Bush administration in the aftermath of 9/11 was that an overzealous response at home—a response that curtailed civil liberties—would be self-defeating. Bush said on many occasions that the Islamicist terrorists hated America precisely for its freedoms. Amen, said civil libertarians, and this is all the more reason why it is inappropriate to curb those free-doms in the name of increasing security. In this way, the nation's civil liberties groups were themselves confirming the universal nature of American freedom—it was the one issue they would not compromise on. This was true of groups ranging from the traditionally liberal American Civil Liberties Union to the Cato Institute, a Washington think tank that favors small government and is considered conservative to the point of being nearly libertarian in its outlook. Yet when Cato's Timothy Lynch showed up at a December 4, 2001, Senate Judiciary Committee hearing to criticize Bush's executive order on military tribunals, Lynch prefaced his criticism with a tip of his hat to Bush's overt Jeffersonianism:

"We must respond to this new threat without losing sight of what we are fighting for," Lynch told the committee. "Our troops over in Afghanistan are not fighting to protect the property and occupants of some geographical location here in North America. They are defending the fundamental American idea that individuals have the rights of life, liberty and the pursuit of happiness."

An *American idea*, but one for all people.

This is accepted wisdom, at least in the world of elective American politics. In the political sphere, notions of cultural relativism have not superseded the doctrine of natural rights. But let us pause in our narrative to note how pervasive such relativism has become in academia, and at all levels. This phenomenon was witnessed in recent times by Ted Kennedy himself, and even the venerable old Massachusetts liberal roused himself to challenge it. The little-known interplay occurred in a class-room at Boston Latin Academy where the senator had gone to accompany Supreme Court Justice Anthony Kennedy in the fifth such session arranged by Justice Kennedy since the attacks of 9/11. The justice, acting in concert with the American Bar Association, designed a program called the "Dialogue on Freedom." It is a dialogue that appears to be necessary.[6]

"Each generation must breathe new life into [the Declaration of Independence]," Sen. Kennedy told the Boston Latin students. But when several of them recited the soothing bromides of multiculturalism until they seemed to have elevated the notion of tolerance for other cultures above the values of freedom and dignity, both of the Kennedys urged the students to think about it some more.[7]

Justice Kennedy gently challenged them: What about societies where women have no rights—and the women themselves seem to acquiesce? "If she wants to give up her freedom . . . then, that's her decision," one high school senior replied. "What's right in our culture isn't necessarily right for everyone."

This student spoke of the "freedom to give up freedoms," but Justice Kennedy nudged her a bit:

"Dictatorships are OK?"

Another student chimed in that he would accept a dictatorship if a majority voted for it. It was at this point that Sen. Kennedy jumped up to his feet and reminded the students that simple majority rule can mean simple tyranny. A majority of lawmakers—and the U.S. Supreme Court—had once enshrined slavery in the Constitution, he noted.

When one student stumbled, saying, "life, liberty . . ." and forgetting what came next, Anthony Kennedy pulled out a pocket-sized copy of the Declaration of Independence that he carries with him.

"You have to read the Declaration of Independence," the justice exhorted. "Read it aloud! It was meant to be read aloud, *was* read aloud to [George Washington's] troops."

Before he left, the Supreme Court justice told the students what the words in the Preamble meant to him. "The pursuit of happiness is [the] self-satisfaction of making a civic contribution to your community," he said, adding that "community" refers not just to Americans, but also to all the people of the world. "It's important to show (others) that they have the time, capacity and inspiration to adopt ideals of freedom."

This is where President Bush resides intellectually, too. America had a right to obliterate the Taliban because a sneak attack was launched on the United States from Afghan soil with the tacit complicity of the Afghan government. But Bush goes farther, much farther. I believe that it is clear from his public speeches, his private comments and his actions that Bush believes America's moral authority to interject itself into Iraq does not—and need not—come from the U.N. Security Council because it derives from a much higher authority. It comes from the Declaration of Independence.

And Bush did not cobble this philosophy together hastily, or after-the-fact—the facts being the changed world after 9/11. Listen to him on July 4, 2001, at Independence Hall in Philadelphia ten weeks *before* he suddenly found himself a wartime commander-in-chief:

> Those new citizens of a nation just four days old heard inspiring
> words, but not original thoughts. Our founders considered them-

selves heirs to principles that were timeless, and truths that were self-evident. When Jefferson sat down to write, he was trying, he said, to place before mankind "the common sense of the subject."

The common sense of the subject was that we should be free. And though great evils would linger, the world would never be the same after July 4th, 1776. A wonderful country was born and a revolutionary idea sent forth to all mankind: Freedom, not by the good graces of government, but as the birthright of every individual. Equality, not as a theory of philosophers but by the design of our Creator. Natural rights, not for the few, not even for a fortunate many, but for all people, in all places, in all times. . . .

Our greatest achievements have come when we have lived up to these ideals. Our greatest tragedies have come when we have failed to uphold them. When Abraham Lincoln wondered whether civil war was preferable to permanent slavery, he knew where to seek guidance. Speaking in Independence Hall, he said, "I have never had a feeling politically that did not spring from the sentiments embodied in the Declaration of Independence." The Declaration, Lincoln said, gave promise that in due time, the weight would be lifted from the shoulders of all men and all should have an equal chance.

If Bush's absolute confidence that this American document, written for an American revolution, supersedes all the laws, treaties and charters of the world strikes many political liberals on both sides of the Atlantic as being arrogant or jingoistic, Bush had an answer: In the first instance, he wondered why so many liberals were so illiberal in their blithe acceptance of a brutal, totalitarian state inside Iraq. Don't the lives and aspirations of Iraqi people count? And why is the lack of discovery of weapons of mass destruction more interesting to these critics than the discovery of mass *graves*?

The notion, advanced subtly by antiwar critics, that Arab culture is unready for democracy also strikes Bush as fundamentally illiberal. The president has asserted on several occasions that freedom is not only one of the "natural rights," but the most basic human yearning. He displays no patience for the idea that there is anything about Arab culture, or Islam, that is incompatible with this desire. "It is presumptuous and insulting to suggest that a whole region of the world—or the one-fifth of humanity that is Muslim—is somehow untouched by the most basic aspirations of life," Bush said at a February 26, 2003, dinner of the American Enterprise Institute. "Human cultures can be vastly different.

Yet the human heart desires the same good things, everywhere on Earth."[8]

Bush noted that such apologists for the status quo have always been among us. "There was a time when many said that the cultures of Japan and Germany were incapable of sustaining democratic values," Bush said. "Well, they were wrong. Some say the same of Iraq today. They are mistaken. The nation of Iraq, with its proud heritage, abundant resources, and skilled and educated people, is fully capable of moving toward democracy and living in freedom."

Here it must be said that George W. Bush was hardly alone in his views, although one wouldn't always know it by some of the news coverage he generated. Before, during and after the war, Bush enjoyed widespread public support in the United States for the invasion. Both houses of Congress voted overwhelmingly to authorize it. Abroad, many more of America's allies supported the president than opposed him as well. The list of prominent American political leaders who supported Bush and Blair included not just Joe Lieberman, but also John Edwards, John Kerry, Dick Gephardt and Hillary Clinton (in other words, the Democrats with the most realistic presidential ambitions), and nearly the entire Republican Party, including John McCain.[9] As Baghdad was falling, 71 percent of Americans told Pew Foundation pollster Andrew Kohut that they favored a "major post-war operation" to rebuild Iraq and establish a stable government there.

And although the debate in Washington became poisoned by name-calling—"chicken-hawk" being the trendy insult—some of the most prominent moral voices in the world also supported the Iraq invasion. These included renowned Holocaust survivor and Nobel Prize–winning author Elie Wiesel,[10] and another Nobel laureate Bernard Kouchner, one of the founders of Médecins Sans Frontières (Doctors Without Borders).[11]

Inside the United States it seemed that there was nearly an inverse relationship between how much people favored Bush's invasion plans and how close they themselves had ever been to living under tyranny. At one extreme was the cabal of cloistered Hollywood millionaires who denounced Bush as a menacing warmonger. At the other end of the spectrum were the working-class Iraqi-Americans living in their Detroit-area enclave who took to the streets in celebration at the news that the U.S. Marines crossed the Kuwait border into Iraq.

This dynamic was common internationally as well in the days before the war: People who had actually lived under Saddam, or people who had been recently freed from tyranny elsewhere in the world, tended to support the United States far more than those who hadn't. "History has shown that the use of force is often the necessary price of liberation," proclaimed Jose Ramos-Horta, the foreign minister of East Timor (and another Nobel Peace Prize winner). He cited his own nation as a recent example, adding pointedly that if antiwar protestors who profess to care about ordinary Iraqis got their way the result would be a lot more murdered Iraqi citizens. "I am unimpressed by the grandstanding of certain European leaders," he added. "If the antiwar movement dissuades the United States and its allies from going to war with Iraq, it will have contributed to the peace of the dead."[12]

Nowhere in the world was this attitude more pronounced than in the badlands of northern Iraq where all that has separated the Kurdish people from annihilation in the past dozen years was the U.S.-operated "no-fly" zones and the Kurdish guerillas known as *peshmerga* ("those who face death"). Jeffrey Goldberg, the intrepid correspondent for *The New Yorker*, visited that inaccessible frontier on the eve of the U.S. invasion of Iraq and found himself besieged for U.S. flags and pictures of George W. Bush. "It is virtually impossible," Goldberg wrote in his magazine, "to find anyone in Kurdistan who is opposed to the war against Saddam's regime."[13]

Europe, however, was nearly evenly divided on the question of an American invasion of Iraq at the outset of 2003. In London, Blair was strongly behind the United States; so were the heads of state in Italy, Spain, Portugal, Poland, Hungary, Denmark and the Czech Republic. But with Russia, Germany, France and Belgium lining up in opposition—and with opponents able to muster millions of antiwar protestors to march in the streets—by February the momentum seemed to be ebbing away from Bush. It was at this point that the remaining nation states of Eastern Europe, all of them former satellites in the Soviet Union, tipped the balance. It came in a joint statement out of Vilnius, the capital of Lithuania, by the ten remaining nations of the old Soviet bloc. The statement, released to the press hours after Colin Powell's February 5, 2003, appearance before the United Nations, said: "The clear and present danger posed by Saddam Hussein's regime requires a united response from the community of democracies."[14]

These developments led to Secretary of Defense Donald Rumsfeld's widely quoted crack questioning the vitality and utility of "old Europe."

They also prompted French President Jacques Chirac to make an even more bizarre comment: The small countries of Eastern Europe "had missed a good opportunity to shut up," Chirac blurted out, adding that they might have jeopardized their impending entry into the European Union. Probably Chirac was venting his frustration, something that was in ample supply on both sides of the Atlantic in the days before the Iraq invasion. But the French leader's fundamentally undemocratic line of argumentation undermined his own position, while sharpening the resolve of the former Soviet-occupied states.

This reality came home to Bush himself twelve days later, on President's Day. Washington was virtually closed down by a snowstorm, and Bush had cancelled a planned speech. But he kept his appointment with one of those ten Eastern European leaders, Latvian President Vaira Vike-Freiberga. He was glad he did so.

"Let me talk to you about Iraq . . ." Bush began when she came into the Oval Office.

"There is no need for that," replied Mrs. Vike-Freiberga. "For fifty years, the democracies slept while we lived under repression and tyranny . . ."[15]

Ms. Vike-Freiberga spent most of her life in Canada following the 1941 takeover of Latvia by the Soviet Union. After the fall of the Soviet Union in 1991, she returned to her home country for a visit, bringing only two suitcases with her—and never left. In her talk with Bush she said it was the plight of the Iraqi people that she couldn't get out of her mind. Another Eastern European statesman, Hungarian Ambassador to the United States Andras Simonyi, made the same point publicly, citing the failure of the West to come to Hungarians' assistance after they briefly threw Soviet troops out of their country in 1956.

"Hungarians perhaps have a better understanding for why democracies might have to go to war," he said in an appearance on C-Span's *Washington Journal.* "In 1956, the international community, democracies, failed to act . . . [and] Hungary got occupied by a foreign power. . . . Hungarians have a pretty good understanding of what happens when democracies fail to move."

Bush himself was aware that such sentiments were prevalent in the capitals behind the old Iron Curtain. In late May of 2003, after Saddam Hussein's reign had ended, but while American soldiers were still dying in Iraq trying to pacify that country, Bush went to Poland, a nation carved up in a secret pact between Hitler and Stalin while the western powers dithered in the hope that more talk would lead to peace. It was in that setting, at Wawel Castle in Krakow, that Bush held forth on the horrors that resulted from the historic failure to confront Nazism. Bush did so in a way that France—and more particularly, Germany—could hardly rebut; that is, he did it after a visit to Auschwitz. "Within an hour's journey of this castle lies a monument to the darkest impulses of man," Bush said. "Today, I saw Auschwitz . . . a place where evil found its willing servants and its innocent victims."

> One boy imprisoned there was branded with the number A-70713. Returning to Auschwitz a lifetime later, Elie Wiesel recalled his first night in the camp: "I asked myself, God, is this the end of your people, the end of mankind, the end of the world?"
>
> With every murder, a world was ended. And the death camps still bear witness. They remind us that evil is real and must be called by name and must be opposed. All the good that has come to this continent—all the progress, the prosperity, the peace—came because beyond the barbed wire there were people willing to take up arms against evil. And history asks more than memory, because hatred and aggression and murderous ambitions are still alive in the world. Having seen the works of evil firsthand on this continent, we must never lose the courage to oppose it everywhere.

Bush made those remarks on May 31, 2003. Standing beside him was one prominent member of the "coalition of the willing," Poland's president Aleksander Kwasniewski. Bush lauded his Polish counterpart, saying he'd given credibility to his nation's motto: *For your freedom—and ours.*[16]

That slogan itself is as good a shorthand as any to describe the Bush doctrine, which, I believe in the aftermath of 9/11 can be described this succinctly: An undemocratic government anywhere is a potential threat to democracies everywhere.

But if that is a disquieting thought because of the huge obligation that it implies, there is another way to look at it, and that is that the inverse is probably true as well: As long as democracy flourishes in the United States, freedom's allure will always be on display. This is certainly how Ronald Reagan, the eternal optimist and the president to whom Bush is most often compared, would have described it.

*　　*　　*

Reagan, in his farewell address to the nation, recalled a time in the early part of the 1980s, when the aircraft carrier USS *Midway* was patrolling the South China Sea on the lookout for boat people from Southeast Asia. The Navy crew spotted a leaky little vessel in the distance. "Crammed inside were refugees from Indochina hoping to get to America," Reagan related. "The *Midway* sent a small launch to bring them to the ship, and safety. As the refugees made their way through the choppy seas, one spied a U.S. Navy sailor on deck and stood up and called out to him. He yelled, 'Hello American sailor! Hello Freedom Man!'"

The sailor was so struck by the greeting that he couldn't get it out of his mind, and he wrote about it in a letter that reached the White House. Reagan couldn't stop thinking about it, either. Later in that speech, Reagan returned to this theme of America as a beacon to the world, invoking the memory of another freedom seeker, a man who was also, in his way, a boat person. Reagan continued:

> The past few days when I've been at that window upstairs I've thought a bit of the shining "city upon a hill." The phrase comes from John Winthrop, who wrote it to describe the America he imagined. What he imagined was important because he was an early Pilgrim—an early "Freedom Man." He journeyed here on what today we'd call a little wooden boat; and, like the other pilgrims, he was looking for a home that would be free.
>
> I've spoken of the shining city all my political life, but I don't know if I ever quite communicated what I saw when I said it. But in my mind it was a tall proud city built on rocks stronger than oceans, wind-swept, God-blessed, and teeming with people of all kinds living in harmony and peace—a city with free ports that hummed with commerce and creativity, and if there had to be city walls, the walls had doors and the doors were open to anyone with the will and the heart to get here.

Other American politicians, and other presidents, have mentioned John Winthrop, who became the first governor of Massachusetts. One of them was John Kennedy, who also cited the "city on the hill" in a 1961 speech. But there was something uncommonly poignant about Reagan's idealized vision of that mythical city. He seemed to identify with an aspect of it that eluded many others: John Winthrop's ode to America was a sermon he wrote while still aboard his flagship *Arbella* as it crossed the Atlantic. ("We must consider that we shall be a city set on a hill," he said, borrowing biblical imagery. The eyes of all people are upon us.")[17] Winthrop was telling his followers that they would be watched by the world, and that if they failed in their faith, they would undermine the very cause of religious freedom. To Reagan, this point had a contemporary application; America was to be an example of the merits of freedom. But perhaps the key point is that when he wrote those words, John Winthrop *had yet to lay eyes on the New World*. America then, Ronald Reagan was reminding his countrymen in his last, wistful speech as president, is not a matter of geography, but a state of mind. And it was one that anyone in the world could aspire to inhabit.

"And if there had to be walls, the walls had doors . . ."

Political scientist Hugh Heclo calls this Reagan's "sacramental vision of America." It was a vision that pulled Reagan into public life, and remained with him even as he changed political parties and allegiances. In 1952, when he still considered himself a liberal Democrat, Reagan put it this way: "I, in my own mind, have thought of America as a place in the divine scheme of things that was set aside as a promised land. It was set here and the price of admission was very simple; the means of selection was very simple as to how this land should be populated. Any place in the world and any person from those places; any person with the courage, with the desire to tear up their roots, to strive for freedom, to attempt and dare to live in a strange and foreign place, to travel halfway across the world was welcome here."

And travel halfway around the world they do. In fact, the chances are not remote in 2003, that the "Freedom Man"—an active duty sailor in the United States Navy—patrolling for boat people would himself be an immigrant. At the outbreak of the war in Iraq, some 37,000 sailors, soldiers and Air Force personnel wore the uniforms of the U.S. armed forces but were not citizens. Some of them fought in the deserts of Arabia, and some of them died there.

One of them was a young U.S. Marine named Ahn Chanawongse, who emigrated from Thailand when he was nine years old, with his mother and older brother. "They wanted to be in the land of the free," his uncle said at the funeral. The six uniformed and armed Marines who accompanied the casket to Arlington National Cemetery were complemented by seven Buddhist monks in saffron robes. His mother was presented with an American flag to complement the Purple Heart her son received posthumously. "He was a proud Marine, and we are the proud parents of a Marine," his mother had said upon learning her son had died in a March 23 ambush. "It is very good when we see Saddam's statue come down by his own people. That means what we are doing is the right thing."

In Charley Company of the 1st Battalion, 2nd Marine Regiment of the 1st Marine Division, the young corporal was known as "Chuckles," for his constant laughter and good humor. Awaiting the war's start, he and his Marine buddies played baseball with a ball of rags and a stick, like the soldiers at Valley Forge. "He had a short life, but he was happy, and he made the best out of that and he died with honor and made everybody proud," his mother said. "Even though he passed away, he passed away as a hero."

The Marine Corps, with its mystique, is a magnet for many of these non-citizen soldiers, most of whom are Latino. And there were more funerals to come, and more Purple Hearts to award. On April 11, 2003, the president and first lady Laura Bush went to National Naval Medical Center in Bethesda, Md., to pay their respects to some of the wounded troops. Among those they visited were two "green card Marines," Lance Corporal O. J. Santamaria, a native of the Philippines, and Master Gunnery Sergeant Guadalupe Denogean, a native of Mexico. Both had asked to be citizens, and on this day their requests were granted. Both Marines took their citizenship oath in the presence of their commander-in-chief. Santamaria stood unassisted, despite the fact that he was in obvious pain and was in the process of receiving a blood transfusion. Bush looked on proudly, as the twenty-year-old Marine struggled unsuccessfully not to cry.

Then, turning to Denogean, who grew up in Arizona and who had already served twenty-five years in the Corps, Bush simply said, "*Mucho gusto*," it's my pleasure to meet you. To Denogean's family, Bush added "*Gracias a ustedes*." Thank you all.[18]

On the eve of the war in Iraq, a twenty-four-year-old Marine named Roger Persad, a native of Trinidad, hunkered in his tent as the wind blew across the dark desert sands, his eyes falling on the American flag before he fell asleep at night. "I believe in fighting for freedom and anything that falls under patriotism and loyalty," he told American journalist Wayne Woolley. "I believe in America."[19]

The immigrants who stream into the United States annually understand this attraction. They have arrived in turn-of-the century-type numbers every year since Reagan's first term, changing the very makeup of their new country. So much so that today one out of seven Americans is foreign-born, the first time that has been true since the heyday of Ellis Island. Although these new pilgrims don't differentiate in bright lines between the political freedom and the economic opportunity they will have in their new home, the truth of the matter is that for most of them the economic chance is probably more immediate. That hardly undermines America's claim to exceptionality. The economic power of the United States, and the opportunity that power affords to newly minted Americans, is a better testament to the efficacy of democracy than any public relations man—or any president—could ever jam into a Fourth of July speech. That people risk their lives to reach these shores is something all Americans can take enormous pride in. In any event, these immigrants are getting both freedom and prosperity in the same bargain.

"We share the vision of Walt Whitman that democracy is the *essence* of American spirit and the *purpose* of America's existence," said Vartan Gregorian, an immigrant born in Tabriz, Iran, who came to this country in 1979. He made these remarks on July 4, 2001, at Monticello to a group of new pilgrims about to take their own oaths as American citizens. "Whether we came to the United States for economic opportunity, political or religious asylum, education, security, or reunification with our families and relatives, we all share a common faith in this country."

At the same Monticello July 4th ceremony the year before, then–Secretary of State Madeleine Albright—herself an immigrant—stated clearly that in their condition of independence and strength Americans are obliged to share freedom with those who don't have it, and to work for its expansion. "If our country is to be secure and prosperous in the new century, we must be more than consumers of liberty, we must be the champions and vindicators of it," she said. "We must join with others who believe in what Jefferson called the 'sacred fire of freedom,' and ensure that the democratic tide remains a rising tide around the world."

Another famous immigrant, movie star Arnold Schwarzenegger, is currently planning a run for governor of his adopted home state. Only in California, some say. But to the man known around the world simply as "Arnold," the moral of the story is that only in America could an Austrian bodybuilder with a thick German accent become a multimillionaire, a political force and an international film icon.

"I came to America because of what I read and watched and heard—that this was the land of opportunity," he said at a June 10,

2003, political dinner in Los Angeles. "That this is the greatest country in the world. That anyone here, if they are willing to work hard can make it. Can make their dream turn into reality. Well, I am proof of that. I came over to this country with empty pockets, but I was full of dreams and full of desire. . . . I went *beyond* my dreams, but only because I was in the right country."

These attitudes are utterly typical of immigrants. In a comprehensive recent poll, one thousand immigrants were asked whether they were "happy" they had come to the United States or "generally disappointed." The answers were unambiguous. Only 2 *percent* said they were disappointed, 55 percent said they were "extremely happy," while 41 percent answered "somewhat happy." Ninety-six percent is simply not a number that pollsters expect to find in answer to any question; statistically speaking, this is almost total affirmation. In this survey, done by a respected polling firm called Public Agenda, the margin of error (3 percent) was actually larger than the negative response of 2 percent.[20]

These results are all the more impressive because 69 percent of the respondents in the Public Affairs poll said they came to the United States with "very little" money. The poll also asked specifically why they immigrated to America. [The sub-categories are Mexican-Americans; those from Latin-American nations other than Mexico; Europeans; Asians; and immigrants from the Caribbean islands.]

Thinking about living in the United States, which of these three things is most important to you personally?

	All	Mexican	Latin-American	European	Asian	Caribbean
The opportunity to work and make a living	37%	48%	42%	27%	32%	37%
The personal freedom to live your life the way you choose	40%	31%	36%	49%	41%	32%
The political freedoms like voting or freedom of speech	18%	18%	19%	21%	20%	24%
Don't know	4%	3%	3%	3%	6%	7%

By a margin of 80–11 the respondents, when given a choice between staying in their home country or emigrating to the United States, said they'd come to America all over again. Small wonder. Asked where it was easier "to earn a good living," 88 percent of the immigrants said America; only 4 percent cited the nation where they were born. But the quality-of-life questions weren't all economic. By a two-to-one margin, the immigrants said that the United States is a better place to raise children than their native country, and by more than three-to-one the immigrants believe the educational system in America is better. By overwhelming ratios, the immigrants said the United States has a more honest government, more reliable police officers, a fairer legal system and better health care than the country they left behind. In answers to non-economic questions about their adopted country, the immigrants reported that America treats women better, is more tolerant of religious freedom and is more receptive to immigration than the nation they left behind. The most instructive answer of all came when the pollsters asked immigrants to choose between two statements:

"The United States is a unique country that stands for something special in the world."

or

"The United States is just another country that is no better or worse off than any other."

Eighty percent of immigrants chose the first statement, with very little variation from ethnic groups. Only 16 percent of immigrants believe America is "just another country."[21]

Once upon a time, such attitudes were known in academic circles as "American exceptionalism." Perhaps in some remote scholarly outposts they still are, although the idea is considered passé in the academy. The notion that America is a special place with a special calling dates to the time of the Puritans, and it used to be taught in American schools as a matter of course. In recent decades college professors have attempted to eradicate the idea of American exceptionalism from their students' minds. It is a myth, they say, or outdated, and certainly racist. Many of these professors are leftists, but not all. Even Irving Kristol, a prominent conservative thinker, questioned whether, two centuries after the founding, American "exceptionalism" was still an appropriate way to look at things. "We are now a world power, and a world power is not 'a city on a hill,' a 'light unto the nations'—phrases that, with every passing year, ring more hollow," Kristol wrote in 1995. Brown University professor Gordon S. Wood, a historian of the American Revolution, picked up on this theme in 1998, writing that he didn't see how any American president would ever use such language again—as Kennedy did in 1961—that Americans should: "Let every nation know, whether it wishes us well or ill, that we shall pay any price, bear any burden, meet any hardship, support any friend, oppose any foe to assure the survival and the success of liberty."

Well, guess what? In the aftermath of 9/11, George W. Bush speaks exactly that way—and deliberately so. Standing aboard the USS *Lincoln* on May 1, 2003, Bush said, "Yet all can know, friend and foe alike, that our nation has a mission. We will answer threats to our security, and we will defend the peace."

The young men and women in the U.S. military have certainly picked up on this theme. When Bush spoke at the U.S. Coast Guard Academy commencement on May 21, 2003, a cadet named Greg Ponzi presented the commander-in-chief with a t-shirt reading, "We will not tire. We will not falter. We will not fail." The words were Bush's—he delivered them on September 20, 2001, in his address to the American people, but they were an echo from an earlier president, and an earlier America that made no bones about its exceptionalism: "We can. We will. We must," said Franklin Roosevelt.

Gordon Wood was one of those who noticed. Even before that USS *Lincoln* speech or the president's appearance at the Coast Guard Academy, Wood delivered a lecture at Stanford University in which he described his early epitaph of American exceptionalism to be "perhaps" premature. "After September 11 it appears that we can no longer be sure that our special role in the world is over," Wood said. "We are seeing a revival of our sense of ourselves as a peculiar nation with a special role to play in the world."

Even before 9/11, 72 percent of Americans reported being "very proud" of their nationality. This was significantly higher than any European nation except Ireland. In addition, 90 percent of Americans polled told University of Chicago researchers that they agreed with the statement, "I would rather be a citizen of America than any country in the world." (After 9/11, this figure shot up to 97 percent.) If the current war has strengthened the idea of American exceptionalism, so have immigrants—and they've been doing so for a long time. To these modern pilgrims, America is still more than a destination. It's also an idea. This is not a cliché, but a literal difference: Nations, even one so vast as the United States, are finite. Ideas need not be. This is a distinction that has been on display for more than one hundred years.

The 1890 census, for many Americans living at the time, was a bracing bit of seemingly bad news. Noting the unbroken line of non-Indian settlements in the West, the superintendent of the U.S. Census Bureau basically proclaimed the great American "frontier" to be no more. One of those who thought this had profound implications for Americans' self-image was a young historian, Frederick Jackson Turner, who produced a seminal book that postulated that American exceptionalism was tied up in the unlimited possibilities implied by the vastness of the western frontier. For that reason, Turner inferred, Americanism was unexportable. Moreover, the demise of that frontier suggested to Turner and his devotees that the values of American exceptionalism were unsustainable even within the United States.

This proved not to be the case, as new waves of patriotic immigrants took the place of the old—each generation bringing with them anew the conviction of America as the shining city on the hill. (And not only immigrants. In 1890, the same year as the fateful census, Mark Twain said in his "Foreign Critics" speech: "We are called the nation of inventors. And we are. We could still claim that title and wear its loftiest honors if we had stopped with the first thing we ever invented, which was human liberty.") Intellectuals tended to quote Twain on other matters, not this one. But Turner clearly needed modernizing, and six decades after his history appeared, he got it. In 1954, another eminent historian, David M. Potter, updated the fading frontier theory in an influential work, *People of Plenty: Economic Abundance and the American Character.*

Potter had much to say in this book, some of it optimistic, some of it decidedly pessimistic. He admired the fact that amid its plenty, America had defined poverty up instead of defining it down. But he also offered up the disquieting idea that consumer capitalism was ultimately dependent on advertising, which he defined as getting people to buy things they really did not need—and then throwing them away, so they could buy more. Potter theorized that when bad times hit the United States, as inevitably they must, American exceptionalism would leave Americans particularly ill-equipped emotionally to handle it. And he suggested that America's message to the world was not freedom, but a sense of entitlement to abundance. His implication was that America couldn't deliver on that promise and that, as a result, it was hardly in a position to export democracy to the rest of the world.

"We conceive of democracy as an absolute value, largely ideological in content and equally valid in any environment," Potter wrote, "instead of recognizing that our own democratic system is one of the major by-products of our abundance—workable primarily because of the measure of our abundance."

This passage was quoted approvingly in 1993 by then–House Majority Leader Richard A. Gephardt, who was using it as an argument against the North American Free Trade Agreement. At this writing Gephardt is a candidate for president in 2004, but he's swimming against the tide when it comes to trying to micromanage globalism: Gephardt's worldview has not been shared by any American president in the last thirty years, Republican or Democrat. It was Ronald Reagan who proposed NAFTA, and Bill Clinton who shepherded it through Congress. Clinton's skillful campaign for the treaty was launched in the East Room at an event featuring guest stars Jimmy Carter, Gerald Ford and the first President Bush. And it should be no surprise that the second President Bush accepts as a matter of political faith that free trade, unfettered commerce and freedom are all linked.

"Recent events have provided the world with a clear and dramatic choice," Bush said on October 29, 2001. "Our enemies—the terrorists and their supporters—offer a narrow and backward vision. They feed resentment, envy, and hatred. They fear human creativity, choice, and diversity. Powerless to build a better world, they seek to destroy a world that is passing them by. . . . We offer a better way. When nations respect the creativity and enterprise of their people, they find social and economic progress. When nations open their markets to the world, their people find new ways to create wealth. When nations accept the rules of the modern world, they discover the benefits of the modern world."

The following summer, at an August 6 event at which he signed the Trade Act of 2002, Bush amplified on this theme. "Free trade is also a proven strategy for building global prosperity and adding to the momentum of political freedom," he said. "History shows that as nations become more prosperous, their citizens will demand, and can afford, a cleaner environment. And greater freedom for commerce across borders eventually leads to greater freedom for citizens within the borders."

Author and journalist Michael Elliott, himself an émigré from

Great Britain, noted that Americans tend to give God credit for their richness instead of their own hard work, or—like Australians are wont to do, their plain "dumb luck" at living in such a bounteous land. Surely, the national work ethic and North America's great natural resources have assisted in America's success story. But what is unique about America is its founding principles. Cognizant of this obvious historic truth, American presidents speak as though David Potter had it precisely backwards: It is, they say, American democracy that produces the free-market system that allows the American economic engine to hum so loudly. America's continuing prosperity, in turn, propels each new wave of immigration to the United States, a steady pool of workers and con-sumers, who keep the cycle going, while repatriating money to their loved ones abroad and perpetuating the narrative of the city on the hill. It is not as far back as John Winthrop, but George Washington would have thought it odd that anyone would deny American exceptionalism. For him it was the point of the Revolution. And the Revolution was won.

"When we consider the magnitude of the prize we contended for, the doubtful nature of the contest, and the favorable manner in which it has terminated, we shall find the greatest possible reason for gratitude and rejoicing," President Washington wrote the state governors on June 8, 1783. "The Citizens of America . . . acknowledged to be possessed of absolute Freedom and Independency [are] from this period to be consid-ered as the Actors on a most conspicuous Theatre, which seems to be peculiarly designated by Providence for the display of human greatness and felicity."

Certainly, this is the view of America's forty-third president, who would generally be considered an unabashed proponent of American ex-ceptionalism. Actually, Bush's views on this point are more nuanced. True, he's been known to pepper his speeches with phrases in which he calls America the world's "greatest nation" and her citizens "the finest people on the face of the Earth."[22] But if one listens closely, Bush is si-multaneously a kind of a universalist. He quotes Jefferson literally, and tends to take him at face value. That is to say, he believes fervently that freedom is not only for Americans. In holding to this view, Bush is falling in formation with a long line of American presidents, something he him-self has alluded to. On February 25, 2002, at an event commemorating the sixtieth anniversary of Voice of America, Bush said, "As President

Reagan said, freedom is not the sole prerogative of the lucky few, but the inalienable right—inalienable and universal right of all human beings."

Five days after the fighting began in Iraq, Bush traveled to MacDill Air Force Base in Florida and put it this way:

> Our entire coalition has a job to do, and it will not end with the liberation of Iraq. We will help the Iraqi people to find the benefits and assume the duties of self-government. The form of those institutions will arise from Iraq's own culture and its own choices. . . . The people of Iraq deserve to stand on their feet as free men and women, the citizens of a free country. This goal of a free and peaceful Iraq unites our coalition, and this goal comes from the deepest convictions of America. The freedom you defend is the right of every person and the future of every nation.
>
> The liberty we prize is not America's gift to the world; it is God's gift to humanity. The Army's special forces define their mission in a motto: *To liberate the oppressed.* Generations of men and women in uniform have served and sacrificed in this cause. Now the call of history has come once again to all in our military and to all in our coalition. We are answering that call. We have no ambition in Iraq except the liberation of its people.

The line about liberty being God's gift to humanity began appearing in Bush's speeches within ten weeks of September 11, 2001, and has been repeated by the president more than a dozen times. It is a logical extension of Jefferson's words. The torch of life, liberty and the pursuit of happiness has been passed over the decades from white men to black men. And then, to women. And to immigrants. To Germans, Japanese and Italians. To the African colonies and to India. To Pakistan. To the people of the former Soviet bloc—and the Russians themselves. To the handicapped. To Central Americans. And now to Kuwaitis, Bosnians, Kosovars, Afghans and, hopefully, to Iraqis.[23]

Bush Forty-One used the phrase *pursuit of happiness* to apply to all these waves of liberation theory. In 1981, he roused an audience at Tuskegee Institute with the phrase. He was appearing there, as vice president, to assure a skeptical audience of African-Americans that the Reagan administration wouldn't turn back the clock on civil rights legislation—that it would update the laws on the books: "As we will not tolerate or condone the irresponsible actions of those who would deprive black and minority Americans of their right to life, liberty and the pursuit of happiness as envisioned by our country's founding fathers."

As President, Bush used the Declaration's language to explain the need for the bill he signed on July 26, 1990, the Americans With Disabilities Act. "Today's legislation brings us closer to that day when no Americans will ever again be deprived of their basic guarantee of life, liberty and the pursuit of happiness," the president said.

The same year, Bush Forty-One applied the phrase to foreigners who yearned to bring freedom to their land. In his 1990 State of the Union address, Bush re-created for American audiences the scene two months earlier in Czechoslovakia, as that nation prepared to throw off forty years of communist rule. A brewery worker dressed in overalls, Zdenek Janicek, rose to speak—and began by reading the Preamble. "We hold these truths to be self-evident . . ." This may have surprised Americans—or maybe not—but it was what Janicek's audience would have expected. During the Cold War, Charter 77, the Czech version of Poland's Solidarity movement, translated Martin Luther King Jr.'s "Letter from Birmingham Jail" and disseminated it to Freedom Men (and women) in the trade union movement that became a democracy movement. "America, not just the nation, but an idea alive in the minds of the people everywhere," Bush said. "Our nation is the enduring dream of every immigrant who ever set foot on these shores, and the millions still struggling to be free. This nation, this idea called America was and always will be a new world, our new world."

Secretary of State Colin Powell, in a July 4, 2002, speech at Independence Hall, expounded on this thesis. "The most famous of these words [in the Declaration] we all know by heart," he said. "*We hold these truths to be self-evident, that all men are created equal.* Thirteen words for the thirteen colonies. Thirteen words that, 226 years later, still throw the light of hope into the darkest corners of tyranny and oppression. Thirteen words conveying truths that need no explanation or analysis or debate. They're not facts; they're truths. They're self-evident. . . ." Powell continued:

> And they are unalienable, meaning no one can take them away. . . .
> There are many other rights that were not mentioned by the signers of the Declaration, but these rights they did mention: God granted us life, God intended us to have liberty, and God expected us to pursue happiness. Everyone knows these lines oh, so well. But it's the

next line of the Declaration that I really love. It says that, "To secure these rights, governments are instituted among men, deriving their just powers from the consent of the governed. . . ."

The Declaration says, "secure the rights." Not protect them. Secure them. If people do not yet have them, the government's responsibility is to secure them, get them, and give all people . . . these God-given rights to life, liberty and the pursuit of happiness.

By choosing those words, secure those rights, Jefferson gave us a glimpse of his vision for the future. Because when he wrote about equality and unalienable rights, he knew that those rights didn't apply to everyone—not at that time, not in this place. They didn't apply to women. They didn't apply to people who owned no land. They didn't apply to black people. They surely didn't apply to the slaves that Jefferson had on his plantation at Monticello. . . .

And it is no less our responsibility as citizens of the world's greatest democracy to ensure that our country, this great country of ours, remains a force for freedom all around the world. After all, unalienable rights were given to all humankind. They belong to every man, woman and child on this earth. . . . So just as we must always stand up for our own rights and the rights of our fellow citizens, Americans must also stand with courageous men and women all around the world who seek to secure the rights of their fellow citizens.

Powell's speech attracted modest attention nationally, but it struck a cord inside the White House. While the newspapers were full of speculation about tension between Powell and Donald Rumsfeld, Powell's Philadelphia speech summed up what other administration aides were trying to explain to the nation. It was touted to me by a West Wing aide in private and cited by top State Department official Richard N. Haass in public. In a December 4, 2002, speech to the prestigious Council on Foreign Relations titled *Towards Greater Democracy in the Muslim World,* Haass said, "The United States will assist other nations to achieve these basic human aspirations because they are universal. These values are not just lifestyles America thinks it ought to export."

Bush himself put it this way in a September 17, 2002, speech: "You see, ours is a history of freedom. One of the most precious ideas we have is freedom for everybody. We love our freedoms. We love the idea of being a free society. And throughout our history, people have fought for freedom. Whether it's been in the Revolutionary War or the heroic struggle to end slavery or civil rights wars in the United States Congress, or whether it's World War II, where we fought to free people from tyranny, the history of this nation has been a history of freedom and justice."

In one sense, this is what any American president might be expected to say. Yet it can also be said that George W. Bush is floating a radical idea here. Although he doesn't say it just this way, the idea appears to be this encompassing: That the attacks of September 11, 2001, showed the civilized world that planet Earth is too small to have *any* dictatorships in it. And in furtherance of this idea, Bush rhetorically places the United States not in the role of architect of this plan, but as a kind of subcontractor in something that he sees as a much grander design.

It is not a surprise that this would strike some people as a bit *too* grand, not to mention dangerous and naïve besides. Tocqueville wrote, after visiting the United States, of this "irresistible revolution" of democracy. But he also complained of Americans' overbearing and brassy brand of jingoism, even if it was employed in the noble cause of freedom. "It is impossible to conceive a more troublesome or more garrulous patriotism," he wrote. "It wearies even those disposed to respect it."

This is still true today.

Charles R. Kesler, a Harvard-trained political scientist who edits the conservative *Claremont Review of Books,* wrote in the summer 2003 issue of his publication: "The president seems sometimes to regard liberty and democracy as synonyms, which they are not. Across the Islamic world, democracy seems to be confused with a species of majoritarian tyranny. The refrain is: Throw out the local despots and let the people rule, even if, perhaps especially if, they lust after an 'Islamic republic' so severe that it would make republican Rome look softhearted. Once in power, the mullahs will solve the problem of majority tyranny—by so arranging things that no future majority can ever vote them out."

This is a pretty accurate description of what happened in Iran, and what may yet happen in Kuwait, Saudi Arabia—even Iraq, if the Bush administration loses its verve or its mandate. As Kesler points out, in his pithy aside: "Democracy doesn't mean 'One man, one vote, once.'"

Yet, what is to be done about the millions of Shiite Muslims in southern Iraq who were persecuted and dispossessed by Saddam, but whose thanks to the Americans for liberating them was to promptly go on a pilgrimage that had been banned for twenty-five years—and denounce American soldiers en route? Those depressing images did not

undo the stirring pictures of American soldiers being kissed and serenaded as they rolled through Iraq, but they certainly undermined Bush's
easy confidence that long-suffering Iraqis would instantly embrace a plu-
ralistic, democratic style of governance.

And while agreeing with Bush's premise that the "desire for freedom" seems universal, liberal Columbia University professor Eric Foner
sounded a couple of other notes of caution about the Administration's
expectation that Iraqis would simply inhale the elixir of "freedom" and
thereby make everything right in their country. Foner's first caveat is that
America's own understanding of what is meant by freedom has evolved
over two centuries—and that it's unrealistic to expect a nation like Iraq
to suddenly be transfigured into a twenty-first century version of the
United States. "Far from being timeless and universal, our own definition of freedom has changed many times," Foner pointed out. "The
story of freedom is one of debates, disagreements and struggles rather
than fixed definitions or uninterrupted progress toward a preordained
goal."[24] Foner's second caveat was that freedom, however much it may
be craved, is "more than a set of ideas" and must take root in a nation's
institutions, popular culture—and laws.

This is the point in the discourse that is the cue for Fareed Zakaria,
author of *The Future of Freedom: Illiberal Democracy at Home and
Abroad*. In the same day's issue of the *Times* in which Foner was reminding Americans of the pitfalls that remain in Iraq, Zakaria was
quoted in another article as saying, "If six months from now America
has packed its bags and left, there's a very small chance that Iraq will be
a real democracy."

Expounding on the theme that freedom and democracy are not
precisely the same thing, Zakaria posits in his book that people need
freedom first, then democracy. If that requires a bit of authoritarianism
for a while, so be it. It's not easy for a nation used to totalitarianism
to embrace the practices embodied in freedom of speech, assembly and
worship, the notion of private property and binding contracts. It's called
the rule of law, and if it's not in place before free elections and free-
market capitalism are instituted, it can lead to the kind of near-anarchy
and lawlessness associated with modern Russia.

That need not be Iraq's fate. "Iraq could well become the first
major Arab country to combine Arab culture with economic dynamism,
religious tolerance, liberal politics, and a modern outlook on the

world," Zakaria wrote in a passage that sounds like it could have come from Bush himself. "And success is infectious."

In hopes that democracy will prove catching, the White House appointed Noah Feldman, an assistant law professor from New York University, to advise Iraq's leaders on how to draw up a Constitution that a majority of Iraqis will embrace. Although he is only thirty-two years of age, Feldman has a Ph.D. in Islamic studies, speaks fluent Arabic, and is quite popular with his students. And he's a democrat, with a small "d." "The critical decisions," he said, "are [to be] made by the [Iraqi] people."

But pessimism can be contagious, too, however, and in the rhythms of modern politics—which means the maw of the twenty-four-hour news cycle—some of the worldwide debate as spring changed to summer of 2003 centered on the failure to find weapons of mass destruction and, in turn, to ascertaining Bush's deepest motivations for the invasion.

Anti-American critics abroad divined such intentions as the United States' desire to steal Iraq's oil, thwart the expansion of Islam, or build an American "empire." These purported explanations were, each in their own way, absurd. First of all, if the United States coveted Iraq's oil, all it had to do was lift the U.N. sanctions (which France and Russia had opposed to begin with), and buy it on the open world market, which it will soon be required to do anyway. As for the second reason, the world's democracies freely allow Muslims to emigrate to their nations and to worship freely. It is the Arab states that restrict the practicing of religion, not the West. The canard about colonialism was put in perspective by Colin Powell when he was asked by the former archbishop of Canterbury if empire-building wasn't really the Yanks' aims. "We have gone forth from our shores repeatedly over the last one hundred years— and we've done this as recently in the last year in Afghanistan—and put wonderful young men and women at risk, many of whom have lost their lives," Powell said tersely. "And we have asked for nothing except enough ground to bury them in. . . ."

Bush himself made this observation earlier, in a Memorial Day visit to Normandy in 2002. "And in all those victories American soldiers came to liberate, not to conquer," Bush said. "The only land we claim as our own are the resting places of our men and women."

Less than a month after the attacks of 9/11, Lynne Cheney, wife of the vice president, gave a speech in Dallas called "Teaching our Children About America." In it, she discussed the palpable fear that stalked Europe during the Second World War. Quoting from historian Stephen Ambrose's book *Citizen Soldiers*, Mrs. Cheney recalled those dark days in the 1940s "when twelve-man squads of teenage boys armed and in uniform struck terror into people's hearts all around the globe. . . ."

> But there was an exception: a squad of GIs, a sight that brought the biggest smiles you ever saw to people's lips, and joy to their hearts. Around the world this was true . . . because GIs meant candy, cigarettes, C-rations, and freedom. America had sent the best of her young men around the world, not to conquer but to liberate, not to terrorize but to help.

This was the other side of the coin from John Hersey's pie-loving Marines who wanted to go home. These were the young soldiers of the United States who helped unshackle a world. But even as Iraq was being freed from a familiar kind of tyrant, Bush-bashers raised repeated questions impugning the president's motives for going to war there in the first place. Although they took care to praise the performance of American troops in the field, these critics harped on the absence of the chemical and biological weapons Bush had all but guaranteed would be found. The president, they said, had committed the nation to an impetuous, if not illegal, war based on trumped-up intelligence briefings that hyped Saddam Hussein's supposed arsenal of weapons of mass destruction. It was, they said, the Gulf of Tonkin all over again.

From his perch as a *New York Times* columnist, Princeton economist Paul Krugman emerged as the most dependable and strident of the Bush critics. Speaking for many on the left, Krugman asserted in column after column that Bush had fabricated evidence against Saddam Hussein simply because he wanted a war, presumably to help his reelection chances in 2004. "It's no answer to say that Saddam was a murderous tyrant," Krugman added.

That rather callous (to Iraqis) sentiment was a minority view, but not a fringe view. A Gallup Poll conducted the same week Krugman wrote his anti-Bush, antiwar columns—the first week of June of 2003—asked Americans how relevant they considered weapons of mass destruction. While a solid majority of 56 percent said the war was justified even if such weapons are never found, 23 percent of those polled said it was justified only if such weapons were found, and 18 percent said it wasn't justified at all. Even more alarming, one-third of Americans told pollsters that they thought Bush had "deliberately" hyped the intelligence information about weapons of mass destruction in Iraq.[25] So Krugman spoke for many Americans. But so, too, did his *Times* colleague, three-time Pulitzer Prize winner Thomas L. Friedman, who opened his April 27 column by commenting on the skull from Iraq that the paper had pictured on page one days earlier.[26] It was a skull that could belong to anyone—Saddam's reign of terror was pretty indiscriminate—and it served as a symbol of the murderous nature of his regime. "Just under the picture was an article about President Bush vowing that weapons of mass destruction will be found in Iraq, as he promised," Friedman wrote. "As far as I'm concerned, we do not need to find any weapons of mass destruction to justify this war."

> That skull, and the thousands more that will be unearthed, are enough for me. Mr. Bush doesn't owe the world any explanation for missing chemical weapons (even if it turns out that the White House hyped this issue). It is clear that in ending Saddam's tyranny, a huge human engine for mass destruction has been broken. The thing about Saddam's reign is that when you look at that skull, you don't even know what period it came from—his suppression of the Kurds or the Shiites, his insane wars with Iran and Kuwait, or just his daily brutality.

Friedman's view, as it often does in Middle East politics, will probably emerge as the prevailing national perspective in the United States. But if the success of what Bush began calling "the battle of Iraq" doesn't hinge for most Americans on its putative legal justification under international law, it certainly *will* be judged on whether a decent society with a functioning government emerges in Iraq. This is entirely as it should be. Bush convinced Americans to go to war in Iraq, and he sent the troops there. If that country does not embrace a democratic constitution guaranteeing life, liberty and the pursuit of happiness to its citizens then Americans will have died in vain, and George W. Bush is the proper person to be held accountable for that failure.

Some days, Bush sounds as if he understands the complexities of bringing this about; some days he doesn't. Speaking in Chicago on June 11, 2003, Bush said flatly, "Thanks to the bravery of our military, and to friends and allies, the regime of Saddam Hussein is no more. The world is peaceful and free. Thanks to their bravery and their sacrifice, the world is more peaceful, America is more secure, and the Iraqi people are now free."

He tossed in an admonition about there still being "work to do in Iraq," but this was your basic upbeat—some would say Pollyannaish—assessment. Bush's hopeful scenarios seemingly knew no bounds. In June of 2003, he opined that "success in Iraq" could pave the way for a "truly democratic Palestinian state"—even as Hamas-directed suicide bombers were turning Israel's civilian buses into slaughterhouses.

Other days, Bush was more pensive, more appreciative of the subtleties involved. He said on a couple of occasions that he believed a representative government would materialize in Baghdad, and he said he hoped the Iraqis realized the importance of the doctrine of separation of church and state—and the need to adopt a Constitution that protected the rights of minorities.

"I'm confident that a government will emerge," he said at one point. "I dismiss the critics who say that democracy can't flourish in Iraq. It may not look like America. You know, Thomas Jefferson may not emerge. . . ."

Bush made those comments in an interview with NBC anchor Tom Brokaw, which aired April 25, 2003. The following night, while attending the annual White House Correspondents' Dinner, the president expressed similar sentiments to the author, including the worry that the Iraqis may not find a Jefferson among their number. "Or a John Adams," Bush added.

Ah, but maybe they will.

The same night, I ran into Jeffrey Goldberg of *The New Yorker* and we discussed this book. He laughed with pleasure when apprised of Bush's remarks—but he wasn't laughing at Bush. Goldberg related that while he was communing in the highlands of Iraq with the leaders of the Kurds, he discovered something so unlikely, so hopeful, that it can only be considered the counterweight to the men of the seventh century who launched this war from their own caves in Afghanistan.

"Oh, the Kurds know all about the Declaration of Independence," Goldberg said. "Some of them have read *Founding Brothers*. They'll tell you who among them reminds them of which Founding Father. Some of them like Adams; some prefer Jefferson."

Later, Jeffrey told me of having dinner at the house of Barham Salih, the English-educated prime minister of one of two rival Kurdish factions. It was Salih who had read *Founding Brothers*, and who reminded the American journalist that even the Founding Fathers had quarreled among themselves, argued, and nurtured grudges. One of them (Aaron Burr) actually shot another one (Alexander Hamilton), yet they had managed to produce this remarkable document and its timeless revolution. Excitedly, Salih opened Joseph Ellis' book and pointed to pages where Jefferson predicts that democracy will eventually replace tyranny everywhere. "This ball of liberty, I believe most piously," Jefferson predicted in a 1795 letter to a friend, "is now so well in motion that it will roll around the globe." Ellis also quotes briefly from the letter Jefferson wrote to Roger Weightman days before his death. A nostalgic Jefferson totes up the accomplishments of the "host of worthies" who met in Philadelphia. "All eyes are opened or opening to the rights of man," Jefferson wrote with pride.

Fifty years earlier, the Argonauts, he was saying, had convinced the world that freedom and self-government were unalienable and undeniable—and Jefferson predicted that this "palpable truth" would ultimately find its way to the far corners of the earth.

The house of Barham Salih, in the town of Sulaimaniya, is just such a remote corner. And a dangerous place for the apostles of liberty. In an assassination attempt against him a year earlier, the Ansar al-Islam terrorist group had detonated a bomb in that dwelling that killed six of Salih's bodyguards and a personal secretary. But on this night, as he pointed intently into the pages of an American book, this Kurdish revolutionary remarked that the ball of liberty set in motion in Philadelphia in 1776 had indeed made its way to his time and to the remote reaches of his lands.

"It's even reached here!" he said. "So, you see, Jefferson was right."

Epilogue and Acknowledgments

In the second week of April 2003, much of the staff of my publication, *National Journal*, was in Boston for the funeral of Michael Kelly, who had been killed near Baghdad when the vehicle he was riding in while embedded with the Army 3rd Infantry Division came under fire and veered into a canal. Michael had been a columnist at our magazine, then our editor, and at the time of his death, was the editorial director of our company, which includes *The Atlantic Monthly*.

To say that Michael was beloved in our newsroom is an understatement. We were lucky to get the magazine out that week. I stayed behind to help accomplish that task, and was sitting at my desk writing Michael's obituary at noon on Tuesday, April 8, when Department of Defense spokeswoman Victoria Clarke opened her televised daily briefing by reciting the names of American military personnel killed in Iraq. This day she cited three Marines. The last one was the name I had been hoping and praying *not* to hear. "First Lieutenant Brian M. McPhillips of Pembroke, Massachusetts," she said.

Brian was twenty-five years old. He was the only son of Julie and David McPhillips, longtime family friends. The last time I'd seen Brian he was a young teenager, but in late March, Julie called to tell me that he had graduated from Providence College and had promptly joined the Marine Corps. Brian, she told me, was a unit commander in the 2nd Tank Battalion, 2nd Marine Division. After hanging up the phone, I asked one of our editors, Patrick Pexton, who was keeping track of the embedded reporters we had in the field, where the 2nd Marines were heading. "Into some very heavy shit," he replied.

So I walked out of our building down the street to St. Matthew's Cathedral, where the body of John F. Kennedy once lay in state. There,

I lit a candle for Brian McPhillips and for Michael Kelly, and said prayers for them both. The Lord had his own ways, however. Michael died on Thursday night, April 3. Brian was killed in a firefight the following day, April 4, 2003.

Both of them believed in the war in Iraq. Brian understood that he was going there to liberate Iraqis and to protect his own country. Michael had written that it had been a mistake for the United States to leave a barbaric, totalitarian regime in power in Iraq twelve years earlier—a tragedy for the people of Iraq. He agitated in his column for America to rectify that omission; and when George W. Bush decided to do just that, Mike shipped himself over there to see the story through. He was putting his money where his mouth was, as men our age used to say.

I think of those two every day, and of the others deployed there as well. I wince now when I read the morning newspapers. One of my fears is that soon after this book is published the number of American servicemen killed in Iraq since Saddam's fall will surpass the number who died during the time it took to invade and occupy the country. I was agnostic about this war, although I tried to keep those misgivings to myself. But I am not agnostic about it now: The invasion took place; the only good result would be for Iraqis to embrace democracy, and to accept a Constitution that guarantees all of the people of that land the right to life, liberty and the pursuit of happiness. I became convinced in the research and writing of this book that those rights *are* unalienable, that the yearning for them is universal as well, and that, ultimately, there is no real safety or satisfaction to be had until all the people of the world are free. I do not expect to live long enough to see such a thing, but Jefferson didn't even manage to free his own slaves. In other words, it's a long process. We only hope that our generation makes some advancement.

That next generation of Americans will derive its authority in that "straight line" that President Bush mentioned in Ripley, West Va. It runs through the early Virginians, Washington, Jefferson, Madison, Mason and then north, through the Adamses of Massachusetts (Abigail, John and John Quincy). The line was strengthened by the words of Abraham Lincoln and Stephen Douglass, and includes the many deeds of the Roosevelts of New York (Theodore, Eleanor and Franklin). It weaves through the lives and careers of Hubert Humphrey, Lyndon Johnson and Martin Luther King Jr., through the Kennedys—yes, Anthony Kennedy, too—and Carter and Reagan and our two most recent dynasties, the Clintons and the Bushes. And the line was held by U. S. Grant and

Dwight D. Eisenhower, and all the twenty-year-olds they commanded from Vicksburg to Normandy.

Paying homage to the American sacrifice on D-Day, French president Francois Mitterrand once said, "The 6th of June sounded the hour when history tipped toward the camp of freedom." In a Memorial Day service at the Normandy American Cemetery in Colleville-Sur-Mer in 2002, Bush told a story of a French woman coming upon the U.S. paratroopers who dropped inland before dawn that fateful day. She implored them not to leave. One trooper said, "We're not leaving. If necessary, this is the place we die." And many did.

There are other ways to serve. My niece enlisted in the Army reserves on the eve of the Iraq war, and was called to active duty. My eldest daughter has decided to become an elementary school teacher. When she mentioned this to President Bush one night, he said, simply, "Thank you." My son is deciding between the military and law school. His interest in constitutional law was sparked by James S. Todd , a lecturer in the political science department at the University of Arizona. I am indebted to Professor Todd for this; also for the vignette in chapter nine about Thomas Jefferson writing to Madison about the poor French woman he met in his travels.

Jefferson's ruminations on market capitalism and the future of self-government served as a reminder to me that the faucet of liberation, once it begins flowing, is not an easy one to turn off. Ronald Reagan and George W. Bush have said that they believe the concept of life, liberty and the pursuit of happiness should—and will—eventually be extended to unborn children. This vision, expressed in the context of partisan American electoral politics, has probably not been given its due in the intellectual discourse of this nation. I suspect Reagan and Bush will be proven right. But that's not all, full human rights for women and girls all over the globe will be a cause that becomes "self-evident." Gay and lesbian rights are being expanded as I write these words. The same American jurist, Tony Kennedy, who pulled the Declaration out of his pocket in a Boston high school, wrote a decision invalidating a Colorado statute that attempted to proscribe gay rights; he also voted in the majority on a June 2003 U.S. Supreme Court that overturned laws prohibiting gay sexual behavior. The latest interest group to employ the Preamble to its cause, however, is not the right-to-life lobby or the gay lobby, but the animal rights movement.

As I write these words, People for the Ethical Treatment of Animals is preparing its "Declaration of Independence t-shirts" for sale on the Fourth of July. PETA as a modern incarnation of Thomas Jefferson may seem a stretch; surely that organization, in particular, has marginalized itself with its absolutist dietary views and the mean-spiritedness— toward humans—of some of its publicity stunts. However, just because *homo sapiens* have been eating meat for fifty millennia doesn't mean we will forever. This July 4th PETA is asking people to issue their "personal declarations" on how they will change their lifestyles "to bring the right *to life, liberty and the pursuit of happiness* one step closer for animals." That might strike some readers of this work as a frivolous use of the language of 1776. I'm no longer sure of that. Writing this book made me less certain of such things.

I began this project also harboring skepticism about the current state of the academic history profession. Plagiarism scandals are one thing—they strike with frequency in my own profession, as well—but the partisanship shown by so many of the nation's elite historians during the current and previous presidential administrations was unsettling. I wasn't impressed by the petition signed by hundreds of historians warning that impeaching Bill Clinton would leave the presidency "permanently disfigured," thereby "undermining the Constitution." I believed that the true motives of the main instigators, Princeton professor Sean Wilentz and Arthur Schlesinger Jr., were revealed by Wilentz's over-the-top threat to House impeachment managers that "history will track you down and condemn you for your cravenness." Clinton *was* impeached, but he defeated conviction in the Senate. In his remaining time in office, Clinton found sufficient energy remaining in the executive branch not only to save Kosovo, but to entangle himself in another scandal, this one involving pardons, on his way out the door. Yet Clinton left the White House with a 65 percent job approval rating, helped install his wife in the Senate, and retained the loyalty of tens of thousands of Democratic Party stalwarts who tend to believe to this day that Al Gore made a mistake in 2000 by putting too much distance between himself and the Man from Hope.

Were the historians chastened? Apparently not. The next petition from their venue that attracted mass support showed up in the autumn of 2002, and it attempted to undercut Bush's march toward Iraq. Only Congress, these historians insisted, has the right to commit U.S. troops to battle. In their petition, these historians called on Congress to vote, up or down, on whether to "declare war on Iraq." With a Republican in the Oval Office, the historian signers had switched sides in the intellectual debate. When Clinton was president, they were all a-twitter about the possibility of weakening the presidency. Four years later, they wanted to reign in the president's authority and give to Congress a dormant power it hadn't exercised since 1941. The most disillusioning aspect of the petition wasn't the obvious partisan nature of the thing, but its naiveté. Neither Bush nor Congress wanted to "declare war on Iraq" because this is precisely what they said they weren't doing—attacking the Iraqi people. Just as Lincoln never acknowledged the legality of the Confederacy, the Bush administration was signaling that it questioned the very legitimacy of Saddam Hussein's dictatorship—of his sovereign right to lead the country.

And yet. . . .

My worries about the state of the history profession did not survive the process of writing this book. James Todd was just the beginning. The first place I went for research was the Papers of George Washington. So much of the work there has been digitized that almost anyone can hack around in them, but there are times when any researcher needs help. I was assisted by the University of Virginia's Philander Chase and Frank E. Grizzard Jr., the papers' editors. Frank sent me the citation for George Washington's baseball watching at Valley Forge; he also knew right where to find the documentation of George Washington's largesse toward the free school in Alexandria.

At Princeton University, in a project that began in 1950, the thirty-first volume of the Papers of Thomas Jefferson has just gone to the printer—and they are only up to the year 1800. The National Archives and the Jefferson Library at Monticello have put a lot of these documents on-line. For material that isn't, Barbara B. Oberg and James P. McClure of Princeton will try and steer a researcher in the right direction. It was Jim McClure who told me that Jefferson made a $100 gift to Princeton when the school was trying to construct a new building. "And that was a pretty fair piece of change," he said. In Boston, Anne Decker Cecere, senior editor of the John Adams Papers, explained the haphazard spelling in Abigail and John Adams' correspondence about women's rights. In Hyde Park, archivist Mark Renovitch was able to dig out precisely how many times Franklin Roosevelt used the phrase *pursuit of happiness*, while supervisory archivist Raymond Teichman unearthed six speeches in which FDR employed the word "ingenuity." Allida Black, director and editor of the Eleanor Roosevelt Papers project at George Washington University, was able to confirm the exact wording—and discern the citation—for an Eleanor Roosevelt quote about true happiness. The best source for accurate Mark Twain quotes has been compiled by website publisher Barbara Schmidt who spends much of her life providing the precise citation for famous Twain quotes—and patiently debunking others. That's a lot of debunking; my father offered half-jokingly to write a book with me called *They Never Said It*. Half the volume would be fake Twain quotes. One chapter would certainly be bogus Tocqueville quotes, which John J. Pitney Jr. of Claremont McKenna College alerted me to. I cannot thank everyone who gave of their time in this way, but I am indebted to all of them.

Often, these academics and other lovers-of-history went out of their way to assist me. Historical societies in Minnesota, Maryland, Maine, Kansas and Ohio were only too happy to fax or mail copies of Civil War letters. Russell Duncan, editor of *Blue-Eyed Child of Fortune: The Civil War Letters of Robert Gould Shaw*, seemed to have disappeared, which was unfortunate because I wanted to ask him if it was true that Shaw sang the John Brown song as he marched into Harper's Ferry. The story *was* true, as I discovered when Duncan, now teaching at the University of Copenhagen, graciously responded by e-mail to my all-points bulletin on his whereabouts. Nancy Unger at Santa Clara University regaled me for a long time with many stories about Bob La Follette; George Mason University professor Roy Rosenzweig shared arcane—but vital—information on Theodore Roosevelt.

It was humbling, as well, how some of the same scholars kept turning up. David McCullough on John Adams; David McCullough on Truman. William Lee Miller of the University of Virginia on John Quincy Adams; William Lee Miller on Lincoln. Stanford's David M. Kennedy on World War I. David Kennedy on the Great Depression—and World War II. Also, a person can read books by people like this and still have further questions. I had them, in particular, for Pauline Maier on the early declarations of independence by local governments in the colonies. She patiently answered my queries by phone and by e-mail, once while she was on vacation. This was typical of the dedication I found in these professors who proved not only knowledgeable, but almost without exception accessible, pleasant and eager to teach. I had been told that George Washington University history professor emeritus Walter Berns was a hopeless grouch. But when I called him he was a peach. And so it went.

Eminences such as David Kennedy, James McPherson and Alan Brinkley had no qualms about answering questions about their scholarship. It didn't take long for me to realize that the very idea that a freshman in college could walk in and take a class from Professor Kennedy or Jack Rakove or David W. Brady is a small miracle—and that's just at Stanford! A student at Columbia can be taught by Brinkley or Eric Foner; a Princeton undergrad can take classes by McPherson, Wilentz Barbara Oberg or, if that student is willing to walk across the quad to the political science department, from the pioneering presidential scholar Fred I. Greenstein. They are all a wonder—and there are thousands more. It's enough to make a person wish he were eighteen again.

I must also thank Charles Green, the editor of *National Journal*, who patiently waited for me to resume my previous presence at the White House beat, and to John Fox Sullivan and David Bradley, our publisher and owner, respectively. The one indispensable person has been Delia M. Rios, who covers a beat she created, the American Identity, for *Newhouse Newspapers*. Delia read every word of this manuscript, twice, made hundreds of suggestions, and did a great deal of research. She was a sounding board, and a friend, and I thank her. My wife Sharon was exceedingly patient and supportive in myriad ways—sometimes by what she did *not* say. She has never mentioned, for instance, that I haven't cut the grass in a year. I suppose she's been doing it herself. Our youngest child, who was six years old when I started this project, is now eight. I owe her several fishing trips.

Readers will have noticed that I tend to quote American political leaders, especially presidents, at length. I did this partly because I observed at the conferences I attended on presidential studies that learned men and women with advanced degrees would discuss "presidential communications" for hours at a time without ever actually quoting presidents themselves, except in snippets. I found the same to be true even in lengthy biographies of presidents. For the purposes of this book, this device of truncation struck me as insufficient. I was writing about how presidents' words help shape public opinion—and the public's perception of great events—during times of war or in the midst of great social movements in peacetime. And Americans often listen to the important presidential speeches, if not in their entirety, for more than a few seconds at a time.

This habit made the book longer than my publisher originally wanted, and I thank Rowman & Littlefield for their forbearance. While

I'm on that subject, I might add as well that when this book was conceived the war I had in mind was the amorphous War on Terror. That quickly turned into the war in Afghanistan, which gave way to the war in Iraq. The upshot was that, whatever his merits or drawbacks as a theorist and a commander-in-chief, George W. Bush made my book late to the publisher. I thank my editor, Jennifer Knerr, for her patience on this front as well.

Pushing deadline was not the only characteristic of journalism that I fell back on. As a professional reporter, not an academic, I eschewed the scholars' practice of compiling an extensive bibliography and citation notes for each chapter. Instead, I used a device common to my craft: identifying the source material as I went along. But this is not a perfect method. For one thing, the attribute-as-you-go school is not always compatible with the narrative writing process. In addition, certain niceties of form—such as the page number or the web site coordinates—of a particular citation often get left behind. To that sin, I plead guilty. I only hope readers find it a venial, and not a mortal transgression. Any mistakes I made are, of course, solely mine and will be corrected in any future editions.

If it is true, as Jessamyn West noted, that writing is a "solitary occupation," it is also true that it is a collaborative effort. For me this list starts with the great deceased presidents, including the first one. "At this auspicious period, the United States came into existence as a Nation, and if their Citizens should not be completely free and happy, the fault will intirely be their own," President Washington wrote in 1783. "Such is our situation, and such are our prospects . . . happiness is ours, if we have a disposition to seize the occasion and make it our own."

Words to live by.

I am also in the debt of the living ex-presidents whose words in my original magazine story formed the idea for this book. A few sentences about them: I first approached the two I actually knew, Gerald Ford and Bill Clinton. President Ford sent word he'd rather do an interview than write an essay, and simply picked up the phone on August 7, 2001—a miserably hot day in Washington—and chirped, "It's going to be 72 degrees here today in Colorado. Come on out!" President Clinton sent word that he would write an essay for the pursuit of happiness issue, but asked if it could be more generally about Thomas Jefferson. That was a welcome wrinkle, actually, and then Clinton surprised me, and his own staff, by faithfully making his deadline. George H. W. Bush, whom I had only met twice, initially declined through his chief-of-staff, Jean Becker. I then sent her an e-mail saying that I believed that any man who, upon losing the presidency said with a smile to the White House "pool" reporters that he was now going big-time into the "grandfather business," and who, just for grins, jumped out of an airplane fifty years after bailing out over the Pacific Ocean, had something to say about *the pursuit of happiness* that Americans needed to hear. This appeal must have touched a cord: Becker replied that the former president would be writing an essay for me that afternoon, a Friday, and that Bush would send it to me on Monday. "Is that OK?" she asked. Yes, it was, Mr. President. Thank you.

Jimmy Carter also initially declined, but when I showed up unannounced at Maranatha Baptist Church in Plains, Ga., where he gives a frequent Sunday school lecture, Carter steered me under a shade tree and talked about the pursuit of happiness in the context of modern politics— and of his religious faith.

Former White House press secretary Ari Fleischer made sure that George W. Bush contributed a statement to my project, too. Anne Womack, Fleischer's deputy, once called me on my cell phone while I was playing centerfield in an over-thirty-eight hardball tournament in Arizona. Someone from my team yelled from the bench, "It's the White House calling!" I waited until the third out, sprinted into the dugout and wrote the comments she relayed from Bush into our team's scorebook. I fancied that the president, a fellow baseball fan, would have approved. I know Mike and Brian would have.

Notes

Chapter 1

1. Bush invoked the image of Disney's Magic Kingdom during a September 27, 2001, rally at United Airlines' corporate headquarters in Chicago. "Get on board," he told the nation. "Do your business around the country. Fly and enjoy America's great destination spots. Get down to Disney World in Florida. Take your families and enjoy life the way we want it to be enjoyed."

2. The 2001 NFL season was epitomized by conspicuous displays of patriotism, the most affecting of which occurred at the Super Bowl, where the names of hundreds of September 11 victims were scrolled across a giant screen at half-time. In a pulp-fiction touch, the Super Bowl champions were—who else?—the New England Patriots. One player in the league, Arizona Cardinals' defensive back Pat Tillman, truly was a patriot: after the season ended, he walked away from a contract that paid him in excess of a $1 million-per-year and, along with his brother (a minor league baseball player), enlisted in the United States Army.

3. But Washington had a pretty good idea about how to go about "the manner of doing it"—that is, ridding the colonies of the British. In the same letter to George Mason—the very next paragraph, in fact—Washington raised the idea of bearing military arms against the Crown. "That no man shou'd scruple, or hesitate a moment to use a—ms (arms) in defence of so valuable a blessing, on which all the good and evil of life depends; is clearly my opinion," Washington wrote.

4. Washington made this observation in an August 15, 1786, letter from Mount Vernon to Theodorick Bland. The Revolutionary War had been over for three years, and General Washington was three years away from assuming the presidency.

5. Japan has sent several pitchers to the U.S. major leagues, beginning with Masanori Murakami, who pitched for the San Francisco Giants in 1964

and 1965. But the stereotype of Japanese ballplayers—in Japan as well as the United States—was that they weren't big enough to compete on an everyday basis with American ballplayers. In 1941, the stereotype was that the Japanese couldn't see well enough to fly high-powered airplanes and were too technologically inefficient to wage war effectively against the United States. Admiral Yamamoto, the commander of the Japanese fleet that attacked Pearl Harbor, shattered that myth; Ichiro took care of the one about Japanese ballplayers.

Chapter 2

1. Jefferson revealed this himself, in an 1823 letter to James Madison.

2. The story of Adams' dying words is so entrenched that even the docents at Jefferson's Virginia home, Monticello, tell it with relish. It is so appealing because Adams and Jefferson died the same day—July 4, 1826, the fiftieth anniversary of American independence. According to Andrew Burstein, author of *America's Jubilee*, the written records reveal that Massachusetts congressman Edward Everett told this story within a month of the two men's deaths, at a eulogy for Adams. The account is also included in John Quincy Adams' diary, but with a qualifying caveat. Here is the entry: "About one [in the] afternoon he said, 'Thomas Jefferson survives,' but the last word was indistinctly and imperfectly uttered. He spoke no more." But John Quincy Adams, who was president at the time, didn't arrive at the Adams family home until July 17, nearly two weeks after his father had died. It appears that he must have gotten the deathbed account from Louisa Smith, the niece and adopted daughter of Abigail Adams. Smith was the only person with the old man when he passed away. Thanks to Burstein's sleuthing one other account comes down through history, though it is third-hand and even less definitive than John Quincy's diary. In the 1861 memoir of Eliza Quincy, the wife of Boston's mayor, Smith is quoted as telling the mayor "that the last words (Adams) distinctly spoke was the name 'Thomas Jefferson.' The rest of the sentence he uttered was so inarticulate, that she could not catch the meaning. This occurred at one o'clock—a few moments after Mr. Jefferson had died." There is, however, no question about what Adams said when visitors came calling earlier on that July 4th before he began lapsing in and out of consciousness. Fully aware of what day it was, he proclaimed, "Independence forever!"

3. McCullough's voice is itself a gift. Many Americans watching filmmaker Ken Burns' eleven-hour documentary on the Civil War initially mistook it for that of former NBC anchorman John Chancellor, but in time McCullough couldn't order in a restaurant or buy an airline ticket without someone stopping him. "Civil War," they would say simply. And he would nod and answer yes—

quite an honor for someone who never appeared on screen in that groundbreaking PBS series.

4. The indignant academic was Cornell University professor emeritus of law Milton R. Konvitz, who accused Maier in a review for *The New Leader* of repeatedly disparaging Jefferson. Anticipating such criticism, Maier playfully concedes in the introduction to *American Scripture* that she once nominated Jefferson in an *American Heritage* survey as "the most overrated person in American history," but insists she bears "no animus" toward Jefferson. Actually, she reveals a grudging affection (like a guilty pleasure?) for the man she believes deliberately nudged Adams off the stage when it came to claiming credit for authorship of the Declaration: She dedicates *American Scripture* to her husband Charles, whom she identifies only as "my Jeffersonian."

5. Maier made these comments, with only minor variations, to several journalists, including my former colleague Carl Schoettler of the *Baltimore Sun* in 1997. She made these observations to me in 2001.

6. Jefferson was an idiosyncratic speller, and in his recollections this name came out "Graaf," a mistake that crops up even today although it was corrected by the ever-thorough Dumas Malone in 1948 in *Jefferson the Virginian*, the first of six volumes on Jefferson. The Graff house, long since torn down when Malone was writing, was rebuilt from photographs in 1975 and is open for tours a couple of hours a day.

7. By the time he retired to Monticello after serving as president, Jefferson owned the finest private library in America. After the British burned the Capitol in 1814—and along with it, the entire collection of the Library of Congress—Jefferson offered his library as a replacement. In 1815, Congress took Jefferson up on this offer, paying $23,940 for some 6,500 books—twice the number lost in the 1814 fire. This contribution is duly noted at the Library of Congress, which today sits across the street from the Capitol.

8. He was right about the desk. William L. Bird, co-curator of the presidency exhibit, believes it is one of the most prized possessions the Smithsonian owns. "It's our first national artifact," he told me when I went to view it.

9. It's easy to see why Richard Henry Lee found common purpose with the Adams clan. Like them, Lee was a visionary on the issue of race. Seventeen years earlier, while in Virginia's House of Burgesses, he proposed attacking the institution of slavery by enacting importation taxes so onerous "as to put an end to that iniquitous and disgraceful traffic within the colony of Virginia." Jefferson would, much later, try this gambit in the Declaration—though it didn't make the final draft. But Jefferson *never* said plainly, as Lee had in 1759, that Africans were "equally entitled to liberty and freedom by the great law of nature."

10. Adams goes on in his letter to gently critique Jefferson for calling King George a "tyrant," a rhetorical attack he found too personal. If *Life, Liberty*

and the Pursuit of Happiness was among the "high tone and flights of oratory" that impressed Adams, he did not mention it.

11. "Life, liberty, property" was, of course, originally John Locke's formulation. It was published in 1690, originally anonymously, in the *Second Treatise on Government*. In it, Locke spoke of the "natural rights" of man—not given him by any king or ruler—and of the State itself as the basis of a social contract between the governed and those who govern them.

12. Otis' *Declaration of Rights* opens this way: "The members of this congress, sincerely devoted, with the warmest sentiments of affection and duty to His Majesty's person and government, inviolably attached to the present happy establishment of the Protestant succession . . ." The contrast with Jefferson's radicalism is implicit from the Declaration of Independence's first sentence: "When in the Course of human Events, it becomes necessary for one People to *dissolve* the Political Bands which have connected them with another . . ." [emphasis added]. There is something else interesting about Adams invoking Otis at this late date: Adams may have been settling an old score, not against Jefferson, but with his own conscience. Adams had been Otis' protégé; the two men had a bitter falling out—over the issue of Otis' wavering in opposition to the Crown. Adams' cruel treatment of his onetime mentor apparently haunted him. In *The Character of John Adams*, historian Peter Shaw writes: "Adams, whose own role lacked definition until 1770, denounced (Otis) with a vigor for which he could never forgive himself."

13. The author of *Common Sense* had been in America just over a year when his blunt pamphlet was published in Philadelphia. He arrived in that city on November 30, 1774. *Common Sense* rolled off the presses for the first time on January 9, 1776. Counting subsequent printings, more than 500,000 were sold, the work inspired the masses—and gave political cover to members of the Second Continental Congress. Paine's classic is well named. His succinct observation: "A government of our own is our natural right."

14. Even references to Aristotle and Cicero are somewhat obscure today, although they wouldn't have been to the men Jefferson was corresponding with. The notion that governments instituted among men must be reformed constantly to avoid subverting their rationale for existing is now widely characterized as a Jeffersonian idea. In Jefferson's day, this concept was recognized properly as Aristotelian. Cicero, the Roman orator and philosopher who lived from 106 to 43 B.C., was a favorite classical scholar of Jefferson's, who enthusiastically collected Cicero volumes. One of them, *Tusculan Disputations*, was among fourteen Cicero titles that came to the Library of Congress in 1815.

15. Their phrase is often rendered as, "Workers of the world unite; you have nothing to lose but your chains." But in German, the language in which *Manifesto* was written, it actually ends this way: *"Die Proletarier haben nichts in ihr zu verlieren als ihre Ketten. Sie haben eine Welt zu gewinnen. Proletarier*

aller Länder, vereinigt euch!" Thus, a more accurate translation is: "The prole-tarians have nothing to lose but their chains. They have a world to win. Work-ing men of all countries unite!"

16. Montesquieu had predicted as early as 1730 that America would rebel against its mother country, asserting, accurately, that the break would come when Britain would seek to put limitations on the colonists' trade.

17. Protagoras' comment was prophetic in a literal sense. After burning his books, the Athenian Assembly banished Protagoras, who drowned while at-tempting to sail to Sicily.

18. Filmer, born in 1588, was knighted by Charles I. By 1680, when *Patri-archa* was published on the authority of Charles II, who had been restored by Parliament to the throne in England after the death of Oliver Cromwell, Filmer was already dead. It was written much earlier, perhaps in 1640. In 1652, this defender of monarchal rule had written a rebuttal to Hobbes. "I wonder," Filmer wrote after citing the version of creation in Genesis, "how the right of nature can be imagined by Mr. Hobbes . . ."

19. This essay appeared on March 29, 1792, in the *National Gazette*. It can be found in Chapter 16, Document 23 in Volume I of *The Papers of James Madison*, edited by William T. Hutchinson, The University of Chicago Press.

20. Drayton did not look to Locke for his inspiration but to another En-glishman, William Blackstone, author of *Commentaries on the Laws of En-gland*, written between 1765 and 1769.

21. The *Pennsylvania Evening Post* published the Virginia Declaration on June 6, the *Pennsylvania Ledger* on June 8 and the *Pennsylvania Gazette* on June 12, the day after Jefferson was tasked to draft the Declaration. The editors of the *Gazette* may have had the welfare of their old publisher in mind, one who had signed on as an editor of sorts for the Declaration of Independence. The *Gazette*, of course, was Ben Franklin's old paper.

22. One of nine Pennsylvanians who signed the Declaration, Wilson had only emigrated to America ten years earlier. He is believed to have written this essay in 1769 or 1770, but didn't publish it until 1774, when the British had responded to the Boston Tea Party with the Coercive Acts and the virtual imple-mentation of martial law in Boston, where General Thomas Gage, commander of the British troops in America, was made governor of Massachusetts. "The die is now cast," King George III wrote to Lord North, Britain's prime minister, "the colonies must now either submit or triumph." After the colonies tri-umphed, James Wilson, one of the king's former subjects, was appointed by President Washington to the United States Supreme Court.

23. The French, being French, tried to improve on Jefferson's formula. They did not succeed. Article 2 of the *Rights of Man and of the Citizen*, the National Assembly of France, on August 26, 1789, amended the French consti-tution to read: "The aim of all political association is the preservation of the

natural and imprescriptible rights of man. These rights are liberty, property, security, and resistance to oppression."

24. Jefferson wrote this to Roger C. Weightman as a response to the invitation to appear at the festivities commemorating the fiftieth anniversary of Independence Day in Washington, D.C. In the letter, dated June 24, Jefferson expresses "regret that ill health forbids me the gratification of an acceptance." He died the day of the ceremonies in Washington.

Chapter 3

1. George Washington Parke Custis, Washington's grandson, wrote in his 1859 memoirs "some officers of the 4th Pennsylvania regiment were engaged in a game of fives. In the midst of their sport they discovered the Commander-in-Chief leaning upon the enclosure and beholding the game with evident satisfaction. In a moment all things were changed. The ball was suffered to roll idly away, the gay laugh and joyous shout of excitement were hushed into a profound silence, and the officers were gravely grouped together. It was in vain the Chief begged of the players that they would proceed with their game, declared the pleasure he had experienced from witnessing their skill, spoke of a proficiency in the manly exercise that he himself could have boasted of in other days. All would not do. Not a man could be induced to move, till the General, finding that his presence hindered the officers from continuing the amusement, bowed, and wishing them good sport, retired."

2. This gem of a toast is recounted in *George Washington: A Biographical Companion*, a 2001 volume compiled by Frank E. Grizzard Jr., editor of the Papers of George Washington at the University of Virginia.

3. From *Blacks in Bondage: Letters from American Slaves*, edited by Robert S. Starobin.

4. In a "Millennium Evening" address at the White House on February 11, 1998, Bailyn discussed the great paradox of the Founders, Jefferson in particular, to a rapt audience that included President Clinton and first lady Hillary Rodham Clinton: "The great goals of enlightened reform in America were set out most vividly by Jefferson. He was, let it be said, a fallible man, and he was a pragmatic, opportunistic politician, who feared power in others but used it deftly himself. But he was also the Revolution's true poet, its deepest conscience, and its most brilliant expositor. His was the most eloquent voice of America's Revolutionary ideology, as he proclaimed—in the face of these brutal realities— the principles of equality before the law, of absolute freedom of conscience, of responsible self-government, of the need for universal diffusion of knowledge and access to education and for freedom from poverty and the fear of poverty.

It was a strange encounter. The distance between these glittering ideals and the sordid realities of Jefferson's world was vast. Slavery brutalized new thousands every year and was poisoning the moral foundation of the nation as the Enlightenment ideals took root. On the frontiers the barbarous, almost genocidal race wars continued."

5. This article helped prompt the formation in Philadelphia a month later of the American Anti-Slavery Society, perhaps the first abolitionist organization in America. "That some desperate wretches should be willing to steal and enslave men by violence and murder for gain, is rather lamentable than strange," Paine's piece began. "But that many civilized, nay, christianized people should approve and be (involved) in the savage practice, is surprising."

6. This exchange was entered into John Quincy Adams' diary on February 24, 1820.

7. Adams' diary lists this conversation as having occurred on March 2nd of the same year, while the two were walking home together, presumably from the Capitol.

8. George Washington became a slave owner at age eleven, inheriting ten slaves and five hundred acres of land upon the death of his father. At twenty-two, when he began farming at Mount Vernon, he had thirty-six slaves; more came to the plantation upon his marriage to Martha Custis, who owned twenty. Washington continued to purchase slaves, who intermarried on the plantation and had children of their own. When Washington died in 1799, Mount Vernon was virtually a small town, albeit a black one, with some 316 slaves living on the property, 123 of whom belonged to Washington. Those slaves were officially freed January 1, 1801, weeks after Martha Washington signed a deed of manumission. But under Virginia law, the slaves Martha owned reverted to the estate of her long-dead husband Daniel Parke Custis. As a result, on Martha's death, they were divided up among her four grandchildren.

9. If one follows that line the other direction, eastward to the Atlantic Ocean, it separates Tennessee from Kentucky and runs between Virginia and North Carolina. Virginia was a slave state to be sure, but because it had been a cradle of freedom, and birthplace of presidents, there was sentiment in the Commonwealth to respect union. Jefferson, in his seventies at the time of the Missouri Compromise, remarked on it—and the question of expanding slavery—in an April 22 letter to John Holmes: "But as it is, we have the wolf by the ears, and we can neither hold him, nor safely let him go. Justice is in one scale, and self-preservation in the other." Jefferson's (and Robert E. Lee's) home state had earlier voted not to join the cotton states, but after Lincoln responded to Fort Sumter with a call for enlistments, Virginial reserved itself. It can be agonizing to contemplate how much shorter the Civil War might have been if Virginia had held fast.

10. The 1830 Census showed that the nation had 2 million slaves. In 1840,

it was 2.5 million, meaning that at the time Hammond spoke, he was referring to approximately 2.3 million people.

11. This story was written by John Aikin, a Scotland-trained physician and member of a prominent London literary clan. The story of the imaginary dialogue between a slave and a slave owner first appeared in an English anthology edited by Aikin and his sister, poet and essayist Anna Letitia Barbauld. The anthology was called *Evenings at Home*.

12. "The paper became my meat and drink," Douglass later wrote. "My soul was set all on fire."

13. "No Union with Slaveholders" proclaimed the masthead of *The Liberator*.

14. Noting that the Founding Fathers had inherited slavery *before* declaring independence and adopting a Constitution, Lincoln suggested that they were embarrassed by it and cites as evidence that it is nowhere mentioned in the Constitution, and that, in fact, the Founders used cumbersome circumlocutions to *avoid* mentioning it. "Thus the thing is hid away, in the Constitution," he said, "just as an afflicted man hides away a . . . cancer." Lincoln gave this speech on October 16, 1854. In it, he called the phrase "all men are created equal" his "ancient faith" and termed the Preamble to the Declaration the "sheet anchor of American republicanism."

15. Smith was an English writer remembered today mainly for a jibe worthy of a French ambassador to the United Nations: "In the four quarters of the globe, who reads an American book? Or goes to an American play? Or looks at an American picture or statue?"

Chapter 4

1. His name was Jehan de Wavrin. An English translation of his account of the famous battle on the eve of St. Crispin's Day in the year 1415 can be found in *Eyewitness to History* by John Carey.

2. The original interview appeared in a front-page article of the *Richmond Times Dispatch* on September 29, 1997. The article was written by Gary Robertson.

3. This review ran in the Book World section of *The Washington Post* on November 17, 2002, a little over a month after Ambrose had died of cancer.

4. In his memoirs, Grant described the scene at Appomattox courthouse on April 9, 1865, this way: "What General Lee's feelings were I do not know . . . but my own feelings, which had been quite jubilant on the receipt of his letter, were sad and depressed. I felt like anything rather than rejoicing at the downfall of a foe who had fought so long and valiantly, and had suffered so

much for a cause, though that cause was, I believe, one of the worst for which a people ever fought, and one for which there was the least excuse."

5. By the time of Lincoln's inauguration, southern politicians had upped this dollar estimate—because of the increase in slaves—to $4 billion.

6. Speech at Peoria, October 16, 1854. Found in *This Fiery Trial: The Speeches and Writings of Abraham Lincoln*, edited by William E. Gienapp.

7. Lincoln did, however, mention Russia at least once in the context of slavery—though not the way Yoder implies: In an 1855 letter to his friend Joshua Speed, a Kentucky slaveholder, Lincoln laments the rise of the nativist Know-Nothing party: "Our progress in degeneracy appears to me pretty rapid. As a nation, we began by declaring 'all men are created equal.' We now practically read it 'all men are created equal except Negroes.' When the Know-Nothings get control, it will read 'all men are created equal except Negroes and foreigners and Catholics.' When it comes to this I should prefer emigrating to some country where they make no pretense of loving liberty—to Russia, for instance, where despotism can be taken pure and without the base alloy of hypocrisy."

8. The editors of Lincoln's paper found this on a scrap kept by Mary Todd Lincoln. The provenance is considered legitimate, but the approximate date—sometime in 1858—is, according to University of Virginia scholar William Lee Miller, author of *Lincoln's Virtues*, only an educated guess.

9. Hammond's quotes are from the same February 1, 1836, Hammond speech in the House of Representatives quoted earlier and cited in Miller's *Arguing About Slavery*.

10. Dew's demeanor in this brief, but weighty book is one of resignation, not glee. He expresses some discomfort that so much of what he was taught about the war as a youth was incomplete, and "profound sadness" at what he later learned. "Although I have taught at a New England college for the past twenty-three years, I am a son of the South," his book begins. "My ancestors on both sides fought for the Confederacy, and my father was named Jack, not John, because of his father's reverence for Stonewall Jackson. On my fourteenth birthday I was given a .22-caliber rifle and Douglas Southall Freeman's *Lee's Lieutenants*. . . . When I went off to high school in Virginia, I packed a Confederate flag in my suitcase and hung it proudly from my dorm room. My grandmother, whom I loved dearly, was a card-carrying member of the United Daughters of the Confederacy. . . . I knew from listening to adult conversations about The War, as it was called, and from my limited reading on the subject that the South had seceded for one reason and one reason only: states rights."

11. The Alabama secession convention began on January 7, 1861. The first order of business was a prayer, the second the reading of the roll. Then came the first resolution, setting the tone for the entire affair. "WHEREAS, a sectional party, known as the Black Republican Party, has, in the recent election, elected

Abraham Lincoln to the office of President, and Hannibal Hamlin to the office of Vice-President of these United States, upon the avowed *principle* that the Constitution of the United States *does not recognise property in slaves* and that the Government should *prevent its extension* into the common Territories of the United States, and that the power of the Government should be so exercised that *slavery, in time, should be exterminated: Therefore, be it Resolved, by the people of Alabama, in solemn Convention assembled,* That *these acts* and *designs* constitute such a violation of the compact, between the several States, as absolves the people of Alabama from all obligation to continue to support a Government of the United States, to be administered upon such *principles,* and that the people of Alabama *will not submit* to be parties to the *inauguration and administration* of Abraham Lincoln as President, and Hannibal Hamlin as Vice President of the United States of America." This document is accessible at the University of North Carolina at Chapel Hill library's Documenting the American South archives.

12. "Black Republicans" was a formulation used by all the commissioners; it was intended as a slur that needed no amplification to Southern listeners. Charles Dew's book contains Harris' full speech, which was delivered December 7, 1860.

13. Hale's letter quoting Jefferson contains a significant editing change: "The primary object of all good governments," he wrote, "is to protect the citizen in the enjoyment of life, liberty, and *property* . . ." In so doing, Hale reverted to Lockean language, bypassing Jefferson as it were. Apparently even such a virulent racist as Stephen Hale couldn't square the everyday realities of slavery with the images evoked by the words "pursuit of happiness."

14. The government may have hanged Brown, but his glorification was not a figment of the South's imagination: Ralph Waldo Emerson told a cheering Boston crowd that Brown was "a new saint" whose hanging "would make the gallows as glorious as the cross."

15. This was, understandably, powerful imagery to a slave-owning audience. Liberation for Haiti's slaves was achieved at a frightful cost in lives for both blacks and whites. The plantations of the island were virtual death camps, as the French earned a reputation for cruelty singular even in the brutal environment of slave-owning societies. Haiti's slave revolt was actually a long, gruesome multisided war for liberation that involved tens of thousands of French, British and Spanish troops. The war began in the 1750s and 1760s with surreptitious poisonings by runaway slaves of white plantation owners, progressed in the 1790s to open insurrection by mobs that gang-raped women and tortured whites to death before burning the hated plantations and cane fields, and ended, finally, in 1804, when French troops quit that half of the island of Hispaniola, leaving the whites who did not go with them to die by the sword after a despotic Haitian ruler decreed that all Europeans were to be exterminated.

16. Charles Dew, recoiling from Calhoun's racialist diatribe, prefaced it in *Apostles of Disunion* with the wry observation that: "Calhoun gave this speech in the State Capitol in Columbia, which was an appropriate setting for what he was about to say." The accounts of this speech were preserved by the following day's editions of the *Columbia Daily South Carolinian*.

17. This letter is in the Hutson Papers owned by the Southern Historical Collection at the University of North Carolina, Chapel Hill.

18. Grimball, one of three brothers from a prominent Charleston planting family who volunteered for military service in the Confederacy, wrote this on November 20, 1860, to his oldest sister Elizabeth, who spent most of the war in Philadelphia. Elizabeth was chastised in another letter by one of her other brothers for her anti-Secessionist sentiments. William Grimball did not survive the war, dying in an army hospital in 1864. The family's letters are stored at the Perkins Library at Duke University.

19. Notice how this letter (dated August 30, 1861, and on file at the Tennessee State Library in Nashville) uses Locke's (and Hale's) formulation—but not Jefferson's.

20. This quote can be found in *Ulysses S. Grant: Soldier and President* by Geoffrey Perret, page 121. Perret's source is a *St. Louis Globe Democrat* article published July 24, 1885.

21. From the foreword to *All for the Union: The Civil War Diary and Letters of Elisha Hunt Rhodes*. Compiled by his great-grandson, Robert Hunt Rhodes.

22. Audiences were so moved by the *Dear Sarah* letter that Burns took to carrying it around with him, and pulling it out and reading it to people when they asked him about it. He did this once for me during a quiet moment at a reception following the White House Correspondents' Association annual dinner, sometime in the early 1990s.

23. From *For Country, Cause & Leader, the Civil War Journal of Charles B. Haydon*, Ticknor & Fields, 1993, p. 212.

24. The Louisiana Native Guards were mustered into service on September 27, 1862, five days after Lincoln read the Emancipation Proclamation to the cabinet, making it the first official colored regiment in the Union army. A Second Louisiana Native Guard came the following month, and the Third the month after that. General Butler, at that time in the heart of French-speaking Louisiana, insouciantly dubbed these regiments of liberated blacks and freedmen the "Corps d'Afrique." Jefferson Davis, a man with little sense of irony, let alone humor, was not amused. On December 23, 1863, he issued a proclamation of his own, declaring Butler and his officers be considered "robbers and criminals, deserving death, and that they and each of them be whenever captured, reserved for execution."

25. Not all of the Union soldiers appreciated the subtlety of Lincoln's posi-

tion. Chauncey H. Cooke, of Company G in the 25th Wisconsin Volunteer Infantry, wrote to his sister on January 6, 1863: "I am awful sorry that Freemont [*sic*] was set down on by Lincoln. I am with Freemont as many of the boys are. I have no heart in this war if the slaves cannot go free. Freemont wanted to set them free as fast as we came to them. I am disappointed in Lincoln." From "Letters of a Badger Boy in Blue," *Wisconsin Magazine of History*, 1920.

26. What McClellan was revealing here is not so much insensitivity to the plight of the slaves or even his shortcomings as a military man, but, rather that he had a tin ear; he believed he was giving Lincoln sound *political* advice. Earlier, on August 9, 1862, McClellan issued an order promulgating Lincoln's executive order of July 22, which had instructed the federal troops operating in southern states to seize property suitable for military purposes, including slaves, and to employ them. McClellan added that fugitive slaves employed by the Union army "have always understood that after being received into the military service of the United States in any capacity they could never be reclaimed by their former holders," and he promised such slaves "permanent military protection against any compulsory return to a condition of servitude." (From *The War of the Rebellion: A Compilation of the Official Records of the Union and Confederate Armies*, ser. 1, vol. 11, pt. 3, pp. 362–64.)

27. From the *Valley of the Shadow* project, Virginia Center for Digital History, University of Virginia.

28. From *Cause and Comrades: Why Men Fought in the Civil War*, Oxford University Press (1997), p. 19.

29. From page 69 of *Mr. Lincoln's Army*, the first volume in Catton's trilogy *The Army of the Potomac*.

30. In this November 12, 1861, letter, housed at the U.S. Army Military Historic Institute in Carlisle, Pa., Ames was writing to his mother. Robert Gould Shaw, in a letter to *his* mother, reveals that he did just that when the Massachusetts 2nd marched into Harper's Ferry in July 1861, where they toured the scene of John Brown's raid—he sang the John Brown tune.

31. Stone's motivations were not animus for fugitive slaves, but the exigencies of the military situation; the Massachusetts units were operating in Maryland and Virginia on both sides of the Potomac in hostile, slave-holding territory. But his pride got the best of him when he publicly tangled with such powerful civilian authorities. In the end, he paid for his intemperance. When some two hundred Union men were killed and seven hundred taken prisoner (most of them from Massachusetts) in a botched operation at Ball's Bluff, Bay State officials called for Stone's scalp—and got it. He was cashiered and jailed for months while the investigation dragged on. Later, Grant brought him back, giving him command of a brigade, but after another disastrous battle Stone was demoted to colonel. He subsequently left the United States army, but was given a commission in the Egyptian military, where he trained soldiers and helped

build up Egypt's coastal fortifications. Stone returned to the United States after thirteen years and was put in charge of building the pedestal for the Statue of Liberty. The statue was dedicated on October 28, 1886, with Stone serving as grand marshal. But his bad luck held; he caught a chill that day and died three months later.

32. From *A Jewish Colonel in the Civil War: Marcus M. Spiegel of the Ohio Volunteers*, edited by Frank Byrne and Jean Powers Soman, University of Nebraska Press.

33. From the *Valley of the Shadow* digital archives.

34. From the private collection of Samuel Vance Dutton, San Jose, Calif.

35. This letter was enclosed in a packet from General McClellan to Secretary of War Edwin Stanton in January 1862, and is contained in the National Archives [A-587 1862, Letters Received, ser. 12, Adjutant General's Office, Record Group 94]. The envelope containing the letter is addressed, in a different handwriting, to "Mrs. Elizabeth Boston Care Mrs. Prescia Owen, Owensville Post Office Maryland." The letter is reprinted in *The Destruction of Slavery*, Cambridge University Press (1986).

36. But the paradox is even greater than that, notes historian Jay Winik, the author of the best-selling book upon which the film was based. "One Confederate soldier put it so trenchantly in March of 1865, 'slavery has received its death blow.' The significance of this could not be underestimated. In the end what the Confederacy most cherished was its independence. And unwittingly, this produced a supreme irony: as April 1865 approached, the two sides, North and South, were closer on the issue of slavery than perhaps they had ever been since the founding of the republic; and yet it no longer mattered."

37. Boritt wrote this in a February 22, 2003, letter-to-the-editor to the *Washington Post*, in which he weighed in on the controversy surrounding Richmond's opposition to erecting a statue of Lincoln and Tad. Referring to the historic bow, Boritt said, "This is the moment the Richmond sculpture should portray."

38. Excerpted from the "Men of Color to Arms!" This essay, written by Douglass, appeared in several places, perhaps as early as March 1863. These quotes are from the May 14, 1863, edition of the *National Anti-Slavery Standard*. "A war undertaken and brazenly carried on for the perpetual enslavement of colored men calls logically and loudly upon colored men to help to suppress it," he wrote. "Action! action! Not criticism, is the plain duty of the hour. Words are now useful only as they stimulate to blows. The office of speech now is only to point out who, where and how to strike to the best advantage."

39. Shaw's body was not returned to the Union, as was customary for officers. "I buried him with his niggers," was the explanation reportedly provided by victorious Confederate Gen. Johnson Hagood. Shaw's parents, prominent Boston abolitionists, replied that there was no more fitting interment place for

their only son than with his men. But the story may have picked up the sheen of legend as it made its way north. James Tatum, a war historian and professor of classics at Dartmouth College, writes that the source for Hagood's comment was John T. Luck, a Federal assistant surgeon taken prisoner during the battle. In *The Mourner's Song*, Tatum writes that what Luck actually said Hagood told him was: "I shall bury him in the common grave with the Negroes that fell with him." Whether that is a distinction with a difference is for the reader to decide; Shaw was the only white officer—and all the officers in the Massachusetts 54th were white—whose body was not returned by the Confederates. Yet, he seems to have been accorded some grudging admiration from the enemy. According to Colonel George P. Harrison Jr., of the Georgia 32nd Shaw's body was laid "without roughness and with respect," and then the burial detail "placed on his body 20 of the dead Blacks whom he had commanded." Hagood, a wealthy planter, went into politics after the war. He served as South Carolina's governor. The football stadium at The Citadel, where Hagood graduated at the top of his class in 1847, is named after him.

40. Douglas Southall Freeman, *R.E. Lee: A Biography*. (Freeman attributes this observation to the memoirs of Colonel Lane, the regiment's commander and cites G.C. Underwood's *History of the 26th North Carolina*.)

41. According to *The Civil War* by Geoffrey C. Ward, Ric Burns and Ken Burns, a companion book to the Burns' documentary, General Butler found *The Bonnie Blue Flag* so inspirational to Southerners that he arrested its New Orleans publisher and threatened to fine anyone overheard singing it $25. "But the North had the best marching songs—*We're Coming, Father Abraham; Tramp, Tramp, Tramp, the Boys are Marching; Rally 'Round the Flag, Boys; John's Brown's Body*," the authors write. "A southern major, who listened to a northern officer sing some of them after the war admitted, 'Gentlemen, if we'd had your songs, we'd have licked you out of boots.'"

42. Steffe's correspondence with John Brown biographer Richard J. Hinton is on file with the Kansas State Historical Society in Topeka.

43. From Howe's autobiography, *Reminiscences 1819–1899*. Her husband was away, but Howe's youngest child, then not yet two years old, must have been in her bedroom when she wrote the verses in the dim light just before sunrise. "I had learned to do this when, on previous occasions, attacks of versification had visited me in the night, and I feared to have recourse to a light lest I should wake the baby, who slept near me," she writes. "I was always obliged to decipher my scrawl before another night should intervene, as it was only legible while the matter was fresh in my mind. At this time, having completed my writing, I returned to bed and fell asleep, saying to myself, 'I like this better than most things that I have written.'"

44. Haydon describes *The Atlantic* as not only his favorite campfire reading, but indispensable to retaining a good state of mind. On April 8, 1862, he

writes: "The coffee & sugar have come. The storm is still pelting us without mercy but the camp is well ditched & the men have bark & boughs enough in their tents to keep them off the damp ground. One of the luckiest hits imaginable was the purchase of the *Atlantic* for April just before I started. Last night & today I have read it nearly through. I should have had a lonesome time without it." On July 26, 1862, he adds: "I have subscribed for the *Atlantic* & shall have it regularly. I cannot do without it."

45. The following year, McCabe had the occasion to sing the song at an Illinois memorial service commemorating Lincoln's death. After the war, Mc-Cabe became an influential Methodist bishop and, later, the second chancellor of the American University in Washington. His life is chronicled in *The Life of Chaplain McCabe* by Frank Milton Bristol, Jennings and Graham (1908).

46. Lincoln to his secretary, John Hay, May 7, 1861.

47. Lincoln's oft-quoted phrasing at Gettysburg was borrowed from the Rev. Theodore Parker, a renegade Unitarian preacher from Boston who became a radical abolitionist. Parker hid fugitive slaves, advocated disobedience to the Fugitive Slave Act, and raised money for anti-slavery militias in Kansas. He provided financial and moral support for John Brown's raid. In the 1850s, Parker defined democracy as being "of *all* the people, by *all* the people, for *all* the people."

48. *Autobiography* by John Stuart Mill (1873), Chapter 7.

49. His letters are on file at the Minnesota Historical Society.

50. These letters can be found at the Ohio Historical Society in Columbus. The intrepid James McPherson unearthed both sets.

Chapter 5

1. "It is particularly gratifying to me to enter on the discharge of these duties at a time when the United States are blessed with peace," Monroe said. "It is a state most consistent with their prosperity and happiness."

2. These observations are from the fourth volume of John Quincy Adams' memoirs.

3. This vivid scene, which comes from the Papers of Woodrow Wilson 19:33, is repeated in several histories of the twenty-eighth president, including August Heckscher's 1991 *Woodrow Wilson: A Biography*. "Wilson was four when the Civil War began, eight years of age at its close," Heckscher writes. "During much of the conflict he was too young to have clear recollections, and was shielded by his family from the more harrowing or unpleasant scenes. Nevertheless, the war persisted as a major influence in Wilson's life and thought. Not only did he struggle with its implications in his early writings, but at a

deeper level a sense of the war's encroaching chaos remained with him in later life. . . ."

4. Wilson made these comments in his August 19, 1914, message to Congress, which ended in this spirited call to neutrality: "We must be impartial in thought, as well as action, must put a curb upon our sentiments, as well as upon every transaction that might be construed as a preference of one party to the struggle before another."

5. Their essay, *The Rise and Fall of Constitutional Government in America*, was published in 2002 by the Claremont Institute, a conservative educational foundation devoted to restoring "the principles of the American Founding to their rightful, preeminent authority in our national life." West is a professor of politics at the University of Dallas. Jeffrey is an administrator at Hillsdale College in Michigan.

6. Upon graduation from Princeton and the University of Virginia law school, Wilson earned a doctorate at Johns Hopkins University, became a widely respected professor of political science and, in 1902, president of Princeton. New Jersey's conservative Democratic machine tapped him to be a gubernatorial candidate in 1910. Wilson accepted their entreaties, if not their platform, running—and winning—as a progressive Democratic candidate. Only two years later, he was elected president of the United States.

7. From *After Virtue*, MacIntyre's immensely respected 1981 book.

8. The cable, signed by Arthur Zimmermann and on file in the National Archives, reads: "We intend to begin on the first of February unrestricted submarine warfare. We shall endeavor in spite of this to keep the United States of America neutral. In the event of this not succeeding, we make Mexico a proposal or alliance on the following basis: make war together, make peace together, generous financial support and an understanding on our part that Mexico is to re-conquer the lost territory in Texas, New Mexico, and Arizona. The settlement in detail is left to you. You will inform the President of the above most secretly as soon as the outbreak of war with the United States of America is certain and add the suggestion that he should, on his own initiative, invite Japan to immediate adherence and at the same time mediate between Japan and ourselves. Please call the President's attention to the fact that the ruthless employment of our submarines now offers the prospect of compelling England in a few months to make peace."

9. This point, which has been a staple of the debate over war and peace since the Vietnam War, is something of a canard. While it is true that the makeup of the military, particularly the Army, is more brown and black than the population as a whole, this is not true of combat units. In Vietnam, 12.5 percent of American servicemen who lost their lives were black at a time when the population of the United States was 13.1 percent African-American. In the Persian Gulf War, the pattern was similar. Blacks comprised 23 percent of the military personnel, but 17 percent of the combat deaths.

10. At the time of the first Persian Gulf War, slightly more than two dozen members of Congress who had voted on the Gulf of Tonkin resolution still served in the House; twelve of them voted to authorize force, fourteen against. "I am eighty years of age," one of the dissenters, Rep. Charles E. Bennett, a Florida Democrat, told his colleagues. "I have been in this chamber forty-three years. Out of the 17,000 votes I have cast, the only one I really regret is the one I cast for the Bay of Tonkin Resolution. I particularly regret it, because I knew it was a declaration of war."

11. The pummeled constituent was a minor league baseball player named Alexander Bannwart, aged thirty-six, who was promptly arrested by the Capitol police. Sen. Lodge claimed to be too busy to press charges—perhaps the fact that he was the aggressor played a role in his thinking—and Bannwart, in a fit of patriotism, subsequently enlisted in the United States Army. Such were the emotions of the time. This story has been preserved for posterity by the office of the Senate historian.

12. That was hardly Theodore Roosevelt's most outrageous riposte. According to George Mason University history professor Roy Rosenzweig, TR proposed, in response to the 1915 hit, "I Didn't Raise My Boy to be a Soldier," that a companion be sung. Its title? "I Didn't Raise My Girl to be a Mother."

13. All of this information, and a great deal more, can be found in Santa Clara University historian Nancy C. Unger's 2000 biography: *Fighting Bob La Follette: The Righteous Reformer.*

14. Romero had only been on the job in the organization's Manhattan headquarters a week when the Twin Towers were attacked, and his staff watched in horror as doomed civilians threw themselves out of those burning buildings. "As the destruction spread, our staff and everyone else caught downtown on that awful day fled the area in fear and desperation, chased by swelling clouds of smoke and debris," he said in that same May 22, 2002, speech. He mentioned this, he said, in response to critics who accuse the ACLU of being "out of touch" with the realities of everyday American life, adding that he believes that "defending liberty during a time of national crisis is the ultimate act of defiance . . . the ultimate act of patriotism."

15. Wellstone died two weeks later in a plane crash in the Iron Range that took the life of his wife, one of his daughters, three staff members and two pilots. After his death, friends recalled how the college-professor-turned liberal senator often invoked the spirit of the Declaration of Independence with an apocryphal story about a fourth-grade teacher in a poor area of Minnesota who asks her class one day, 'How many of you in here had a big breakfast this morning?' Half the kids raised their hands. The teacher then said, 'How many of you in here had any breakfast today?' Six more raised their hands. She then said, 'What about the other four, what about you?' Silence. Finally, one little girl explained shyly: 'It wasn't my turn to eat today.' Variations of this parable

abound, but in Wellstone's telling, the punch line was always the same. "When the Founders of our republic said that life, liberty and the pursuit of happiness were the unalienable rights of all Americans, they didn't say anything about taking turns!"

16. In 2002, this torch was carried by the Green Party and various anti-globalization groups worldwide, who never wavered from their claim that the war against Saddam Hussein was somehow motivated by the Bush administration's coveting of Iraqi oil. In 2003 this conspiracy theory gave way to another: the lust by Republican-affiliated corporations for rich rebuilding contracts in Iraq.

17. Interviewed on February 19, 2003.

18. Dennis was charged under the Alien and Sedition Act, known then as the Smith Act, for advocating the overthrow of the government by force. Dennis, future CPUSA president Gus Hall, and nine other defendants were convicted in a ten-month trial and sentenced to five years in federal prison. This anachronistic conviction, upheld by the U.S. Supreme Court in 1951, was obtained on evidence of speech and organizing activity that could be observed today in any faculty lounge on college campuses all over the United States. But if the conviction was discreditable, it must be said that Dennis most decidedly *was* dedicated to the overthrow of the United States government, and was probably a spy for the NKVD, the Soviet forerunner agency to the KGB. He emerged from prison a frail man, his health broken. Hall, who roomed at Fort Leavenworth in a cell adjacent to Machine Gun Kelly, spent his time in stir adding muscle to his stocky frame by lifting weights. He emerged from the penitentiary a stronger man, politically and physically, and took over the leadership of the party from Dennis, running it for four decades until he died in 2000 at age ninety. By the time of his trial, the Stalin-Hitler pact had already all but ended the Communist Party in this country, but Hall's loyalty was so complete that even the fall of the Soviet Union didn't faze him. In 1991, he held a press conference to denounce McCarthyism and witch hunting—in Russia, which he had just visited. Asked if he planned to go back, Hall said he had another destination in mind: "If you want to take a vacation, take it in North Korea," he gushed about the world's last remaining Stalinist regime. "The world should see what North Korea has done. In some ways it's a miracle." Thus had Gus Hall come full circle: while out on bail awaiting his appeal he had, in 1950, challenged President Truman at a "Hands off Korea" rally.

19. Pine was also one of three federal judges in the Washington, D.C., circuit who ruled the "Hollywood Ten" in contempt of Congress for refusing to name members of the Communist Party active in the movie business. Presidential scholars remember Judge Pine as the judge who handled the lawsuit against President Truman for ordering the federal government to seize several steel mills in an effort to avert a crippling steel strike in 1952. During oral arguments, As-

sistant Attorney General Holmes Baldridge asserted that, unless the Constitution expressly takes it away from him, a president has all the powers of King George III. That claim caused a public relations disaster for the White House. Judge Pine apparently wasn't impressed with it, either. He ruled against Truman, as did the Supreme Court when it heard the case on appeal.

20. From an article "Are We Overlooking the Pursuit of Happiness," which appeared in the September 1936 issue of *Parents Magazine*. Mrs. Roosevelt was writing in support of such programs as health insurance and on behalf of a proposed new federal agency that would, in time, become the Department of Health, Education and Welfare. Today, that agency is the Department of Health and Human Services, education becoming a function served by the Department of Education, created under President Jimmy Carter.

21. Some political reporters still remember Miss McGovern from the 1972 campaign. Then twenty-two years old, she gave the most passionate of the Democratic speeches delivered that year on behalf her dad. She died on December 13, 1994, of hypothermia after drinking and falling asleep in a snow bank in Madison, Wis. Teresa Jane McGovern left behind two daughters, aged seven and nine. Her father, eulogizing Terry, said he believed she would have succumbed to the ravages of alcoholism sooner but for her devotion to her girls.

22. This became liberal dogma, but four years later (and before it became law) Gene McCarthy would offer a withering critique of the McCain-Feingold bill: "The American Revolution wasn't financed with matching funds," McCarthy said. "We should change our Declaration of Independence, and a lot of Fourth of July speeches, because you still wind them up with Jefferson, saying, 'We pledge our lives, our fortunes, and our sacred honor.' And if [the reformers] had been there [they'd] say, 'Well, that's pretty good, Tom, but why don't you change it to say, 'We pledge our lives, our sacred honor, and up to a thousand dollars?'"

23. Carter made these remarks in his farewell address to the nation on January 14, 1981. It seems fitting, somehow, that a man whose tenure in the White House is not highly regarded either by voters or historians—but who is widely considered one of the great ex-presidents in history—would be so eloquent on his way *out* of office, and into a future that won him such pervasive respect.

24. Thus did Carter, in what should have been his shining moment, find the prize he had coveted tarnished by the very people who were awarding it to him. While accepting it, Carter had the good graces not to join in bashing Bush, and Bush himself was courteous enough to phone Carter and congratulate him.

25. Roosevelt made these assertions in a veto message to Congress on May 22, 1935. The full quote: "The Herculean task of the United States Government today is to take care that its citizens have the necessities of life. We are seeking honestly and honorably to do this, irrespective of class or group. Rightly, we give preferential treatment to those men who were wounded, disabled, or who

became ill as a result of war service. Rightly, we give care to those who subsequently have become ill. The others—and they represent the great majority—are today in the prime of life, are today in full bodily vigor. They are American citizens who should be accorded equal privileges and equal rights to enjoy life, liberty, and the pursuit of happiness—no less and no more."

26. Reagan may have had his founding documents mixed up, but his meaning was clear. This debate, held in Louisville, Ky., is remembered for something else, however. It was the session that prompted the first serious questions about Reagan's age. A tired-looking Reagan appeared every bit his seventy-three years, especially near the end of the one-hundred-minute session, which ran ten minutes longer than scheduled. Although poll numbers didn't change, Mondale's camp was buoyed for the first time in their uphill campaign. Their euphoria was short-lived, however. Two weeks later, at their second debate in Kansas City, Reagan was asked bluntly by Henry Trewhitt of the *Baltimore Sun* if at his age he might lack the stamina to see the nation through an international crisis. Reagan scoffed at the notion he couldn't stay in the White House situation room as long as necessary, then made his famous quip. "I will not make age an issue," he said with a pause. "I will not exploit my opponent's youth and inexperience." The line, delivered with the impeccable timing of a professional actor, got a big laugh in the hall; even Mondale joined in. David Broder of the *Washington Post* wrote that night, "It may well have been that the biggest barrier to Reagan's reelection was swept away in that moment."

Chapter 6

1. In June of that year, Japanese troops landed in the Aleutian Islands, killing thirty-eight in an event that didn't matter strategically, but which had considerable impact psychologically. It was the first time American territory had been occupied in that fashion since 1814.

2. In New York, a radio announcer interrupted his broadcast of the New York Giants' football game on December 7, 1941, with these words, "Japanese bombs have fallen on Hawaii and the Philippine Islands. Keep tuned to this station for further details. We now return you to the Polo Grounds."

3. Many others hadn't waited that long. When England put out an SOS for experienced pilots, thousands of young men from the United States and Canada answered that call. Of those, 244 were inducted into the Royal Air Force, and when the Battle of Britain broke out, ten of the earliest American volunteers were already flying in RAF units. Six of them would not survive the war. Three of the doomed Yanks, Vernon C. Keogh, Andrew Mamedoff and Eugene Q. Tobin, went to Europe with the intention of fighting with the French. But

France's air corps was kaput before they got there. The first American pilot to die in combat defending England was William M. L. Fiske III, an Olympic gold medal winner on the 1928 and 1932 U.S. bobsled team. Fiske's plane burst into flames as he landed during a Stuka raid at Tangmere airfield. Seriously burned, he died in the hospital forty-eight hours later. He was twenty-nine.

4. As the incorruptible "Jefferson Smith," Stewart's famous filibuster begins with him reading the Declaration's preamble. Stewart/Smith then adds: "Now that's pretty swell, isn't it? I always get such a kick outta those parts of the Declaration—especially when I can read 'em out loud to somebody. . . ."

5. Pearl Harbor effectively killed the "America First" movement in this country. At a fateful meeting in Pittsburgh, Pa., two hours *after* the attack, isolationists jeered at the mention of Roosevelt's name, booed down and then physically ejected a colonel in the Army reserves who happened by the meeting and who'd tried to tell the crowd that the Japanese had attacked Hawaii and Manila. Sen. Gerald P. Nye, a North Dakota Republican and leading isolationist, withheld what he knew from the assembly—even though he'd been told about it before the rally began. The following day, Pittsburgh's newspapers dutifully chronicled Nye's deceitful performance. He was vilified and ultimately voted out of office in 1944. Famed aviator Charles Lindbergh, also at the Pittsburgh meeting, had already marginalized himself with an anti-Semitic speech on September 11, 1941, and when Lindbergh offered to serve as a pilot in the war, the White House refused to reinstate his military commission. More astute isolationists showed better sense in those months, but the judgments of time can be unforgiving. Here is legendary *Christian Science Monitor* reporter Richard L. Strout, recording the appearance of California Sen. Hiram A. Johnson at the White House the night of the Japanese attack: "What a sight! The great isolationist, Hiram Johnson, immaculately dressed, stalks across our little stone stage on the White House portico. All the ghosts of isolationism stalk with him, all the beliefs that the United States could stay out of war if it made no attack. . . . Johnson walks by, refusing to comment, looking straight ahead through the crowd of reporters, who are silenced for a minute with the sense of history passing and a chapter closing."

6. "On my trip across the continent and back I have been shown many evidences of the result of common sense cooperation between municipalities and the Federal government, and I have been greeted by tens of thousands of Americans who have told me in every look and word that their material and spiritual well-being has made great strides forward in the past few years," Roosevelt said. "And yet, as I have seen with my own eyes, the prosperous farms, the thriving factories and the busy railroads—as I have seen the happiness and security and peace which covers our wide land, almost inevitably I have been compelled to contrast our peace with very different scenes being enacted in other parts of the world."

7. Deaver made this revelation in a January 2001 interview with the author. "[Reagan] said that no government should be allowed to embarrass the president of the United States," Deaver told me. But if Reagan's impulse was generous, it was ultimately futile. The hostages had not cleared Iranian airspace until minutes after the ceremony ended.

8. Reagan wrote two autobiographies. The first, *Where's the Rest of Me*, was published in 1965, and is the more revealing of the pair. This passage is taken from the second set of memoirs, *Ronald W. Reagan: An American Life*, published by Simon & Schuster in 1990.

9. Grey made the defense of France the cornerstone of Great Britain's foreign policy, but he didn't make this clear to Germany, the nation that most needed to know it. Those who opposed Britain's entry into the Great War argue that if Grey had made it clear that a declaration of war against France (which Germany made on August 3, 1914) was tantamount to a war on England, the Kaiser might have pressured Austro-Hungary to settle its differences with the Serbs short of war. Conversely, if Britain had stated unequivocally that it had no intention to enter the war, France and Russia might have been less belligerent in their dealings with Germany. By the time Roosevelt sent this letter to Grey, those chances had been lost, and Grey's own fear, "The lamps are going out all over Europe; we shall not see them in our lifetime," was proving prophetic.

10. Roosevelt may have been saved by his own verbosity: The bullet fired by a deranged gunman struck a metal eyeglass case in his breast pocket and was slowed further by a folded copy of a *fifty-page* speech.

11. The timing of heroes' epiphanies is not predictable. For Dwight D. Eisenhower, all it took was standing on the plain at West Point for the first time as a cadet. "The feeling came over me," he said much later, "that the expression 'the United States of America' would now and henceforth mean something different than it ever had before. From here on, it would be the nation I was serving, not myself."

12. "Theodore Roosevelt was larger than life," McCain added. "Theodore Roosevelt believed in reform. He took the politics of America out of the hands of the robber barons, and gave it back to the people. He put the United States of America on the world's stage, in the international arena, which made way for our ever-expanding role in the world. He established our national parks system. He was an activist. He was a reformer. And he was a man of great vision . . . (and) a truly wonderful father and family man as well—who happened, by the way, to lose a son in World War I. . . ."

13. McCain had not been a president, of course, and is not likely to become one. But because of his special place in the history of his generation I thought he had standing. My editors agreed.

14. Roosevelt used the phrase "pursuit of happiness" six times after the United States entered the war. This one was December 15, 1941. The additional

dates were January 1 and September 4 of 1943; January 11 and May 17 of 1944 and, for the last time, on January 30, 1945, the last birthday of Roosevelt's life. He used the phrase a total of fourteen times in his presidency. The author is indebted to FDR Library archivist Mark Renovitch for this trove of detail.

15. According to Doris Kearns Goodwin in *No Ordinary Time*, Eleanor Roosevelt actually answered one curmudgeonly anti-Thanksgiving letter writer. "I can think of a thousand things for which I am deeply thankful," the First Lady replied. "I am grateful for the fact that my country is made up of many peoples; that I have an opportunity to show that I really believe that all men are created equal; that our boys whom I love had not fallen [in the war]; for my husband's strength and for his belief in God."

16. The two prominent anglers landed no trout. "[Roosevelt] was placed with great care by the side and sought to entice the nimble and wily fish," Churchill related. "I tried for some time myself at other spots. No fish were caught, but [FDR] seemed to enjoy it very much, and was in great spirits for the rest of the day."

17. In the years since Roosevelt, other American presidential candidates have been tagged with the "Happy Warrior" sobriquet, including Hubert H. Humphrey and John McCain. In each case this was certainly a legitimate appropriation of the phrase.

18. And that level of pay reflected a substantial wartime increase for the American fighting man. In 1940, the American League's Most Valuable Player was Hank Greenberg. It was his last season for a while. "Hammerin' Hank," who was Jewish, enlisted in the Army in May of 1941—before the draft took effect—thereby trading an annual salary of $55,000 for a monthly stipend of $21. Upon reporting for duty at Fort Custer, Michigan, Greenberg told the *Sporting News*, "If there's any last message to be given to the public, let it be that I'm going to be a good soldier." Greenberg, who was thirty, was discharged after a new law lowered the draft age to twenty-eight. He re-enlisted two days after Pearl Harbor, telling reporters, "This doubtless means I'm finished with baseball." It actually wasn't. Despite his age, he returned to the game with a flair, hitting a homer in his first at-bat in 1946, a year in which he slammed forty-four home runs.

19. His eyes narrowing somewhat, Bush then asked me suspiciously, "You're not a Yankee fan are you?" Assured that I still rooted for my hometown team, the San Francisco Giants, Bush began talking about his—and my—boyhood favorite, Willie Mays.

Chapter 7

1. FDR must have had a premonition about *Yank*. Identifying himself as "your Commander-in-Chief," Roosevelt paid homage to the magazine in its

May 28, 1942, maiden issue. "In *Yank*, you have established a magazine which cannot be understood by your enemies," Roosevelt said. "It is inconceivable to them that a soldier should be allowed to express his own thoughts, his ideas and his opinions." Roosevelt's—and Trimmingham's—faith in *Yank* was well placed. The magazine published the corporal's letter on April 28, 1944, as well as a follow-up a month later in which the black soldier reported that he had received 287 written replies, most of them from white soldiers. "Another strange feature about these letters is that most of these people are from the Deep South," Trimmingham wrote in his second letter. "They are all proud that they are from the South but ashamed to learn that there are so many of their own people playing Hitler's game." *Yank* itself acknowledged receiving thousands of responses from GIs, "almost all of whom were outraged by the treatment given the corporal."

2. This interview was done by Lou Cannon, who covered Governor Reagan for the *San Jose Mercury News* and President Reagan for the *Washington Post*. The author is indebted to Mr. Cannon for this account—and, it's probably not necessary to say, for a whole lot more as well.

3. Art has a way of circling back around on life. In the 2001 Touchstone Pictures' *Pearl Harbor*, African-American actor Cuba Gooding Jr. reenacted the famous scene, manning the machine gun as Dorie Miller had done sixty years before.

4. In a 2003 essay in *The New Yorker* about The Library of America's recent, two-volume anthology *Reporting Civil Rights: American Journalism 1941–1973*, Nicholas Lemann observed: "One reason that the Montgomery bus boycott was a breakthrough was that it made Martin Luther King the movement's first true media star. King was shockingly young and oratorically spectacular, and the national press—in particular, *Time* and *Life*—conferred a celebrity status on him that it had never given . . . any of the movement's earlier leaders.

5. Liberals were dismayed when Truman replaced Francis Biddle with Clark after FDR's death. But Clark went on to play a pivotal role in the history of fighting racism: He was one of five justices who voted to end school segregation in the landmark 1954 case *Brown v. the Board of Education of Topeka, Kansas*.

6. Of course, it was a less litigious society then. Woodward collected nothing through the courts, despite the efforts of the NAACP, which sued Greyhound for $50,000. The VA gave Woodward a pension, and in several civil rights rallies across the country money was raised for him; the largest of these was in New York, attended by Woody Guthrie, Paul Robeson and heavyweight champion of the world Joe Louis. Guthrie composed a song, *The Blinding of Isaac Woodward*, and performed it for twenty thousand people.

7. "He attempted to take away my blackjack," the police chief told a

local newspaper. "I grabbed it away from him and cracked him across the head." This was the comment that was characterized as boasting.

8. These figures have been compiled by Tuskegee Institute, which began documenting lynching cases in 1892, and the NAACP, which followed some time later. An October 2002 conference on lynching held at Emory University revealed that the definition of this chilling word itself varies. For purposes of this book, I use the four criteria historically required by the NAACP: (1) There is clear evidence someone was killed; (2) The killing was done illegally; (3) Three or more persons took part in the act; (4) The killers claimed to be serving justice or tradition. The act does not necessarily involve hanging. Even so, it is easy to understand why this definition is unsatisfying to some modern scholars of black history. It does not, for example, include Isaac Woodward, but it does include the hanging of murderers and cattle thieves in parts of the Old West. On the other hand, perhaps that's as it should be. Lynching is an American crime with deep roots. It took its name in Revolutionary times from Col. Charles Lynch, who assembled "lynch" mobs to target and sometimes kill colonists loyal to the British crown. The first president to call for a federal anti-lynching law was Benjamin Harrison, outraged over the hanging of eleven Italian immigrants in New Orleans in 1891. Republican William McKinley found the practice so horrid that he called for its abolition in his first inaugural address.

9. Randolph related all this to Thomas H. Baker, an interviewer with the Lyndon Baines Johnson Library oral history project. The interview took place in Randolph's office in Harlem on October 29, 1968.

10. When he ran for governor in 1946, as a dashing bachelor and World War II veteran, Thurmond's campaign was largely free of race-baiting. According to University of Alabama history professor Kari Frederickson, author of *The Dixiecrat Revolt and the End of the Solid South, 1932–1968*, Thurmond argued for abolishing the poll tax, and as governor, mobilized state law enforcement to prosecute whites who perpetrated a 1947 lynching. So what was Thurmond doing in Birmingham? His biographer, Nadine Cohodas, suggests it was part impulse and part opportunism: he was eyeing the 1950 Senate race. Thurmond was elected senator in 1954, serving forty-eight years until he was nearly one hundred years old and changing allegiances one final time to become a Republican. But he demonstrated, even late in life, a deftness on race that escaped many of his fellow conservative southern Democrats-turned-Republicans, including—most famously—Mississippi Sen. Trent Lott.

11. This comes from *Master of the Senate*, the third volume of Robert A. Caro's massive history of Johnson's life. Corcoran's warning came in a phone call; Rowe's in writing. "To keep [LBJ's presidential ambitions] alive, Rowe's memorandum said, it was necessary for Johnson not merely to vote for a civil rights bill, but to fight for one," Caro explained.

12. The six were: the NAACP; the Urban League; the Congress of Racial

Equality (CORE); the Negro American Labor Council; the Student Nonviolent Coordinating Committee, founded by Stokely Carmichael and other students, including future Georgia congressman John Lewis; and the Southern Christian Leadership Conference, which King headed. The march was conceived by Randolph, fulfilling a dream he had long had, and organized by Bayard Rustin, who was instrumental in the creation of both CORE, and King's SCLC.

13. In the late eighteenth century American spelling was an inconsistently practiced art, and because she had no formal schooling Abigail Adams' spelling tends to be even more erratic than her husband's—or Jefferson's. "But my personal opinion is that she did pretty well for the time and her situation," Anne Decker Cecere, associate editor of the John Adams Papers, said in an e-mail. "I'm not sure if she was self-conscious about it or not. We do know that she often drafted a letter first, and then copied it over before sending it."

Chapter 8

1. McCain told me this in a 2003 interview. He also reminded me that some American POWs learned of the moon landing when they received letters from home with postage stamps featuring Neil Armstrong in his space suit taking the first step from the Eagle onto the moon's surface. The news heralded on the stamps is unmistakable: Earth itself is clearly visible in the stamp's background.

2. Jefferson's ideas about educating women were liberal by the standards of his day, but hopelessly retro by ours: "A plan of female education has never been a subject of systematic contemplation with me," Jefferson wrote in 1818 to Nathaniel Burwell. "It has occupied my attention so far only as the education of my own daughters occasionally required. Considering that they would be placed in a country situation, where little aid could be obtained from abroad, I thought it essential to give them a solid education, which might enable them, when become mothers, to educate their own daughters, and even to direct the course for sons, should their fathers be lost, or incapable, or inattentive. . . ." But Jefferson had definite opinions on the primary obstacle preventing women from developing their minds. It was, he said, the gentler sex's "inordinate passion" for romantic fiction. "When this poison infects the mind," Jefferson wrote, "it destroys its tone and revolts it against wholesome reading. Reason and fact, plain and unadorned, are rejected."

3. Professor Mackenzie made these observations at a midterm review of the George W. Bush presidency, held in early May 2003 at the University of London, and in subsequent interviews with the author.

4. This author is indebted for this detail to the redoubtable Ray Teichman, archivist at the Franklin D. Roosevelt Library in Hyde Park, N.Y.

5. The British and American pilots were fortunate: The reason these deadly German planes didn't have a more determinative outcome in the war was because they weren't deployed properly—or in a timely way. This failure was Hitler's own. Hitler initially approved mass production of the Me-262, but he envisioned them as being used for bombing. When they were built as fighters—their highest and best use—Hitler ordered them retrofitted as bombers. Delays begat more delays, as Germany began to run short of spare parts and trained pilots. In 1944, hundreds of the Messerschmitts waiting to be refitted were destroyed on the ground by the very Boeing-built American bombers they were designed to kill.

6. The P-51, built by North American, was originally developed for the RAF. The maneuverable, versatile plane was deployed in every theater of the war. Some 15,000 Mustangs were sent airborne, serving as high-altitude escorts to bombers in Europe and engaging Japanese Zeroes in dogfights all over the Pacific. By war's end, they had destroyed 4,950 enemy planes in the air.

7. O'Hare, a national hero for whom Chicago's airport is named, was flying a Hellcat the night of November 27, 1943, when he was killed in a low-altitude dog fight with incoming Japanese torpedo bombers attacking the USS *Enterprise*.

8. The Grumman-built Avengers sunk some thirty-one German submarines during the war and two of Japan's largest battleships, the *Yamoto* and the *Musashi*. The plane is also the answer to a trivia question among science fiction aficionados: In 1945, a navy squadron of five Avengers took off from Ft. Lauderdale on a routine training mission, flew into the Bermuda Triangle, and were never seen again. Thirteen lives were lost, as well as another twenty-two men aboard a rescue plane that exploded and crashed.

9. "Listen now," an NBC radio network announcer told his audience that night, "for the sound that forevermore separates the old from the new."

10. Although he was out of office when it happened, Teddy Roosevelt became the first president to fly in an airplane, going for a four-minute ride at a height of fifty feet in a Wright Brothers biplane on October 11, 1910, at a St. Louis air show. The pilot was Arch Hoxsey, who had been a trick cyclist before signing on with the Wright Brothers. Hoxsey was killed in a plane crash on December 31, 1910—eleven weeks after taking Roosevelt up. Apparently undaunted, Roosevelt undertook another kind of exploration, personally navigating an uncharted tributary of the Amazon so foreboding it was called the River of Doubt. It is now named Theodore Roosevelt River.

11. From *Lyndon: An Oral Biography* by Merle Miller, p. 470.

12. On the day the *Challenger* exploded, Reagan was expecting to give the State of the Union address. He and congressional leaders agreed to postpone it

a week. House Speaker Thomas P. "Tip" O'Neill Jr. had squared off with Reagan in the Oval Office earlier in the day over the budget. O'Neill later recalled that he had seen Reagan at his worst and at his best in the same day. "It was a trying day for all Americans," O'Neill recalled, "and Ronald Reagan spoke to our highest ideals."

13. SDI stands for Strategic Defense Initiative, the name Reagan chose, and which is still in use at the White House and in congressional budgeting documents. In the early days of the controversial program it became known in some circles of the media and Capitol Hill, not altogether kindly, as "Star Wars."

14. Lou Cannon unearthed the gem of Powell's reaction while researching his acclaimed Reagan biography, *Role of a Lifetime*. This author explored the issue further with unnamed former Reagan administration sources in 2000 while writing about President Clinton's interest in the same subject.

15. But, if historian Garry Wills' hunch is right, the modern Jefferson might be the wrong man to ask. In 1981, Colorado Sen. Gary Hart was so impressed by Wills' *Inventing America: Jefferson's Declaration of Independence* that he called the author and met him for breakfast on a trip to Chicago. Implicit in many of Hart's queries, Wills later told David Maraniss of the *Washington Post* was, "What would Jefferson be doing if he were running for president today?" Wills replied that he didn't think Jefferson would even be in politics if he were living today. "What would he be doing?" Hart asked. "He would be a research scientist," replied Wills.

16. This interview took place on April 24, 2003. "I don't bring God into my life to be a political person," Bush told Brokaw. "I ask God for strength and guidance. I ask God to help me be a better person. But the decision about war and peace was a decision I made based upon what I thought were the best interests of the American people. I was able to step back from religion, because I have a job to do. And I, on bended knee to the good Lord, asked Him to help me to do my job in a way that's wise."

Chapter 9

1. Speaking at the National Archives, Ford also lauded music and art as keys to a good life. "We have exported America's happiness to the world with our gramophones, our movies and our own talented performers," he said. "We took all of the arts of those who came to join the American adventure and made new arts of our own. No nation has a richer heritage than we do, for America has it all."

2. Eleanor wrote this in her May 31, 1939, "My Day" newspaper column.

3. From *You Learn by Living*, by ER, 1960.

4. The son of a Scottish missionary to Ireland (where he was born) Hutcheson was professor of moral philosophy at the university in Glasgow in 1729. Among his students was Adam Smith. During the week, Hutcheson lectured, in English, on moral philosophy, religion and natural law. On Sundays he taught classes (in Latin) on Hugo Grotius' *On the Truth of the Christian Faith*. Presbyterian elders rebuked Hutcheson for teaching that moral goodness came from attending to others' happiness; and his advocacy of the beneficial effects of laughter put him at cross-purposes with the stern Thomas Hobbes. Hutcheson has been called "the father of the Scottish Enlightenment."

5. From *Mark Twain's Notebook*.

6. Bush's biblical allusions are frequent, although in today's secular journalistic and political culture this is not always recognized. It is, for example, a matter of modern political lore that the epitome of public service is the motto of the Kennedy clan: "To whom much is given, much is required." But this lesson was preached in the Bush family for generations as well—as it was in millions of other families. That's because this animating ethic originates, not from any particular Democrat or Republican patriarch, but with the Gospels themselves—from the book of Luke.

7. Harvard-trained historian Sheldon Stern, writing in the *New England Journal of History* (Fall 1998), noted that influential Kansas journalist William Allen White repeated the "the business of America is business" line ten times in books and articles published between 1925 and 1938. Accompanied by a cardboard cutout version of Coolidge, it was also repeated by influential New Deal–era historians, some of whom joined the New Deal itself. Given the idealistic nature of Coolidge's speech to ASNE, the effort to discredit him by misquoting him—and, worse, quoting him wildly out of context—seems a willful misrepresentation.

8. Churchill also said, "The inherent vice of capitalism is the uneven division of blessings, while the inherent virtue of socialism is the equal division of misery."

9. Boesky was giving the 1985 commencement address at the University of California-Berkeley School of Business when he made his famous remark. "Greed is all right, by the way," he told the newly minted MBAs to general laughter and applause. "I want you to know that. I think greed is healthy. You can be greedy and still feel good about yourself."

10. Gardner, a professor at the Harvard Graduate School of Education, was assisted by two other prominent researchers. They were Mihaly Csikszentmihalyi of Claremont Graduate University, and William Damon of Stanford University. Their work was published in the book: *Good Work: When Excellence and Ethics Meet*, Basic Books, 2001.

11. All the vouchers were repaid, except for $400 worth, solidifying Hoover's faith in the American people—and, fatefully, in the efficacy of private (not governmental) acts of good will.

12. The definitive account of this effort is *The Humanitarian*, the 1988

work by George H. Nash. That is the second volume of Nash's multivolume series, *The Life of Herbert Hoover.*

13. FDR made this comment in a 1920 letter to his friend Josephus Daniels. This letter was quoted by Carl Degler's essay "The Ordeal of Herbert Hoover" published in the 1963 summer edition of *Yale Review.*

14. "In reviewing the incidents of my administration, I am unconscious of intentional error," Washington wrote in 1796. Lexicographer Frank Abate, president of Dictionaries International, is the source of this gem, as well as for most of the presidential linguistic and semantic "firsts" I cite here.

15. On the occasion of Jefferson's birthday in 2001, George W. Bush made fun of himself on this score, noting in a lighthearted East Room ceremony that the Sage of Monticello had coined words such as *debarrass* and *Barbaresque* (after the Barbary pirates), while the best he could do was *misunderestimate.* "It's not quite in Jefferson's league," Bush quipped, "but I'm giving it my best shot."

16. Nancy Reagan may have been the first Republican to realize Bush had actually coined a self-rebuke that could boomerang, not just on Reagan's reputation, but on the entire GOP. At Bush's 1989 swearing-in, Nancy quietly seethed over the phrase after Bush repeated it in his inaugural address. Ever protective of her husband, she turned to an aide and said tersely, "Kinder and gentler than whom?"

17. In his last will and testament, Washington left $4,000—a huge sum in those days—to the school. And while lamenting in the will itself that freeing his slaves is too complicated to accomplish outright, Washington also directs that they be "taught to read and write" as well as trained in a "useful occupation."

Chapter 10

1. Capt. LaCroix's words were reported by Evan Osnos of the *Chicago Tribune,* who was in Iraq covering the war.

2. Buckley literally gave his life helping others: He died when he fell from an Army truck while throwing food to hungry Iraqis.

3. Alexandra Tychnowitz' missive was printed by the *New York Daily News* as part of its "Letters from Home" feature launched by the paper on March 27, 2003, to honor the U.S. troops in Iraq.

4. In his last e-mail to her, Bitz, a member of the 2nd Assault Amphibious Battalion of the 2nd Marine Division, told his mother he was "her warrior" and that he loved her. Bitz, thirty-one, also left behind a young wife Janina, a two-year-old and newborn twins whom he never saw. The Marine also had a seven-year-old son, Christian, from a previous marriage.

5. The same fate befell George W. Bush's father. In 1991, Bush Forty-One had registered an unheard-of 90 percent job approval rating in the wake of the

Persian Gulf War. A year later, in his three-way race against Bill Clinton and Ross Perot, Bush tallied just under 38 percent of the vote, the lowest percentage for a sitting president since Teddy Roosevelt threw a monkey wrench into the 1912 presidential election.

6. On September 17, 2002, Bush paid homage to Anthony Kennedy's efforts—and David McCullough's efforts—at encouraging American schoolchildren to study their own history. "Our history is not a story of perfection," Bush said in the Rose Garden event. "It's a story of imperfect people working toward great ideals. This flawed nation is also a really good nation, and the principles we hold are the hope of all mankind. When children are given the real history of America, they will also learn to love America."

7. The Kennedys were accompanied to the school by local journalists. The accounts here are drawn from three April 30, 2002, articles; two in the *Boston Herald* and one in the *Boston Globe*. Sandy Coleman covered for the *Globe*. The *Herald* scribes were Karen E. Crummy and Wayne Woodlief.

8. Democrat Bob Kerrey, a frequent Bush critic, agreed with him on this point—and on the rationale for war. In an interview with *Salon*, the liberal online magazine, Kerrey dismissed the argument that democracy won't work in Iraq as "racist and condescending." He added, "In 1998 . . . [I] had people saying in response to me, 'There's no Thomas Jefferson in Iraq.' Well, there's no Thomas Jefferson [currently] in the United States. Our job isn't to pick an Iraqi leader; it's to let Iraq pick a leader."

9. McCain, as is his talent, cut to the heart of things in a June 15, 2003, *Washington Post* op-ed piece. "Like many Americans, I am surprised that we have yet to locate the weapons of mass destruction that all of us, Republican and Democrat, expected to find immediately in Iraq," he wrote. "But do critics really believe that Saddam Hussein disposed of his weapons and dismantled weapons programs while fooling every major intelligence service on earth, generations of U.N. inspectors, three U.S. presidents and five secretaries of defense into believing he possessed them, in one of the most costly and irrational gambles in history?" McCain ended his piece this way: "It is too early to declare final victory in Iraq. But we're well past the point of knowing that our war to liberate Iraq was right and just. The discovery of mass graves filled with the bodies of murdered children should have convinced even the greatest skeptic. We made America more secure, liberated millions from a reign of terror and helped create the prospect for the establishment of the first Arab democracy. That should make Americans proud—and critics of the administration's decision to go to war a little more circumspect."

10. In the March 11, 2003, *Los Angeles Times* Wiesel noted that only armed force prevented widening bloodshed in the Balkans—and only force could have stopped genocide in Rwanda. "Had Europe's great powers intervened against Adolph Hitler's aggressive ambitions in 1938 instead of appeasing

him in Munich, humanity would have been spared the unprecedented horrors of World War II," he added. In a 1996 interview with the author, Wiesel revealed that he made the same point to President Clinton in urging him to intervene in Bosnia. Clinton confirmed this account—and credited Wiesel for helping focus his attention on the crisis.

11. In the March 3, 2003, issue of *Le Monde*, Kouchner said that he detests war as much as anyone he knows, and that war is "a very bad" solution. "But there is something worse than a very bad solution, which is leaving in place a dictator who massacres his people," Kouchner wrote.

12. This chilling prediction was contained in a February 25, 2003, *New York Times* op-ed.

13. Perhaps most telling was the testimonial of Sherko Bekas, described to Goldberg as the Kurds' unofficial poet laureate. Bekas was appalled by the noisy efforts of American poets to embarrass first lady Laura Bush as a way of registering opposition to the war. "Saddam is the god of war," Bekas told Goldberg. "He is the killer of poetry. I say to these poets that if they lived for two weeks under Saddam's rule they would write verse in reverse. They would write poems asking Bush to attack Saddam sooner."

14. The nations in the group, dubbed the "Vilnius Ten," were Romania, Bulgaria, Slovenia, Slovakia, Croatia, Latvia, Estonia, Lithuania, Albania and Macedonia.

15. This conversation was unearthed by *U.S. News & World Report*.

16. These attitudes were not limited to former Soviet colonies. Italian prime minister Silvio Berlusconi, on the eve of war in Iraq, came to the White House and said: "We will never forget that we owe our freedom [and] our wealth to the United States of America. And our democracy. And we also will never forget that there have been many American young lives that were lost and sacrificed themselves for us. . . . Every time I see the U.S. flag, I don't see the flag only representative of a country, but I see it as a symbol of democracy and freedom."

17. Winthrop was alluding, as his listeners would have known, to a passage from the New Testament book of Matthew. And if one consults the passage, it becomes clear where, many years later, Reagan would get his adjective "shining"—for that imagery is there as well: "You are the light of the world," the verse reads. "A city set on a hill cannot be hid. Nor do men light a lamp and put it under a bushel, but on a stand, and it gives light to all in the house. Let your light so shine before men, that they may see your good works. . . ."

18. I am unsure of the origin of the phrase "green card Marines." The *Los Angeles Times* wrote a series beginning May 25, 2003, about the "Green Card Marines" from California who died in the fighting. Others have used the expression as well. It appeared in a headline in the *Newark Star-Ledger* two months earlier, on March 17, and was also used in early April by Ernesto Portillo Jr., a columnist for the *Albuquerque Tribune* in New Mexico.

19. Woolley was an embedded reporter for the *Star-Ledger*, traveling in Kuwait and Iraq with the 1st Marines.

20. Public Agenda was in the field for its data in October and November of 2002. The poll was commissioned by the Carnegie Corp. of New York. It surveyed 1,002 adults who came to the United States when they were at least five years old.

21. Although in the wake of September 11, 2001, there was very little room for doubt in Americans' minds, whether they were native-born or émigrés, about their loyalty to the United States. In October of that year, a *Washington Post* poll found that 97 percent of Americans would rather be citizens of the United States "than of any other country."

22. He used both of those expressions in a speech at the White House on September 26, 2002.

23. Bush would add, as did Reagan, "the unborn" to that litany. In January 2003, via telephone from St. Louis, Bush declared to marchers at an anti-abortion rally in Washington: "You all are gathered today on the National Mall, which is not far from the monument to Thomas Jefferson who, as you all know, is the author of our Declaration of Independence. And the March for Life upholds the self-evident truth of that Declaration—that all are created equal, given the unalienable rights of life, and liberty, and the pursuit of happiness. . . . In our time, respect for the right to life calls us to defend the sick and the dying, persons with disabilities and birth defects, and all who are weak and vulnerable. And this self-evident truth calls us to value and to protect the lives of innocent children waiting to be born."

24. The piece quoted from here ran as an op-ed in the April 13, 2003, editions of the *New York Times*.

25. This is quite a conspiracy theory, if one thinks about it. As Robert Kagan, a senior associate with the Carnegie Endowment for International Peace has pointed out, it is a conspiracy that would necessarily have to include Bill Clinton, Al Gore, former Defense Secretary William Cohen, Tony Blair, U.N. inspector Hans Blix, Jacques Chirac and many others—all of whom have said categorically in recent years that Saddam possessed such weapons. It also conveniently ignores the thousands of Kurds gassed to death by Saddam's troops—they died of something—and it entirely begs the question of why Saddam would forfeit his regime and most likely his life in a defiant effort to protect something he did not possess.

26. The *New York Times* was criticized in many quarters, and not only by conservatives, for sounding as though it was engaged in an old-style newspaper crusade to drum up opposition to war. This was said to be in keeping with the paper's modern reputation as a liberal voice. But in fairness to the paper—and despite the palpable animus of its editorial board toward Bush and his policies—the *Times* presented a wide range of views on Iraq in its news columns, op-ed page, and its Sunday magazine.

Index

About the Author

Carl M. Cannon is the White House correspondent for *National Journal,* Washington's authoritative nonpartisan weekly journal on politics and government.

Before joining the magazine in May of 1998, Mr. Cannon worked for six newspapers over a twenty-year span. Prior to coming to Washington in the first Reagan term, he covered police, courts, local and statewide politics, education and race relations during stints at newspapers in Virginia, Georgia and California.

In California, Mr. Cannon's reporting on a 1937 Los Angeles murder helped secure a pardon based on innocence in 1982 for the man wrongfully convicted, then-eighty-year-old Pete Pianezzi.

While on vacation in San Francisco in 1989 to see the Bay Area World Series, Mr. Cannon found himself covering the Loma Prieta earthquake instead of watching baseball. He was a member of the San Jose *Mercury News* staff awarded the Pulitzer Prize for that coverage.

As a reporter in the Washington bureau of Knight-Ridder Newspapers from 1982 to 1993, he covered the California congressional delegation, technology policy, western lands issues, politics and the presidential campaigns of 1984, 1988 and 1992.

In 1993, he was hired by the *Baltimore Sun* to cover the White House. He remained on the beat after switching to *National Journal* in 1998. The following year, Mr. Cannon was honored for his White House coverage by winning the prestigious Gerald R. Ford Prize for Distinguished Reporting of the Presidency. He is currently the president of the White House Correspondents' Association and also serves as the in-house writing coach at *National Journal.*

Mr. Cannon is a co-author of *Boy Genius,* a recent biography of top Bush White House aide Karl Rove. Mr. Cannon has also written for numerous magazines, including *The Atlantic Monthly, New Republic, Forbes, Business Month, Working Woman, Brill's Content, George, Mother Jones,* the *National Review* and the *Weekly Standard.*

A native of San Francisco, Carl attended the University of Colorado, majoring in journalism. He lives in Arlington, Virginia. He and his wife, Sharon, have three children ranging in ages from eight to twenty-two. Carl's pursuits include fly-fishing in Montana, thoroughbred racing, opera and playing amateur baseball in an adult hardball league.

AMERICAN POLITICAL CHALLENGES
Larry J. Sabato, *Series Editor*

The American political process is in trouble. Although we witnessed a movement toward specific electoral reforms in the aftermath of the 2000 election debacle, the health of our political system is still at risk. Recent events have altered the political landscape and posed new challenges, and reforms are much needed and wanted by the American public. Diligence is required, however, in examining carefully the intended and unintended consequences of reforms as we look toward the 2004 elections and beyond.

Series Editor Larry J. Sabato of the University of Virginia Center for Politics is a leading political scientist and commentator who has clear ideas about what needs to change to improve the quality of our democracy. For this series, he taps leading political authors to write cogent diagnoses and prescriptions for improving both politics and government. New and forthcoming books in the series are short, to the point, easy to understand (if difficult to implement against the political grain). They take a stand and show how to overcome obstacles to change. Authors are known for their clear writing style as well as for their political acumen.

Titles in the Series

Chesapeake Bay Blues: Science, Politics, and the Struggle to Save the Bay
  Howard R. Ernst

The Pursuit of Happiness in Times of War
  Carl M. Cannon

Forthcoming

The Presidential Nominating Process: A Place for Us?
  Rhodes Cook